Catholic Thought and Catholic Action:

Scenes from Australian Catholic Life

James Franklin

Connor Court Publishing Pty Ltd

Published in 2023 by Connor Court Publishing Pty Ltd.

Copyright © James Franklin

All rights reserved. Not to be reproduced without the permission of the Copyright holders.

Connor Court Publishing Pty Ltd.
PO Box 7257
Redland Bay QLD 4165
sales@connorcourt.com
www.connorcourt.com

ISBN: 9781922815361

Cover Design by Maria Giordano

Front cover: Catholic boy scouts at St Patrick's College Manly, Corpus Christi, 7 June 1934, photographer Ted Hood. (State Library of New South Wales, https://collection.sl.nsw.gov.au/record/nM7BVKKY).

Printed in Australia.

Acknowledgement:

I am grateful to Gerald O Nolan for extensive editing work.

Contents

Introduction	vii
1 Sydney, 1803: The experiment in toleration of Catholics	1
2 1821: A new beginning for the Church in Europe and Australia	16
3 Catholic missions to Aboriginal Australia: an evaluation	24
4 F. X. Gsell: The missionary with 150 Wives	46
5 Catholic rural virtue in Australia: ideal and reality	56
6 Catholic Scholastic philosophy in Australia	82
7 Catholic thought and Catholic Action: Dr Paddy Ryan MSC and the Red Peril	105
8 Convent slave laundries? Magdalen asylums in Australia	128
9 Catholics versus Masons	153
10 Archbishop Mannix and the politics of social justice	171
11 Memoirs by Australian priests, religious and ex-religious	188
12 Calwell, Catholicism and the origins of multicultural Australia	207
13 Catholic Action, Sydney style: Lay organisations from friendly societies to the Vice Squad	222
14 Gerald Ridsdale, pedophile priest, in his own words	259
15 Natural law ethics and the *Mabo* decision	272
16 Random thoughts	285
Index	295

Introduction

The last recorded words of Jesus are his message to his followers at the beginning of the Acts of the Apostles, "you will be my witnesses in Jerusalem, and in all Judea and Samaria, and to the ends of the earth." Acts continues the story up to St Paul's arrival in Rome. That is well beyond Judea and Samaria, but it is not the ends of the earth.

The story of the Catholic Church at the actual ends of the earth resumed in 1803, when officials in the Vatican received an unexpected letter via Irish connections in Rome. The letter described events in a recently established British colony on the far side of New Holland. It revealed that an Irish priest forcibly sent there, Fr Dixon, was exercising his ministry. Despite the major disruption to Church activities resulting from the French Revolution followed by Napoleon's occupation of Rome, the church functionaries acted enthusiastically in response. They sent Fr Dixon an official letter. It excused him from any defects in canonical forms that may have proved necessary in his difficult circumstances, urged him to organise where possible the conversion of the Pacific Islands, and granted him the impressive title, "Prefect Apostolic of New Holland." (The story is told in ch. 1)

Fr Dixon returned to Ireland in 1809 and Australia was left without priests. But lay Catholic devotion continued and an organised Catholic community was ready in Sydney to welcome government-approved priests in 1820 (ch. 2). In the two centuries since, a vigorous church, first Irish and then multicultural, developed into a distinctive section of Australian society, comprising one fifth to one quarter of the population. Through its sacraments, sermons, tight ecclesiastical organisation and especially through its own education system, the Australian Catholic community embodied a tradition of ideas and ideas-led action different from the rest of the population.

Australian Catholic history is the story of that unique community and its contributions to the wider society.

The present book is not a complete overview of Australian Catholic history. It presents a series of vignettes which, on their relatively small scale, illustrate the variety of the doings of the Catholic faithful. Those actions were not random or ill-considered, but informed by a tradition of faith and ideas that implied a definite view on metaphysical, theological, moral and political issues.

The Catholic tradition differs from both Protestant and secular ones in two main respects, one theological and one philosophical. Theologically, it emphasises the sacraments and the visible unified institutional Church centred on the Pope and taking orders from Central Command. It is thus embodied in a more definite way than rival traditions; and, just as we can choose our friends but are stuck with our family, so Catholics must live in the same Church as other Catholics, whatever they may think of their views, actions and devotional practices.

Philosophically, Catholic theory differs from both Protestant and most secular theory in its commitment to a natural law ethics – that what is right follows from the inherent nature of things, especially human nature. That was the central tenet of the scholastic philosophy that dominated Catholic philosophy and education for the first half of the twentieth century (ch. 6). And on a Catholic view, objective ethics applies not only to the actions of individuals, but to the collective arrangements of society; the theory of social justice of Leo XIII's encyclical *Rerum Novarum* requires that arrangements like a minimum fair wage be instituted – as explained by Archbishop Mannix (ch. 10). The Catholic tradition has too a strong sense that ethics is not only objective but demanding. If children are not being educated, or women are destitute on the streets, or Communists are taking over the unions, someone should do something about it urgently. If I am on the spot and have relevant talents and resources, "someone" is me. God requires me to take action, and to organise with others to make action effective.

That perspective, explicitly or implicitly, has been behind the Catholic contributions to Australian life described in this book. Catholic remote-area missions were premised on a belief that aboriginal Australians were entitled not only to hear the word of God but to be protected against toxic aspects of both black and white culture (chs 3-4). A commitment to the inherent equality of the worth of persons was behind the Mabo decision of the Catholic-dominated High Court, which declared that indigenous Australians had rights in land that could not be ignored by the white colonisers (ch. 15). Similar views were behind Arthur Calwell's 1940s plan for mass immigration, which held that refugees in war-torn Europe had some right to Australia's unused spaces (as well as being good for Australia) (ch. 12). The untiring anti-communist organising of Dr Ryan (ch. 7) reflected not only knowledge of Stalinist atrocities, but a presumption that a materialist philosophy like Leninism could only result in a view of humans as expendable, fit only to be shovelled into mass graves if they were not on the side of "history". If Freemasonry was a godless ideology, as Catholics believed (not entirely correctly) then it was certainly unsatisfactory if society were dominated by Freemasons (ch. 9).

It is also characteristic of the Catholic tradition to act communally and institutionally as well as individually. The mass is a communal celebration, not a collection of people praying privately, and Catholic action for good is also typically collective. The poor Catholic communities of 1821 and the later rural ones portrayed in "John O'Brien's" *Around the Boree Log* overcame the challenges of sparse populations to create a virtuous and faithful common life (chs 2 and 5).

Catholic religious – priests, brothers and nuns – were trained in isolated seminaries and convents to be a special class of dedicated workers wholly devoted to the church cause; their memoirs testify to a unique institutional culture very different from the way of life of most Australians (ch. 11). Charitable action for the worst-off in society was done on a large scale through institutions such as the Magdalen laundries that took in destitute girls (ch. 8). In the fight against communism, Catholics provided not only the intellectual firepower but the organised foot soldiers to fight in the unions (ch. 7). Calwell's action for European refugees was successful because solidly supported by the Catholic-dominated Labor Party of his day. The Cahill government was effective partly because it was based on organised Catholic lay mass societies (ch. 13).

There are lessons to be learned. History is not *for* lessons, and historical study must be pursued on its own terms in an effort to understand what really happened, not what one would like to have happened. Nevertheless, once that has been done, there may be lessons arising which it would be stupid to ignore.

The story contains both extraordinary role models to inspire imitation and avoidable disasters that stand as warnings.

St Mary MacKillop is the perfect exemplar of a type of sanctity seen again and again in Australian Catholic history – practical, inspired by faith and well-informed on theory, energetic, institutionally organised in a way that created benefits for many, especially the worst off. Her model was followed by missionaries such as Bishop Gsell (ch. 4), country priest and poet "John O'Brien" (ch. 5), anti-communist speaker and organiser Dr Ryan (ch 7), Archbishop Mannix (ch. 10), immigration minister Arthur Calwell (ch. 12), and the early Sisters of Charity who took in large numbers of destitute girls (ch. 8). Confident, larger than life and outward-looking figures, they got action. A comparison with the present day shows up too many contemporary Catholics as lazy, soft, uncommitted, ignorant of Catholic ideas and culture, afflicted by modern nervousness and over-concerned with internal church disputes. The lessons are obvious.

But along with those achievements, something went seriously wrong. The Royal Commission into Institutional Responses to Child Sexual Abuse was probably the world's most intensive external investigation of the Catholic Church, and most of its adverse findings were justified. The sexual abuse crisis and its cover-up were the most prominent but not the only devastating outcome of a religious culture that became ingrown, self-satisfied and inaccessible to outside or inside scrutiny. The ability of the serial pedophile priest Fr Ridsdale to continue his offending although it was known to his superiors (ch. 14) depended on the Church acting in a coordinated way to "protect its reputation" without regard to the welfare of victims. Less well known but also with severe impacts on powerless victims was the near slave labour endured by young women in Magdalen laundries (ch. 8) and the persecution of homosexuals by a Catholic police commissioner (ch. 13). Those events were not one-off mistakes but the results of an unaccountable institution implementing a body of ideas not subject to internal or external criticism. Again, the lessons are obvious.

Australia is by world standards a notably successful state and culture. Its Catholic tradition has been one contributor to that success. Cardinal Moran's vision of the Australian Church as a base for the Christianisation of Asia and the Pacific and a counter to secularisation at home is a live one. It needs to be informed by knowledge of the two centuries of Australian Catholic history, which put into perspective the shallow disputes and discouragements of the present day.

1

Sydney, 1803: The experiment in toleration of Catholics*

Abstract: In 1803, Governor King's authority over the raw colony of New South Wales faced serious threats, including from Irish convicts. On the instructions of Lord Hobart, King allowed the convict priest Father Dixon to minister to Catholics. The reasoning behind this decision is explained, in the light of the Irish background. Hobart's earlier success in negotiating with Irish bishops is essential for understanding developments in New South Wales. The experiment in toleration of Catholics was short-lived, in view of the Castle Hill convict rebellion, but nevertheless was a limited success that set the tone for later respectful Catholic-government relations.

On March 1st, 1804, Governor King wrote with satisfaction to his superior in London, Lord Hobart, of the success of his proclamation of toleration for Catholics a year earlier:

> The indulgence proposed by your Lordship respecting the Rev'd Mr. Dixon performing the functions of his clerical office as a Roman Catholic … has had the most salutary effects on the number of Irish Catholics we have, and since its toleration there has not been the most distant cause for complaint among that description, who regularly attend Divine service.[1]

He spoke too soon. Three days later, the Castle Hill Rebellion broke out.

How did it happen that for a brief period in the early colony, Catholicism was tolerated and its clergyman paid a government salary? What was the result of this unlikely experiment?

The Irish rebels

The four hundred convicts sent to New South Wales for complicity in the Irish rebellions of 1798 to 1803 were agreed by those in authority

---

* Edited extract from 'Sydney 1803: When Catholics were tolerated and Freemasons banned', *Journal of the Royal Australian Historical Society* 107 (2) (2021), 135–155.

to be the most desperate, dangerous and unreformable characters imaginable, threatening the colony with destruction at any moment. Memories were fresh of atrocities on both sides in the rebellion of the United Irishmen in 1798, when at least 10,000 had been killed, probably many more.

Both the authorities and the convicts spoke as if revolution would resume in New South Wales where it had left off in Ireland. King reported in 1801,

> we have been very quiet until the arrival of the *Ann*, transport, from Cork, with 137 of the most desperate and diabolical characters that could be selected throughout that Kingdom, together with a Catholic priest of most notorious, seditious, and rebellious principles – which makes the numbers of those who, avowing a determination never to lose sight of the oath by which they are bound as United Irishmen, amount to 600, are ready, and only waiting an opportunity to put their diabolical plans into execution.[2]

In King's first two years, 1800 and 1801, interrogations were conducted, plots uncovered, floggings ordered, ringleaders hanged and others sent to Norfolk Island. But the ratio of talk and rumours to real action was high. The evidence is contaminated by the use of flogging to extract confessions – though interrogatory torture was and is illegal under British law – and the knowledge by informants of what government wanted to hear. Some of the evidence extracted by the Reverend Samuel Marsden's questioning was thin: Hester Stroud, convict, has heard talk of pikes hidden, and "this Depon't further saith from what she saw of the Irishmen being in small Parties in the Camp at Toongabby and by their walking about together and talking very earnestly in Irish. Deponent verily believes they were intent upon something that was improper on Saturday afternoon."[3] Finding any pikes proved difficult.

François Péron, visiting with Baudin's expedition in 1802, was convinced, or said he was convinced, by the Irishmen's bloodthirsty talk. "Their eyes bathed in tears, pouring out curses against England, imploring Bonaparte and calling for the moment of vengeance on their oppressors[4] … it would have been more difficult for the French to prevent the massacre of the English than to conquer the colony."[5] "The Irish in chains are silent now, but if our country's government, alarmed by the rapid increase of this colony, planned to seize or destroy it in the name of France, all the Irish arms would rise."[6] Or, as with the French invasion of western Ireland in 1798, they might not.

The Castle Hill rebellion in 1804 was certainly real and showed that King's fears were not groundless. But even there, no soldiers, volunteers or settlers were killed or injured, while just some thirty insurgents were killed then or later. The troubles of Ireland did not repeat themselves in the colony.

Toleration of Catholics: for and against

The question for Hobart and King was, whether a Catholic priest was a net positive or negative for controlling the Irish convicts. The answer was not obvious.

Significantly for the question of toleration of religious ceremonies, a distinction was drawn between the ordinary Irish and gentlemen, a category taken to include priests. Governor Hunter wrote "we can scarcely divest ourselves of the common feelings of humanity so far as to send a physician, a former respectable sheriff of a county, a Roman Catholic priest, or a Protestant clergyman and family to the grubbing hoe or timber carriage."[7] They had to be supported on the government stores. So from the beginning, a potential commonality of interest between government and priests was possible.

As often in Australian history, what happened was a reflection of events back home. This question has an Irish background in the previous decade. The Protestant Ascendancy had vigorously persecuted Catholics with penal laws for a century after the Battle of the Boyne in 1690, with some attenuation by the 1780s. Then it was suddenly realised in the 1790s that His Majesty's Government and the Irish Catholic hierarchy faced a common and pressing enemy, the French Revolution. Dublin Castle needed the Catholic bishops' support against the spread of revolutionary ideals among the laity, while the bishops wanted progress on Catholic emancipation and help with replacing the Irish seminaries destroyed by revolutionary forces in Europe (which had to that time educated almost all Irish priests). In 1793, the year of the Terror in Paris, the Irish Parliament passed the major reforms of the Roman Catholic Relief Act. It was piloted through Parliament by the Lord Lieutenant's Chief Secretary, Lord Hobart, against local Protestant opposition and was sometimes called "Hobart's Relief Act".[8] Archbishop Troy of Dublin met Hobart at Dublin Castle. He suggested to Hobart that even if seminaries were restored in France after a counterrevolution, "our clerical youth would be exposed to the great danger of imbibing seditious maxims and propagating them afterwards in this kingdom." He reminded Hobart of attacks on clergy following their support for order in recent disturbances, and laid out the advantages of British permission for clerical education in Ireland. Then he asked the British to pay for it.[9]

While Hobart left Ireland shortly after, the negotiations were successful and the Irish bishops, though disappointed over lack of further progress towards Catholic emancipation, did receive Maynooth Seminary ("The Royal College of St Patrick") in 1795, at government expense. When the 1798 Rebellion broke out, the government received an excellent return on its investment in the Archbishop. He excommunicated the United Irishmen, called for loyalty and gratitude, instructed his priests to preach restraint, and referred at least privately to those few clergy implicated as "the very faeces of the church".[10] The Irish Catholic hierarchy has continued to solidly oppose the cause of revolution to the present day, with the sole exception of a later President of Maynooth, Daniel Mannix.

That is not to say that Hobart was pro-Catholic. He was not himself in favour of Catholic emancipation. In 1805 he argued strongly in the House of Lords against emancipation for Catholics, on the grounds of their loyalty to a foreign power.[11] Indeed, he is the only person in the whole story other than Marsden who shows concern for the Protestant interest as such. Nevertheless, he was very familiar with the benefits of concessions for Catholics for strategic reasons and the possibility of priests restraining revolutionary hotheads.

The other reason in favour of toleration in Sydney lay in the person of Fr James Dixon. He was widely agreed, then and later, to be a mild-mannered man and well-educated (at Salamanca and Louvain) with no interest in revolution and undeservedly transported.[12] He was thus of the same mind as Archbishop Troy – indeed, much of the surviving evidence for Dixon's innocence is in letters to Troy. Even on the voyage out, he had gained a name as a moderating influence. The journal of the ship's captain's wife says of the convicts on board:

> It was fortunate both for themselves and us, that there were amongst them men of education and sense; who doubtless contributed to restrain the others from evil and violence; one was said to be a Roman Catholic clergyman, and we trusted that his influence was beneficial.[13]

Governor King soon came to agree that "the conduct of Dixon, the Catholic priest, has been exemplary since he has been here."[14] If a priest was to be tolerated at all, Fr Dixon was the ideal candidate – as well as, by 1803, the only candidate.

The opposite opinion on toleration of Catholics was represented by the Rev Samuel Marsden, the senior Church of England clergyman as well as flogging magistrate and sheep farmer. His views on the risks of toleration appear in a manuscript of his of 1807, bound with two others, one describing the spirit trade as the downfall of the colony and the other calling almost all of the colony's unmarried females prostitutes. The essays were apparently intended for publication on his visit to England but that did not occur.[15] While he understood that some believed that toleration would quiet the minds of convicts,

> But whoever is acquainted with the real National Character of the Irish Convicts, and the local Situation of the Colony, will be of a very different Opinion. It is more than probable that if the Catholic Religion was once allowed to be celebrated by Authority, that the Colony would be lost to the British Empire in less than one year. The number of Catholic convicts is very great in the Settlement; and these in general composed of the lowest Class of the Irish Nation, who are the most wild, ignorant and savage Race that were ever favoured with the Light of Civilization; Men that have been familiar with Robberies Murders and every horrid Crime from their Infancy. Their minds being destitute of every Principle

of Religion & Morality render them capable of perpetrating the Most Nefarious Acts in cool Blood. As they never appear to reflect upon Consequences; but to [be] governed entirely by the Impulse of Passion and always alive to Rebellion and mischief they are very dangerous members of Society … The low Irish Convicts are an extraordinary Race of Beings; their Minds are depraved beyond all Conception … Should the Catholic Religion ever be tolerated in the Settlement, that will immediately give them that Opportunity they wish for. At the Celebration of the Mass they would assemble from every part of the Colony; reveal their Intentions, and gain one another's Confidence. Measures would be immediately concerted to overturn the present Government. …

Marsden is particularly concerned about the future, securing which will need the authorities to make sure children are all brought up Protestant. At the moment Catholics fortunately have little knowledge of their religion. Therefore:

> If none but the Protestant Religion should continue to be established or tolerated, in a few years there will be very few Catholics, to what there are now in the Settlement. The rising Generation will be Protestants and Strangers to all other religious Opinions, if Attention is paid to their early Education and for want of the public Celebration of the Mass the common People will think little of it … should the Morals and Education of the Children of the Irish Catholic Convicts be neglected, many of them will walk in the Footsteps of their wretched Parents, the Boys will be idle and rebellious, and the Girls infamous – the former living by plundering the industrious, and the latter by Prostitution.[16]

King's own initial opinion was closer to Marsden's than Hobart's, and he is unlikely to have considered a policy of toleration of his own accord. In reporting as above in 1801 on "the most desperate and diabolical characters" foisted on him, he advised against "any more of those violent Republican characters being sent here for some time, and particularly the priests (of whom we have now three)."[17]

(Of the three priests, Fr James Harold and Fr Peter O'Neil were soon sent to Norfolk Island, though the "most notorious, seditious and rebellious" Fr O'Neil had to be sent home when news of his exoneration arrived, doubts having arisen about his confession after 275 lashes.[18] Only the tractable Fr Dixon was left in Sydney.)

The proclamation of toleration of Catholics

King's views were behind the times. The recipient of his letter, the Home Secretary Lord Portland (in charge of both Ireland and the Colonies) had favoured Catholic emancipation in principle although he had had to recall in 1795 an ally who as Lord Lieutenant in Ireland had been felt to have moved too precipitately on the question.[19] By the time of the official reply to King, he had been succeeded, now with the title of Secretary of State for War and the Colonies, by Lord Hobart. Hobart's reply to King on 29 August 1802 politely informed him that policy had changed:

> The Catholic priests Dixon, O'Neal, and Harrold, and a man named Abraham Gough, have been represented to me as persons who may not be undeserving of the conditional emancipation above explained: if their conduct should have justified this representation, and you should be of opinion that these priests may be usefully employed either as schoolmasters, or in the exercise of their clerical functions, you may avail yourselves of their services.[20]

Hobart set policy. King followed orders. His proclamation in the *Sydney Gazette* of 19th April 1803 announced toleration for Dixon's masses:

> Whereas I have judged it expedient and admissible, in consequence of a Communication from His Majesty's Principal Secretary of State for the Colonies and War Department, to Grant unto the Reverend Mr. DIXON, a Conditional Emancipation to enable him to Exercise his Clerical Functions as a Roman Catholic Priest: which he has qualified himself for by the regular and exemplary Conduct he has manifested since his residence in the Colony; and his having taken the Oath of Allegiance, Abjuration, and Declaration, prescribed by Law.[21]

Appended is a series of regulations which show the intended advantages and attendant fears of the authorities:

Regulations

To be observed by the Rev. Mr. DIXON, and the CATHOLIC CONGREGATIONS in this Colony:

FIRST. They will observe, with all becoming gratitude, That this Extension of liberal Toleration proceeds from the Piety and Benevolence of OUR MOST GRACIOUS SOVEREIGN, to Whom, as well as our Parent Country at large, we are (under Providence), indebted for the Blessings we enjoy.

SECOND. That the Religious Exercise of their Worship may suffer no hindrance, it is expected that no Seditious Conversations that can anywise injure HIS MAJESTY's Government, or affect the Tranquillity of this Colony, will ever happen, either at the Places prescribed for their Worship, or Elsewhere. But that they will individually manifest their Gratitude and Allegiance, by exerting themselves in Detecting and Reporting any impropriety, of that or any other nature, that may fall under their observation.

THIRD. As Mr. Dixon will be allowed to perform his Clerical Functions Once in Three Weeks at the Settlements at Sydney, Parramatta, and Hawkesbury, in Rotation, the Magistrates are strictly forbid suffering those Catholics who reside at the places where Service is not performing, from resorting to the Settlement and District at which the Priest officiates for the day.

FOURTH. The Catholic Service will be performed on the appointed Sundays at 9 o'clock in the morning.

FIFTH. No improper behaviour, during the time of Service, is to be allowed by the Priest, who will be responsible to the Magistrates for his Congregation's going regularly and orderly to their respective homes, after the Offices are ended.

SIXTH. And to the end that strict Decorum may be observed, a certain number of the Police will be stationed at and about the places appointed, during the Service.

SEVENTH. Every Person throughout the Colony will observe, that the Law has sufficiently provided for the Punishment of those who may Disquiet or Disturb any Assembly of Religious Worship whatever, or Misuse any Priest, or Teacher, of any Tolerated Sect,

(Signed) JAMES DIXON.

Subscribed before Us, this 19th Day of April, 1803.

RICHARD ATKINS

THOS. JAMISON[22]

It remained to be seen whether the hoped-for gratitude would outweigh the feared seditious plotting.

Fr Dixon held the first public mass in Australia at Sydney on 15 May 1803.[23] The exact location is not known. The *Sydney Gazette* officially recorded him as conducting a marriage and attending an execution in 1803,[24] indicating official acceptance of the normal range of a clergyman's duties.

Through the offices of the head of St Isidore's Irish College in Rome, a petition from Fr Dixon to Rome reached Vatican authorities. Despite the chaotic conditions resulting from Napoleon's invasions, they responded enthusiastically to the unexpected news of missionary activity at the ends of the earth. They forwarded faculties (official permissions to operate) for the three priests, and for Fr Dixon appointment with the impressive title "Prefect Apostolic of New Holland".[25]

The experiment seemed to King to go well in the subsequent months. In September 1803 he reported with satisfaction:

> The Irish, of whom we have so great a proportion, in general behave well, which I cannot but attribute to their being indulged with the exercise of their religion, in performing the functions of which Mr. Dixon conducts himself and his congregation so well that I have availed myself of your Lordship's permission in giving him £60 per annum.[26]

Then as we saw, on 1 March, 1804 he reported that Fr Dixon's work "has had the most salutary effects on the number of Irish Catholics we have, and since its toleration there has not been the most distant cause for complaint among that description, who regularly attend Divine service."[27]

Revolution

The Castle Hill rebellion broke out on 4 March. Two to three hundred rebels led by Philip Cunningham, a veteran of 1798, seized farms and weapons and advanced towards Parramatta. Major Johnston acted decisively and with a forced march reached Parramatta and then caught up with the rebels near Castle Hill. He took Fr Dixon with him.

After deceiving the leaders with a parley he captured them and the rest fell apart. Fr Dixon's appeals to lay down arms (depicted in a contemporary watercolour) fell on deaf ears. Some thirty rebels were killed then or executed later.[28]

Watercolour of Castle Hill Rebellion[29]

Aftermath

When the revolution was over, the Governor regretted the toleration experiment. He wrote that he has "also been necessitated to withhold the salary from the Romish priest Dixon, for very improper conduct, and to prevent the seditious meetings that took place in consequence of the indulgence and protection he received."[30] The "improper conduct" is not specified.

Nevertheless, when it came to the point Fr Dixon had supported the government in the crisis and risked his life addressing the rebels.

Detail: Fr Dixon pleads "Lay down your Arms my deluded Countrymen"

Some believed he had had some good effect; a compilation of local sources published in 1811 says that he "proved to be of some utility in bringing back the insurgents to a proper sense of their duty. It cannot be too much to say, that the conduct of Mr. Dixon, before and after this business, has been exemplary."[31]

In fact from 1804 Fr Dixon was allowed to practice privately for some years. In January 1809 he performed the marriage of William and Catherine Davis, both to be leaders of the Church in the future.[32] The deposed Governor Bligh complained to Lord Castlereagh in 1809 that among the laxities of the provisional government that had replaced him, indulgences were granted to the Irish rebels and "the Romish Priest is now wildly following his functions, which were before kept within proper bounds, and must be again limited by wise and mild measures."[33]

Fr Dixon was permitted to return to Ireland in 1809 and later said very little about his time in Australia. Fr Harold, returned from Norfolk Island, continued the ministry for another year, according to himself with success and happiness though according to a local, "avaricious and petulant to a degree." He was pardoned and left in 1810.[34]

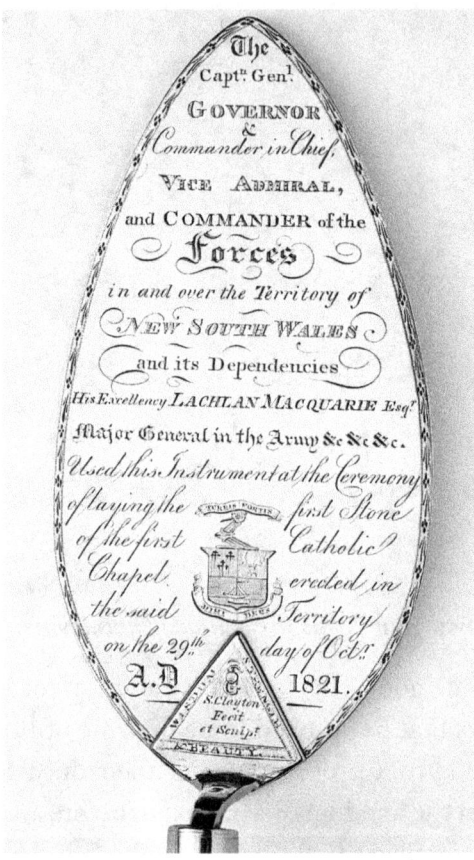

The ceremonial trowel Governor Macquarie wielded when laying the foundation stone of St Mary's church, at which time he made a joke about being a mason.

Marsden took events to have justified his stance, claiming that meeting at mass was a cover for planning insurrection, and that it was not the want of mass that caused their rebellious spirit, but "their Natural Ferocity, which nothing can ever eradicate."[35]

Macquarie too was to accept Marsden's false view of history, saying "those Disturbances being entirely occasioned by the Machinations of a Couple of unprincipled Catholic Priests" and "the only Insurrection among the Convicts, which ever took place here, was instigated several years ago by Irish Popish Priests," who therefore should be excluded from the colony.[36]

Meanwhile, a successful revolution had taken place with the "Rum Rebellion". The United Irishmen took no part in the event.

Thereafter, peace and a degree of practical goodwill ensued, and from Macquarie's arrival in 1810, respectability reigned. For both the rebels of 1798 in Ireland and those of 1808 in Sydney, bygones were allowed to be bygones. The perpetrators of the Rum Rebellion escaped any severe punishment, and it was by then years since there had been any violence from the Irish. Everyone who remained in the colony received a land grant, or several land grants. Most grants were surveyed by the Deputy Surveyor, James Meehan, a rebel who had been transported on the same ship as Fr Dixon.

Four of the men of '98, William Davis, James Dempsey, James Meehan and Michael Hayes, became wealthy and respected citizens and the leaders of the Catholic community in the priestless years of Macquarie's time. When two priests finally arrived with official approval in 1820, a committee was formed to raise funds for a church. It comprised the two priests and seven laymen. Six were rebels of '98 and included Davis, Meehan, Hayes and Dempsey.[37] When the foundation stone of St Mary's church was laid, on a handsome plot of land chosen by Meehan,[38] Governor Macquarie wielded the ceremonial trowel and made a joke about being a mason.[39]

Just twenty years after the rebels had been transported, it was becoming clear that things would be done very differently in the new country.

---

[1] King to Hobart, 1 March 1804, in *Historical Records of Australia* [hereafter *HRA*], series 1 vol. 4, 470.

[2] King to Portland, 10 Mar 1801, *HRA*, series 1 vol 3, 9.

[3] Evidence of Hester Stroud to Samuel Marsden, 29 Sept 1800, *HRA*, series 1 vol 2, 641.

[4] François Péron, Tableau militaire des colonies anglaises aux *Terres Australes*, quoted in Edward Duyker, *François Péron: An Impetuous Life: Naturalist and Voyager*, Miegunyah Press, Melbourne, 2006, 144.

[5] François Péron, Mémoire sur les établissements anglais à la Nouvelle Hollande, à la Terre de Diemen et dans les archipels du grand océan Pacifique …, présentation, édition et notes de Roger Martin, transcription du manuscrit avec le concours de Jacqueline Bonnemains, préface de Joël Eymeret, *Revue de l'Institut Napoléon,* No. 176, 1998, vol I, 1–187, at 147, quoted in Michael Connor, 'The secret plan to invade Sydney', *Quadrant* 53 no. 11, Nov, 2009, 38–41.

[6] Francois Péron, Report to General Charles-Mathieu-Isidore Decaen on the colonisation of New Holland, 1803, quoted in Duyker, *François Péron,* 205.

[7] Hunter to Portland, 20 March 1800, *HRA*, series 1 vol 2, 475.

[8] Thomas Bartlett, *The Fall and Rise of the Irish Nation: The Catholic Question 1690–1830*, Gill and Macmillan, Dublin, 1992, 165.

[9] Troy to Hobart, 29 November 1793, Dublin Archdiocesan Archives, in Vincent J. McNally, 'John Thomas Troy, Archbishop of Dublin, and the establishment of St Patrick's College, Maynooth, 1791–1795', *Catholic Historical Review* 67, 1981, 565–588.

[10] Dáire Keogh, 'John Thomas Troy (1739–1823)', *Archivium Hibernicum* 49, 1995, 105–110; similar from the Bishop of Cork, in Edward D'Alton, 'Francis Moylan',

Catholic Encyclopedia, Appleton, New York, 1911, vol 10, http://www.newadvent.org/cathen/10609b.htm.

11. *House of Lords Hansard*, 13 May 1805, https://api.parliament.uk/historic-hansard/lords/1805/may/13/roman-catholic-petition#S1V0004P0_18050513_HOL_4

12. Harold Perkins, *The Convict Priests*, Thistle Press, Gardiner, Vic, 1984, 51-57; Vivienne Keely, *Dixon of Botany Bay: The Convict Priest from Wexford*, St Paul's Publications Strathfield, 2003; James Waldersee, 'Father James Dixon and the 1798 Wexford Rising', *Journal of Religious History* 6, 1970, 27–40.

13. Mary Ann Reid, 'Cursory remarks on board the Friendship', *Asiatic Journal and Monthly Register for British India and its Dependencies* 8, Dec 1819, 556, repr. In Col Graham, Perry McIntyre and Anne-Maree Whitaker (Eds), *The Voyage of the ship Friendship from Cork to Botany Bay 1799-1800*, PR Ireland, Sydney, 2000, 27.

14. King to Hobart, 9 May 1803, *HRA*, series 1 vol 4, 82.

15. Michael Saclier, 'Sam Marsden's colony: notes on a manuscript in the Mitchell Library, Sydney', *Journal of the Royal Australian Historical Society* 52, no 2, June 1966, 94–114.

16. Samuel Marsden, 'A Few Observations on the Toleration of the Catholic Religion in New South Wales', memorandum; c. 1807, Ms. 18, Marsden Papers, Mitchell Library, Sydney: http://acms.sl.nsw.gov.au/_transcript/2015/D06597/a2105.html

17. King to Portland, 10 Mar 1801, *HRA*, series 1 vol 3, 9.

18. Vivienne Parsons, 'O'Neil, Peter (1757–1835)', *Australian Dictionary of Biography*, http://adb.anu.edu.au/biography/oneil-peter-2524/text3419

19. David Wilkinson, 'The Fitzwilliam episode, 1795: A reinterpretation of the role of the Duke of Portland', *Irish Historical Studies* 29, 1995, 315–339.

20. Hobart to King, 29 Aug 1802, in *HRA*, Series 1 vol 3, 564.

21. *Sydney Gazette and New South Wales Advertiser*, 24 Apr 1803, https://trove.nla.gov.au/newspaper/article/625538

22. *Sydney Gazette and New South Wales Advertiser*, 24 Apr 1803, https://trove.nla.gov.au/newspaper/article/625535

23. 'Sydney', *Sydney Gazette*, 22 May 1803, https://trove.nla.gov.au/newspaper/article/625581

24. 'Married', *Sydney Gazette*, 15 May 1803, https://trove.nla.gov.au/newspaper/article/625572; 'Execution', 9 Oct 1803, https://trove.nla.gov.au/newspaper/article/625811

25. Perkins, *The Convict Priests*, 59-60; appeal to Propaganda Fide on behalf of Fr Dixon and letter of Propaganda Fide to Dixon of 25 February 1804 transcribed in Cathaldus Giblin, 'James Dixon and Jeremiah O'Flynn, Two prefects apostolic in Australia', *Collectanea Hibernica* 25, 1983, 63–85.

26. King to Hobart, 17 September 1803, *HRA*, series 1 vol. 4, 394.

27. King to Lord Hobart, 1 Mar 1804, in *HRA*, series 1 vol 4, 470.

28. Anne-Maree Whitaker, *Unfinished Revolution: United Irishmen in New South Wales, 1800-1810*, Crossing Press, Sydney, 1994, ch 5.

29. National Library of Australia (nla.pic-an5577479)

30. King to Hobart, 14 Aug 1804, *HRA*, series 1 vol. 5, 99.

31. George Paterson, *The History of New South Wales from Its First Discovery to the Pre-*

sent Time, Newcastle upon Tyne, 1811, p 388; identical text in D.D. Mann, *The Present Picture of New South Wales,* London, 1811, 4.

[32] 'Notice', *The Australian,* 1 Apr 1826, https://trove.nla.gov.au/newspaper/article/37071792

[33] Bligh to Castlereagh, 8 July 1809, *HRA,* series 1 vol 7, 163.

[34] Harold Perkins, 'Father Harold: the story of a convict priest,' *Journal of the Australian Catholic Historical Society* 3, no. 3, 1971, pp 1–14; Perkins, *Convict Priests,* 14.

[35] Marsden, 'A few observations'.

[36] Macquarie to Bathurst, 12 December 1817 and 18 May 1818, *HRA,* series I vol 9, pp 710 and 801; discussion in Vivienne Keely, *Michael Hayes: The Life of a 1798 Wexford Rebel in Sydney,* Anchor Books, Melbourne, 2019, 95.

[37] G. M. Cashman, 'A Catholic Who's Who from 1788 to Polding', *Journal of the Australian Catholic Historical Society* 5, no. 3, 1977, 23–42; 'Roman Catholic Chapel', *Sydney Gazette* 15 July 1820, https://trove.nla.gov.au/newspaper/article/2179608

[38] Michael Sternbeck, 'For a Godly purpose: planning Saint Mary's Chapel in old Sydney-town,' *Journal of the Australian Catholic Historical Society* 43 (2022), 1-24.

[39] Columbus Fitzpatrick, 'Catholic religious and social life in the Macquarie era: St Mary's Cathedral [As portrayed in the Fitzpatrick letters (1865)]', *Journal of the Australian Catholic Historical Society* 2, no. 1, 1966, 13–45, at 17–18.

2

1821: a new beginning for the Church in Europe and Australia*

Abstract: The year 1821, when Governor Macquarie laid the foundation stone for the first Catholic church in Australia, was a pivotal one both in Australia and in the Old World. The poor Irish Catholic community at the ends of the earth was part of a world Christian revival in the aftermath of the persecutions of the French Revolution and Napoleon.

The year 1821 saw two notable events, one marking the end of the old order and the other the beginning of the new.

In that year Napoleon died in British captivity on St Helena, a remote island in the South Atlantic. His death marked the end of the upheavals of the French Revolution and his invasions of most of Europe. That era of mass destruction, which had threatened the existence of the Church as much as civil society, ended with Napoleon's defeat at Waterloo in 1815 and the restoration of the monarchist European order at the Congress of Vienna. The new political order would last largely unchanged for a hundred years, until destroyed in the First World War.

In that time the fate of most of the world was dominated, for both good and ill, by the European powers. For a distant region like Australia, it was significant that Britain, the country most responsible for defeating Napoleon, was unchallenged as a world power. And in the second significant event of 1821, the British Parliament passed an act for the building of the first public railway line with steam locomotives. The Industrial Revolution would power Britain to world economic leadership. Australia, protected for a century by the undefeated Royal Navy, would become an integrated part of the British Empire. Its language, customs, laws and institutions were "a chip off the old block".

---

* *Catholic Weekly* commemorative edition for the bicentenary of St Mary's, Sydney, 23 October 2022

The revival of faith

The new conditions proved to be fruitful for an extraordinary wave of revival of the Catholic faith and of Christianity more generally.

The eighteenth century was a low point in the history of the Church. The atheist ideas of the French "Enlightenment" seemed to be the way of the future and the Church was identified with decrepit political regimes like that of Louis XVI. When the Revolution swept those away, violent persecutions of the Church ensued.

When Pope Pius VI died as a captive of the French in 1799 and Rome was still occupied by revolutionary armies, the Church was possibly at its lowest ebb in recent centuries. The next papal conclave almost did not take place, but enough cardinals were assembled in Venice to elect a successor. Pius VII proved adept in reaching an accommodation with Napoleon and lived to see the restoration of an acceptable political order after Waterloo.

Catholicism regained the intellectual as well as the political initiative. With Enlightenment ideas tainted as sources of the disasters of the Revolution, the way was open for a renewed appreciation of more conservative and traditionalist ideas such as those of Joseph de Maistre. To Rousseau's naïve and corrosive slogan, "Man is born free and everywhere he is in chains," de Maistre replied "You might as well say that sheep are born carnivorous and everywhere they eat grass." He means that a due respect for authority is not only widely observed but is natural to humans and essential to common life.

With the world freed from tyranny and more stable government in place, a new wave of faith began. In France and Ireland especially, a burst of spiritual energy transformed people's lives.

Australians will recognise the names of some of the leaders of the French Catholic revival because the organisations they founded have played such a crucial role here: especially Marcellin Champagnat, who founded the Marist Brothers in 1816. The Society for the Propagation of the Faith followed in 1822, St Vincent de Paul Society in 1833 and the Missionaries of the Sacred Heart in 1854.

A physical symbol of the revival was Viollet-le-Duc's restoration of the Cathedral of Notre Dame in Paris. Although the medieval walls survived, the inside of the Cathedral was derelict after the destruction of the Revolution. The spire that collapsed spectacularly in the fire of 2019 was a creation of the restoration of the mid-nineteenth century.

The British Empire, opportunity for Irish evangelisation

In Britain, too, the fortunes of religion took a turn for the better in the nineteenth century. An Evangelical Revival contributed to the abolition of slavery, and legal restrictions on Catholics in Britain and Ireland eased. Although the British crown was linked to the Anglican Church, official toleration of Catholics was well advanced by 1821 and Catholic Emancipation was completed by the Duke of Wellington's government in 1829. Catholics then had all normal legal and political rights.

It became clear to Church leaders that the British Empire, though governed by a regime considered heretical, was an opportunity as well as a problem. That arose from the Irish diaspora. Millions of Irish, most of them English speakers, left poverty-stricken Ireland and settled in the countries of the British Empire and the United States. If they could be provided with priests and nuns to preserve and strengthen their faith, they would be the seeds of extensive communities of faith in those large parts of the world.

Ireland itself, like France, was experiencing a religious revival. Australians gratefully remember the Christian Brothers, founded in 1802, the Sisters of Charity, founded in 1815, who provided the first religious sisters to come to Australia in 1838, and the Sisters of Mercy, founded in 1831. The Irish orders long provided much of the man- and woman-power of the Australian church.

While the high point of the "Irish ecclesiastical empire"[1] was reached in the late nineteenth century with the appointment of such leaders as Cardinal Moran in Sydney, the process was well under way earlier. The arrival of the Irish priests Fathers Therry and Conolly in Sydney in 1820, and their cautious welcome by Governor Macquarie, set the scene for the Catholic Church in Australia – an Irish piety flourishing under state toleration. In distant Australia, on its smaller scale, a new beginning was being made that would in the rest of the century turn that remote land into a major stronghold of the Church.

Land of economic opportunity

One aspect of the new Industrial Revolution strongly impacted Australia. A crucial product of English industry was fine wool, which was not easily grown in the cool and wet conditions of England itself. When Napoleon's invasion of Spain threatened the supply of Spanish merino wool, John Macarthur touted the strategic advantages of a replacement source. Millions of sheep on the plains of the distant British colony of New South Wales could replace dependence on European sources.

It was a dubious claim at the time but turned out to be true. Wool survives a long sea voyage and with safe sea lanes, Australian wool took a large share of the British market. The Australian colonies changed from loss-making convict settlements to economically buoyant magnets for immigrants – though often at the expense of the indigenous inhabitants. Convicts from the poorest British classes and poor Irish immigrants found a land with, for many, opportunities they could never have found at home. The large proportion who maintained their faith were able to support a vigorous growth of churches, schools and religious charitable organisations.

The years around 1821 were an auspicious time for establishing the Catholic Church in Australia. That is because they were a time of new beginnings – political, economic and spiritual – across the world.

Reflection on those years will give insights into the opportunities for reviving faith in today's world.

The Catholics of New South Wales in 1821

The white population of the colony of New South Wales in 1821 was about 30,000. Most lived in Sydney and nearby towns and rural areas. The Census of 1828 showed 30 per cent were Catholics, and a similar proportion can be inferred for 1821.

Who were those pioneers of the Australian Church?

They were overwhelmingly Irish and poor. Many were still convicts serving the long sentences that had earned them transportation across the globe. Some worked in gangs on government projects but many were assigned servants in individual households and farms. The rest were mostly ex-convicts who had served their sentences and now were establishing themselves in menial occupations. The adults among both classes were mostly male, as only a small proportion of convicts sent to Australia were women. A first generation of children was growing up and their education was an urgent task.

There was only one priest, the energetic but sometimes irascible Father John Joseph Therry. Two priests had arrived with official recognition in 1820 but the other, Fr Conolly, soon moved to Van Diemen's Land (Tasmania). Father Therry was left and he served the whole colony by himself, from Sydney to the remotest bush, for years.

The "men of '98"

A leading position in the Catholic community was occupied by the "men of '98", a group of ex-convicts who had been transported for alleged involvement in the Irish rebellion of 1798. By 1821 they had long served their sentences and in many cases had become leading citizens. Some of them took leadership of the well-organised lay Catholic community that awaited Fr Therry when he stepped ashore – they formed nearly all of the committee that undertook the appeal for the first St Mary's Church after Fr Therry's arrival. Most prominent as a religious leader was James Dempsey, a supervisor of government building works, in whose house in Kent Street the Catholic community met regularly to pray. Also significant was James Meehan, the deputy government surveyor. His official work led to many land grants to Catholics in the area beyond Campbelltown, which eventually led to a high proportion of Catholic settlers in the Goulburn and Riverina areas. His role in acquiring the site of St Mary's was crucial.

Joining them as a lay leader was Catherine Fitzpatrick, a schoolteacher who had come to Sydney with her convict husband. She trained a choir which later developed into St Mary's Cathedral Choir. The Choir is older than not only the Cathedral itself but the first church in Sydney.

Although the early Catholics were overwhelmingly Irish, multiculturalism has been part of the story from the start. The French Royalist exile, Gabriel Louis Marie Huon de Kerillau, "a Catholic gentleman and scholar", was employed as tutor to the sons of John and Elizabeth Macarthur, the colony's leading citizens. "Louis Peter, a native of India and Roman Catholic" was recorded as a witness in a legal case in 1810. In 1814 a convict, Angelo le Rosse, was accompanied to the gallows by a lay Catholic appointed in place of a priest, as there were no priests in the colony. As far as is known, there were no indigenous Catholics in 1821 (although in 1827 the second chaplain, Fr Power, baptised an aboriginal man on the scaffold).

Protestant attitudes

The attitudes of the Protestant population to their Catholic fellows varied widely. The Reverend Samuel Marsden, "the flogging parson", believed that Irish Catholics were ignorant and savage and their children needed to be forcibly educated in Protestantism. On the other hand, there was considerable Protestant goodwill towards the building of the first St Mary's Church, to the extent that a special committee was formed to handle Protestant donations.

Governor Macquarie, though he had earlier believed that religious uniformity was better for public order, accepted policy from London that Catholic priests be sent to the colony and officially recognised, including payment of a salary. His list of instructions of 1820 to the newly-arrived Fathers Therry and Conolly is welcoming, but cautions them that they are permitted to marry Roman Catholics only and must not proselytise.[2] Father Therry treated the Governor's "instructions" as loose guidelines to be ignored when pastoral necessity demanded it.

Individual voices

It is hard to hear the individual voices of the earliest Catholics, as most of them can be known only through basic convict and census records and the occasional newspaper articles. They have not left writings of their own.

However, there are just a few exceptions, where we can hear from them directly. One is the merchant Michael Hayes, one of the "men of '98" and the subject of Vivienne Keely's biography.[3] He prospered for a time in the 1810s and several letters of his give insights into the difficulties of business and his family life. His letters to his brother, a priest in Rome, were significant in gaining attention to the needs of Catholics in Sydney.

Another source is the collection of notes and letters received by Father Therry. The State Library of New South Wales website has a page displaying a number of urgent and poignant requests sent to him.[4] One says:

> Sydney Gaol March the 16th 1822
>
> Revd,
>
> Mr. Terry we beg your assistance at the Last Day we are anxious to see you in hope it may Reconcile us, for god sake come, as we hope in the almighty god we are to Die in a few Days.
>
> Francis Murphy
>
> James Fallen

It is a reminder of the harsh times and desperate situations of many in early Sydney.

The most extensive eyewitness account is that written in old age by Columbus Fitzpatrick, Catherine's son, who remembered the lay community of the late 1810s.[5] He was an altar boy to Fr Therry at Governor Macquarie's laying of the foundation stone of the first St Mary's on 29th October 1821. He recalled holding the ceremonial silver trowel before Fr Therry handed it to the Governor, and claimed to remember a good deal of the inscription on it. Remarkably, his account can be checked – he has it almost right – because the trowel still exists. It is held by the State Library.

At the time of the centenary celebrations of the colony in 1888, the Sydney Catholic newspaper, the *Freeman's Journal*, was able to interview the aged but alert Ambrose Fitzpatrick, the younger brother of Columbus.[6] He was by then one of the last persons alive able to remember the time before 1820. He testified to the reservation of the Blessed Sacrament in Dempsey's house where it was left by Fr Jeremiah O'Flynn, who had been expelled by Governor Macquarie in 1818 after arriving in Sydney without permission.

There is much still to discover about the early years of Catholicism in the colony. Dr Damian Gleeson, the State Library of New South Wales Australian Religious History Fellow for 2022, is engaged on Fr Therry's papers and is finding many yet untold stories of our Irish forebears.

Many well-researched and beautifully illustrated stories from the early days are available on Michael Sternbeck's marvellous *In Diebus Illis* blog.[7]

We pray for the souls of, especially, the anonymous pioneers who founded our Australian Catholic community.

---

[1] Colin Barr, *Ireland's Empire: The Roman Catholic Church in the English-Speaking World, 1829–1914* (Cambridge University Press, Cambridge, 2020), reviewed by Jeff Kildea in *Journal of the Australian Catholic Historical Society* 41 (2020), 212-15.

[2] Copy of instructions from Governor Macquarie to the Reverend Messrs. P. Connolly and J.J. Therry, Roman Catholic chaplains, 14 October 1820, https://trove.nla.gov.au/newspaper/article/2186564

[3] Vivienne Keely, Michael Hayes: *The Life of a 1798 Wexford Rebel in Sydney* (Anchor Books, Melbourne, 2019), reviewed by Michael Sternbeck in the *Journal of the Australian Catholic Historical Society* 41 (2020), 199-201.

[4] State Library of New South Wales Archive, John Joseph Therry, https://www2.sl.nsw.gov.au/archive/discover_collections/history_nation/religion/catholics/therry/

[5] 'Catholic religious and social life in the Macquarie era', *Journal of the Australian Catholic Historical Society* 2 (1) (1966), 13-45, https://australiancatholichistoricalsociety.com.au/wp-content/uploads/2022/10/columbusfitzpatrick.pdf

[6] 'The Church and the Centenary', *Freeman's Journal*, 21 Jan 1888, https://trove.nla.gov.au/newspaper/article/115461422

[7] *In Diebus Illis*, https://inthosedayes.blogspot.com/

3

Catholic missions to Aboriginal Australia: an evaluation*

Abstract: The paper gives an overview of the Catholic Church's missionary efforts to the Aboriginal peoples of northern and western Australia up to 1970. It aims to understand the interaction of missions with native culture and the resulting hybrid culture created on the missions. It describes the differing points of view of missionaries and the generations who grew up on the missions.

It is argued that the culture created on the missions by the joint efforts of missionaries and local peoples was by and large a positive phase in Australian black history, between the violence of pre-contact times and the dysfunctionality of recent decades. Criticisms of the missions are considered, such as those arising from their opposition to aspects of native culture and from their involvement in child removals.

Introduction

There is no overview available of the Catholic mission effort to Aboriginal Australia (or of the Christian missions overall. A short article cannot fill that gap, but it can make a start by indicating the topics that need to be covered, the questions to be answered and the sources available.[1]

Here, "missions" is taken in the traditional sense, where a group of white clergy and helpers establish themselves in a remote location and preach and provide other services to local black people who have had little contact with whites. Such initiatives as apostolates to urban black communities are excluded.

The topic is important because the history of Aboriginal interaction with missions is quite different from the history of other white-black interactions in Australia, and because many present-day remote communities are former missions which still have strong connections with their mission past.

---

* *Journal of the Australian Catholic Historical Society* 37 (1) (2016), 45-68, edited. The original article included a bibliography which is omitted here.

Mission foundations

While Catholic church authorities in earlier times were mostly fully occupied with establishing the Church in white society, the needs of the Aboriginal people were not entirely forgotten. The first Catholic bishop and archbishop in Australia, John Bede Polding, wrote:

> White men have too often been apostles of Satan, have riveted his chains and confirmed his kingdom. It seems now almost a necessity that Christian missionaries should isolate themselves from all intercourse with white men. We want missionaries equal to the glorious exiles of those members of the Society of Jesus, who preached and taught the Gospel of old in the reduction of Paraguay, and, perhaps, this country will never be fully purified and absolved until such men have arisen within it.[2]

Polding sent a small number of Italian missionaries to Stradbroke Island in the 1840s, but the mission failed through lack of resources and difficulties with the local population,[3] as did a roving mission in Queensland by Fr Duncan McNab.[4]

The missions founded in the nineteenth century[5] are indicated in Fig 1 (next page).

New Norcia was a Benedictine Abbey with an Aboriginal ministry that was successful in the long term. Much has been written about it[6] and much was written by the founders themselves.[7] Following an unsuccessful Jesuit mission at Rapid Creek near Darwin,[8] the Jesuit mission on the Daly River, at one time led by Mary MacKillop's brother Donald MacKillop, had some initial success but failed because of financial difficulties and a disastrous flood.[9] Beagle Bay was founded by French Trappists and later run by German Pallottines.[10] Its pearl shell altar is still a noted tourist attraction. Thursday Island was not a mission in exactly the traditional sense, as Thursday Island was a European port settlement, but it conducted missionary activities with the Torres Strait Islander people.[11]

Drysdale River (Kalumburu) was an offshoot of New Norcia.[12] Lombadina was associated with the Trappist/Pallottine mission but largely founded by the Filipino Thomas Puertollano.[13] Balgo was es-

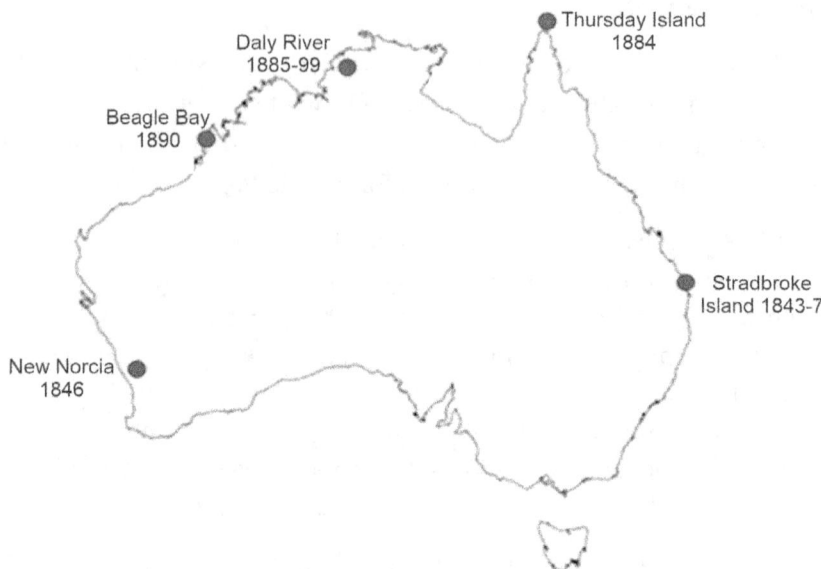

Figure 1 Catholic missions in Australia in the nineteenth century

The missions in the twentieth century are indicated in Fig 2:

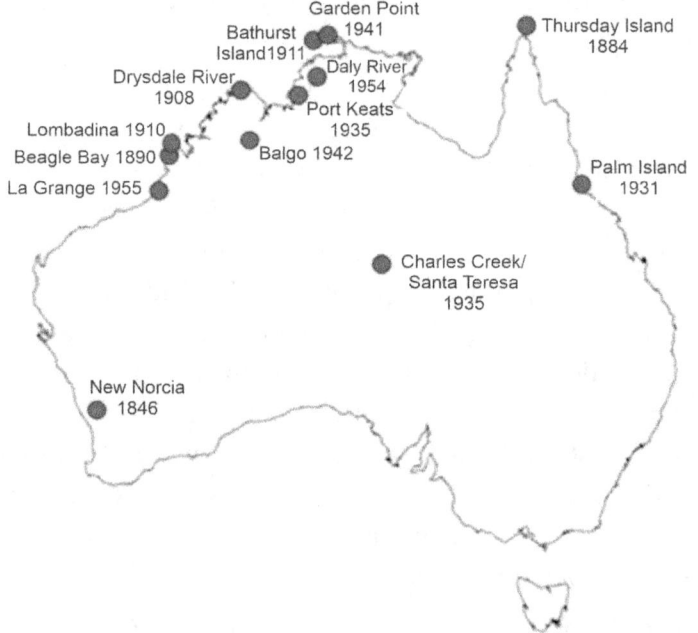

Figure 2 Catholic missions in Australia in the twentieth century

tablished in cattle country in the Kimberley and operated as a cattle station,[14] and there were some other shorter-term missions in the Kimberley. Bathurst Island (Nguiu, now Wurrumiyanga) was founded in 1911 by Father (later Bishop) Francis Xavier Gsell of the Missionaries of the Sacred Heart.[15] A mission in the Alice Springs area existed in several locations, eventually settling at Santa Teresa.[16] The Palm Island mission ministered to those dumped there from other Queensland locations.[17] Garden Point on Melville Island (described further in the next chapter) was not a traditional mission but was established by Gsell to care for children of mostly mixed race, some of them removed from their families under government policy.[18] Port Keats (Wadeye) was established in 1935.[19] A mission was re-established on the Daly River. La Grange (Bidyadanga) was established near Broome in 1955.[20]

Fr Richard Docherty MSC and friends, Port Keats, 1930s
Missionaries of the Sacred Heart

In addition to the missions, religious sisters staffed three leprosariums, most of the patients of which were Aboriginal. At Derby WA, Channel Island NT, and Fantome Island near Palm Island, they were originally established as government facilities and handed over to orders of nuns.[21]

Something of the tone and point of the missions, as conceived by the missionaries, is encapsulated in the most celebrated story

Derby Leprosarium Orchestra, 1948
– Stuart Gore Collection, State Library of WA

Bathurst Island mission sawmill, 1958
Australian Archives, image no. A1200, L25645

from them, Francis Xavier Gsell's dramatic account of Martina, a Bathurst Island mission girl who objected to an arranged marriage with an older man and was "bought" by him. (The story is told more fully in the next chapter.) Over the following decades, Gsell "bought" in similar fashion a hundred and fifty promised girls, all of them, according to tribal law, his wives. He became known as the "bishop with 150 wives".[22]

Those who grew up as children on the missions learned a monastically-ordered lifestyle that contrasts with Aboriginal life before and since. Betty Lockyer, of mixed Aboriginal and Malay parentage, believed that her removal by government action was unjustified, but was positive about her life at Beagle Bay Mission in the 1940s:

> The men had their jobs to do, each going to their own workplace, whether it was the bakery, gardens or checking the windmills. The women stayed at home to look after the babies and little ones, or worked elsewhere for a few hours. Some helped out at the church, convent, presbytery or the Brothers' houses. There was no such thing as idle hands. They all knew their jobs and did them well … Our people were shown how to live an orderly lifestyle and in that short time they learned to conform.[23]

(Lockyer does however think the life was rather too ordered for everyone's good.)

In a rare letter from a young person on a mission, Hilda, a girl from Drysdale River, wrote to the Abbot at New Norcia about the return of the nuns after World War II:

> Since the Sister are here everything very nice. We are having the meals on the table we ate doing in turns to wash the plates and set the table also we the three big girls we help the sisters to set the table for the Fathers do the cleaning and feed the fowls and some other little things; the young married women are helping in the kitchen washing iron and mending. I sometimes help the sister to make the bread fry de eggs in the morning and to take the diner to the Fathers. I'm still going to the school which I like very much because the most I learned the most useful I will be to the Sisters.[24]

As a single illustration of what it was like for the missionaries "on the ground", Sister Antoninus recalls the early days at Garden Point:

> In those wonderful tea chests that Sister Annunciata had packed in Sydney there was a pile of discarded Sacred Heart sodality banners that had really seen better days but the linings, albeit faded and streaked were made of strong sateen. These, Mother ripped up and made into pants for the small children and believe me they needed a supply for they certainly were not toilet trained. Marie and John had the habit of dirtying their trousers and discarding them anywhere, the little imps would never say where. Many a night, Sister Eucharia and I would sally forth with a hurricane lamp searching the yard for the offending articles, wash them so that the scamps would have something to put on in the morning.[25]

And of course the heat was appalling.

Generalities

Some general points, mostly obvious, help to put the story in perspective.

The story of the missions (both Catholic and Protestant) is quite different from the story of other interactions between black and white Australians. Earlier settlers, pastoralists and miners forcibly occupied the country and did as they wished, while the Aboriginal population had to accommodate themselves to the situation as best they could. Missions did not operate on those principles. Although the missionaries invited themselves to a remote location, after that their success depended on local cooperation. They were usually unarmed, they were unable to impose their will on the locals (at least, until much later times), and they occupied only the area of the mission. If the local people did not like it, they needed only to avoid contact – indeed, that is largely what happened at the first mission on Stradbroke Island (and initially at Drysdale River, where there was briefly armed conflict). On the missionaries' side too, a cooperative spirit was needed, in ways not necessary for the rest of white Australia. Their aim was to persuade the objects of missionary endeavour of the benefits of Christianity and civilisation, so basic research into the

Aboriginal way of seeing things was necessary,[26] and there was no reason to attack those aspects of native culture that were considered compatible with Christianity.

Understanding the initial interaction is difficult because we lack the perspective of one of the actors. The story involves three groups of actors – the missionaries, the first generation of the local population who dealt with them, and later generations who grew up as children on the missions. There is plenty of information coming from the first and third of these, but in the nature of the case very little from the second.

We can nevertheless make certain inferences about the cooperation that the first generation afforded to the missionaries. The first necessary cooperation was linguistic. Local populations did communicate with the missionaries, often in a combination of sign language and pidgin; those missionaries who learned the local language relied on the patience of locals to teach them. Locals were aware of the advantages of white technology such as fishhooks and knives, and knew that the missions could provide food security in bad times, and for people facing threats of violence, physical security. Tobacco (that is, chewing tobacco) and sugar products proved attractive,[27] but alcohol was avoided.

The local populations did not, by and large, cooperate in the way the missionaries most desired, by becoming converted to Christianity. Gsell, one of the most successful missionaries, had not a single adult convert in his first thirty years. Some "conversion" was more like an assimilation of parts of the missionary message to local spiritual understandings.[28] But time was on the side of the missionary endeavour, because of the most momentous decision in favour of cooperation that the local communities made. It was to allow the missionaries to bring up later generations of children. The reasons for that decision are not entirely clear.

As a result the missions have had a great impact on Aboriginal history. The biggest remote communities today are former missions. The largest is Wadeye, the former Catholic mission of Port Keats.

The missionaries operated under a model that was more monastic than assimilationist. New Norcia was literally a monastery, but in other cases too it was considered best to, as Polding said, go as far away as possible from white society with its temptations and risks ("where the evils of our European civilization had not yet penetrated", as Salvado put it;[29] Gsell said "Bathurst had no white settlers and was completely free of interference".[30]) The communities were to be as far as possible isolated and self-sufficient.

Not many missionaries undertook anthropological or linguistic work on Aboriginal cultures. There is no Catholic counterpart to the Strehlows' work at the Lutheran mission in Hermannsburg. But Fr Ernest Worms made extensive studies of Kimberley and other Aboriginal languages and religions.[31] Donald MacKillop's work on local languages has not been much investigated.[32]

The history of the missions is an Australian Catholic story largely without Irish. Whereas much of Australian Catholic history before recent times was dominated by the Irish, the mission field saw very few. Spanish, Germans, French, Italians, Filipinos and native Australians provided the mission personnel.[33] A rare exception is the unusual figure of Fr John Creagh, who enjoyed a successful ecclesiastical career in the Kimberley after inciting an antisemitic riot in Limerick in 1904.[34] A number of Irish nuns worked at Beagle Bay.[35]

The Catholic story ought to be compared to the story of Protestant missions. That is beyond the scope of the present chapter, but the careful multi-decadal study of Mornington Island in the anthropologist David McKnight's books such as *From Hunting to Drinking* shows similar patterns. A period of relative calm in mission times separates a violent traditional past from an equally violent and alcohol-fuelled period since the 1970s.

Evaluations

Evaluations of the missions have ranged widely. An extreme view is that deriving from Comintern policy which declared tribal peoples an oppressed class in the Marxist sense and hence identified the missionaries as agents of colonial oppression. That theory was sent to

Australia and appeared with local embellishments in the *Workers' Weekly* of 25 September 1931:

> The Aboriginal race, the original inhabitants of Australia, are among the most exploited subject peoples in the world. Not only are inhuman exploitation, forced Labor and actual slavery forced upon the Aborigines, but a campaign of mass physical extermination is being and has been carried on against them, until to-day less than 60,000 full bloods have survived the murder drive ... setting up organisations of crawlers and kidnappers, known as "Aborigines Protection Boards" to enslave the remaining members of the tribes, and "Mission Stations," under dope-peddlers to muster the youth so that they can be sold into slavery – such truly British methods were used, and are still being used to enslave the Australian Aborigines and to totally exterminate the race ...

The *Workers' Weekly* includes in its demands:

> (11) Liquidation of all missions and so-called homes for Aborigines, as these are part of the weapons being used to exterminate the Aboriginal race by segregating the sexes and sending the young girls into slavery.[36]

No evidence of allegations of slavery was provided then or since, making it difficult to understand why Comintern propaganda of 1931 resembles so closely contemporary views in some parts of the political spectrum of the past interaction of whites and blacks in Australia.

Views based on closer observation have generally been more positive. An example comes from Mark Nevill, a teacher and geologist who was familiar with the Balgo mission in the East Kimberley over a number of decades, both during and after the mission era.

> In Mark [Nevill]'s view the work of the Pallottines and the St John of God sisters in the Kimberley is an heroic chapter in our State and national history. Mark sees the strength of Balgo then, compared with now, as being:
>
> - Better policing, no alcohol,
> - Better education, no truancy,
> - Better health,

- Better diet, supplemented with much bush tucker,
- Organised work and the learning of skills. The policy was no work, no tucker!
- Industry developed, horses, cattle, etc.,
- There was a role for men,
- The Aborigines were free to move around, and,
- Minimal impact on Aboriginal culture – they were free to practice their customs outside the immediate Mission area.

Negative change in Aboriginal communities in the Kimberley is often attributed to the introduction of the equal wage. Yet, while pastoralists were concerned about the possibility of higher wages, little displacement occurred as a result. The other factors that Mark identified as causing an exodus from the stations were:

- Access to child endowment and unemployment benefits, or 'sit-down money' as it was called,
- Rising costs due to the first oil price hike, and,
- Changes in the pastoral industry, which displaced the need for labour. Changes such as mechanisation - mustering planes, motorbikes, portable pumps, better fencing, steel cattle yards, etc

The result is that many Aboriginal people lost the structure they had in their everyday lives, a structure that was there in the traditional lifestyle in the desert, on the missions and on the stations. The increased disposable income gave them increased access to alcohol and nutritionally poor food.[37]

Negative views of the effect of the missions have come from two directions – one suggesting they were contemptuous of and destructive of native culture, and the other criticising their involvement in government child removal policies.

An example of the former is an article, 'The Catholic Church's toll on Aboriginal Australia'.[38] It criticises elements of Frank O'Grady's *Francis of Central Australia*, a biography of lay missionary Francis McGarry who worked at the Alice Springs/Arltunga mission (later moved to Santa Teresa). "O'Grady quotes McGarry ordering the children that they 'were not to speak Arunta [sic] in church or in school otherwise they would be sent home without tucker'. McGarry also sought to 'work quietly towards the elimination' of adherence to Arrernte cultural practices."

That is not convincing as criticism as it stands. The context involves children who have recently begun to attend the presbytery and go home every day, so they are not isolated from their own language. To learn any language, one needs have a space in which that language must be spoken. Speaking in a form of English also allows McGarry to know what is going on.[39] The reference to "cultural practices" mainly concerns corroborees. McGarry regarded some as unobjectionable but did campaign against initiation corroborees that involved high levels of mutilation.[40]

One aspect of traditional culture the missionaries certainly did work to eliminate, namely the high levels of violence. McGarry intervened to reduce levels of traditional "payback" violence.[41] Brother John Pye tells similar stories on the Daly River, and as evidence of success tells of only one murder or manslaughter being committed in mission times, 1938–1972.[42] Gsell took little interest in cultural practices in general and for their own sake, but worked to eliminate those of the kind now called abuses of human rights, such as enforced child marriages and the burying alive of decrepit old people.

In general, present-day attitudes take it, without further argument, that the breaking down of native culture is a bad thing in itself.[43] That is a thoughtless methodological stance. Aboriginal society, like Western society or any other, can contain features that are dysfunctional and anti-human. Claims of the missionaries that certain practices were evil and needed to end are neither self-justifying nor self-refuting. They need to be taken seriously and evaluated in the light of universal principles of human rights. It is still true that putting stress on a culture can have evil effects such as chaos from the breakdown of authority. There is no problem with debating that in any particular case. The problem arises from the unargued assumption that criticism of aspects of another culture and efforts to change it are inherently wrong. Gsell writes of those who criticise in principle the missionaries' attempts to change culture:

> ... these fine talkers, few of whom have given the subject any deep thought, themselves enjoy the benefits of Christian civilization: and they enjoy this security because, in day[s] of old, missionaries brought these benefits to their forebears. The heathens are men as we are men and, as such, they have the same right that we have to the benefits of Christianity.[44]

It is true however that some missionaries did behave arrogantly towards cultural practices to which there could be no reasonable objection. The Tiwi on Bathurst Island remember Fr John Fallon destroying Pukamani, the sacred burial poles. Fallon later described himself as fired by zeal to convert souls and destroy idolatrous practices, and expressed regret.[45]

The second source of criticisms of the missionaries comes from their involvement in child removals and the "Stolen Generations". Government child removal policies, especially in the Northern Territory and the Kimberley, relied on cooperation from the missions to bring up the removed children. The policy of large-scale removal of children of mixed blood was pioneered in the Kimberley after the Aborigines Act of 1905, as a partnership between state officials and the Beagle Bay mission.[46] It was driven initially by concerns about tribes prostituting women to lugger crews and the resulting needs of the "unfortunate half-caste and black children who are to be seen in Broome streets, acquiring all the worst vices of Asiatics and blacks"[47] and the church was allowed to take and educate them. From 1909, government policy was to remove all part-Aboriginal children in the Kimberley, described as " 'rescuing of waifs and strays from the bad contaminating influence of natives' camps".[48] Beagle Bay looked after and educated them at little cost to the government.

Many of the mothers came too and lived in the mission compound, separately from their children in the dormitory. Some contact was allowed and it was not the purpose of the mission to separate the children entirely from their mothers or culture. Father Walter's 1928 account says

> It is not the duty of a Missionary to repress a child's Aboriginal nature and for this reason the children are given as much freedom as possible to follow their customs and practices. From time

to time all children are allowed to attend ordinary corrobborees (under supervision) and to hold their own corrobborees. Outings are utilised to make them sufficiently familiar with bush craft to survive, and one competes with another to catch snakes, lizards, kangaroos and other game, and to study animal trails.[49]

Nevertheless the education was almost entirely Western and children were locked in the dormitory at night.

Debate on past child-removal policies has been vitiated by a high level of moral indignation combined with a low level of attention to the evidence from those involved such as patrol officers on the reasons for what they did. Bishop Gsell, who as Bishop of Darwin was in charge of Catholic involvement in child removal in the Northern Territory in the 1940s, writes of "half-caste" children removed from camps, "these creatures roam miserably around the camps and their behaviour is often worse than that of native children. It is an act of mercy to remove them as soon as possible from surroundings so insecure."[50] (The quotation is given more fully in the next chapter.) Gsell's phrase "worse than that of native children" refers to the fact that removal policies were aimed mainly at children of mixed blood, who were considered to be especially at risk. As the Northern Territory patrol officer Colin Macleod explained it, referring to the late 1950s,

> A person brought up without the protection of the tribal life, without any supporting family other than a very young mother, who almost certainly had been abused at its birth, was going to be kicked from arsehole to breakfast time.
>
> These children were often the butt of cruelty not only from whites but also from the full-blood Aboriginals. Brother Pye of the Catholic mission at Garden Point once saw a six-year-old part-coloured boy speared by a full-blooded Aboriginal, almost as a joke, just because the boy was a "yella fella". Brother Pye took this boy under his wing, probably saving his life.
>
> Half-caste kids would now and again turn up at missions with spear marks and signs of horrific beltings. Babies were occasionally abandoned and young children left to fend for themselves. "Yella fellas" could find themselves in a no-man's land and a no-

win situation. No-one will ever know how many were left to die, killed or simply pined away ... Many of the children taken away were being given a chance to live and not die, to have a life beyond childhood without being permanently maimed. Garden Point ... was a preferred destination ... [Brother Pye] felt that in many cases these children were saved from real danger and abject misery by being sent to Garden Point.[51]

(Macleod does believe that before his time, in the 1940s, removals were sometimes undertaken for more ideological reasons.)

Debate on the intentions and results of child removal policies ought to proceed, and it is certainly arguable that the policy of removing virtually all mixed-blood children did not allow for individual cases to be properly considered. But debate can only proceed on the basis of considering the relevant evidence from all the interested parties.

Other criticisms of the missionaries arise from negative memories of some who grew up on the missions. *The Bringing Them Home* report contains an allegation of sexual abuse at Garden Point and there have been later apologies for abuse suffered there.[52]

Aftermath

Around 1970, control of the missions was handed over to governments and many changes occurred through new government policies such as welfare payments, self-determination and land rights, and the general encroachments of modernity. Despite the changes being individually reasonable, the generally disastrous effects of the whole are now well-known. As detailed in books like Stephanie Jarrett's *Liberating Aboriginal People from Violence*, Peter Sutton's *The Politics of Suffering*, Geoffrey Partington's *Hasluck Versus Coombs*, Rosemary Neill's *White Out* and David McKnight's *From Hunting to Drinking*, remote Aboriginal communities were swept by a wave of violence, alcoholism and cultural disintegration. Optimistic present-day talk of "closing the gap" covers up extreme and continuing levels of domestic violence, alcohol and drug consumption, chronic health problems and low school attendance. If the missions are to be evaluated by comparison to what happened later, the bar is low. As Sutton, the leading expert in indigenous violence, writes, "Public recognition of mission time as far happier and safer than the post-liberation era, in the segregated communities, came not just from Indigenous people but was increasingly being recognised by others, even academics ... There is, in fact, much complaint that life was substantially better under the old pre-1970 mission regimes. Even if we discount the distorting factor of Golden Age nostalgia here, for many settlements this is the uncomfortable truth."[53]

Catholic involvement with the former missions did not cease with the changes of around 1970, although it was in a lower key. A visitor to a former mission today will find an active Catholic community with mass being said regularly. According to census data (2011), they are the most Catholic places in the country:

Parish	Diocese	Total Catholics	Per cent Catholic
Santa Teresa	Darwin	490	88.8
Wadeye	Darwin	2322	86.6
Bathurst Island	Darwin	1400	86.5
Melville Island	Darwin	799	83.1
Balbo Kutjungka	Broome	939	66.3
Daly River	Darwin	765	63.6
Kalumburu	Broome	461	62.7
Dampier Peninsular	Broome	629	60.9
Horsley Park	Sydney	2669	57.2

Table 1. Parishes with the highest percent Catholic, 2011 Australian Census[54]

Although there were no ordinations to the priesthood of former mission residents, there were a number of Aboriginal nuns.[55] Bishop Raible set up a short-lived order of Aboriginal nuns in the Kimberley.[56] Boniface Perdjert of Port Keats was Australia's first permanent deacon.[57]

A very colourful tribute to mission days was the 1990 comedy-drama musical and 2009 movie *Bran Nue Dae*.[58] As in *Star Wars*, the man in black is revealed to be father of one of the younger characters.

A celebrated Aboriginal Catholic image was that used on vestments in World Youth Day in 2008. It was given by Marjorie Liddy, a former resident of Garden Point, who saw it in a vision while driving at night.[59] Liddy commented on the "Stolen Generations" in an ABC News item on the centenary of the Bathurst Island Mission:

> MARJORIE LIDDY, STOLEN GENERATIONS: I had to grow up at – we were taken to Garden Point. They was collecting part-coloured children, to look after us there.
>
> FATHER JOHN MULRONEY: I wanted to say to you today that if any MSC has hurt you in any way, or has in anyway done you any harm, in anyway has misunderstood your culture and in any way harmed your culture I say to you sorry unreservedly.
>
> MARJORIE LIDDY, STOLEN GENERATIONS: Probably they feel from us being taken away, they might feel a little bit responsible about it. I don't know what they feel, but we had a beautiful upbringing. But no they did, gave us everything in life, taught us everything.
>
> PAULINE COMPTON, PROVINCIAL OLSH SISTERS: Again I would also like to say we are sorry if we have hurt you, or misunderstood your culture.[106]

A just evaluation of the missions will need to prioritise the testimony of those who were there, not the view of those seeking to impose later agendas.

---

[1] 2022 note: This gap has now been filled by Regina Ganter's impressive and massively well-informed 2018 book, *The Contest for Aboriginal Souls: European missionary agendas in Australia* (ANU Press), which covers both Catholic and Protestant missions.

[2] John Bede Polding, 'Pastoral letter of the Second Provincial Council of Australia, 1869', in P. O'Farrell, ed, *Documents in Australian Catholic History* (G. Chapman, London, 1969), Vol I, 413–6; authorship discussed in Girola, Stefano, 'The Italian connection: new historical sources on European-Aboriginal relationships', *Australasian Catholic Record* 87 (2010), 92–106.

[3] Osmund Thorpe, *First Catholic Mission to the Australian Aborigines* (Pellegrini, Sydney, 1950); Ganter, Regina, *The Stradbroke Island Mission*, http://missionaries.griffith.edu.au/qld-mission/test-stradbroke-island-mission-1843-1847#The_Catholics_in_Australia

[4] H. J. Gibbney, Duncan McNab, (1820–1896), *Australian Dictionary of Biography*, vol. 5 (1974): https://adb.anu.edu.au/biography/mcnab-duncan-4131

[5] Survey in Stefano Girola, 'Catholic missions among indigenous Australians in the 19th century', in Girola, S. & R. Pizzini, eds, *Nagoyo: The Life of Don Angelo Confalonieri among the Aborigines of Australia, 1846–1848* (Trentino Historical Museum Foundation, Trento, 2013), 85–104.

[6] G. H Russo, *Lord Abbot of the Wilderness: The life and times of Bishop Salvado* (Polding Press, Melbourne, 1980); James Flood, *New Norcia* (Burns & Oates, London, 1908); Anna Haebich, 'No man is an island – Bishop Salvado's vision for mission work with the Aboriginal people of Western Australia', *New Norcia Studies* 9 (Sept. 2001), 20–28; Kenneth B Williams, 'To what extent did Bishop Rosendo Salvado seek to preserve Aboriginal culture in the conduct of his mission at New Norcia?' *New Norcia Studies* 9 (Sept. 2001), 29–35; Anouk Ride, *The Grand Experiment: Two boys, two cultures* (Hachette, Sydney, 2007); Tiffany Shellam, 'A mystery to the medical world: Florence Nightingale, Rosendo Salvado and the risk of civilisation', *History Australia* 9 (1) (2012), 110–135; Théophile Bérengier, *New Norcia: History of a Benedictine Colony in Western Australia, 1846–1878*, trans. P. Gilet (Abbey Press, Northcote, Vic, 2014); Bob Reece, 'The Invincibles: New Norcia's Aboriginal cricketers, 1879–1906', (*Histrionics*, Perth, 2014); Katharine Massam, 'Missionary women and work: Benedictine women at New Norcia claiming a religious vocation', *Journal of Australian Studies* 39 (2015), 44–53.

[7] Rosendo Salvado, *The Salvado Memoirs* (University of Western Australia Press, Nedlands, 1977), *Report of Rosendo Salvado to Propaganda Fide in 1883*, trans. and ed. Girola Stefano (Abbey Press, Northcote Vic, 2015); *The Torres Diaries 1901–1914: diaries of Dom Fulgentius* (Anthony) Torres y Mayans, O.S.B. Abbot Nullius of New Norcia, Bishop Titular of Dorylaeum, Administrator Apostolic of the Kimberley Vicariate in North Western Australia, ed. R. Pratt and J. Millington (Artlook Books, Perth, 1987).

[8] Regina Ganter, *Rapid Creek*: http://missionaries.griffith.edu.au/mission/rapid-creek-1882-1891.

[9] G. J. O'Kelly, *The Jesuit mission stations in the Northern Territory 1882–1889*, BA Hons thesis, Monash University, 1967; John Pye, *The Daly River Story: A river unconquered* (John Pye, Darwin, 1976); Feehan, H.V., 'Donald MacKillop SJ – advocate and apostle of Aboriginals', *Footprints* Nov 1981, 35–38; Lan Gray, 'Aboriginal fertility at the time of European contact: the Daly River baptismal register', *Aboriginal History* 7 (1/2) (1983), 80–89; Deborah Bird Rose, 'Signs of life on a barbarous frontier: intercultural encounters in north Australia', in *The Archaeology of Difference: negotiating cross-cultural engagements in Oceania*, ed. R. Torrence and A. Clark (Routledge, London, 2000), 215–37; R M Berndt, 'Surviving influence of Mission contact on the Daly River, Northern Territory of Australia', *Neue Zeitschrift fur Missionswissenschrift*, 8 (2/3) (1952), 1–20; Regina Ganter, *Daly River (1886–1899)*: http://missionaries.griffith.edu.au/mission/daly-river-1886-1899

[10] George Walter, *Australia: Land, People, Mission*, trans. I. Danaher (Bishop of Broome, Broome, 1982); Remi Balagai, et al, *This Is Your Place: Beagle Bay Mission, 1890–1990: Birthplace and cradle of Catholic presence in the Kimberley* (Pallottine Centre, Rossmoyne WA, 2001); Brigida Nailon, *Emo and San Salvador* (Brigidine Sisters, Echuca, 2005) Christine Choo, 'The role of the Catholic missionaries at Beagle Bay in the removal of Aboriginal children from their families in the Kimberley region from the 1890s', *Aboriginal History* 21 (1997), 14–29; Betty Lockyer, *Last Truck Out* (Magabala

Books, Broome, 2009); Pat Jacobs, *Living on the Kimberley Pearling Coast: Sisters of St John of God in the Early Twentieth Century* (Sisters of St John of God Heritage Centre, Broome, 2014); Regina Ganter, *Beagle Bay (1890–2000)*: http://missionaries.griffith.edu.au/mission/beagle-bay-1890-2000

11 Tyrone Deere, *Stone on Stone: Story of the Hammond Island Mission* (Our Lady of the Sacred Heart Church, Thursday Island, 1994).

12 Anselm M Catalan, *Lecture on the origin and development of the Drysdale River Mission, Western Australia, from 1908 to 1934* (Co-operative Printing Works, Perth, 1935); Eugene Perez, *Kalumburu: The Benedictine Mission and the Aborigines 1908–1975* (Kalumburu Benedictine Mission, Wyndham WA, 1977); Hilton Deakin, *The Unan cycle: a study of social change in an Aboriginal community*, PhD, Monash University, 1978; Eugene Perez, *Kalumburu War Diary*, ed. R. Pratt and J. Millington (Artlook Books, Perth, 2001); Mary Pandilow, 'The coming of the missionaries to Kalumburu: an Aboriginal view of a West Australian Catholic Mission', *Nungalinya News* 46 (1987), 4–5; Christine Choo, 'Conflict between value systems: marriage laws and the Drysdale River Mission', *New Norcia Studies* 2 (1994), 59–65; Ambrose Mungala Chalarimeri, *The Man From the Sunrise Side* (Magabala Books, Broome, 2001); Seraphim Sanz de Galdeano and Dolores Djinmora, *Metamorphosis of a Race: Kuíni and Kulári tribes of Kalúmburu Mission* (Hesperian Press, Carlisle WA, 2006).

13 Regina Ganter, *Lombadina*, http://missionaries.griffith.edu.au/mission/lombadina-1911-1975 and Thomas Puertollano: http://missionaries.griffith.edu.au/biography/puertollano-thomas-1869-1942; Regina Ganter, *Balgo (1940–1965)*: http://missionaries.griffith.edu.au/mission/balgo

14 D. Choules Edinger and G. Marsh, *Reassessing the missions: Balgo – its history and contributions, Kimberley Society*: http://www.kimberleysociety.org/oldfiles/2004/REASSESSING%20THE%20MISSIONS%20Nov%2004.pdf

15 P. H. Ritchie, *North of the Never Never* (Angus and Robertson, Sydney, 1934); A Barclay, 'Life at Bathurst Island Mission', *Walkabout* 5 (8) (1939), 13–19; Francis Xavier Gsell, *The Bishop with 150 Wives: Fifty years as a missionary* (Angus and Robertson, Sydney, 1955); F Lancaster Jones, *A Demographic Survey of the Aboriginal Population of the Northern Territory, with Special Reference to Bathurst Island Mission* (Canberra: Australian Institute of Aboriginal Studies, 1963); Owen Stanley, *An Aboriginal Economy: Nguiu, Northern Territory*, Australian National University, North Australia Research Unit, Casuarina, NT, 1984; Diane Bell, 'Choose your mission wisely: Christian colonials and Aboriginal marital arrangements on the northern frontier', in *Aboriginal Australians and Christian Missions*, ed. Tony Swain and Deborah Bird Rose (Australian Association for the Study of Religions, Bedford Park SA, 1988), 338–352; Colin Macleod, *Patrol in the Dreamtime* (Victoria Mandarin, Kew, 1997), 115–22; John Morris, 'The Japanese and the Aborigines: an overview of the efforts to stop the prostitution of coastal and island women', *Journal of Northern Territory History* 21 (2010), 15–36; John Morris, *The Tiwi: From isolation to cultural change* (NTUP, Darwin, 2001), ch. 6; James Franklin, 'The missionary with 150 wives', *Quadrant* 56 (7/8), (July/Aug 2012), 31–32: https://quadrant.org.au/magazine/2012/07-08/the-missionary-with-150-wives/ (edited version in this collection); Regina Ganter, *Bathurst Island Mission 1911–1938–1978*, http://missionaries.griffith.edu.au/mission/bathurst-island-mission-1911-1938-1978

16 Frank O'Grady, *Francis of Central Australia* (Wentworth Books, Sydney, 1977); John Pye, *Santa Teresa and East Aranda History* (Colemans Printing, Darwin, 1989); Jolien Harmsen, *You Gave Us the Dreaming: Aboriginal law and Catholic law: changing*

religious identities of Arrernte people at Charles Creek, Arlthunga and Santa Teresa in Central Australia, 1936-1991 (Centre for Pacific Studies, Nijmegen, 1993).

17. Hilary Carey, 'Subordination, invisibility and chosen work: Missionary nuns and Australian Aborigines, c.1900-1949', *Australian Feminist Studies* 13 (28) (1998), 251-67; John Maguire, 'Catholic missions to the Aborigines in North Queensland', in *Lectures on North Queensland History no. 4*, ed. B. J. Dalton (James Cook University, Townsville, 1984), ch. 3: https://espace.library.uq.edu.au/view/UQ:241819/Lectures_on_NQ_History_S4_CH3.pdf

18. Thecla Brogan, compiler, *The Garden Point Mob: Stories about the early days of the Catholic mission and the people who lived there, to celebrate the 50th anniversary of the mission* (Historical Society of the Northern Territory, Darwin, 1990); John Leary, 'Out bush in the NT: further reminiscences in the life of an outback priest: the Garden Point people', *Nelen Yubu* 69 (1998), 17-27; John Pye, *The Tiwi Islands* (J. R. Coleman Printers, Darwin, 1977), 77-92; John Pye, 'Garden Point people: 1941-1968', *Nelen Yubu* 70 (1998), 16-18; Regina Ganter, *Garden Point, Melville Island 1940-1962*, http://missionaries.griffith.edu.au/mission/garden-point-melville-island-1940-1962

19. John Pye, *The Port Keats Story* (John Pye, Kensington NSW, 1973); Graeme K Ward, and Mark Crocombe, 'Brother Rexford John Pye OAM MSC 1906-2009', *Australian Aboriginal Studies* 2 (2009), 157-9; W E H Stanner, *The Murinbata - 1935-1953*, paper delivered in section F (Social Anthropology) at ANZAAS 1954; Martin J Wilson, 'Father Richard Docherty MSC', *Tracks 2* (1979), 4-8: http://chevaliercentre.org/documents/NY02.pdf; Martin J Wilson, *Remembering Founding of Port Keats Mission: 75 years ago 1935-2010* (Nelen Yubu, Kensington NSW 2010).

20. Kevin McKelson, 'Japulu Kankarra (The Father in Heaven): Part 2: Early years at La Grange', *Nelen Yubu* 60 (1995), 1-8.

21. Charmaine Robson, *Care and control: the Catholic religious and Australia's twentieth-century 'indigenous' leprosaria 1937-1986*, PhD, UNSW, 2012.

22. Gsell, *The Bishop with 150 Wives*, 43, also recounted in Ritchie, *North of the Never Never*; John Pye, *The Tiwi Islands* (J. R. Coleman Printers, Darwin, 1977), 41-2, and a hostile view in Tony Scanlon, '"Pure and clean and true to Christ": black women and white missionaries in the North', *Hecate* 12 (1/2) (1986), 82-105.

23. Lockyer, *Last Truck Out*, 51; similar recollections in Christine Choo, *Mission Girls: Aboriginal Women on Catholic Missions in the Kimberley, Western Australia, 1900-1950* (University of Western Australia Press, Crawley, 2001), 153-5; Margaret Zucker, 'Open hearts: The Catholic Church and the stolen generation in the Kimberley', *Journal of the Australian Catholic Historical Society* 29 (2008), 23-37.

24. Christine Choo, *Mission Girls*, 77.

25. Thecla Brogan, compiler, *The Garden Point Mob: Stories about the early days of the Catholic mission and the people who lived there, to celebrate the 50th anniversary of the mission* (Historical Society of the Northern Territory, Darwin, 1990), 61-2.

26. E.g. Kenneth B. Williams, 'To what extent did Bishop Rosendo Salvado seek to preserve Aboriginal culture in the conduct of his mission at New Norcia?' *New Norcia Studies* 9 (Sept. 2001), 29-35.

27. I. M. Crawford, 'The Benedictine Mission at Kalumburu', *Studies in Western Australian History*, 3 (1978).

28. Laura, 'Going Native: Converting narratives in Tiwi histories of twentieth-century missions', *Journal of Ecclesiastical History* 70 (2019), 98-118.

29. Rosendo Salvado, *The Salvado Memoirs* (University of Western Australia Press, Nedlands, 1977), *Report of Rosendo Salvado to Propaganda Fide in 1883*, trans. and ed. Stefano Girola (Abbey Press, Northcote Vic, 2015).

30. Regina Ganter, *Bathurst Island Mission 1911–1938–1978*: http://missionaries.griffith.edu.au/mission/bathurst-island-mission-1911-1938-1978.

31. E. A. Worms, *Australian Aboriginal Religions* (Spectrum Publications, Richmond Vic, 1998); Bindon, Peter, 'A century of effort: contributions to the study of Aboriginal ethnology and linguistics by Pallottine missionaries in Northwest Western Australia', *Nelen Yubu* 78 (2001).

32. Donald MacKillop, 'Anthropological notes on the Aboriginal tribes of the Daly River', *Transactions of the Royal Society of South Australia* 17 (1892–3).

33. Stefano Girola, 'The Italian connection: new historical sources on European-Aboriginal relationships', *Australasian Catholic Record* 87 (2010), 92–106.

34. Anne Dolan, 'Irish Lives: John Creagh 1870–1947', *Irish Times* 17 Apr 2010, http://www.irishtimes.com/life-and-style/people/irish-lives-1.653625

35. Mary Durack, *The Rock and the Sand* (Corgi Books, London, 1971), chapters 17 and 18; Siobhan McHugh, 'Beagle Bay: Irish nuns and stolen children', *ABC Radio documentary, 2000*; transcript at: https://siobhanmchughwollongong.files.wordpress.com/2012/02/transcript-beagle-bay-documentary1.pdf; Pat Jacobs, *Living on the Kimberley Pearling Coast: Sisters of St John of God in the Early Twentieth Century* (Sisters of St John of God Heritage Centre, Broome, 2014). The Sisters of St John of God Heritage Centre in Broome commemorates their work.

36. 'Communist Party's Fight for Aborigines', *Workers' Weekly* 25 September 1931, p. 2: https://trove.nla.gov.au/newspaper/article/209418403; further at: https://trove.nla.gov.au/newspaper/article/209418294

37. Edinger D. Choules and G Marsh, *Reassessing the missions: Balgo – its history and contributions, Kimberley Society*: http://www.kimberleysociety.org/oldfiles/2004/REASSESSING%20THE%20MISSIONS%20Nov%2004.pdf

38. Mike Bowden, 'The Catholic Church's toll on Aboriginal Australia', *Eureka Street* 24/6/2013, http://www.misacor.org.au/emagazine/current-news/201-reappraising-aspects-of-mission-activity

39. Frank O'Grady, *Francis of Central Australia* (Wentworth Books, Sydney, 1977), 28.

40. Ibid., 41–2, 45, 58, 65–6.

41. Ibid., 43, 46, 114.

42. Pye, *The Daly River Story*, 23, 30, 44.

43. Tony Scanlon, '"Pure and clean and true to Christ": black women and white missionaries in the North', *Hecate* 12 (1/2) (1986).

44. Gsell, *The Bishop with 150 Wives*, 38–39.

45. John Fallon 'The good old days', *Nelen Yubu* 48 (1991), 12–16, https://www.misacor.org.au/images/Documents/NelenYubu/NY48.PDF

46. Christine Choo, *The role of the Catholic missionaries*, 14–29; Choo, *Mission Girls*, ch. 5; Margaret Zucker, *From Patrons to Partners and the Separated Children of the Kimberley: A history of the Catholic Church in the Kimberley, WA* (University of Notre Dame Press, Fremantle, 2005).

47 Letter of Fr Emo of 1904, quoted in Choo, *The role of the Catholic missionaries*, 19.

48 Choo, *The role of the Catholic missionaries*, 24.

49 Walter, George, *Australia: Land, People, Mission*, trans. I. Danaher (Bishop of Broome, Broome, 1982), p. 24; quoted in Choo, *The role of the Catholic missionaries*, 18.

50 Gsell, *The Bishop With 150 Wives*, 154–5

51 Macleod, *Patrol in the Dreamtime*, 175–6, 229; generally confirmed in Doreen Mellor & Anna Haebich, eds, *Many Voices: Reflections on experiences of indigenous child separation* (National Library of Australia, Canberra, 2002), ch. 8 and Cubillo v. Commonwealth [2000] FCA 1084. A first-hand account of a 1965 child removal to Beagle Bay in Tony Thomas, 'Genuinely stolen?' *Quadrant Online* 15/12/2013, http://quadrant.org.au/opinion/tony-thomas/2013/12/genuinely-stolen/

52 Mohammad Ali McKee, 'Garden Point testimony', *Bringing Them Home Report*, 1997, ch. 9: http://stolengenerationstestimonies.com/index.php/testimonies/1016.html; *Bringing Them Home report (Report of the National Inquiry into the Separation of Aboriginal and Torres Strait Islander Children from Their Families)*, 1997: https://www.humanrights.gov.au/sites/default/files/content/pdf/social_justice/bringing_them_home_report.pdf; later apologies at: https://www.abc.net.au/news/2021-06-09/garden-point-abuse-survivors-get-justice/100201550; earlier suspicions in Ganter, *Contest for Aboriginal Souls*, 57-8.

53 Peter Sutton, *The Politics of Suffering: Indigenous Australia and The End of the Liberal Consensus*, Melbourne University Press, 2011, 16, 48–9.

54 National Catholic Census Project: http://pro.catholic.org.au/pdf/ACBC%20PRO%20E-News%20Bulletin%202021.pdf

55 Moya Hanlen, Sr Beatrice FDNSC (Demkardath Kilingkiling Thardim) 10.05.40-12.04.99, *Nelen Yubu* 72 (1999), 14–19.

56 Choo, *Mission Girls*, ch. 6.

57 Anon, 'Aboriginal elder who became Australia's first permanent deacon turns 80', *Catholic Leader* 7 June 2016: http://catholicleader.com.au/slideshow/Aboriginal-elder-who-became-australias-first-permanent-deacon-turns-80; He was ordained the first permanent Deacon in Australia at Port Keats on 19 July 1974 by Bishop John O'Loughlin, the Bishop of Darwin: https://www.natsicc.org.au/a-tribute-to-deacon-boniface.html

58 Jimmy Chi and Kuckles, *Bran Nue Dae: A musical journey* (Currency Press, Sydney, 1991).

59 Fiona Basile, 'Holy Spirit inspires Indigenous painting and storytelling', *Parish and School News, Catholic Archdiocese of Melbourne*, 5 August 2011: http://www.cam.org.au/News-and-Events/News-and-Events/Parish-and-School-News/Article/3629/holy-spirit-inspires-indigenous-painting-and-storytelling-view-gallery#.V-n0LPl97IU

60 Lemke, Laetitia, '100 years of Catholicism', *ABC News*, 27 July 2011: http://www.abc.net.au/news/2011-06-10/100-years-of-catholicism/2754734

4

F. X. Gsell: The missionary with 150 Wives*

Abstract: Bishop Gsell, the founder of the Bathurst Island mission in 1911, was the most celebrated Catholic missionary in Northern Australia. Known as the "Bishop with 150 wives" for his "purchase" of girls promised to older husbands according to tribal law, he opposed indigenous customs which he believed violated human rights. The success of his missions in creating peace and prosperity contrasts with the chaos of post-1970 government policies of self-determination.

In 1956 there was published in Sydney a remarkable memoir, *The Bishop with 150 Wives*. The author, Bishop François Xavier Gsell, describes in vivid detail his decades as a missionary in the Northern Territory. In view of the gross and continuing failures of Aboriginal policy since the time of the missionaries, it is well worth a look to understand how the missions created oases of peaceful and productive activity where others have failed.

Gsell was born in Alsace in 1872, apprenticed as a cotton-spinner, joined the Missionaries of the Sacred Heart and studied in Rome with Eugenio Pacelli (later Pope Pius XII). After a dispiriting time in administration in Randwick, he spent a few years in Papua before being appointed Apostolic Administrator of the Northern Territory, charged with re-founding the Church there.[1] He did so with success but was keen to move on to strictly missionary work among Aborigines. In 1911 he established a mission at Nguiu, Bathurst Island, with the help of several Filipino assistants and later nuns.[2] Naturally conditions were at first very difficult, but he made it a success. In contrast to the failures

---

* *Quadrant* 56 (7/8), (July/Aug 2012), 31–32, with additions from other articles.

of recent times in those regions, he ran a peaceful settlement with children attending school and with real economic activity, including a market garden and a sawmilling business.[3] Gsell had some strokes of good luck (or, as he took it to be, help from God). On arrival he dug a well and, despite the appearance of a rainbow which the local people believed was a warning to stop, found water without being struck dead. A few years later, he spent a large part of his funds having a schooner built at Thursday Island. The Filipino crew, disobeying their instructions to bring it along the coast of the Gulf of Carpentaria, tried to sail directly to Arnhem Land. Missing it, they were about to die of hunger and thirst near the Cocos Islands. Fortunately (for them), World War I had just broken out and the Australian Navy was combing the area for the German cruiser *Emden*. They fed the crew, pointed the schooner towards the Western Australian coast and all was well.

His book shows a close attention to Aboriginal culture. His interest is not anthropological, and he is neither interested in nor concerned by aspects of native culture that he sees as morally neutral, such as ceremonies. What he takes a negative view of are those aspects of traditional society that are severely incompatible with Christianity – as we would now say, violations of human rights. The perfect communism of Aboriginal society – "demand sharing", as it is now called – has, he says, the same result as communism in Europe: it does not lead to equality, since everything is run in the interests of the Party (that is, the elders).[111] Women are chattels, and he especially objects to the practice of betrothal of female infants and their addition to elders' harems at young ages. (Other evidence suggests Gsell may have underestimated the independence of older women, but his picture of betrothal of the very young agrees with that of others.)

Actual missionary success was slow. There was not a single adult convert up to the time he left in 1938. But in 1921 there occurred a remarkable event, the first of the incidents that give the book its title. Gsell describes it as follows:

> Little Martina belonged to the Maolas tribe and she came from the north of the island. An intelligent, lively little girl and quite clever at small tasks, she was not, perhaps, distinguished from

Bathurst Island school, c 1920s?[4]

other little ones about the mission …

There came to me a hairy anonymous man who said, "I have come to fetch my wife."

"And who is your wife?", I asked.

"That one," he said, and he pointed to Martina.

Nothing could be done, I knew. No one might challenge the law of the tribe. No one had ever thought of doing so. Martina, not yet baptised, must go with this hairy, anonymous man and be lost in the sad company of tribal women, slaves, owned body and soul by the men of the tribes … the light we had tried to direct towards little Martina would be darkened for ever …

But now a most extraordinary thing happened. Martina said, "No, I will not go with that man."

I am astonished, and to myself I say, "But the little one may not resist the tribal law … Can I resist a strong custom of these people? I cannot." … as her little fingers clutch my cassock she cries, "Oh, help me, Father. Do not let me go with this old man who is ugly. Please, I want to stay with the Mission …" … the little one accepts her fate and, trying to stifle her sobs, she goes with that man to begin a life which, I know, has less joy than that of the lowest beasts of the forest. The incident passes …

But in five days' time Martina is back. The man has taken her to his district, more than forty miles from the Station … She has resisted her man and he has driven a spear into her leg to drive a right spirit into her small body; and then, when it was dark, she has escaped …

It is evening, and they come – an ugly mob of muttering, gesticulating tribesmen – and they are at the Mission gates. Martina is in my arms; she believes, poor little one, that I can save her … I am deeply distressed and call on God to help …

"You," I said, "have come a long way: and so you are very tired. And also, you are very hungry. But come, you are welcome and there is flour and tobacco for you … they eat their fill, and they smoke, and then they sleep. …

I pray that God, now, will guide me … There comes to me an idea. I will buy Martina from these men. But this is not the custom. For payment – tobacco, flour, calico – they will lend Martina to any unscrupulous brute who may desire her, but … they will not sell her …

Now I proceed with great cunning. On a long table in front of the Mission House, … I place a good blanket, a sack of my best flour, a hatchet of good-quality steel, a mirror, a handsome teapot, some gaily coloured beads, a pipe and some good tobacco, some yards of brightly patterned calico, some tins of meat and pots of treacle. It is all worth perhaps two pounds sterling … tribal custom, often so inexorable, makes the price these sleeping men must pay when they awaken a high one, but my table carries for them untold riches …

My guests are early risers and I, hidden behind a fence … watch them approach … At once they see my stall and they crowd near it chattering like monkeys, gazing at my merchandise longingly …

Finally, I say carelessly to hide my deep anxiety, "It is all very easy for you: you may have everything … the calico, the flour, the tobacco … but in return, you must let me have the girl … The men are struck dumb with astonishment … They begin a discussion in

> low, urgent tones ... they can be severely punished by their tribal elders if they make this bargain ... they may win the enmity of spirits ... on the other hand, would they, they ask themselves, be wise to let such a windfall slip by? ...
>
> Although the council seems to sit interminably, at last it ends and now there comes to me that hairy anonymous old man who claimed Martina as his wife, quite justly according to native law. His face seems slit from ear to ear in a grin as he approaches.
>
> "Everything is good," he declares happily. "We sell the girl, but there is a condition: you must keep her for yourself always; she must not be passed on to any other man."[6]

Martina grew up a Christian with the nuns and chose a Christian husband from the Mission. (Gsell appreciates that an attraction of the mission to young men is that they can marry without waiting for the elders to die off and free their harems.) She had five children and eventually died of leprosy. Gsell bought another hundred and fifty betrothed females in the years following, all considered under tribal law as his wives.

A remarkable footnote to this story: on 23 October 2012 the new member for Arafura in the Northern Territory Parliament, Francis Xavier Kurrupuwu, paid tribute to Gsell in his maiden speech. Mr Kurrupuwu is named after Gsell and is Martina's great-grandson.[7]

As Bishop of Darwin in the 1940s, Gsell was ultimately responsible for the Catholic Church's share of the policy of child removal of "half-castes", now called the Stolen Generation. He has this comment:

> But, I may be asked, is it not cruel to tear these children away from the affectionate environment of their homes? The question is naïve. What homes and what natural affection have these little ones? Yes, if they had families, and if they were surrounded by that love and affection family life offers to the young even amongst primitive peoples, it might be cruel. But these creatures roam miserably around the camps and their behaviour is often worse than that of native children. It is an act of mercy to remove them as soon as possible from surroundings so insecure. After

that, I think, they must be kept at school until they marry, when they can establish a home ...[8]

Although Gsell was sceptical of certain native customs, he was not exactly in favour of assimilation, in the sense of integration into wider white society. That is because he was sceptical of white society as well. The missionaries always preferred sites away from other white settlements, so that those on the mission were not subject to exploitation by unscrupulous whites or to the temptations of an idle life on the fringes of white society. Gsell's ideal, a self-sufficient semi-monastic community well away from cities, might seem to modern economic rationalists a touch communistic.

Gsell had trouble from real Communists. According to Comintern policy as laid out in the Australian *Workers' Weekly* in 1931, Aborigines have been the subject of a campaign of mass physical extermination. The missions are party to a plan to kidnap children and sell them into slavery. Missions must be liquidated.[9] In the late 1930s, Sydney communists, followed by those in Prague, attacked Gsell for buying native girls. As he put it, "Since, to the communists, the Aborigines as an 'oppressed colonial people' are already in a state of communistic grace, it naturally follows that the missionary is Enemy Number One." Nothing much came of Communist complaints at that time and the missions retained the support of government authorities. (At one point a telegram arrived from Canberra, "Please

Martina with husband Agau and daughters Elizabeth and Mary

explain purchase of women", but he had the support of the Northern Territory administration.) When the Communists accused him of destroying native customs, Gsell replied that indeed he sometimes did that, especially sorcery and the burying of unwanted children and old people alive.[10]

Although the invasion of the mission by Japanese troops portrayed in the movie *Australia* is grossly unhistorical, Gsell did experience a Japanese invasion of another kind. In the late 1930s a Japanese pearling fleet visited Bathurst Island and outbid Gsell for women, resulting in the mission having to take on the care of twenty-five half-Japanese babies. To accommodate these and other mixed-race children, a settlement was made at Garden Point on Melville Island (Melville and Bathurst are the two islands in the Tiwi group) and after a period of difficulties Gsell reports visiting "my little City of Co-operation" and seeing houses and gardens built and industry well under way, and writes "Garden Point seems well on the way to inaugurating a Golden Age."

Bishop Gsell (centre) with Fr John McGrath MSC and Fr Paul Fleming MSC and mission boys: Photo courtesy of *Annals Australasia*

Is his account self-serving and inaccurate? It would be very desirable if there were a memoir by one of the inhabitants. There seems to be no such extended individual account (although ex-Garden Point people became prominent in Territory society). But there is a set of generally positive shorter recollections in the 1990 book, *The Garden Point Mob*,[11] and Nova Peris describes her mother receiving care there when her family were in difficult circumstances.[12] Some former residents have negative memories and there have been apologies for abuse.[13]

The Communists won. Although the Communist Party of Australia passed into history, the missions were liquidated and the Comintern's theory of child removals became official policy. Their view of Aborigines as an oppressed colonial people needing self-determination was passed on to a later generation of activists such as Judith Wright and "Nugget" Coombs. Coombs was given his head with Aboriginal policy, resulting in the decades of disaster recounted in books like David McKnight's trilogy about Mornington Island,[120] Geoffrey Partington's *Hasluck Versus Coombs* and Gary Johns' *Aboriginal Self-Determination: The Whiteman's Dream*. In place of "no such thing as idle hands", the ineffectual "job creation" and "training" schemes of CDEP and its successors. In place of Gsell's sawmill, the collapse in 2009 of the timber scheme in the Tiwi Islands. In place of schools teaching literacy in English, a generation of children too tired from noise all night to even get to school. In place of vegetables and melons, alcohol and kava. In place of relative peace, endemic violence.

Afterword: *Northern Territory News*, 20 May 2012

YOUNG KIDS STEAL PETROL TO GET HIGH

A remote shire council will not consider banning unleaded petrol from an island town—despite young kids stealing fuel from its work yard to "get off their trolley".

Ten children were busted sniffing on the roof of the Wurrumiyanga [formerly Nguiu] primary school, on Bathurst Island, on Friday.

It's the latest in an outbreak that began in January, police say.

Dressmaking class at Roman Catholic mission, Garden Point, Melville Island 1958: John A. Tanner, National Library of Australia nla.obj-137819334.

However, the Tiwi Islands have not become known for the extreme levels of dysfunction and violence found in some mainland communities.

---

[1] Peter Donovan, Gsell, Francis Xavier (1872–1960), *Australian Dictionary of Biography*: https://adb.anu.edu.au/biography/gsell-francis-xavier-6502

[2] Regina Ganter, *The Contest for Aboriginal Souls: European missionary agendas in Australia* (ANU Press, Canberra, 2018), 138–9.

[3] 'The Bathurst Island Mission', *Catholic Press* 22/7/1920, p. 14: https://trove.nla.gov.au/newspaper/article/105972918

[4] Missionaries of the Sacred Heart, Kensington.

[5] Francis Xavier Gsell, *The Bishop with 150 Wives* (Angus and Robertson, Sydney, 1956), 32.

[6] Gsell, *The Bishop with 150 Wives,* 80–86; later cultural understandings in Laura Rademaker, 'Challenging Indigenous marriage from within: Memories of the Tiwi's Martina and the figure of Malinche', in *Engendering Transnational Transgressions: From the intimate to the global*, ed. Eileen Boris, Sandra Trudgen Dawson and Barbara Molony (Routledge, London, 2020), ch. 7.

7. Legislative Assembly of the Northern Territory, Debates Day 1 – Tuesday 23 October 2012: https://territorystories.nt.gov.au/10070/438465/0/32
8. Gsell, *The Bishop with 150 Wives*, 154–5; a negative view in Michael Philip Francis, '"The Bishop with 150 Wives": Interrogating the Missionary and Ecclesiastical Career of Monsignor Francis Xavier Gsell MSC (1872–1960)', PhD thesis, University of Melbourne 2020 (access embargoed until 10/9/2022).
9. 'Communist party's fight for Aborigines: Draft program of struggle against slavery,' *Workers' Weekly*, 25/9/1931, p. 2: https://trove.nla.gov.au/newspaper/article/209418403
10. 'Communist attacks aboriginal missions: Bishop Gsell's reply,' *Catholic Press* 4/1/1940: https://trove.nla.gov.au/newspaper/article/106341758 ; comment in Ganter, *Contest*, 192–3.
11. *The Garden Point Mob: stories about the early days of the Catholic mission and the people who lived there, to celebrate the 50th anniversary of the mission*, compiled by Thecla Brogan (Historical Society of the Northern Territory, Darwin, 1990).
12. Nova Peris with Ian Heads, *Nova: My Story* (ABC Books, Sydney, 2003).
13. https://www.abc.net.au/news/2021-11-19/garden-point-mission-stolen-generation-survivors-receive-apology/100631712
14. James Franklin, The cultural roots of Aboriginal violence, *Quadrant* 52 (11) (Nov, 2008), 22–25.

5

Catholic rural virtue in Australia: ideal and reality*

Abstract: The poems of "John O'Brien's" *Around the Boree Log* portray a poor, Irish, and devout Catholic community, living a life of simple virtue far from the hurry and temptations of the city. Such communities really existed. They connected with older models of European peasant virtue, praised by leaders such as de Valera, Salazar and B.A. Santamaria, but were themselves organic growths of Irish migration patterns followed by evangelisation efforts by the Australian Church. As well as saints they did produce their sinners, such as Ned Kelly.

On St Patrick's Day 1943, Éamon de Valera, Taoiseach of Ireland, broadcast on Raidió Éireann a remarkable speech on 'The Ireland that we dreamed of'. It begins:

> The ideal Ireland that we would have, the Ireland that we dreamed of, would be the home of a people who valued material wealth only as a basis for right living, of a people who, satisfied with frugal comfort, devoted their leisure to the things of the spirit – a land whose countryside would be bright with cosy homesteads, whose fields and villages would be joyous with the sounds of industry, with the romping of sturdy children, the contest of athletic youths and the laughter of happy maidens, whose firesides would be forums for the wisdom of serene old age. The home, in short, of a people living the life that God desires that men should live.[1]

In 1921, "John O'Brien" (Father Patrick Hartigan) published his book of poems on rural Australian Catholic life, *Around the Boree Log*. A verse from 'The Little Irish Mother' is:

> *There's a Little Irish Mother that a lonely vigil keeps*
> *In the settler's hut where seldom stranger comes,*

---

* *Journal of the Australian Catholic Historical Society* 40 (2019), 39–61.

> *Watching by the home-made cradle where one more Australian sleeps*
> *While the breezes whisper weird things to the gums,*
> *Where the settlers battle gamely, beaten down to rise again,*
> *And the brave bush wives the toil and silence share,*
> *Where the nation is a-building in the hearts of splendid men –*
> *There's a Little Irish Mother always there.*[2]

That too is the "life that God desires that men should live." Both visions are rural, Catholic, Irish, virtuous, poor (actually, virtuous *because* poor) (and somewhat gendered, but not grossly: men are intended to be virtuous as well as women).

The world context of the rural ideal

There is a very long back-story in Western civilisation to the idea that the old virtues are preserved among simple rural people, in contrast to the many vices indulged in by rootless cosmopolitans and cynical city intellectuals. We will treat it very lightly here by way of background.

Les Murray recalls the ancient Greek contrast between rural Boeotia and urban Athens. Fashion-conscious and frenetic Athens is contemptuous of Boeotia as slow-moving and old-fashioned, but poetry, Murray says, does not work so well in the Athenian mode: "Conflict and resolution take the place, in a crowded urban milieu, of the Boeotian interest in celebration and commemoration, modes that perennially appear in spacious, dignified cultures."[3]

Probably the most admired hero of ancient Rome was the farmer Cincinnatus. With the early Republic in grave danger, the envoys of the Senate find him at his plough. They give him absolute power as dictator. He saves the state and immediately relinquishes power and returns to his farm. Such classical ideals were revived in the eighteenth century. Thomas Jefferson wrote (in a passage quoted by B.A. Santamaria):

> Those who labor in the earth are the chosen people of God, if He ever had a chosen people, whose breasts He has made His peculiar deposit for substantial and genuine virtue ... Corruption of

morals in the mass of cultivators is a phenomenon of which no age or nation has furnished an example.[4]

Robert Burns' poem 'The Cotter's Saturday night' (praised in Robert Menzies' 'Forgotten people' speech of 1942)[5] includes the lines:

Long may thy hardy sons of rustic toil
Be blest with health, and peace, and sweet content!
And O! may Heaven their simple lives prevent
From luxury's contagion, weak and vile![6]

The political tone of rural virtue tends to the conservative. It is a familiar fact that rural political parties are generally conservative.[7] The British Marxist Raymond Williams, in his *The Country and the City* (1973), remarks acidly that every writer praising the unchanging tradition of rural virtue seems to agree that that timeless order broke down under the stress of imported city vices and radical ideas at just the same moment, namely, when the writer was a child.[8]

Rurality as a political ideal can also be expensive. The Common Agricultural Policy that at one stage soaked up 73% of the European Union's budget, producing wine lakes and butter mountains, was premised on a "rural fundamentalism",[9] especially French. The 1958 Stresa conference founding the Policy "expressed their unanimous wish to preserve the character of European farming, which was predominately based on small-size, family holdings".[10]

The rural ideal played well in Australia too, though here it competed with a more left-wing rural narrative of the "Australian bushman" and noble shearers founding the Labor Party. The idea that small landholders would find frugal prosperity and simple happiness working their land was behind early government visions for convicts, propaganda encouraging emigrants, and legislation allowing selection.[11] Albert Facey's *A Fortunate Life* portrays the result – a hard life but one many were grateful for.

The European Catholic ideal of rural virtue and piety

The Catholic version of the rural ideal was somewhat different from the classical one, naturally emphasising the piety as well as virtue of rural people, and connecting with older medieval and early modern "ages of faith" when the population of Europe was mainly rural. As the Church in countries such as France failed to retain the allegiance of the new industrial working classes, popular Catholicism in Europe came to be increasingly rural. Millet's painting of peasants praying the Angelus captures the image nineteenth-century Parisians had of simple rural piety.

Jean-François Millet, *The Angelus* (1857–9)[12,13]

In film, the classic version is the Italian movie 'The Tree of Wooden Clogs'.[14]

In the mid-twentieth century, the ideal of Catholic rural virtue was particularly associated with two regimes in Europe, those of Salazar and De Valera. B.A. Santamaria spoke in 1940 of

> the great inspiration which Salazar in Portugal and de Valera in Ireland have drawn from the social doctrines of the Church ... [in] two countries, at least, a determined effort is being made to reorganise the national economy on Christian lines, to break

the shackles of anarchic and irresponsible capitalism, and to make economics subordinate to human happiness.[15]

Salazar was especially articulate about his model of Catholic rural virtue,[16] so it is worth quoting him at some length as an example of the international nature of the Catholic rural ideal.

In contrast to contemporary assumptions that a main business of governments is economic development, Salazar took at least some degree of rural poverty to be not a bug but a feature. That is because "material life, economic development, and the unceasing rise in living standards" would "leave in darkness all that is spiritual in man".[17] (De Valera too preferred frugal comfort.[18]) Technological improvement is not wrong, but needs to be done in ways not destructive of traditional society:

> Neither by wealth nor by the luxury of technology are we satisfied ... Without distracting ourselves from the activity that gives everyone a greater share of goods and with these, more material comfort, the ideal is to flee from the materialism of our time: make the field more fecund, without silencing the songs of the girls; weave cotton or wool on the most modern loom, without weaving class hatred into the threads and without expelling from the workshop of the factory our old patriarchal spirit.[19]

Governments should instead be encouraging traditional rural culture:

> The Casa de Povo [House of the People] should be major centres for a corporative education of the people, and a home or hearth for the village or the town. There the country people should meet after their daily toil, in innocent games, for simple plays, theatre or choirs.[20]

Salazar explains what is wrong with city life:

> Misery seems a secretion of progress, civilization. It is not in the countryside (even in full crisis) where life is simple and without ambition, that misery turns afflictive, dramatic. Its great tragedy without remedy first develops in the cities, the big capitals, as insensitive and tough as they are civilised. Mechanization, automatization of progress which turns men into machines, isolates

them brutally substituting their desires and affective impulses with complicated and cold interactions.[21]

That does not just apply to factory workers, but to white-collar workers, the habitués of city cafés:

> Men who have been brought up and who live exclusively between the school, the government office, and the café – and it is from among them that most of our public men have been recruited – must not take umbrage if we believe that their education has been defective. I do not say, as many do, that city life is a false type of life: it is what it is, vigorous and real despite its artificiality and its defects. I say that it is incomplete, especially if we would judge the life of the nation by it, and if we assume that the life of one class in a city is the genuine life of the city itself. When we go from the capital to the provinces, from the town to the village, from the club, the newspaper office or the drawing-room to the countryside, the workshop and the factory, the horizon of social realities widens before our eyes and we form quite a different opinion of what constitutes a nation. The distance which separates us who haunt the cafés, who frequent public offices, who have become Ministers and have a share in what may be called the omnipotence of power, drawing up ideal schemes of reform, tracing the lines of important schemes, almost deciding the fate of the world – the distance which separates us from the real nation is immense. The sense of unlimited power which the town gives us because it is dealing with abstract ideas, can find no sustenance in Nature, itself so calm and so retiring, challenging with a smile our impatience and our pride in our creative power.[22]

Naturally, rural smallholders will be politically conservative and reject Communism:

> See how the self-interest of States, overall the so-called capitalist States, is to create the greatest number of small property-holders who, far from favouring Communism or Socialism, tend to constitute the conservative reserve of the Nation, that which most opposes the development of libertarian ideas.[23]

Unlike Europe, colonial lands such as the United States and Australia had no peasantry with roots stretching back to the Middle Ages. Attempts were made to create a Catholic rural America, with a small degree of success.[24] These efforts too were admired by Santamaria.[25]

Santamaria and the National Catholic Rural Movement

In his early working life, Santamaria was not the head of a vast and multifaceted anti-communist "Movement" but Secretary of the National Catholic Rural Movement, which he described as "the most personally rewarding work in which I have ever engaged".[26]

As with many of Santamaria's projects, it was a development of Archbishop Mannix's ideas. A sermon of Mannix's on a visit to the country in 1940 summarises his and Catholic views on the positives of rural life:

STAY IN THE COUNTRY: ARCHBISHOP MANNIX'S ADVICE

A plea for the welfare and development of country life which is vital to Australia was made by the Archbishop of Melbourne (Most Rev. D. Mannix, D.D.) in addressing a large country gathering in Victoria. His Grace said it was consoling to know that all the Catholic people were not confined to the city, but that a considerable sprinkling of them was to be found in the country. Families in the city after two or three generations seemed to die out; they did not seem to last long for one reason or another. He hoped none of those residing in the district to which he was talking would think of going to the city. People should remain in the country as long as they could make a living ... those who were now there should stick to their holdings. Large tracts of land were not vitally necessary; the main thing was to have a sufficiency to make a decent living. Those who got a decent living should not be anxious to turn their backs on the country for the lights, cinemas and other so-called attractions of city life.[27]

Mannix was right about city families having fewer children. A study found that rural Catholic married women had one and a half times as many children as city Catholic married women.[28] So differences between urban and rural behaviours are not purely a matter of perception.

We now know the NCRM mostly through the perspective of later years, when it became another branch of Santamaria's suite of anti-Communist front organisations funding his crusade in the unions.[29] Our view may also be obscured by later leftist caricature of it as about settling peasants with three acres and a cow, a picture specifically disavowed by the movement itself.[30] But in its heyday in the 1940s, when membership grew to 6000, it was neither of those things but a serious movement with economic and philosophical arguments in favour of encouraging self-owned rural smallholdings.[31] It did have a specifically Catholic vision:

> The life on the land is one which is most suited to the practice of the Christian virtues. Therefore, to defend and propagate the life on the land is a definite work of Catholic Action. As Catholic citizens, we have a vital interest in this matter, since the Catholic Church alone possesses the principles which will place rural life on a solid basis.[32]

Santamaria's 1945 manifesto, *The Earth Our Mother*, despite the romantic title, is a work of serious economic reasoning on how rural smallholdings can be made a success in the face of capitalist pressures to consolidate land in large estates.[33]

As it turned out, economic forces proved hostile. The model of small owner-operated businesses has continued to be viable in the suburbs but in the country has been mostly driven out by industrial-scale highly-capitalised enterprises. As Santamaria put it, "If the agrobiologists were to make their fantasies come true, we might have almost no farmers."[34] So it is. Australia could have had a version of the Common Agricultural Policy but chose not to. "O'Brien's" Hanrahan had the last word – "we'll all be rooned", and not by floods and drought but by economic forces unopposed by government intervention.

Irish settlement of rural Australia

Santamaria and Mannix were city theorists with a vision, which may or may not have coincided with or influenced reality. We now turn to the reality itself, the real Catholic rural communities of Australia.

Fr Therry's and Bishop Polding's long days on horseback are well-remembered features of early Australian Catholic history. The communities they visited had grown up through a process of settlement described in a neglected classic of Australian Catholic history, James Waldersee's *Catholic Society in New South Wales, 1788-1860*. Through the efforts of James Meehan, the most active surveyor in the colony in Macquarie's time, many of his fellow transportees from the revolution of 1798 and other Catholics received land grants in the Camden and Campbelltown areas and beyond.[35] Favourable reports sent back to Ireland resulted in chain migration and a swathe of Catholic settlers in the Goulburn, Yass and Boorowa areas and along the Murrumbidgee.[36] Caroline Chisholm helped supply Irish women to marry the Irishmen in those regions. According to her evidence,

> There is a very great demand for them as wives there. An Irishman likes to marry his own countrywoman; and there are a great number of Irish there who are doing extremely well, who formerly got into what is called a little bit of trouble; and they think that their own countrywomen will understanding [sic] them best.[37]

Boorowa was known as the most obviously Catholic region in New South Wales. The Protestant John Dunmore Lang, visiting the town in 1862, wrote,

> Burrowa is one of the most thoroughly Roman Catholic districts in New South Wales. As everybody in the Duke of Argyle's county at home is called Campbell, so everybody in and around Burrowa is called Ryan. This, at least, is the general rule, although there are particular exceptions. Burrowa, in short, is the head-quarters and paradise of the Ryans, and might almost be supposed to be a veritable slice of the county Tipperary.[38]

Galong even had Ryans as grandee squattocrats.[39] (By and large the squattocracy were Protestants to a man.[40]) Bathurst and the Lachlan also had high proportions of Catholic settlers,[41] while the Hunter

St Patrick's Church, Boorowa (completed 1877)
(Mattinbgn, Wikipedia commons)

Valley in NSW was home to a significant number of Catholics, who often settled "beyond the established villages and towns".[42] Other areas of strong Catholic rural settlement were found in southwest and northeast Victoria[43] (sometimes speaking Gaelic[44]).

One aspect of rural Catholicism noted by several observers was its generally anti-sectarian character. Fenian scares, Orangeism and conflicts about jobs and education were largely city phenomena and in the country a spirit of tolerance and cooperation be-

The Warrnambool potato harvest, 1881
(State Library of Victoria)

tween different denominations was regarded as normal.⁴⁵ The *Yass Courier* reported:

> On Saint Patrick's Day 1859 the Yass solicitor George C. Allman addressed a banquet of the town's most prominent men and women. In his address, Allman, the son of a Protestant Irish settler, Captain Francis Allman, praised his town as a 'successful experiment', a place where people 'of all opinions, grades and religions may meet and remember that they belong to a common country'. His sentiments were echoed by the Reverend Patrick Bermingham, one of the town's two Roman Catholic priests, who described the evening's celebration as one 'calculated to make the inhabitants of the southern districts appreciate the sterling good qualities of each other without reference to race or creed'.⁴⁶

Fr Hartigan ("John O'Brien") was a strong supporter of good relations among Christians, both in words and actions.⁴⁷

The mixing of populations and the low density that meant everyone needed to help one another in hard times encouraged a lack of sectarianism. Everyone had to attend everyone else's ball or bazaar or there wouldn't have been enough people to go round. Father Carragher, parish priest at Ungarie in the 1930s and certainly well imbued with Catholic culture after studying philosophy and theology at Valladolid, said "If we didn't support one another out here, we'd all have to close our doors."⁴⁸ Sparse populations also encouraged the evil (from the clerical point of view) of mixed marriages.⁴⁹

Catholic education and culture in the bush

It was one thing to settle remote regions with people nominally Catholic, another to develop Catholic devotion, education and culture in those areas with so little contact with the "outside world". For all the days spent on horseback by pioneer priests, bush people's contact with formal religion was inevitably spasmodic. A letter home to Ireland in 1862 says

> I know some people living (what we call the bush) in the Interiour far in the country. They might be catholics if they hapen to have a family they cant run to a Priest to get them christened

they come down here some times with as many as half a Dozen at a time and get them Baptized and the whole of them well able to talk to the Priest. Catholics has the worst chance for anny such thing in the bush.[50]

A similar theme (with some stereotyping of the Irish) is the point of Banjo Paterson's poem 'A Bush Christening' (1893) which gives an outsider's view of the Irish community. It sets the scene with the tenuous hold of religion in the outback:

On the outer Barcoo where the churches are few,
   And men of religion are scanty,
On a road never cross'd 'cept by folk that are lost,
   One Michael Magee had a shanty.

A priest finally arrives to baptise Magee's son but by then he's aged 10. He concludes that christening must be something like branding horses so he heads for the bush. The priest has to baptise him by throwing a bottle of whisky after him. By then he's forgotten what name he's supposed to christen him with so he takes the one on the whisky bottle and it's "Maginnis Magee."[51]

Waldersee suggests that the first generation of rural Catholics were often not very devoted to their faith. But there are plenty of recollections in later times of major efforts by rural families to reach what masses were available. Kathleen Fitzpatrick recalls the world of her grandparents in rural Gippsland around the 1850s:

> One of the deprivations the Irish colonists felt most was that of the familiar offices of the Catholic Church. A priest came to Nar Nar Goon every six months, arriving on Saturday and staying until Monday morning. When it was known that he was coming Irishmen from miles around bundled their families into buggies and saddled their own horses and converged on Nar Nar Goon on Saturday, when they all went to confession and spent the night at the Limerick Arms or with friends or just camping. On Sunday morning there was Mass, held alternately at the Limerick Arms and the farm of Mr John Dore, a shipmate of Daniel O'Brien's in the olden days; and after mass there were weddings and baptisms. When these were over there was a splendid banquet for everyone

> at the Limerick Arms. A great day for the Irish, from which they returned to their farms nourished spiritually and physically, socially and, no doubt, alcoholically.
>
> Nothing astonishes me more, in the history of Daniel and Brigid O'Brien, than the tenacious campaign they waged to bring their children up as civilised people …[52]

Of course a certain amount of self-help is possible in religion, as in "John O'Brien's" poem in which the little Irish mother in her slab hut expands more and more the "trimmin's on the rosary".[53]

It was difficult to project Catholic education into remote communities. The woeful standard of knowledge is a theme of "John O'Brien's" poem 'Tangmalangalloo':

> *There everything is big and grand, and men are giants too –*
> *But Christian Knowledge wilts, alas, at Tangmalangaloo.*

The imposing bishop visits the bush school. He asks the unfortunate pupil "Why is Christmas day the greatest of the year?" and gets the answer "It's the day before the races out at Tangmalangaloo."[54]

The tendency of the first post-Irish generation in remote regions to lose its religion is lamented in an address to the Australasian Catholic Congress of 1909:

> In the Australian bush how rarely is the Catechism completely mastered, simply because a priest is rarely seen … The youth of Ireland have the Martyrs of Faith as the heroes of their dreams … On the other hand, the youth of the Australian bush, when seeking for some hero, must select from his scanty acquaintanceship either some silent, uneducated bushman, ignorant of many things, but particularly of religion … This portrayal of the bushman's unfavourable religious environment is strongly expressed, for if it is not wholly true of the first generation of Irish Australians, it becomes increasingly true of each succeeding generation. In the former it is largely corrected by the Irish tradition imbibed from the Irish father, thanks to the God-given ability for picturesque narrative and vivid explanation that is the birthright of every son of Erin. On the other hand, the Australian bushman is a silent man, like the children of all the lonely places of the earth

> ... Moreover, many of our Catholic women are ignorant of their Faith and totally incapable of either influencing a careless husband or instructing their sturdy children.[55]

(At least Protestantism in the bush is not much of a contender, he says, as out there they don't know whether Luther was born before Christ or not.)

The task of basic religious instruction in the bush fell mainly to the nuns. Mary MacKillop began her work in Penola, a typical tiny bush community far from anywhere. She said "We are for the backblocks ... it is our business to gather in poor children abandoned in out-of-the-way places; when that is over, we ought to make way for others."[56] The rural dioceses usually had convents even in the smallest towns.[57] When cars became available, some roving nuns like the "caravan sisters" were able to move beyond the constraints of convent life and meet people where they were.[58]

Courtesy of the massive subsidy to rural postal services that kept rural postage as cheap as in the cities, written material could nourish remote faith. The tens of thousands of subscribers of magazines like the Jesuit *Messenger* and Missionaries of the Sacred Heart *Annals* included many in rural areas. In 1914 a distributor of *The Messenger* wrote, "In some of our Catholic homes in the bush *The Messenger* is the only thing that keeps the Faith alive. The people live in the mountains and cannot come to Mass."[59] Correspondence courses for the bush were also developed to substitute for the school and adult education available in cities.[60]

Catholic culture in a more general sense included guilds, friendly societies and social events like race meetings. They needed the support of towns, but not big ones:

> In January 1875 the general meeting of the Boorowa Holy Catholic Guild met and heard reports of a most successful first year of operation in which membership, attendances, and the financial position of the Guild had all been strong. The Chairman, the Reverend J. Dunne outlined plans to strengthen the Guild's library in the following year. The Guild was instrumental in the organization of the Saint Patrick's Day celebrations in Boorowa the same year. The proceedings commenced with

a procession from the town to John Nagle Ryan's neighbouring paddock, where 600 people gathered to attend a race meeting and games.[61]

Not many of the leading figures of the Australian church came from truly rural backgrounds. Two of the conservative intellectuals of the Australian church did so. The Thomist philosopher and anti-communist crusader Dr P. J. (Paddy) Ryan came from a farm near Albury.[62] Sydney's other celebrated Thomist philosopher, the founder of the Aquinas Academy for laity, Dr Austin Woodbury, came from the Hawkesbury.[63]

Eileen O'Connor's two main associates came from poor rural backgrounds. Her co-founder of Our Lady's Nurses for the Poor was Fr Edward McGrath, from a difficult childhood in Kelly country in Victoria,[64] while her first recruit and successor, Theresa McLaughlin, came from an equally poor farm near Lithgow.[65]

Tim Fischer, Deputy Prime Minister and Ambassador to the Vatican, played up his origins as the "boy from Boree Creek", which is in the Narrandera area, "John O'Brien" country.[66]

Around the Boree Log

"John O'Brien's" picture of a "simple folk and hearty", happy and devout rural people is dismissed as "glutinous sentiment" by some supercilious modern intellectuals.[67] That is surely too dismissive of the report of someone who was on the spot and recorded in fine detail what he saw. It is perhaps not all that was happening, but certainly part of it. His picture of life 'At Casey's after mass' is directly based on the observation of someone who was there:

> *Past the kitchen door they rattled and they took the horses out;*
> *While the women went inside at once, the menfolk hung about*
> *Round the stable down at Casey's, waiting dinner down at Casey's;*
> *And they talked about the Government, and blamed it for the drought,*
> *Sitting where the sunlight lingers, picking splinters from their fingers,*
> *Settling all the problems of the world beyond a chance of doubt.*

*From inside there came the bustle of the cheerful wholesome hustle,
As dear old Mrs. Casey tried all records to surpass;
Oh, there's many a memory blesses her sweet silver-braided tresses;
They were "lovely" down at Casey's – always joking down at Casey's –
Spending Sunday down at Casey's after Mass.*[68]

"O'Brien's" most famous creation, Hanrahan whose catchphrase is "We'll all be rooned", is a depressive, but his pessimism is mocked in the poem.[69] Everyone else is positive.

Cullenbenbong

"John O'Brien" was not an insider of his community and was producing poetry, not memoir. It could be suspected that his somewhat rose-coloured picture has some degree of propagandist purpose. So it is valuable to read a straightforward memoir that in effect says the same thing. This is *Cullenbenbong,* by Bernard O'Reilly, who later became an authentic Australian hero by leading a difficult expedition that saved victims of a plane crash.[70]

Cover of the 1968 edition of Around the Boree Log.

The tiny farming community of Cullenbenbong lay in a valley at the western edge of the Blue Mountains. His picture matches "John O'Brien's" exactly:

When the riding party reached the top of Tinkers Hill, where it joined the Ganbenang road they came up with other families on horseback, for it wasn't merely the baby's christening day, it was the one Sunday of the month when Father Hogan drove out from Hartley to the little wooden church at Lowther.[71]

On went the cavalcade. Yarning comfortably they splashed through the gravelly shallows of Marsden's Creek, while the horses kicked spray high in the air and the warm sun slanted down through a fairyland of willows in their tender spring dress. Then the climb up to the Divide amongst the new-blooming black-thorn, with other families joining in until the party was at full strength—the various Cullen and O'Reilly families, the McAvineys and McAuleys, the Flanagans, Ryans and Kellys – all ages, on all types of horses, sometimes double and treble banked, yarning and smoking and singing and acting the goat, drinking in the spring sunshine, the breath of clematis and the songs of the birds – lovely old people, lovely old days.[72]

"John O'Brien" (Fr Patrick Hartigan)

He recalls his father's prayers when by himself:

> Presently with the help of the family Dad would be ready, and we would all trail out to where the horses were tied under the acacias and see him off ... Then would come the patting of the pockets: "Matches, tobacco, knife, glasses, rosary beads." The beads were always in his pocket, even if he were only going up the hill for a hearth log; not for the sake of displaying his religion, but for company he'd tell you; like the glasses he was forever breaking and mending them with bits of fine wire. It was Dad's practice if riding at night to say his prayers as he rode, and then he'd be all ready for tea and bed when the destination was reached. It wasn't a bad idea, and we still keep it up.[73]

O'Reilly even has a spontaneous touch of De Valera and Salazar's view that prosperity can be a bad thing:

> Too soon a little prosperity came to the valley and the sulkies which were the first expression of it hastened the destruction of one of the happiest features of the valley life. So it was in many other quiet valleys. Later still came the motor car, a cold nasty thing which took all the comradeship from the road, and made every fellow traveller a nuisance or a potential enemy.[74]

Kelly Country

While "John O'Brien" and Bernard O'Reilly were telling the truth, it was not the whole truth. They weren't all saints out there. Original sin was not absent in rural parts, nor subsequent sins.

The low density of population in rural areas could mean a distance from civilising influences, including the rule of law, which the less saintly might take advantage of. According to an opinion piece in the Catholic press of 1859, it was well-known that rural morals were terrible, and the clergy were not on top of the problem.[75]

Take the case of Ellen Quinn. Born in County Antrim about 1832, she was something of a truant at school. The family arrived in Port Phillip as assisted migrants in 1841 and moved to a farm outside Melbourne. She became pregnant to and married John ("Red") Kelly, an Irishman who had been transported to Van Diemen's Land for stealing pigs.[76] Her *ADB* article continues:

> The extensive Quinn and Kelly clans tended to skirt the fringes of the law, and for Ellen and Red financial difficulties, several moves, further births and mounting police attention set a definitive pattern. Red began drinking heavily. In 1865 he stole a calf and served four months in gaol. The following year he died, an alcoholic, of oedema, leaving Ellen with seven children aged from 18 months to 13 years.
>
> As she struggled to raise her children on inferior farmland, she became notorious for her sometimes-violent temper, resulting in several court appearances. After moving her family into the far north-east of Victoria to stay near relations, she leased a selection of 88 acres (35.6 ha) there and sold 'sly grog' to make ends meet. The bushranger Harry Power became a family friend, introducing 14-year-old [son] Ned to the life of a bandit. In 1869 Ellen took a lover, Bill Frost, and became pregnant, he promising marriage. The baby—her ninth—was born in March 1870, but Frost did not keep his word. Trouble with the law increased, with several of Ellen's siblings and offspring suffering periods of imprisonment.
>
> Late in 1872, with Ned in prison, she met George King, a 23-year-old Californian horse-thief, and once more fell pregnant ...[77]

And so on ...

Things went from bad to worse when young Ned turned out to be a psychopathic killer well outside the range of the usual rural petty crims.[78] Ellen was conveniently in prison to see Ned before his execution. Big crime then went back to Melbourne where it belonged. Ellen Kelly became respectable in old age though never well-off, and died in 1923.

Ned Kelly's few writings show a more than Irish-sized chip on the shoulder. Like Brenton Tarrant, he was given to writing spiels of garbled history in manifestos full of imported resentments to "justify" his murders:

> I have been wronged and my mother and four or five men lagged innocent and is my brothers and sisters and my mother not to be pitied also who has no alternative only to put up with the brutal and cowardly conduct of a parcel of big ugly fat-necked wombat headed big bellied magpie legged narrow hipped splaw-footed sons of Irish Bailiffs or English landlords which is better known as Officers of Justice or Victorian Police who some call honest gentlemen.[79]

That is from Kelly's "Jeriliderie letter", written at the time he held up Jerilderie from Saturday to Monday (allowing mass to be said on the Sunday).[80] In another letter he wrote, "thank God my conscience is as clear as the snow in Peru."[81]

While the Kelly gang were certainly not church-going folk, the clergy did manage to insert themselves into the story at the last moment. On 28 June 1880, the Irish-born priest Fr Matthew Gibney was travelling by train through Glenrowan. He learned that Ned and his gang had been surrounded in Mrs Jones' Hotel and were shooting it out with police. He left the train and tended the apparently seriously wounded Kelly, heard his confession and gave him the last rites. Although Kelly advised against it, Gibney entered the burning hotel to minister to the remainder of the gang. He found three of them dead and anointed the remaining one shortly before he died.[82]

The Kelly clan were by no means typical of the community among which they lived, the poor selectors of north-east Victoria. Methodist and Catholic farmers who mostly got on well, they were generally law-abiding and patriotic folk, contributing to one another's churches and charities. They saved money by not throwing it away on alcohol, and when they did have a quiet drink it was mostly in licensed premises, not in illegal shanties like Mrs Kelly's. Two respectable Protestant selectors went bail surety for Mrs Kelly when she was in Beechworth jail with a newborn baby.[83] Even in Kelly country, respectability was the norm.

Child slavery?

Other than horse thieving, one sin for which rural Australia provided particular opportunities was child slavery. In Australia's best-known rural memoir, *A Fortunate Life*, Bert Facey is sold into slavery aged 8 by his grandmother, though he doesn't use that word.[84]

Child slavery could occur in closed institutions, such as the agricultural schools for migrant orphans, Tardun and Bindoon.[85] But equally hidden from prying eyes were remote farms, where there was little to prevent poor farmers working young relatives non-stop.

Mary Ann Corrigan, born in Enniskillen, arrived in Australia aged 21 on an assisted passage in 1878 and gained employment on a pastoral property in south-eastern New South Wales. Because of some unspecified problem, she went to the newly-established convent of St Benedict in Queanbeyan and was taken in and did housework for them. On a visit to relatives in Bathurst she met her future husband, a blacksmith, and they married in the Catholic cathedral there in 1884. She named her firstborn Joseph Benedict, the rather unusual second name believed to indicate gratitude for her time at the convent; the nuns embroidered his christening robe. When young Ben was five and with two younger brothers, his paternal grandfather called and suggested Ben come to stay with him for a while on his small farm at Limekilns, a tiny village well out of Bathurst on the Sofala Road. He was to stay there for nine years, and it was not a pleasant time. Old Patrick Chifley had come from the bottom of the heap in County Tipperary and as a boy barely survived the potato famine. He had not long before buried the last of three wives. A daughter kept house but labour was needed to work the considerable number of acres (by Irish standards) that Patrick had accumulated. "The old Tartar", as

Ben later called Patrick, was demanding and Ben's life for nine years was a tough round of milking cows, cutting firewood, bagging potatoes and general dogsbody. He slept on a chaff-bag bed in a four-roomed wattle and daub shack with earth floors. He did attend the local state school (as was compulsory) but its quality was poor and better schools in Bathurst were not considered. At home he learned he was "the descendant of a race that fought a long and bitter fight against perjurers and pimps and liars".[86]

Ben survived to become an educated man, economic theorist and prime minister. But with some residual resentment against banks.

Conclusion

Catholic rural Australia did maintain a distinctive culture – distinct both from rural Protestant culture and city Catholicism. Forged in poverty and Irish heritage, it also took advantage of economic opportunities and freedoms not available in Ireland. Those who wished to maintained a strong Catholic devotion in circumstances where churches were distant and priests present only intermittently.

---

[1] Eamon de Valera, 'The Ireland that we dreamed of', 1943, https://www.rte.ie/archives/exhibitions/eamon-de-valera/719124-address-by-mr-de-valera/

[2] John O'Brien, *Around the Boree Log* (London: Angus & Robertson, 1978); http://www.middlemiss.org/lit/authors/obrienj/poetry/littleirishmother.html; discussion in Jeff Brownrigg, 'Irish mothers and Mother Ireland in the verses of "John O'Brien" and other poetical priests', in J Brownrigg, C Mongan and R Reid, eds, *Echoes of Irish Australia: Rebellion to Republic* (Galong: St Clement's Retreat and Conference Centre, 2007), 167–181.

[3] Les Murray, 'On sitting back and thinking about Porter's Boeotia', in *The Peasant Mandarin* (St Lucia: University of Queensland Press, 1978), 172–184, at 173.

[4] Thomas Jefferson, *Notes on the State of Virginia*, quoted in BA Santamaria, *The Earth Our Mother* (Melbourne: Araluen Publishing, 1945), 30; later developments in Kevin M. Lowe, *Baptized with the Soil: Christian Agrarians and the Crusade for Rural America* (New York: Oxford University Press, 2015).

[5] http://www.liberals.net/theforgottenpeople.htm

[6] http://www.robertburns.org/works/82.shtml

[7] E.g. in Australia, Marc Brodie, 'The politics of rural nostalgia between the wars', in *Struggle Country: The rural ideal in twentieth century Australia*, ed. Graeme Davison and Marc Brodie (Clayton: Monash University Publishing, 2015), ch. 9; Elizabeth

Michael J. Woods, *Cultivating Soil and Soul: Twentieth-century Catholic agrarians embrace the liturgical movement* (Collegeville MN: Liturgical Press, 2009); Allan C. Carlson, '"Flee to the fields": Midwestern Catholicism and the last agrarian crusade, 1920-1941', *Chesterton Review* 33 (2018), 53-75.

[25] Richard Doig, A 'New Deal' for Australia: The National Catholic Rural Movement and American agrarianism, 1931-49', *Rural Society* 10 (2000), 139-152.

[26] Bruce Duncan, *Crusade or Conspiracy? Catholics and the anti-Communist struggle in Australia* (Sydney: UNSW Press, 2001), 30-32, 86-89, 154-5.

[27] 'Stay in the country: Archbishop Mannix's advice', *Bunyip* (Gawler), 24/5/1940: http://trove.nla.gov.au/ndp/del/article/96698982, in James Franklin, Gerald O. Nolan and Michael Gilchrist, *The Real Archbishop Mannix: From the sources* (Ballarat: Connor Court, 2015), ch. 10; Mannix perhaps understates the problem described in the American song of 1919 about soldiers returning from WWI: 'How Ya Gonna Keep 'em Down on the Farm (After They've Seen Paree)?'.

[28] Lincoln H. Day, 'Fertility differentials among Catholics in Australia', *Milbank Quarterly* 42 (2) (1964), 57-83.

[29] Kevin Peoples, *Santamaria's Salesman: Working for the National Catholic Rural Movement, 1959-1961* (Mulgrave Vic: John Garratt Publishing, 2012); Race Mathews, *Of Labour and Liberty: Distributism in Victoria 1891-1966* (Clayton: Monash University Publishing, 2017), 224-6; Duncan, *Crusade or Conspiracy?*, 155.

[30] Tony Ayers, 'Cottage Catholicism: Young Santamaria and the lure of the pastoral', *Arena Magazine* 34 (Apr/ May 1998), 20-23.

[31] Kathy Madden, Dreams and Realities: Some insights into the National Catholic Rural Movement, Master of Humanities thesis, University of Tasmania, 1994, https://eprints.utas.edu.au/20338/1/whole_MaddenKathy1995_thesis.pdf

[32] Catholic Rural Movement, *Catholic Freeman's Journal*, 23/1/1941, https://trove.nla.gov.au/newspaper/article/146374103. Attempts to found rural Catholic communities described in David De Carvalho, 'Whitlands 1941-1951: An Australian experiment in utopian Catholicism', *Australasian Catholic Record* 80 (2003): 145-163; Gael Smith, *Maryknoll: History of a Catholic rural settlement* (Maryknoll: Artistic Wombat, 2002); a utopian vision in Denys Jackson, *Australian Dream: a journey to Merrion* (pamphlets, Melbourne: Australian Catholic Truth Society, 1947-8).

[33] Discussion in Duncan, *Crusade or Conspiracy?*, 87-88.

[34] Santamaria, *The Earth Our Mother*, 23.

[35] Bernard Dowd, 'James Meehan', *Journal of the Australian Catholic Historical Society* 3 (2) (1970), 8-12.

[36] James Waldersee, *Catholic Society in New South Wales, 1788-1850* (Sydney: University of Sydney Press, 1974), chs 4-5; Brian Maher, 'The Catholic communities of southern New South Wales', *Journal of the Australian Catholic Historical Society* 11 (1989), 18-32; Brian Maher, *Planting the Celtic Cross: Foundations of the Catholic Archdiocese of Canberra and Goulburn* (Canberra: Brian Maher, 1997).

[37] Report of Select Committee of the House of Lords on Colonization from Ireland (1848), quoted in James Waldersee, 'Pre-famine Irish emigration to Australia', *Journal of the Australian Catholic Historical Society* 4 (2), (1973), 23-35.

[38] John Dunmore Lang, *Notes of a Trip to the Westward and Southward, in the Colony of*

Kenworthy Teather, 'The Country Women's Association of New South Wales in the 1920s and 1930s as a counter-revolutionary organisation', *Journal of Australian Studies* 18 (1994), 67–78.

[8] Raymond Williams, *The Country and the City* (London: Chatto and Windus, 1973), ch. 2.

[9] Ian R Bowler, *Agriculture Under the Common Agricultural Policy: A Geography* (Manchester: Manchester University Press, 1985), 16

[10] Rosemary Fennell, *The Common Agricultural Policy: Continuity and Change* (Oxford: Oxford University Press, 1997), 20–21; John Gray, 'The Common Agricultural Policy and the re-invention of the rural in the European Community', *Sociologia Ruralis* 40 (2000), 30–52.

[11] James Franklin, *Corrupting the Youth: A history of philosophy in Australia* (Sydney: Macleay Press, 2003), 238–244; Coral Lansbury, *Arcady in Australia* (Carlton: Melbourne University Press, 1970).

[12] Wikipedia commons, https://en.wikipedia.org/wiki/The_Angelus_(painting)#/media/File:JEAN-FRAN%C3%87OIS_MILLET_-_El_%C3%81ngelus_(Museo_de_Orsay,_1857-1859._%C3%93leo_sobre_lienzo,_55.5_x_66_cm).jpg

[13] Similar in Jules Breton's Song of the Lark and Blessing the Wheat; see Maureen Ryan, 'The peasant's bonds to Gaul, God, land and nature: The myth of the rural and Jules Breton's Le Chant de l'alouette', *RACAR (Revue d'Art Canadienne/Canadian Art Review)*, 19 (1/2) (1992), 79–96.

[14] https://www.filmcomment.com/article/on-earth-as-it-is-in-heaven-ermanno-olmi/

[15] B. A. Santamaria, What the Church Has Done for the Worker, pamphlet, 1940, quoted in Gerard Henderson, *Santamaria, A most unusual man* (Melbourne: Miegunyah Press, 2015).

[16] Felipe Ribeiro de Meneses, *Salazar: A political biography* (New York: Enigma Books, 2009), 339, 623.

[17] A. O. de Salazar, *Discursos e notas politicas* (Coimbra: Coimbra Editora, 1965), vol. 6, quoted in Michael Sanfey, 'Salazar and Salazarism', *Studies: An Irish Quarterly Review* 92 (2003), 405–411.

[18] Mary E Daly, 'The economic ideals of Irish nationalism: frugal comfort or lavish austerity?', Éire-Ireland 29 (4) (Winter 1994), 77–100.

[19] A. O. Salazar, *Discursos e notas politicas* (Vol. 2 1935-1937) (Coimbra, 1945), 276. (Thanks to Robert Stove for translation)

[20] *Entrevistas de Antonio Ferreira a Salazar* (2 edition, Lisboa: Parceira A.M. Pereira, 2003, with introduction by Fernando Rosas), interview of 1938, 153. (Thanks to Jean Page for translation.)

[21] Salazar, *Entrevistas*, 171.

[22] F. C. C. Egerton, *Salazar: Rebuilder of Portugal* (London: Hodder & Stoughton, 1943), 151–2.

[23] Salazar, *Entrevistas*, p. 41 (interview of 1932).

[24] David S Bovée, *The Church and the Land: The National Catholic Rural Life Conference and American Society, 1923-2007* (Washington DC: Catholic University of America Press, 2010); Christopher Hamlin and John T McGreevy, 'The greening of America, Catholic style, 1930–1950', *Environmental History* 11 (2006), 464–499;

New South Wales; in the months of March and April, 1862 (Sydney: Hanson and Bennett, 1862), 27; full story in Malcolm Campbell, *The Kingdom of the Ryans: The Irish in Southwest New South Wales, 1816–1890* (Sydney: UNSW Press, 1997); Waldersee, *Catholic Society,* 120–1; Brian Maher, *A Slice of Tipperary: A story of Boorowa N.S.W. Catholic community* (Bruce ACT: Brian Maher, 2016).

39 Max Barrett, *King of Galong Castle: The story of Ned Ryan, 1786–1871* (Weston Creek ACT: Genie Publishing, 2000).

40 Don Aitkin, *The County Party in New South Wales* (Canberra: Australian National University Press, 1972), 103, 140.

41 Malcolm Campbell and Robert Tierney, 'The missing Catholics: Religion and population decline in the Lachlan district, 1870–1890', *Journal of Australian Colonial History* 18 (2016), 115–138; a detailed local history in Gavin Cashman, *Avoca: The faith of the pioneers* (Black Springs NSW: The Centenary Committee of the Church of St Vincent de Paul, 1988).

42 Beverley Zimmerman, *The Making of a Diocese: Maitland, its Bishop, Priests and People, 1866–1909* (Carlton South, Vic: Melbourne University Press, 2000): 44–45; earlier Michael Belcher, The Catholics of Wallis Plains 1820-1835: Catholics in a pre-institutional environment, *Journal of the Australian Catholic Historical Society* 34 (2013), 2-17.

43 Terry G. Jordan and Alyson L Greiner, 'Irish migration to rural Eastern Australia: a preliminary investigation', *Irish Geography* 27 (1994), 135–142; Regina Lane, *Saving St Brigid's* (Carlton South: Bridin Books, 2014), ch. 2.

44 Val Noone, *Hidden Ireland in Victoria* (Ballarat: Ballarat Heritage Services, 2012), 43-48.

45 Confirmed by James Logan, 'Sectarianism in Ganmain: a local study, 1912–1921', *Rural Society* 10 (2000), 121–138.

46 *Yass Courier,* 19/3/1859, in Malcolm Campbell, 'A 'successful experiment' no more: the intensification of religious bigotry in Eastern Australia, 1865–1885', *Humanities Research* 12 (1) (2005), 67–78.

47 Frank Mecham, *"John O'Brien" and the Boree Log* (Sydney: Angus & Robertson, 1981), 72, 161, 171, 187, 269.

48 Fergus Cloran, *I Saw the Bay First* (Glebe: Fast Books, 1993), 79; also in Jack Waterford, 'On being rural, Irish and Catholic', *Canberra Times* 10/9/1983, p. 13, https://trove.nla.gov.au/newspaper/article/116405831.

49 P. M. Lynch, 'The apostolate of the back-blocks: how to advance the interests of religion in remote country districts', *Proceedings of the Third Australasian Catholic Congress,* 1909 (Sydney: St Mary's Cathedral Book Depot, 1910), 89–102, at 92.

50 Michael Normile (N.S.W.) to his father Michael Normile (Clare), 18 Apr 1862, in David Fitzpatrick, "'That beloved country, that no place else resembles': connotations of Irishness in Irish-Australasian letters, 1841–1915', *Irish Historical Studies* 27 (1991), 324–351, at 337.

51 *The Bulletin,* 6 December 1893; http://www.middlemiss.org/lit/authors/patersonab/poetry/christen.html

52 Kathleen Fitzpatrick, *Solid Bluestone Foundations: Memories of an Australian girlhood* (Ringwood: Penguin, 1986), 36–37.

53 http://www.middlemiss.org/lit/authors/obrienj/poetry/trimminsonrosary.html

54 http://www.middlemiss.org/lit/authors/obrienj/poetry/tangmalangaloo.html ; a true story: JA Mecham, 'The biography of 'John O'Brien': Father Patrick Hartigan', *Journal of the Australian Catholic Historical Society* 7 (1) (1981), 24–27; Mecham, *"John O'Brien"* ..., 143.

55 T. Maguire, 'The soul of the pioneer', *Proceedings of the Third Australasian Catholic Congress,* 1909 (Sydney: St Mary's Cathedral Book Depot, 1910), 103–111, at 105–6.

56 George O'Neill, *Life of Mother Mary of the Cross (MacKillop) 1842–1909: Foundress of the (Australian) Sisters of Saint Joseph* (Sydney: Pellegrini, 1931), 394.

57 Marie Crowley, 'The contribution of women religious in rural Australia', *Australasian Catholic Record,* 87 (2010), 20–29; Marie Crowley, *Women of The Vale: Perthville Josephites 1872–1972* (Richmond Vic: Spectrum Publications, 2002); Mary Ryan, *For Whom Alone We Go Forward or Stay Back: A History of the Sisters of Mercy Wilcannia-Forbes Congregation 1884–1959* (Allawah, NSW: Sisters of Mercy Wilcannia-Forbes, 2004); M Assumpta O'Hanlon, *Dominican Pioneers in New South Wales* (Sydney: Australasian Publishing, 1949), ch.7; a biography in Margaret M. Press, 'Leehy, Mary Agnes (1873–1960)', *Australian Dictionary of Biography*, vol 10, http://adb.anu.edu.au/biography/leehy-mary-agnes-7153/text12351.

58 Edmund Campion, *Australian Catholics* (Ringwood Vic: Penguin, 1987), 192–4; Penelope Edman, *Around the Kitchen Table with the Missionary Sisters of Service* (Rangeview Vic: Missionary Sisters of Service, 2008).

59 Campion, *Australian Catholics,* 131.

60 Campion, *Australian Catholics,* 192; John T McMahon, *College, Campus, Cloister* (Nedlands: University of Western Australia Press, 1969), ch. 7; Janice Garaty, *Providence Provides: Brigidine Sisters in the New South Wales Province* (Sydney: NewSouth Publishing, 2013), 169.

61 Campbell, *Kingdom of the Ryans,* 158; more on Boorowa's Catholic culture in 'James McDonald, Henry Curran, bushrangers and a Boorowa dream', *Journal of the Australian Catholic Historical Society* 38 (2017), 20–33.

62 James Franklin, 'Ryan, Patrick Joseph, 1904–1969', *Australian Dictionary of Biography,* vol. 16 (2002), http://adb.anu.edu.au/biography/ryan-patrick-joseph-11591

63 Julie Thorpe, *Aquinas Academy 1945–2015: A very personal story* (Adelaide: ATF Theology, 2016), 2.

64 John Hosie, *A Lonely Road: Fr Ted McGrath, a great Australian* (Hindmarsh: ATF Press, 2010), ch. 4.

65 Jocelyn Hedley, *Hidden in the Shadow of Love: The story of Theresa McLaughlin and Our Lady's Nurses for the Poor* (Strathfield: St Paul's, 2009), 12–18.

66 Peter Rees, *The Boy from Boree Creek: The Tim Fischer story* (Crows Nest: Allen and Unwin, 2001), ch. 2.

67 Fitzpatrick, 'That beloved country', at 330; even Patrick O'Farrell speaks of "O'Brien's" "cloying" and "nostalgic sentimentality": *The Irish in Australia* (rev. ed, Kensington: University of New South Wales Press, 1993), 149, 192.

68 http://www.middlemiss.org/lit/authors/obrienj/poetry/atcaseys.html

69 "John O'Brien", 'Said Hanrahan', *Catholic Press,* 31 July 1919, https://trove.nla.gov.au/newspaper/article/106072280

[70] David Stove, 'A hero not of our time', in D Stove, *Cricket Versus Republicanism* (Sydney: Quakers Hill Press, 1995), 4–13.

[71] Bernard O'Reilly, *Cullenbenbong* (Brisbane: WB Smith & Paterson, 1944), 25–6.

[72] O'Reilly, *Cullenbenbong*, 29

[73] Ibid., 136–7.

[74] Ibid., 29

[75] 'Rural morals', *Freeman's Journal* 10/12/1859, https://trove.nla.gov.au/newspaper/article/114837871

[76] Grantlee Kieza, *Mrs Kelly* (Sydney: HarperCollins 2017), chs 1–2.

[77] Jacqueline Zara Wilson, 'Kelly, Ellen (1832-1923)', *Australian Dictionary of Biography*, Supplementary Volume (2005), http://adb.anu.edu.au/biography/kelly-ellen-13021

[78] Russ Scott and Ian MacFarlane, 'Ned Kelly – stock thief, bank robber, murderer – psychopath', *Psychiatry, Psychology and Law* 21 (2014), 716–746.

[79] Ned Kelly, Jerilderie letter (1879), p. 30, https://www.nma.gov.au/explore/features/ned-kelly-jerilderie-letter/transcription

[80] https://trove.nla.gov.au/newspaper/article/5932022; Mecham, *"John O'Brien"*..., 116–7.

[81] Ned Kelly, Cameron letter (1878), http://kellygang.asn.au/wiki/Cameron_Letter

[82] V. E. Callaghan, 'Gibney, Matthew (1835–1925)', *Australian Dictionary of Biography*, http://adb.anu.edu.au/biography/gibney-matthew-6305/text10873; a fictional story of priest and horse-thief in Banjo Paterson, 'Father Riley's horse', http://www.wallisandmatilda.com.au/father-rileys-horse.shtml

[83] Doug Morrissey, *Ned Kelly: Selectors, squatters and stock thieves* (Redland Bay: Connor Court, 2018), especially chs 2–3.

[84] A. B. Facey, *A Fortunate Life* (Fremantle: Fremantle Press, 2018), ch. 5.

[85] Barry M. Coldrey, *The Scheme: The Christian Brothers and childcare in Western Australia* (O'Connor WA: Argyle-Pacific Publishing, 1993), ch. 12; Royal Commission into Institutional Responses to Child Sexual Abuse, Case Study 11: Christian Brothers, 2014, https://www.childabuseroyalcommission.gov.au/case-studies/case-study-11-christian-brothers; general discussion of institutions in Richard Hil, Joanna Penglase and Gregory Smith, 'Closed worlds: Reflections on institutional care and child slavery in Australia', *Children Australia* 33 (2008), 12–17.

[86] David Day, *Chifley: A life* (Pymble: HarperCollins, 2002), 3–37; DB Waterson, 'Chifley, Joseph Benedict (Ben) (1885–1951)', *Australian Dictionary of Biography*, vol. 13 (1993), http://adb.anu.edu.au/biography/chifley-joseph-benedict-ben-9738

6

Catholic Scholastic philosophy in Australia*

Abstract: Catholic theory strongly supports the consonance of faith and reason. In the first half of the twentieth century, "reason" was taken to mean, centrally, the scholastic philosophy of St Thomas Aquinas. It informed seminary teaching, adult education, controversies in print and on radio, advice in the confessional, and, to an extent, the teaching of religion in schools. Its core ethical doctrine, that moral truths are fully objective and based on natural law, has survived the demise of scholastic teaching in general since the 1960s.

Catholic schools, training-ground of philosophy

In his autobiography, B. A. Santamaria recalled his schooldays at Melbourne's St Kevin's College around 1930:

The type of Catholic "apologetics" which was the strength of religious teaching at St Kevin's prepared my mind for John Henry Newman and later C. S. Lewis, who both provided confirmation of my religious beliefs. To the professional philosopher, Newman and C. S. Lewis might appear to be no more than popularizers of other men's ideas. Yet I do not despise the popularizer, since it seems that there are few new objections to religious belief. What one normally encounters are new formulations of the old objections – except, of course, for those contemporary philosophic systems which, in complete self-contradiction, pretend to prove the useless-

---

* From *Corrupting the Youth: A history of philosophy in Australia* (Macleay Press, 2003), ch. 4, edited.

ness of reason as a mechanism in the search for truth ... In the last analysis, the "apologetics" we absorbed could not lift religion above dependence on an act of faith, but an act of faith sustained by, and consonant with, reason. It was not an act of faith standing, as it were, unsupported or contrary to reason ... Sheehan's *Apologetics and Christian Doctrine* provided me, as a schoolboy at matriculation standard, with the rational justification for my act of faith in Catholic Christianity. When I examine what so many Catholic students at the same level are offered today, I stand appalled not merely at the intellectual poverty of the offering but at the ease with which so many so-called teachers of religion dismiss the intellect as a convincing support for religious belief in favour of highly subjective "religious experience". I can understand why so few students believe anything at all: for that which reason does not sustain rests on most unsubstantial foundations when confronted with the challenges of the "new morality" (which, as someone remarked, is only the old immorality writ large).[1]

Santamaria here describes a time when Catholic intellectual life, from primary school up, was informed by a complete official philosophy, the scholasticism of St Thomas Aquinas. Thomas Keneally's memoirs at the corresponding point also describe the impact of the "nifty" arguments for the existence of God in Sheehan's *Apologetics*, and represent the author as briefly inspired to combat the evil forces of atheistic Sydney University philosophy.[2] The Catholic childhood of legend was more than guilt and incense, and one of the essential extra ingredients was philosophy.

The Catholic Church has always been more hospitable to philosophy than other religious bodies. It has taken the view that if "reason" is a danger to faith, as it obviously is, then the solution is not less reason but more. It is true that the Australian Church has always had at least its fair share of anti-intellectuals, and some leaders of the local church have regarded the pursuits of the mind as an irrelevance and a nuisance. But others argued the opposite, as a response to the pluralism of a colonial society. According to a writer of 1896:

> The simple rudimentary Christian knowledge which was sufficient for the poor exile of Erin while yet in his own saintly island village, where his humble home was perhaps sheltered by

the ivy-clad ruins of some ancient church or monastery, where he saw 'books in the running brooks, sermons in stones, and good in everything,' did not suffice when he found himself in a land where both press and pulpit teemed with calumny against his Holy Faith, and where there were then few shepherds to ward off the wolf from the fold.[3]

In any case, decisions on such matters were made in Rome. Official policy was to ensure that even primary school children understood their faith as clearly as possible, through instruction in the Catechism. At a time when tertiary and even upper secondary education was a rarity, the Catechism was the text that did most to create a difference between a Catholic and a secular education. It began on an abstract note:

Q. Who made the world?

A. God made the world.

Q. Who is God?

A. God is the Creator of heaven and earth and of all things and the Supreme Lord of all.

Q. How do we know that there is a God?

A. We know that there is a God by the things that He made ...

Q. If God be everywhere, why do we not see Him?

A. We do not see God, because He is a pure Spirit, and therefore cannot be seen by us in this life ...

Q. Had God a beginning?[4]

And that is just part of the first page. The later parts of course do not deal in such abstract and philosophical issues, but the precision of the definitions is notable throughout. They are a philosophical education for those with an ear for such things:

Q. What is man?

A. Man is one of God's creatures, composed of a body and soul, and made to God's likeness.

Q. How do you know that you have a soul?

A. I know that I have a soul because I am alive, and because I can think, reason and choose freely.[5]

Q. What is sin?

A. Sin is any wilful thought, word, deed or omission contrary to the law of God.[6]

Q. What is presumption?

A. Presumption is the expectation of salvation without making proper use of the means necessary to obtain it.[7]

Q. What is a lie?

A. A lie is the saying of anything that we believe to be false.[8]

As an intellectual training, it was not without effect either. Little girls came up with curly questions like "How could Our Lady have free will if she couldn't sin?"[9] and "How could a God of intrinsic goodness create evil?"[10] The risk in relying on argument, of course, is that the audience may not be convinced. "I remember Sister Amard who tried to teach me the philosophical proofs of the existence of God, and thereby destroyed my faith completely because she didn't know them; rather, she did know them but they weren't valid", says Germaine Greer. She adds, "the nuns were dreadfully incompetent at teaching Catholic philosophy. The Jesuits on the other hand were very good at it, and if I'd been taught by Jesuits I'd probably still be a Catholic."[11] The reputation of the Jesuits for increasing the validity of arguments is no doubt exaggerated.

Thomas Aquinas, official philosopher to the Catholic Church

The passage from Santamaria refers to the two central themes of Catholic philosophy, the consonance of faith and reason, and the objectivity of ethics. The Church has welcomed the search for arguments for the existence of God,[12] and has tried to resolve the apparent incompatibilities of faith and reason, such as conflicts between science and religion, and the problem of evil. It has also been committed to natural law ethics. The reason murder is wrong, on this view, is neither an arbitrary command of God (or of society, or of our genes), nor a free-floating rule, nor some fact about the greatest happiness of the greatest number, but the intrinsic worth of persons, which makes their destruction wrong. As explained by the philosopher Dr "Paddy" Ryan (whose story will be told in the next chapter):

> Ultimately, then, the morality of human acts is not to be explained by the civil legislation, public opinion and tradition, nor the authority of great men, nor mere utility, nor by gradual evolution from brute beginnings, nor their relation to the production of the super-man, but by their conformity to the law of God, founded in the nature and essential relationships of things, and known by reason. On the other hand, the morality or immorality of our acts does not depend wholly on God's will. In other words, a thing is not always bad because God forbids it; God forbids it because it is bad.[13]

The two themes themselves stem from a more basic doctrine, also mentioned by Santamaria. Thomas Aquinas inherited from Aristotle an unusually optimistic view of reason's ability to know important truths. While sense knowledge may be subject to manifold errors, the human mind, it was believed, has an ability to understand with certainty important matters of principle, like mathematics, philosophy and ethics. It is this capacity to understand objective general facts about the world that grounds both our reasoning about God and our ethical conscience.

While these positions have been part of Catholic tradition at all times, the Church went further in the period of about ninety years from 1880. It officially adopted a very particular philosophy, the scholasticism of Aquinas, taught it to all seminarians and anyone else who would listen, and based school education on it as far as possible. There had been very little attention to Aquinas or other medieval thinkers earlier in the nineteenth century. When the first Catholic Bishop and Archbishop of Sydney, John Bede Polding, taught metaphysics before coming to Australia, it was Scottish "commonsense" realism that formed its basis, Aquinas being then little known north of the Alps.[14] But in the obscure recesses of the Vatican, changes were under way.[15] One of the earliest enthusiasts for the new order was Roger Bede Vaughan, author of the first biography of Aquinas in English and later second Archbishop of Sydney and leader in the fight against secular education.[16] Sydney did not get a philosopher Archbishop again until the bioethicist Anthony Fisher in 2014, though it came close in 1940, when the Sheehan whose *Apologetics* so impressed the young Santamaria and Keneally almost succeeded to the see. He had been appointed Coadjutor Archbishop with right of succession some twenty years earlier, but the survival of the incumbent Archbishop to the age of 90 prevented realisation of his right.[17] Much the same happened in Melbourne, where the scholastic philosopher Justin Simonds[18] was Coadjutor to Daniel Mannix until the latter's death at 99.

The advantage of running a Church through a centralised bureaucracy is that when change comes, it comes quickly; what was forbidden yesterday is permitted today and may be compulsory tomorrow. An 1879 encyclical made St Thomas Aquinas philosopher By Appointment to the Catholic Church, and study of his philosophy was instituted in seminaries everywhere. That applied even in distant Australia, and especially to Manly seminary, Australia's largest. The seminary continued to teach long courses in philosophy to all its students, though the production of genuine enthusiasts for the subject was perhaps low.[19] The seminary's official journal records formal debates in Latin in 1923 and 1924 on such topics as "That God knows himself and knows all other things through himself" and "There exists in man an intellective faculty which is inorganic and immaterial."[20] An effort was certainly being made.

The difficulty for seminary philosophy perhaps lay not so much in its content as in its being compulsory. Philosophy, in Latin, for people whose interests lay primarily in getting to parish work as soon as possible, was an uphill task;[21] philosophy is not an ideal choice as a compulsory subject in any circumstances. The less committed student's sensation of an incoherent jumble of terms is well caught in the recollections of Gerard Windsor, a Jesuit seminarian in the 1960s, one with a mind more literary than philosophical:

> I heard a confident, unprepared burble about Ethics or a detached, alienated display of Metaphysical Psychology. Principles and tags and maxims and terms bobbed past. None of them seemed to possess or be possessed of any urgency. They floated

on, in a rolling, half exposed way, doing the circuit of some river of tradition where every seminarian, as far back and as far forward as imagination reached, paddled fitfully and then stepped out. The mind was forever being dipped in the magical stockpot of the Church's Styx.[22]

The scholastic industry in seminaries had virtually no impact on Australia's universities. There were a few Catholics among the university philosophy staff, but they were not of a scholastic orientation. The only official post in scholastic philosophy at a university was created at the University of Queensland in 1953, when the Archbishop leaned on the University Senate.[23] The appointee, Father Durell, was not welcomed with open arms by the philosophy department, and experienced difficulty in having credit given to his courses.[24] There was a scholastic philosopher briefly appointed at Sydney University in the same period – accidentally, according to rumour, as he confused everyone by knowing about modern symbolic logic as well as scholastic philosophy.[25]

As with any live intellectual movement, scholasticism was subject to a number of schisms, feuds and long-drawn-out wars between opposing camps. Like the Marxists of the same era, the scholastics naturally arranged themselves on a continuum from "left" to "right".[26] The "left" included such figures as Bernard Lonergan who sought some kind of *rapprochement* with modern thought, by which they understood mainly post-Kantian continental philosophy. While Lonergan was studied in Jesuit circles, this stream of scholasticism has not been strongly represented in Australia.[27] There have been few followers of the 'Trotskyist' Scotist, Ockhamist and Suarezian splinter groups that occasionally appeared in Europe.[28] The scholastic "centre" was represented by two French laymen, Jacques Maritain and Etienne Gilson. While Maritain was part of the general European Catholic thought that inspired the Campion Society in Melbourne,[29] and Gilson was also widely read in the English-speaking world, Australian scholasticism has been almost exclusively of the "right". The far right was strongest among ecclesiastics, especially those at the Gregorian and Angelicum universities in Rome. Its dominant figure was the Genghis Khan, so to speak, of the Thomist spectrum, Réginald Garrigou-

Lagrange, professor of theology and philosophy at the Angelicum University in Rome from 1909 to 1960. Late in life, Garrigou-Lagrange supervised the doctoral thesis of Karol Wojtyla, later Pope John Paul II and the world's most famous philosopher (even if not most famous *qua* philosopher). The isolationism to which ecclesiastical institutions are prone made this an inward-looking brand of Thomism, which regarded virtually all philosophical thought since 1600 as a mistake and saw even the scholastic "left" as sadly deluded semi-Kantian deviationists. It was this milieu that produced Sydney's most remarkable scholastic philosophers, two priests who, in different ways, brought their philosophy out of the seminary and into the "world". They were Dr P. J. ("Paddy") Ryan, of Kensington, and Dr Austin Woodbury, of the Aquinas Academy.

The story of Dr Ryan, philosopher and anti-Communist organiser, is told in the next chapter.

Dr Woodbury and the Aquinas Academy, Sydney

Dr Austin Woodbury was a Marist priest from the Hawkesbury Valley of New South Wales.[30] A student of Garrigou-Lagrange in Rome in the 1920s, he founded the Aquinas Academy in Sydney in 1945[31] and headed it for thirty years. It was primarily an evening school, aimed principally at the laity, and was for long a remarkably successful operation. In 1961, for example, it was running nineteen classes a week, with a total enrolment of some 500.[32] Like his counterpart and rival a few miles away at Sydney University, John Anderson, "the Doc" was a charismatic classroom teacher. The artist John Ogburn recalls

Dr Austin Woodbury
(Marist Fathers Australia)

> Frequently Woodbury would send me to the canvas with his answer and I responded to this as a miner greets the fresh air after working a double shift underground. Through the teaching

of these two men [Woodbury and the artist Orban] I had at last found the source of that clear stream of loveliness and beauty, the Being from which or in which all other beings are. I could now start to paint seriously.[33]

The historian and theologian Tim Suttor also writes of the immediate impact of a single evening of Woodbury's lecturing, which freed him from dissatisfaction with modern philosophers and oriented him towards Thomism.[34]

After his return to Australia Woodbury became rather isolated from the world scene. He never published a book summarising his thought – though there were a few pamphlets and many volumes of lecture notes[35] – and he did not tolerate dissent, discussion or questions. His opinion of Anderson's philosophy was much the same as Anderson's of his, an opinion he expressed freely and often in his lectures. The cold war between the Academy and Anderson's department entered a brief hot phase in 1952, when Woodbury claimed publicly, "The department of philosophy in the University of Sydney is a cancer at what ought to be the heart of the scholastic life of this city. It is a disgrace to the University of Sydney, and would be a disgrace to any university anywhere. I would warn students, and the parents of students, that a grave risk to their future intellectual and moral life is incurred by students who follow the course of philosophy at the University of Sydney without at the same time taking courses at this academy." Anderson deigned to reply, at least briefly, describing Woodbury's attack as "sheer rubbish and propaganda". "Dr Woodbury not only knows nothing about philosophy, but he knows nothing about the department of philosophy at the University."[36] As for debate between the two positions, none was forthcoming.

This skirmish was only a curtain-raiser to the later "Gough-Kinsella affair" of 1961, when the Anglican Archbishop of Sydney publicly attacked the atheist philosophy of Sydney University on the basis of allegations made by the Aquinas Academy student Dr Kinsella.[37] The Aquinas Academy entered the limelight briefly once more in 1966 at the time of the "Mother Gorman affair", a confused scuffle over the television appearance of an American nun of "advanced" views,[38] but generally simply pursued its teaching role in the background. Attendance waned as Dr Woodbury's health failed in the 1970s. After Woodbury's death in 1979, the Academy was continued for some time by his followers, but then fell to a coup by Jungians, who changed the character of its teaching entirely. The defeated party set up and long maintained a small Centre for Thomistic Studies, which preserved whole and unreconstructed the authentic deposit of ancient days.[39]

Fr Farrell and the problem of evil

One other scholastic philosopher gained some prominence in the fight against the godlessness of university philosophy. Father Farrell, a Dominican and brother of the historian of Catholic Australia, Patrick O'Farrell,[40] took the unusual step of submitting an article to the leading "enemy" journal, *Mind*; *Mind* took the even more unusual step of printing it.[41] It was a reply to an article on the problem of evil by John Mackie of Sydney University (a student of Anderson and later famous for his theory that there is no such thing as moral obligation[42]). It is recognised by most religious philosophers that the problem of evil is the most serious rational objection to religion: how can a good God cause, or even allow, evil in the world he creates? Or at least, how can a good God allow the never-ending tragedies that actually exist in this world: if people have an obligation to prevent evil when they can, why not God? The problem is a very obvious one. In the only philosophical interlude in Albert Facey's *A Fortunate Life*, he writes, "Anyone who has taken part in a fierce bayonet charge (and I have), and who has managed to retain his proper sanity, must doubt the truth of the Bible and the power of God, if one exists."[43] The thought is reasonable, even inevitable. Still, experiences of great evils have been interpreted very differently by those with different philosophical ideas. Mackie posed the problem in its traditional form: how can it be held simultaneously that God is omnipotent, that God is wholly good, and that evil exists? For surely if he were good and had the power to remove the evils, he would do so? Are there then any excuses that can be made on God's behalf? Mackie argued that various excuses offered by believers all amount to implicitly denying one of these three propositions. For example, the idea that evil is due to human will, or that the universe as a whole is better with some evil, or that evil is necessary as a means to good, he argued to be incompatible with true divine omnipotence, as a truly omnipotent God would be able to remove the evils while retaining the goods.[44]

Father Farrell replied that designing universes is not as easy as Mackie makes it sound, even for an omnipotent God. If the universe is not to be extremely simple, the result must be an interconnected whole in which what happens in one part necessarily restricts what can happen in another. The corruption and decay of living things is an evil, for example, but it is simply impossible for God to create corruptible goods like living things, in such a way that they do not corrupt. So omnipotence is compatible with evil because, though it is not obvious to us, eliminating evils while retaining goods is logically impossible. No doubt the abstractness of the treatment may give an impression of lack of feeling in the face of suffering. On the other hand, the problem posed was an abstract one, and the alternative to an abstract treatment is to start speculating on reasons for the existence of particular evils, which is bound to end in farce. Fr Farrell shows himself aware of the pitfalls by mentioning that the point of the existence of "certain groups of bacteria, e.g." in the divine plan remains obscure to us. Plainly, whatever necessities there may be connecting the parts of creation, we cannot expect to discern them with any confidence. But it is just the *possibility* of such necessary interconnections that explains why one can consistently believe all three of the propositions: God is omnipotent, God is wholly good, evil (even a great deal of it) exists. There is no better excuse for anything than absolute necessity; nor will anything less do as an answer.

The same line of reasoning had been developed for a more popular audience in Sheehan's *Apologetics*: "The notion that there are defects in the work of God is due, not to the imperfect character of His design, but to our imperfect understanding of it." He appears at first to overstep the mark in offering to explain God's design, on such questions as why there are so many useless things in the world. "if the animals called labyrinthodonts which belong to the early geological ages had been endowed with intelligence, they might have made a strong case against the wisdom of Providence from the lavish waste of fern spores." Yet, all that vegetable waste has given us our coal. The animals would have judged wrongly "from their not being able to foresee events of what was to them an incalculably remote future."[45] The example is bizarre but the point is a fair one: it is the abstract possibility of long-range trade-offs in the design of the universe that is being argued for, rather than the explanation of this or that evil.

In 1961, Farrell took the fight to the public, publishing in the Catholic newspapers an attack on the academic standards of Mackie and certain other university philosophers. Mackie's article, he claimed, was defective in claiming to have refuted all existing attempted solutions to the problem of evil, while ignoring those put forward by Aquinas. He complained further about a later article by another Melbourne University philosopher,[46] which had agreed with Mackie's article but not referred to Farrell's or considered the kind of argument he had put forward. Since university philosophers were attacking Christianity while ignoring its counter-arguments, Farrell concluded, the public ought to complain and Catholic students should avoid philosophy at universities. The debate dragged on inconclusively for months, with the Catholic philosophers of Melbourne and elsewhere being mostly concerned to draw a *cordon sanitaire* around Farrell and any like-minded Dominican inquisitors.[47] Parents were assured that studying philosophy at respectable universities like Melbourne was no danger to their children's faith. Max Charlesworth, a philosopher in the liberal tradition of Melbourne Catholicism, was goaded into expressing his real opinion of scholastic philosophers: "If we were to apply Father Farrell's test of philosophical competence to contemporary scholastic philosophers' treatment of modern philosophical positions, we would be forced to declare the majority of them to be flagrantly 'incompetent.'"[48] Another university Catholic philosopher involved was Selwyn Grave, whose story of conversion to Catholicism appears to provide a counterexample to the commonly-asserted theory that no-one is converted by pure argument.[49] Grave had himself written an answer to Mackie.[50] His opinion of the scholastics is evident in his later *History of Philosophy in Australia*, which gives them not so much as a single footnote. No mention was made during the debate of the fact that, except for Fr Durell's tenuous position in

Queensland, none of the Catholic philosophers employed in Australian universities were scholastics. The Sydney University philosophers did not join the debate, and there was no substantial discussion of Farrell's actual charges against Mackie.

James McAuley and *The End of Modernity*

As Grave's case shows, not all converts to Catholicism have been enthusiastic about scholastic philosophy, thinking perhaps that they have taken on board quite enough new doctrines already. James McAuley, on the contrary, understood that in a sense Catholicism with its philosophy asked for less belief than the faith alone, since the philosophy provided a few principles from which a great deal follows. The Christian tradition, he says, is "confined to a few bare principles of natural law and a meagre deposit of revealed teaching."[51] After phases of Marxism, Andersonianism and anarchism in youth,[52] he was converted to Catholicism, and was happy to accept the whole package. He admired Gilson in particular,[53] though he was distressed that both Gilson and Maritain were admirers of modern art.[54] McAuley expressed his own view of the essence of Catholic philosophy in a well-known passage in his 1959 book, *The End of Modernity*:

> While the Greco-Christian tradition remained intact, it was possible to give an intelligible account of human personality and show in what its eminent dignity and worth consist. To be a person means to be capable of reason and choice; able therefore to apprehend objective values and become a bearer of those values. What the Renaissance did was to begin to fritter away this conception of man as a rational being oriented to real values, in favour of a cult of individualism and personal idiosyncrasy. Today our publicists deafen us with proclamations of the 'value' or 'sacredness' of 'personality'; but which of them can give us a rational account of these terms? Scientism, the contraction of science to empirical knowledge, presents us with an impoverished reality in which *persons* have no theoretical charter to exist. In its rigorously determinist from, scientism leaves no room for free will, values, or rational judgement itself. As Etienne Gilson says: 'This is the reason why, for want of a rational metaphysics by which the course of science could be regulated, the liberal

philosophers had no other choice than to attack science itself and to weaken its absolute rationality. The source of modern agnosticism is the fear of scientific determinism in the hearts of men who, by breaking metaphysical rationalism, had broken the very backbone of human liberty.' The notion of the value of personality, whose banishment the totalitarians have gladly accepted from the hands of scientism, survives for the liberals only as an irrational sentiment, and under these circumstances the very meaning of personality is corrupted.[55]

He also drew some lessons for poetry. In particular, he thought, the common exaltation of imagination over intellect by poets is a mistake: "deep waters of feeling are stirred, and imagination induced to disclose its hidden treasures, only under the regnant star of intellectual ideas."[56] These ideas were displayed in the poetry of his classical and intellectual period of around 1960, such as the epic 'Captain Quiros'.

Casuistry and applied ethics

The aspect of scholastic philosophy with the widest impact on ordinary life, and the source of its most widespread controversies, was moral philosophy and its offshoot, the "science" of casuistry. The promise of objectivity in ethics, combined with the expectation that confessors should provide detailed and consistent advice on any matter that penitents cared to raise, created a vast body of reasoning on the application of moral principles to particular "cases".[57] Dr Woodbury used to tell the story of Franco asking his advisers in moral theology whether it was permissible to make war on the Spanish republic, to which the answer was, "not only licit but obligatory". During the Vietnam War, too, Catholics created some bemusement among outsiders by debating whether the War fulfilled the traditional conditions for a just war.[58] Some of the stranger cases of conscience arose from complications in Church rules, rather than from natural law, but even those were supposed to be solved as reasonably as possible. May one deliberately confess to a deaf priest? (Of course not, since that defeats the essential purpose of confession.)[59] Is an excommunicate obliged to attend Mass? (A more realistic case than it looks, as there were many who considered themselves Catholics but who had incurred automatic excommunication by marrying in a Protestant Church: Ben Chifley, for example.[60] The answer is tricky.[61]) The most important cases, though, were ones involving matters of ethical principle, which ought to apply equally to everyone, whether Catholic or not. Outside the Catholic (and Jewish) tradition, there has been a general feeling that it is not appropriate to confine ethical principle to such detailed 'rules',[62] but this perhaps rests on a misunderstanding of casuistry. Moral dilemmas, like legal cases, come up of their own accord, each with its own collection of properties and circumstances. To decide what is right in those circumstances, there is hardly any choice but to look at how all applicable ethical principles bear on the case and perhaps conflict with one another.

The crunch for casuistry came, as far as the general Catholic population was concerned, with the prohibition of the Pill on the grounds that artificial contraception defeats one of the essential purposes of sexual activity. Since the subtle deductions of casuistry did permit sex for the infertile, as well as contraception by the rhythm method, the boundary between the licit and the illicit was a very thin one, and the reasoning did not carry the conviction hoped for even among experts.[63] The large number of Catholics who ignored the Pope's 1968 encyclical on the Pill tended to blame and reject the whole apparatus of casuistry and confession.. The resulting "crisis of authority" was taken to concern not only the commands of the Pope but the scholastic deductions behind it. Both lay obedience and seminary training divested themselves of explicit scholastic philosophy, even though there was little effort devoted to refuting its arguments.

Aftermath

On the surface, scholasticism has virtually disappeared. After the Second Vatican Council of the 1960s, much of Catholic opinion lost sympathy with systems of thought identified with the *ancien regime*. Circles eager for change, in which "before the Council" became a term of abuse, were hardly likely to approve of an intellectual structure that dated from before the Council of Trent. It was certainly true that scholasticism had in some ways left itself in a weak position to survive the onslaught, by taking little notice of so many developments in modern thought. It had made little attempt to come to terms with modern scientific thought, for example.[64] That was despite the fact that modern science itself grew out of a scholastic matrix, which gave it its initial vocabulary, set of questions, most general concepts and methodology.[65] By contrast, new ideas in general were the weak point of modern scholasticism. It was said that the way to stop the charge of a man-eating Thomist was to ask what questions not dealt with by Aquinas Thomists were about to work on.[66]

Catholic philosophy since the 1960s has gone through a post-scholastic phase. It rejects the details of scholasticism but hopes to preserve a distinctively Catholic orientation. This means that a concern for objective morality and the general reliability of reason has been grounded on a synthesis, or attempted synthesis, of some of the basics of scholasticism with ideas from modern philosophy.[67] There have continued to be defenders of the need to base Catholic education on a commitment to intellectual values, though, as Santamaria said, the results have not always been evident in Catholic schools.[68]

All these attempts are interesting, and not without their successes. From the scholastic point of view, though, they are like trying to have one's cake after eating the ingredients. Or perhaps more exactly, they are like trying to have Euclid's theorems without the axioms.

In some ways, the demise of scholasticism has been much exaggerated. Survivals of it are widespread. Casuistry is back, for example, and not just in Catholic circles. It is now called "applied ethics" and has created a host of employment opportunities for philosophers.[69] Distinctively Catholic views on ethics are also visible in the recent debates on topics in bioethics, for example in Anthony Fisher's *Catholic Bioethics for a New Millennium*.[70] On some issues most Catholics still maintain views which descend from the core doctrines of the old moral philosophy. A properly conducted sociological study of Australians' attitudes to abortion showed that opposition to abortion depended strongly on "deductive moral reasoning from basic Christian beliefs", and little on such attitudes as obedience to the Pope or ("contrary to received wisdom") a desire to keep women tied to the kitchen sink.[71] In the philosophy of religion, there have also been several substantial books by Catholic philosophers who added to rather than subtracted from the scholastic legacy.[72]

Even more surprisingly, just as scholasticism was being consigned by most Catholics to the scrapheap of history, the realist metaphysics at its core was becoming respectable in mainstream philosophy, and nowhere more so than in Australia. The main event in its acceptance was the publication in 1978 of David Armstrong's *Universals and Scientific Realism*, which defends a strongly and explicitly Aristotelian position in the old scholastic debate, the problem of universals.[73]

And as we will see in a later chapter, scholastic philosophy of law underwent a strange revival in the High Court of Australia, resulting in the 1992 Mabo decision.

---

[1] B. A. Santamaria, *Santamaria: A Memoir* (Melbourne, 1997), 8.

[2] T. Keneally, *Homebush Boy* (Melbourne, 1995), 37, 43, 45; similar in *Sweet Mothers, Sweet Maids*, ed. K. & D. Nelson (Ringwood, 1986), 168–9.

[3] M. J. Treacy, 'The necessity of being able to give a reason for the faith that is in us', *Australasian Catholic Record* 2 (1896): 412–24, at 415–6.

[4] *Catechism of Christian Doctrine: Adapted for Australia by 2nd and 3rd Plenary Councils* (4th ed, Sydney, 1944), 11 (1938 ed available at https://nla.gov.au/nla.obj-254085965/view?partId=nla.obj-254086276#page/n2/mode/1up) ; almost identical, but lacking the third question, in *Catechism: Approved for General Use by the Cardinal Delegate, Archbishops and Bishops* (Sydney, 1905), 9; see M. Sheehan, 'Some remarks on the catechism problem', *Australasian Catholic Record (hereafter ACR)* 14 (1937): 182–9; recollections in J. Redrup, *Banished Camelots: Recollections of a Catholic Childhood* (Sydney, 1997), 127–8.

[5] *Catechism*, 1944, 12.

[6] *Catechism*, 1905, p. 25, 'actual sin' in 1944, 29.

[7] *Catechism*, 1944, 34.

[8] *Catechism*, 1944, 38; cf. A. Coady, 'The morality of lying', *Res Publica* 1 (2) (Winter, 1992): 6–9.

[9] Nelson, *Sweet Mothers, Sweet Maids*, 130; a serious answer to a similar question in T. Muldoon, 'Christ's free will and the Father's command', *ACR* 23 (1946): 169–85; also on the Cathechism as intellectual training, R. McLaughlin, 'Humanity', in *On Being Human*, ed. V. Nelson (Melbourne, 1990), 127–140, at 127.

[10] J. Arnold, *Mother Superior Woman Inferior* (Melbourne, 1985), 101, cf. 143–4.

[11] G. Greer in *There's Something About a Convent Girl*, ed. J. Bennett & R. Forgan (London, 1991), 88, 92; also in C. Packer, *No Return Ticket* (Sydney, 1984), 88.

[12] Arguments for the existence of God in the apologetic style in L. Rumble, *Radio Replies in Defence of Religion* (Sydney, 1936), ch. 1, http://www.radioreplies.info/radio-replies-vol-1.php?t=1; L. Rumble, *Questions People Ask About the Catholic Church*

(Kensington, 1972), ch. 1; L. Dalton, *Can We Prove There Is A God?* (Kensington, 1939); P. J. Ryan, *The Existence of God: The Argument from Design*, (Kensington, 1950); analysis in C. Roberts, 'St Thomas's world and his "ways" ', *ACR* 27 (1950): 311–6.

[13] P. J. Ryan, 'he fundamental tenets of scholasticism', *Catholic Press* 17/5/1934, 12, https://trove.nla.gov.au/newspaper/article/104375893 & 7/6/1934, 6, https://trove.nla.gov.au/newspaper/article/104374216 ; cf. H.B. Loughnan, 'Scholasticism versus realism in ethics', *Australasian Journal of Psychology and Philosophy* 11 (1933): 141–53; other introductions to scholastic philosophy: T.V. Fleming, *Foundations of Philosophy* (Sydney, 1949) (on Loughnan and Fleming, D. Strong, *Australian Dictionary of Jesuit Biography* (Sydney, 1999), 107–8, 198–9).

[14] W. B. Ullathorne, *From Cabin-Boy to Archbishop: The Autobiography of Archbishop Ullathorne* (London, 1941), 38, 41; T. Suttor, 'Polding's intellectual formation, *ACR* 54 (1977): 360–70; on the philosophy degree of the first bishop of Brisbane, see G. Roberts, 'James Quinn's Roman background', *ACR* 37 (1960): 11–16.

[15] Brief accounts in E.J. Howley, 'Neo-scholasticism', *ACR* 19 (1913): 403–9; N.M McNally, 'Scholasticism', *Austral Light* 13 (1912): 775–84.

[16] J. T. Donovan, *The Most Reverend Roger Bede Vaughan* (Sydney, 1883), 24–6, 35–41. R. B. Vaughan, *The Life and Labours of Saint Thomas of Aquin* (2 vols, London, 1871–2); also R.B. Vaughan, Science and Religion: Lectures on the Reasonableness of Christianity and the Shallowness of Unbelief (Baltimore, 1879); Arguments for Christianity Delivered in St Mary's Pro-Cathedral (Sydney, 1879); Address at St John's College, Sydney University, 1878, in R.B. Vaughan, *Occasional Addresses Delivered in New South Wales* (Sydney, 1881), 38–44; G. Haines, 'The Catholic mind of Roger Bede Vaughan', Tjurunga 25 (1983): 133–46; A.E. Cahill, 'Archbishop Vaughan and St John's College', *Journal of the Australian Catholic Historical Society* 14 (1992): 36–47; 'Philosophy lectures delivered by Archbishop Vaughan, St John's College, Sydney University', student notes (Fisher Library, Sydney University, Rare Book Library uncatalogued mss, single ms. no. 139.)

[17] G. Byrnes, 'Archbishop Sheehan – a biographical sketch', *Journal of the Australian Catholic Historical Society* 14 (1992): 24–35; M. Sheehan, *Apologetics and Catholic Doctrine* (Dublin, 1926, 4th ed, Philadelphia, 1951; 6th ed, ed. P. M. Joseph, London, 2001), (review in *ACR* 7 (1930): 272–5); M. Sheehan, *The Origin of Life: The Case For and Against Evolution* (Dublin, 1952).

[18] M. Vodola, *Simonds: A Rewarding Life* (Melbourne, 1997), 8–16; *ADB* vol. 16 243–4; M. Vaughan, 'The philosopher archbishop of Melbourne', *Bulletin* 30/11/1963, 28–31; J.D. Simonds, 'Laughter', *ACR* 8 (1931): 289–96; 'Evolution and theology', *ACR* 10 (1933): 12–19; 'Free will and modern psychology', *ACR* 10 (1933): 289–93; 'Einstein and the Prima Via', *ACR* 11 (1934): 11–16; 'Maurice de Wulf', *ACR* 11 (1934): 353–6; 'A new theological series', *ACR* 36 (1959): 78–81; another Louvain philosophy graduate in K. Coen, *Monsignor John Leonard and the Catholic Youth Organisation* (Strathfield, 2000), 19, 31–2.

[19] F. P. Kissane, 'A plea for philosophy', *Manly* 5 (2) (1936): 73–8; F. P. Kissane, 'St. Thomas Aquinas and Aristotle', *Manly* 6 (1) (1939): 53–7.

[20] *Manly* 2 (2) (1923): p. 192 and 2 (3) (1924): 266–7; content of Melbourne seminary philosophy c. 1960 described in V. Noone, 'Post-war Catholic intellectual life: A view

from a seminary', *Footprints* 16 (1) (June 1999): 2-28.

[21] J. Hill, 'Philosophy and the priesthood', *Metaphilosophy* 10 (1979): 215-26; also J. Rheinberger, 'The teaching of ethics in seminaries', *ACR* 47 (1970): 242-5; H. Ramsay, 'Philosophy, teaching and the academic vocation', *ACR* 78 (2001): 131-40.

[22] G. Windsor, *Heaven Where the Bachelors Sit* (St Lucia, 1996), 117; similar in C. Geraghty, *Cassocks in the Wilderness* (Melbourne, 2001), 102-5, 110-5; C. Geraghty, *The Priest Factory* (Melbourne, 2003), 37-42; J. Hanrahan, *From Eternity to Here* (Melbourne, 2002), 69, 139-40, 173-4; G. Dening, *Performances* (Melbourne, 1996), 17-19; I. Guthridge, *Give Me a Child When He Is Young* (Melbourne, 1987), 47-66, 76-80; on Jesuit philosophy teaching, see the articles in *Australian Dictionary of Jesuit Biography* on Daniel, Egan, Fleming, Flynn, Fynn, Gleeson, Gryst, Hehir, Keane, Loughnan, McEntegart, McEvoy, McInerney, Murphy, O'Brien, O'Neill and Stormon.

[23] T. P. Boland, *James Duhig* (St Lucia, 1986), 345; T. Truman, *Catholic Action and Politics* (Melbourne, 1960), 61.

[24] 'University course in scholastic philosophy', with complaint by Durell to Duhig, c. 1959; I am grateful to T.P. Boland for providing a copy.

[25] 'New philosophy lecturer on university standards', *Honi Soit* 23 (14) (5/7/1951), 3, https://digital.library.sydney.edu.au/nodes/view/3294#idx8572 ; *One Hundred Years of the Faculty of Arts* (Sydney, 1952), 31; J. J. Wellmuth, 'Philosophy and order in logic', *Proceedings of the Catholic Philosophical Association* 17 (1941): 12-17; J. J. Wellmuth, 'Some comments on the nature of mathematical logic', *New Scholasticism* 16 (1942): 9-15; 1940 thesis at https://www.proquest.com/docview/301760765 ; also J.J. Wellmuth, *The Nature and Origins of Scientism* (Milwaukee, 1944).

[26] Overseas background in G. A. McCool, *From Unity to Pluralism: The Evolution of Modern Thomism* (New York, 1989); H. J. John, *The Thomist Spectrum* (New York, 1966).

[27] But see W. Ryan, 'The philosophy of Aquinas', *AJPP* 2 (1924): 272-82; 'McEvoy, Patrick', in *Australian Dictionary of Jesuit Biography*, 220-2; on Lonergan, *Lonergan and You: Riverview Reflections 1985* (Pymble, 1987); *Australian Lonergan Workshop*, ed. W.J. Danaher (Lanham, 1993); W.J. Danaher, *Insight in Chemistry* (Lanham, 1988); Windsor, *Heaven Where the Bachelors Sit*, 116; Dening, *Performances*, 22-3.

[28] E. J. Stormon, 'Scotus redivivus', *ACR* 19 (1942): 24-37; F.A.R. Misell, 'Francis Suarez', *Newman* (Newman College, Melbourne) 1943, 38-41; complaints of Ockhamist persecution of Thomists in D.D. Smith, 'A report on philosophical teaching given at St Paschal's Franciscan College, Box Hill, Melbourne, Australia, in the year 1947', typescript (copy in Ryan Archives, St Paul's Seminary, Kensington); the Ockhamist's ideas in S. Day, *Intuitive Cognition: A Key to the Significance of the Later Scholastics* (St Bonaventure, NY, 1947).

[29] Santamaria, *Santamaria*, 11; C. H. Jory, *The Campion Society and Catholic Social Militancy in Australia 1929-1939* (Sydney, 1986), 33; meeting of Kevin Kelly and Maritain, with comments on Maritain's influence in Australia in the 1930s in K. T. Kelly to M. McInerney, 26/1/1958, comments in A. Calwell to G. Heffey, 20 June 1958 (in possession of Kelly family), also B. Duncan, *Crusade or Conspiracy?* (Sydney, 2001), 40-4, 385; for Brisbane see G. Harwood, *Blessed City* (Sydney, 1990), 152, 193, 205, 241, 244, 246, 252.

[30] 'Friend of philosophy', *Catholic Weekly* 15/2/1945, 9; *ADB* vol. 16, 580-1; obituary in *SMH* 6/ February 1979, 4; brief summary of his philosophy in A.M. Woodbury,

'What is metaphysics?', *Catholic Weekly* 14/2/1946, 11, 21; introduction to Academy philosophy in J. Young, *Reasoning Things Out* (booklet, Parramatta, 1975, repr. Fort Worth, 1981).

31 Julie Thorpe, *Aquinas Academy 1945-2015: A very personal Australian story* (Hindmarsh SA, 2016); J. Thornhill, Woodbury, Austin Maloney (1899–1979)', *Australian Dictionary of Biography*, 2006; 'School of philosophy to be opened here in March', *Catholic Weekly* 25 /1/1945, 1; 1 March 1945, 2; 1 March 1945, 6; 21 June 1945, 1; 27 March 1947, 6; courses detailed in *Catholic Weekly* 3 April 1947, 2 and 8 May 1947, 6; on the Academy's teaching on the philosophy of economics, see H.G. Pearce, *Value, Normal and Morbid: An Exposition of Economic Value* (Sydney, 1948, 2nd ed, Eastwood, 1987); D. G. Boland, *Economics Science and St Thomas Aquinas* (St Louis, 2016); cf. J. P. Kelly, *Aquinas and Modern Practices of Interest Taking* (Brisbane, 1945); A. J. Walsh, *A Neo-Aristotelian Theory of Social Justice* (Aldershot, 1997); on Thomist economic principles and the Cain government's policies, see M. Simons, 'Hard times for local heroes', *Eureka Street* 1 (2) (April 1991): 13–15.

32 *The Academician* 2 (5) (June 1961), 3; 2 (10) (Nov 1961); further in 'The dream that came true: The story of the Aquinas Academy', *Catholic Weekly* 28 April 1960. 400 normal at the start of most years, J. Ziegler to author, 12 April 1995.

33 N. Turner, *Catholics in Australia: A Social History* (Melbourne, 1992), vol. II, 286.

34 T. Suttor, 'Austin Mary Woodbury', *ACR* 55 (1978): 142–50, at 149–50; cf. T. Suttor, introduction to Thomas Aquinas, *Summa Theologiae*, vol. 11 (London, 1970).

35 Many available at https://www.austinwoodbury.com/

36 *Catholic Weekly* 13/3/1952, 1:, https://trove.nla.gov.au/newspaper/article/146743272 ; also 'Atomic age no threat to perennial philosophy', *Catholic Weekly* 13/3/1952, 15; reply in *Sun* 9/3/1952, 12:, https://trove.nla.gov.au/newspaper/article/229632003.

37 J. Franklin, *Corrupting the Youth: A history of philosophy in Australia* (Sydney, 2003), ch. 5.

38 'Dr Muldoon and Mother Gorman', *Nation* 10/12/1966, 9–10; Campion, *Rockchoppers*, 172–6.

39 J. Ziegler, 'A brief history of the CTS'; *Universitas* 3 (1) (1999) (https://web.archive.org/web/20000831210749/www.cts.org.au/1999/ctshistory.htm); support for Thomism also from Opus Dei in P. Grant, 'Metaphysics', *ACR* 63 (1986): 412–5.

40 P. O'Farrell, *Vanished Kingdoms* (Kensington, 1990), 99–100, 185–196; occasional writings in *Current Affairs Bulletin* 22 (9) (1958), 30 (6) (1962), 31 (1) (1962).

41 P. M. Farrell, 'Evil and omnipotence', *Mind* 67 (1958): 399–403; further in 'Freedom and evil', *AJP* 36 (1958): 216–21.

42 J. L. Mackie, *Ethics: Inventing right and wrong* (Harmondsworth, 1977).

43 A. B. Facey, *A Fortunate Life* (Fremantle, 1981), 317.

44 J. L. Mackie, 'Evil and omnipotence', *Mind* 64 (1955): 200–12; Farrell is unmentioned in Mackie's later *The Miracle of Theism*, but there is a brief mention in J.L. Mackie, 'Theism and utopia', *Philosophy* 37 (1962): 153–8, and a polemical reply in *Prospect* 5 (3) (1962): 23.

45 Sheehan, *Apologetics and Catholic Doctrine*, 41–2; a similar argument in J. Franklin, 'The global/local distinction vindicates Leibniz's theodicy', *Theology and Science* 20 (4) (2022), 445-462.

[46] H. J. McCloskey, 'God and evil', *Philosophical Quarterly* 10 (1960): 97–114.

[47] *Advocate* 26/10/1961: 18; 2/11: 18; 9/11: 18; 16/11: 18; 23/11: 18; 30/11: 18; 7/12: 18; 21/12: 12; 14/12: 18; *Catholic Weekly* 12/10/1961: 12–13; 16/11: 20; 30/11: 13; 21/12: 22; 11/1/62: 12; *Prospect* 5 (1962): 26; J. Kovesi, 'The temptation of absolute truth', *Twentieth Century* 16 (1962): 216–22; R.M. Gascoigne, 'A comment on a controversy', *Twentieth Century* 17 (1962): 17–24; J. Kovesi, 'An answer', 25–41; cf. T. Suttor, 'Australian Catholic culture', *Manna* 4 (1961): 122–36.

[48] M. Charlesworth, 'Academics and Christianity', *Advocate* 30 November 1961: 18.

[49] S. Grave, 'A discovery of the Church', in *Treasure Hidden in a Field*, ed. M. Elliott (Melbourne, 1971), 149–58.

[50] S. Grave, 'On evil and omnipotence', *Mind* 65 (1956): 259–62.

[51] J. McAuley, *The End of Modernity* (Sydney, 1959), 12.

[52] M. Cook,, 'McAuley and Anderson', ch. 4 of 'James McAuley's Encounter with Modernism', PhD thesis, Sydney University, 1993; R. J. Page, , "So many voices urging:" Transformation, Paradox and Continuity in the Poetry of James McAuley, PhD thesis, University of Lisbon, 2018, chs. 1-2; J. McAuley, 'Realist aesthetics', reported in *Union Recorder*, 1/10/1936, repr. in *Heraclitus* 41 (May 1995): 6; 'Metaphysical poetry', *Union Recorder* 2/7/1936, reported in *Heraclitus* 40 (Mar 1995): 4–5; G. Balzidis, 'James McAuley's radical ingredients', *Meanjin* 39 (1980): 374–82; Horne, *Education of Young Donald*, 200–1.

[53] Cook, 'McAuley's Encounter', 274–82; Page, So many voices', ch. 6; J. McAuley, letter, *Australian Quarterly* 24 (2) (1952): 76–8; J. McAuley, 'A small testament', *Quadrant* 20 (12) (1976), repr. in *James McAuley*, ed. L. Kramer (St Lucia, 1988); with comment in *Quadrant* 25 (9) (Sept 1981): 79 and 25 (11) (Nov 1981): 76; N. Rowe, 'James McAuley and the grammar of existence', *Australian Journal of Law and Society* 9 (1993): 107–17; G. Melleuish, *Cultural Liberalism in Australia* (Cambridge, 1995), 181–6.

[54] J. McAuley, 'A note on Maritain's views', in *The End of Modernity*, 111–6.

[55] 'The loss of intellectuality', in *The End of Modernity* 86–9, at 88–9; cf. 35; similar in J. McAuley, 'Friend of permanent things', *Quadrant* 14 (2) (Mar/Apr 1970): 40–3; discussion in C. Pybus, *The Devil and James McAuley* (St Lucia, 1999), 139–40; his views on university philosophy in 'A letter to John Dryden', *Collected Poems* (Sydney, 1994), 104–17.

[56] McAuley, *End of Modernity*, preface, vii.

[57] J. Franklin, *The Science of Conjecture: Evidence and Probability Before Pascal* (Baltimore, 2001), ch. 4.

[58] V. Noone, 'Melbourne Catholics and the 1965 increase in Australian military intervention in Vietnam', *Journal of Religious History* 16 (1991): 456–81, section III; M. Charlesworth & V. Noone, 'Christians, Vietnam and the theory of the just war', in *War: Australia and Vietnam*, ed. K. Maddock & B. Wright (Sydney, 1987), 148–59; J. Fox, 'Can war ever be justified?', in *Catholics in Revolution*, ed. P. Ormonde (Melbourne, 1968), 113–8; opposite Catholic view in Bob Breen, *First to Fight* (Sydney, 1988), 23; V. Noone, ed, *Catholics and Nuclear War* (Melbourne, 1982).

[59] J. J. Nevin, 'Purposely confessing to a deaf priest', *ACR* 20 (1943): 258–9 (on the author: K.J. Walsh, *Yesterday's Seminary: A History of St Patrick's Manly* (Sydney, 1998),

190–218); cf. J. Passmore, *Memoirs of a Semi-Detached Australian* (Melbourne, 1997), p. 45; P. Mullins, 'Looking back on the way we were', *ACR* 75 (1998): 264–70.

60 D. Day, *Chifley* (Sydney, 2001), 92–4; P. Hasluck, *The Chance of Politics* (Melbourne, 1997), 29.

61 J. J. Nevin, 'Is an excommunicate bound to go to Mass on Sunday?', *ACR* 22 (1945): 232–5; on the relevant metacasuistical principles, see H. McDermott, 'Probabilism vindicated', *ACR* 12 (1905): 374–84; Walsh, *Yesterday's Seminary*, 133–4; T. F. Roche, 'St. Alphonsus' probabilism', *ACR* 19 (1942): 146–53.

62 E. N. Merrington, The Possibility of a Science of Casuistry (Sydney, 1902); Anon, Roman Catholic Morality as Inculcated in the Theological Class-Books Used in Maynooth College (3rd ed, Dublin, 1836, repr. Sydney, 1839).

63 Earlier Catholic views in S. Siedlecky & D. Wyndham, *Populate and Perish* (Sydney, 1990), 15–16; J.C. Thompson, *Lectures on Medical and Legal Ethics Given at St John's College, University of Sydney* (Sydney, 1933); later debate in J. Finnis, 'Natural law in Humanae Vitae', *Law Quarterly Review* 84 (1968): 467–71; N. Ford, 'Humanae vitae — twenty-five years on and beyond', *ACR* 70 (1993): 139–60; N. Tonti-Filippini, 'Postpartum contraception', *ACR* 71 (1994): 82–8; J. Young, *Catholic Thinking* (Merrylands, 1990), 104–5; F. Mobbs, *Beyond its Authority? The Magisterium and Matters of Moral Law* (Sydney, 1997); G. Gleeson, 'The scope of the Church's moral teaching', *ACR* 75 (1998): 264–70.

64 Some Australian attempt in G. Ardley, *Aquinas and Kant* (London, 1950); G.W.R. Ardley, 'Prolegomenon to any natural science which can be called philosophical', *Modern Schoolman* 32 (1955): 101–13; V. A. Garten, 'Physics and the goodness of creation', *Divus Thomas*, no. 4 of 1985, 276–88; D. Rockey, 'Some fundamental principles for the solution of terminological problems in speech pathology and therapy', *British Journal of Disorders of Communication* 4 (1969): 166–75; J. B. T. McCaughan, 'Capillarity — a lesson in the epistemology of physics', *Physics Education* 22 (1987): 100–6.

65 J. Franklin, 'Science by conceptual analysis: the genius of the late scholastics', *Studia Neoaristotelica* 9 (2012), 3–24; J. Franklin, 'Mental furniture from the philosophers', *Et Cetera* 40 (1983), 177–91; J. Franklin, *What Science Knows: And How It Knows It* (New York, 2009), ch. 4.

66 F. J. Sheed, *The Church and I* (London, 1974), 104.

67 Examples in R. Gascoigne, *Freedom and Purpose: An Introduction to Christian Ethics* (Sydney, 1993); N. Brown, *The Worth of Persons: A Study in Christian Ethics* (Manly, 1983); T. Rowland, *Culture and the Thomist Tradition: After Vatican II* (London, 2003); N. Ford, 'The meaning of intrinsic moral norms for persons', *ACR* 60 (1983): 186–97; J. Hill, 'Natural sanction and philosophical theology', *Sophia* 17 (1978): 27–34; J. Hill, 'Christian moral education', *Journal of Religious Ethics* 9 (1981): 103–17; J. Hill, 'The methodology of Veritatis splendour', *ACR* 71 (1994): 145–61; J. Hill, 'Can we talk about ethics anymore?', *Journal of Business Ethics* 14 (1995): 585–92; E. Hepburn, *Of Life and Death: An Australian Guide to Catholic Bioethics* (Melbourne, 1996).

68 E. D'Arcy, 'The intellectual apostolate', *ACR* 62 (1985): 349–58. J. Franklin, 'Secular versus Catholic conceptions of values in Australian education;, in *Catholic Values and Australian Realities* (Ballan, 2006), 111–127; B. Tobin, 'The Catechism of the Catholic Church and the role of cognition in Christian life', *ACR* 71 (1994): 411–8.

69 Franklin, *Corrupting the Youth*, 408–10.

70 A. Fisher, *Catholic Bioethics for a New Millennium* (Cambridge, 2012); a recent example in X. Symons, *Why Conscience Matters: A Defence of Conscientious Objection in Healthcare* (London, 2022).

71 J. Kelley, M. D. R. Evans & B. Headey, 'Moral reasoning and political conflict: the abortion controversy', *British Journal of Sociology* 44 (1993): 589–612; work on the topic from a Catholic orientation in J. Finnis, 'The rights and wrongs of abortion', in M. Cohen *et al.*, eds, *The Rights and Wrongs of Abortion* (Princeton, 1974), 85–113; N. Ford, *When Did I Begin?* (Cambridge, 1988); A. Fisher & J. Buckingham, *Abortion in Australia* (Blackburn, 1985); B. F. Scarlett, 'The moral status of embryos', *Journal of Medical Ethics* 10 (1984): 79–80; P. Drum, 'Hylomorphism and abortion', *Australian Journal of Professional and Applied Ethics* 2 (1) (2000): 71–4; T. Keneally, *Three Cheers for the Paraclete* (Sydney, 1968), 110–3; Les Murray, 'Who's Ignatius, whose Loyola?', *Kunapipi* 1 (2) (1979): 149–54.

72 P. Forrest, *God Without the Supernatural: A Defense of Scientific Theism* (Ithaca, NY, 1996); P. Forrest, *Developmental Theism: From Pure Will to Unbounded Love* (Oxford, 2007); B. Miller, *A Most Unlikely God* (Notre Dame, 1996), especially ch. 9; cf. R. J. Kearney, 'Analogy and inference', *New Scholasticism* 51 (1977): 131–41; earlier B. Miller, *The Range of Intellect* (London, 1961); *From Existence to God* (London, 1992).

73 D. M. Armstrong, *Universals and Scientific Realism* (Cambridge, 1978); see esp. vol II p. 75 n. 1; earlier Catholic view in D. Gallery, 'Nominalism and realism', *ACR* 10 (1904): 145–51.

7

Catholic thought and Catholic Action: Dr Paddy Ryan MSC and the Red Peril*

Abstract: Dr P. J. "Paddy" Ryan, of the Missionaries of the Sacred Heart, Kensington, was both a philosopher and a man of action. Trained in scholastic philosophy, his abilities as a controversialist led to extensive work on radio, in pamphleteering and in adult education. His dramatic anti-Communist speeches in the late 1940s complemented his secret activities as leader of the Sydney branch of the anti-Communist "Movement".

Philosopher and controversialist

Melbourne in the 1930s was the scene of the vigorous Catholic intellectual life of the Campion Society.[1] Sydney was quite different, and for reasons much debated but still far from clear, its version of Catholic Action was much less impressive, and there was not much in the way of a public or lay Catholic intellectual life.[2] In Sydney, Catholic philosophy, apologetics and controversy in the 1930s and early 1940s was almost a one-man show. The man was Father Paddy Ryan. If it was a question of attacking Communists, or replying to objections on radio, or debating philosophers, or setting up Catholic adult education, or writing a pamphlet to prove the existence of God, one contacted the Sacred Heart Fathers at Kensington and got Father Ryan on the job.

Born near Wodonga in 1904, he had studied at the Gregorian University in Rome, earning in 1929 doctorates in theology and philosophy with the highest honours, with work on the "Question of God" in modern European philosophy.[3] He taught philosophy, of a strictly scholastic orientation, at the Kensington seminary thereafter. A series of lectures for the Catholic Evidence Guild at Sydney University which summarise scholasticism were printed in full in the

---

* *Journal of the Australian Catholic Historical Society* 17 (1996), 44–55, with updates.

Dr P. J. Ryan (centre), 1948
MSC Archives

Catholic press, at that time more hospitable than later to the discussion of intellectual topics.[4]

His ability as a controversialist was first widely recognised in a debate with the celebrated atheist Professor of Philosophy at Sydney University, John Anderson, in a symposium on "Science, philosophy and Christianity" in 1936. Anderson argued that "in so far as religion sets up a doctrine of meaning or explanations above the facts ('supernature') it is unscientific", and that Christian morality wrongly "takes the standpoint of the individual recipient of benefits" instead of exalting cultural achievement. Ryan then summarised the scholastic position on the knowability of God by natural reason, the reasonableness of faith, and the evils of taking scientific theories beyond their limits. He argued that inconsistencies between the Catholic faith and modern philosophies, such as materialism, were due to the faults of the latter.[5]

Anderson and Ryan met again in 1939, in a symposium with two biologists on "The origin of life", the topic of which was really the theory of evolution. The largest hall in the University was packed with 500 people; others were turned away. Ryan here defended one of the most controversial assertions of mid-century scholasticism, one in which he took a special interest: it was that spontaneous generation of life from the non-living is impossible, whether now or in the distant past, for purely philosophical reasons. Ryan argued that the "immanent nature of activity in living things" meant there was a difference in kind, not degree, between the living and the non-living, which could not be crossed without divine intervention.[6] Though Catholic philosophy generally was giving up the fight against evolution by the 1940s,[7] Ryan did not. In his later pamphlet on the existence of God, he did however argue that if the theory of evolution were true, God would be even more needed, since "the Author of world order would have endowed the primitive organisms with the powers necessary to produce, by gradual development, the present order of the plant and animal kingdoms."[8] Donald Horne recalled attending the debate as a convinced Andersonian of long standing, and still being surprised at the position Anderson took:

> I had been a believer in Darwinism ever since I had read in *Cassell's Book of Knowledge* that 'The protoplasm was the beginning of the wonderful story of evolution', and when Pritchett and I stayed back at the university one night to attend a symposium on evolution at which Anderson would be speaking I expected that, since a Catholic priest was to be one of the other speakers, Anderson would launch all his fury against the ignorance and superstition of this clerical bigot. The large lecture theatre was brimming with people, and Anderson sat intent, silent and sad-eyed, while the priest jumped on the theory of evolution and a scientist picked it up. Anderson sprang into the ring and floored the priest with a couple of blows. I was astounded when, after an obeisance towards Darwin because, like Freud, he had rejected the dualism of man and nature, he then pummelled evolutionary ethical theory, on, blow after blow, because it was full of progressivist illusions. Things might not get better. They might get worse. With Anderson one did not know where one was.[9]

There is a much greater sense of the cut and thrust of live argument in the report of a debate Ryan held, also in 1939 and at Sydney University, on freewill. His opponent was A.G. Hammer, a lecturer in psychology at Sydney Teachers' College, later Professor of Psychology at the University of New South Wales. An audience of 500 was again estimated. Hammer claimed that "all our decisions are as necessary as the explosion of a bomb", and asserted that "we can predict all human acts with absolute certainty, granted a sufficient knowledge of a man's heredity, environment, and other factors extrinsic to the will." Ryan took his stand on the "clear and unmistakable testimony of consciousness that it is very often in his power to choose freely amongst various actions which he has motives to perform." He is reported, in perhaps a moment of overkill, as having "proceeded to prove that the testimony of consciousness is absolutely reliable." Some interesting exchanges during the discussion are reported, which give some sense of Ryan's ability to argue on his feet – as well as the style of public trading of certainties that has come to play less part in the tradition of public debate:

> *Mr O'Neill, an ardent determinist*: Dr Ryan assumes the 'self' or 'ego' to be an abiding reality. But as a mere succession of states, the 'ego' could not be self-determining.
>
> *Dr Ryan*: My appeal is to facts of experience. We have the direct and immediate experience of the 'self' as an abiding reality and the subject of successive states quite distinct from it. The facts cannot be explained away by futile indulgence in metaphysical speculations concerning the nature of the 'ego'.
>
> *Mr O'Neill*: Your proof from the validity of consciousness means that all illusions are impossible. Yet there are illusions.
>
> *Dr Ryan*: How do you know that there are any illusions except from your consciousness of them? But the objection is pointless because I appeal, not to the testimony of consciousness merely as testimony, but as presenting objective evidence which enables us to distinguish between illusion and reality, between deliberate and indeliberate acts.

The chairman of the debate, John Passmore, perhaps less well-informed about the history of philosophy than in his later *A Hundred Years of Philosophy*, then intervened with a historical point. "Relinquishing his duties as chairman", he accused Ryan of reviving Descartes' philosophy, and "attacked the notion of a self-determining principle, declaring it to be absurd." Ryan said that Descartes' philosophy was not the same as Aristotelico-Thomistic philosophy.

Mr Passmore: The only person other than Descartes who adopted Dr Ryan's line of approach was St Augustine, a man not regarded as a philosopher by anyone outside a certain religious organisation.

Dr Ryan: Not one word of that is correct.[10]

Ryan did not confine his campaign to open debate. After collecting statements from students at Sydney Teachers' College, he had a letter written by his superior to the Director of Education demanding that something be done about the immoral teaching at the College. The determinism taught by the Andersonians at the College was the focus of the complaints. Dr Rumble's *Radio Replies* was used to publicise the campaign.[11] Ryan's interest in Sydney University continued. He claimed:

> I personally have argued for hours with graduates of Sydney University in a futile endeavour to convince them of their own existence, —so deeply had their very reason been undermined by scepticism and sophistry.
>
> In condemning things of this sort, we are not condemning critical or progressive thought. We are condemning a perverse negation which spells the suicide of thought and makes all progress impossible.
>
> In defending self-evident truths like one's own existence and personality, or easily demonstrable truths like the existence of God, we are merely defending the foundations without which all talk of justice and injustice is so much meaningless twaddle.[12]

Donald Horne had the opportunity to tangle personally with Ryan in 1941, when Horne, as editor of *Honi Soit*, was a representative at a "Youth Parliament" which saw a clash between Stalinists and Catholics. Horne recalls, "In the evening I drank beer with some of the Stalinists, infuriated by the unscrupulous red-herring tactics of the clerical fascists, who were not concerned with the constructive work of the Youth Parliament but with disrupting it by obscurantist Gestapo methods … Whenever the name 'Catholic Action' was mentioned I would fall quiet with hate. We didn't know much about it, but there were rumours of hysterical meetings and secret plottings in some kind of conspiratorial Catholic anti-Communist campaign that was going on in Sydney. Any Catholic student who wore a Holy Name badge seemed a servant of a black and unscrupulous clerical reaction which, under the subterfuge of anti-communism, represented an ambition of Francoism in Australia."[13]

The Catholic resolution which particularly offended the "Parliament" was one affirming "its complete adherence to the principles of democracy; its repudiation of the Totalitarian ideologies whether Nazi, Fascist or Communist". As Ryan said, Catholic Action, like any genuine democratic Australian, would be in favour, so it was fair to ask why the "Youth Parliament" rejected it. "Characteristic in this respect", Ryan adds, "is the letter by Mr D.R. Horne, published in '*Honi Soit*' issue of 27 June 1941. Mr Horne writes with deep emotion—with more heat than light. I gather from the references to the 'unbalanced priest' who speaks over Radio 2SM, 'the vaporisings of Dr Ryan', the 'Catholic papers' and sundry threats of Blitzkriegs to come, that he is making some sort of attack on me. But he does not face the real point at issue ... A genuinely democratic Youth Parliament really representative of the Youth of Australia would deserve support. But the same cannot be said of a Youth Parliament which provides a convenient cloak for anti-democratic and anti-British propaganda."[14] Rumours of Catholic plots, Stalinists exposed ... much more was to be heard of these themes in the coming years.

Ryan gave a series of lectures on campus in 1943 which provoked the usual polarisation of opinion.[15] A thoughtful reply to his arguments for the existence of God came from medical student Doug Everingham, later Minister for Health in the Whitlam Government.[16]

Ryan was employed by the Church in a huge range of activities during the 1940s and 50s. In 1936, during one of the hierarchy's periodic wringings of hands over the loss of young Catholics after they left school, lecture courses on apologetics and social theory were instituted, with Ryan as director.[17] He was again involved, providing much of the study material, when the movement was reformed, with great but temporary success, in 1938.[18] After the War, he headed a "Workers' School of Social Reconstruction".[19] In 1954, the problem was as unsolved as ever ("There is practically no such thing in Australia as the Catholic mind," according to Ryan[20]) and an Adult

Education Institute (Director, Dr Ryan) was set up in the city to offer courses in apologetics, theology and public speaking (but not philosophy, where it was presumably not thought worthwhile to compete with the Aquinas Academy). Enrolments, however, were never more than a few score. He debated on the radio on more or less anything; in a single broadcast of 1941, he dealt with the permissibility of moderate consumption of alcohol, the idiocy of chain letters ("shows the depth of absurdity to which people can fall when they lack genuine religion") and the responsibility of H.G. Wells for the War ("If people teach, as Mr Wells does teach, that the Ten Commandments are so much junk, they have no right to complain if Hitler presents them with a working model of their own philosophy").[21] Radio Replies were one area where Ryan did have a rival, however. His colleague at Kensington, Dr Rumble, specialised in the genre, and books of his replies sold millions in Australia and overseas.[22]

Tragically, in 1943 Ryan shot dead a man in mistake for a rabbit.[23]

Anti-Communist speaker

It was the Red Peril, however, that came to take up most of his energy. Catholic emotional involvement in the Spanish Civil War had resulted in Catholics being more concerned than most Australians about the perils of international Communism. While many Australians maintained a generally favourable view of the USSR at the time when Stalin was on the same side during the war against Hitler, and the membership of the Communist Party of Australia reached a peak in 1944, Catholic circles remained solidly hostile to Stalinism.

In 1943, Ryan answered one of the most effective leftist pamphlets of the day, Dean Hewlett Johnson's *Socialist Sixth of the World*.

This was the pamphlet which had converted to Communism the young Frances Bernie, hitherto active in Catholic youth organisations, leading to her leaking papers from Dr Evatt's office to the Communist Party and later to her appearance before the Petrov Royal Commission.[24] Ryan's answer, concentrating on the lack of freedom of religion in Russia,[25] sold some 45,000 copies.[26] There was a reply by the indefatigable Communist, Lance Sharkey, long-time General Secretary of the Communist Party of Australia. Sharkey says that Lenin is as much in favour of a moral way of life as Father Ryan. But the fact that employers and their press laud the strike-breaker as a hero, while the workers regard him as a scab ("the most immoral creature on earth"), "refutes Father Ryan's standpoint that there is a general, fixed system of morals that applies to all conceivable conditions." Further, Sharkey says, it is not part of Communism to attempt to uproot religion. It must be allowed to wither away with the "improvement of the material conditions of the masses" and "the development of knowledge of nature through scientific investigation".[27] Ryan replied in a series of articles, collected into a pamphlet with the title *Said Comrade Sharkey*. It is a superior piece of propaganda. The chapter on "Comrade Sharkey's 'Truth' about Spain" is illustrated with pictures of murdered priests in Spain; that on "Religion in Soviet Russia" has an enormous amount of evidence about the truth of Stalin's persecutions.

Ryan's finest hour came with a public debate at Rushcutters Bay Stadium on 23 September 1948, on the topic "That Communism is in the best interests of the Australian people".

His opponent was Edgar Ross, a member of the central committee of the Party. Despite rain, 30,000 turned up, clogging the trams. Half of the crowd had to hear the debate outside through loudspeakers. Ross opened with a quotation from Pope Leo XIII on the need to find a remedy for the misery and wretchedness of the working class. He went on to condemn monopoly capitalism, Imperialism, atomic bombs, American bases. "Against this, the Soviet Union stood strong, secure, stable and prosperous (applause and boos)." "The family was the bulwark of Soviet society (Laughter). In no country of the world

Crowd at the Ryan-Ross debate, 23 September 1948
(Australian Communist Party)

were human rights so explicitly acknowledged. The Catholic Church in Russia enjoyed complete freedom of activity. (Dr Ryan scribbles furiously and waves a gently protesting hand to shush the audience)."

Ryan then spoke. He alleged Communism was based on a degraded philosophy of life, that its programme necessarily involved ruthless and unlimited dictatorship, and that the Australian Party had no loyalty to God or country but only to Moscow. "The audience broke out into coughing as Dr Ryan went measuredly into the influence of the philosopher Hegel on the thought of Karl Marx," but perked up when he waved the Communist Manifesto and discussed the possibility of getting a divorce in Russia simply by sending a card through the post to the registrar. Even more shockingly, he alleged that workers in Russia were forbidden to strike. Ross, in reply, "claimed that Dr Ryan had given a lot of generalisations on philosophy, a few lies about the Soviet, but nothing about the practical tasks confronting the worker in the real situation today." Catholic preaching about the evils of society was like trying to cure cancer with an aspro. To Ryan's claim that all the Catholic bishops in Russia were dead, in exile or missing, Ross replied that the churches were open "in thousands" in Russia. "To the laughter he shouted, Do you think I would pull the wool over your eyes?' One solitary shrill feminine voice shouted: 'Yes.'" Ryan asked what reliance could be placed on Ross's word, when "according to Lenin, Communist morality was wholly subordinated to the class struggle of the proletariat." "In saying that the Catholic Church supported Fascism, Mr Ross was (again the quiet unimpassioned voice) a liar. The Catholic Church was the deadliest enemy of Fascism, and of Red Fascism, too (Wild applause)."[28]

Ross writes briefly of the occasion in his memoirs. He complains that "both sides were supposed to have equal rights in admittance to the Stadium and ring-side seats. But when the doors were thrown open the ring-side and many rows back were already stacked with nuns, priests and students from catholic institutions, who led the cheering and booing." (According to others, the Communist Party Central Committee had done its best to round up all available members of the Eureka Youth League and the New Housewives Association.[29]) Ross writes, "A report of the event took up half the front page of the *Sydney Morning Herald* and had the positive effect of introducing communism to thousands of people."[30] He omits to mention that the other half of the page was taken up with the latest news on the Soviet blockade of Berlin. An ability to put an upbeat construction on the facts was becoming increasingly necessary to Party members, and would become more so. Ross was one of the leaders of the Coal Strike the next year that did so much to assure Menzies' election victory.

Ryan's wish to spend some of his time in such an abstruse matter as the influence of Hegel on Marx is a perfect example of what Frank Knopfelmacher was later to call the "seminarian-deductive" attitude to political doctrines. It is characterised, according to Knopfelmacher, by a "naïve" kind of intellectualism, which is pre-Freudian and pre-Marxist in believing in the "authentic force and causal efficacy of intellectual convictions".[31] Ryan certainly did believe that, though whether it is naive is arguable. In any case, Australia has cause to be grateful for the "intellectualism" that led to the Cold War being fought here, not with the bloodshed and imprisonments of many other countries, but by nothing much worse than Dr Ryan lecturing the Communist housewives of New South Wales on Hegel.

Ryan continued to speak against Communism to large audiences, notably at the time of the Coal Strike.[32] During the campaign for Menzies' anti-Communism referendum of 1951, he toured the country, earning headlines in local papers like "'Peace' movement part of Communist plot for war" (*Armidale Express*), "Big audience hears Dr. P. J. Ryan talk on the Red menace" (*Goulburn Evening Post*), "Anti-Communist authority in Walcha" (*Walcha News*).[33] These speeches, and Ryan's study materials, are the prototypes of the thousands of Evils of Communism speeches in emotion-charged church halls that are such a central element in the Catholic Childhood of legend. An interesting feature of Ryan's own treatment of the issue, not always imitated, was his insistence on the positive aspects of Catholic social philosophy and its incompatibility with *laissez-faire* capitalism:

> What we need is not less capital, but more capitalists: not the abolition of property, but the wider distribution of it among private owners. We want this to enable the worker to become an owner so that he might achieve economic independence and political freedom. The industrial capitalist admitted in theory the right of personal property, but denied it in practice to the great majority of his fellow men.[34]

Ryan is not saying anything unusual here. His programme is in line with the "corporatist" or "distributist" view of society, as a potentially homogeneous whole of organisations representing various interests, which also found expression in the Catholic bishops' social justice statements.[35] The project aroused little enthusiasm outside the Catholic Church and was eventually allowed to lapse as the fight against Communism took centre stage; the Hawke government's "politics of consensus" has some resemblances to it. Ryan's position was average, except possibly for his support for bank nationalisation, which did not find much support from other Catholic leaders.[36]

Secret action of the Sydney Movement

The public speeches were only the tip of the iceberg of Ryan's anti-Communist crusade. He had been during the 1930s a leading proponent of "Catholic Action", a phrase with a range of meanings covering any lay action from prayer to politics.[37] Party political action was excluded, but political action to combat Communism was not. As early as 1940, or possibly even in 1937, he had investigated the possibility of setting up Catholic cells in the unions,[38] and around the end of the War he was effectively the founder of the Movement in Sydney.[39] B. A. Santamaria credited Ryan with having achieved the difficult task of convincing Cardinal Gilroy that enthusiastic support for secret anti-Communist action was necessary.[40] Gilroy appointed Ryan the Sydney director of the Movement about 1946, with the title "Director of the Catholic Social Science Bureau" and an office in the city, though without much in the way of money to run it.[41]

The story of the success of the Movement and its allies in Sydney is still far from written. Suffice it to say that in 1949 there were many Communist-controlled unions and within a very few years there were almost none. Facts have come to light, however, about one comparatively small but interesting aspect of the Movement's activities in Sydney, their collaboration with the security services. The matter casts some light on Ryan's opinions on the morality of various actions.

The records of an ASIO investigation of 1953 into leaks of information from the Commonwealth Investigation Service, the forerunner of ASIO, to Catholic Action in the late 1940s provides an insight into contacts between the security services and Ryan's operation. A senior officer, in the course of denying that he had passed any information to Catholic Action, writes:

> 1. I was an officer of Commonwealth Investigation Service from March, 1933, to October, 1949, when I transferred to ASIO. I had official contact with Catholic Action over the greater part of this period and visited the office of that organisation regularly up to about 1946. My dealings were with Dr Ryan, [deleted] and two persons whose names I do not now recall who were employed by the organisation prior to [deleted]. I was aware that Brigadier Galleghan and Mr Barnwell, of Commonwealth Investigation Service, were in contact with Catholic Action in that period also.
>
> 2. From approximately 1946 my C.I.S. duties became supervisory and I ceased to visit Catholic Action office, although I was in telephone contact from time to time. Brigadier Galleghan was also in

contact, I think mainly by telephone, but Dr Ryan visited Commonwealth Investigation Service's office on at least one occasion to see him.⁴²

(Brigadier "Black Jack" Galleghan, earlier commander of the Australian troops in Changi, was at this time Deputy Director of the C.I.S. in Sydney, and was soon to go to Europe to select nearly 200,000 anti-Communists, mostly Catholics, for Calwell's immigration program.⁴³ Bill Barnwell was also an anti-Communist specialist and also went to Europe to select refugees.⁴⁴)

Further documents in the same ASIO file indicate that the C.I.S., and later ASIO, continued to employ an officer at Catholic Action headquarters, with Ryan's approval, for the purpose of acquiring information about suspected Communists which came from Catholic Action members. (Payment, £2, subtracted by Catholic Action from the officer's salary.) Catholic Action felt the security forces were ill-informed, especially about union matters, and were happy to fill the gap.⁴⁵ The relationship between the two organisations was not close, and had its vicissitudes. From the point of view of ASIO, the aim was to get information without giving any in return, and Catholic Action sometimes resented giving high-quality information, such as shorthand records of high-level Party meetings, without sufficient reward in terms of information usable for propaganda purposes. On the other hand, C.I.S. and later ASIO suspected that information they gave sometimes returned to them from other sources. To check this, in 1948 an officer supplied some false information, which was received back via Naval Intelligence. More disturbing was a leak of security information in 1948, though its nature is not disclosed. The investigation of 1953 revealed that a Catholic Action officer had actually worked form ASIO's office at Edgecliff.

> It will be appreciated that if [deleted] used the Edgecliffe (*sic*) ASIO office for the purpose of carrying out Catholic Action organisational work, it left ASIO open to grave repercussions, if this became known to persons unkindly disposed toward this organisation. Such persons could imply that ASIO and Catholic Action were 'hand in glove', and working in common to the point of sharing the same office.⁴⁶

The case of "Diver" Dobson

More alarmingly for all concerned, some information about the liaison was publicly exposed. On 6 August 1949, W.T. Dobson, secretary of the Industrial Group in the Federated Clerks Union, dragged himself from Sydney Harbour into Nielsen Park, rang the police, and claimed that Communists had thrown him from a Manly ferry and stolen a bag containing secret documents relating to Catholic Action.[47] Two days later, he changed his story, confessing that he was a fanatical anti-Communist and had made the story up to smear Communists.[48] Dobson's confession was a relief to both sides. The Communists enjoyed portraying "Diver" Dobson as typical of anti-Communists, and escaped any suspicions that their political methods might include throwing their opponents off ferries. The Catholics and security gained a general scepticism about any documents that might be associated with Dobson. That was just as well, because the Party still had the documents (though no story as to how they came to have them), and proceeded to splash photostats of them in *Tribune* and *Labour News*. They led with a particularly choice item, an official letter to Calwell agreeing to his request that a phone line be urgently installed for Dobson in his hotel room.[49] Calwell made no attempt to deny its authenticity and was compelled to explain in Parliament:

> Mr. CALWELL. – I did make representations to the Postmaster-General at the request of Mr. Dobson. He came to see me, and fooled me. He came to me as the assistant secretary of the industrial group of the Federated Clerks Union and said he had the blessing of the head-quarters of the Labour party in New South Wales. I plead those facts in extenuation of my lapse. He was accompanied by another prominent representative of the industrial group, and he told me that he was carrying on certain work which, I believed, was of national importance. I made representations to the Postmaster-General to the effect that Mr. Dobson might be given telephone facilities, if that were possible, and a silent number to enable him to carry on the work of the industrial groups inside the union.
>
> Mr. BEALE. – Was that work of national importance?

Mr. CALWELL. – That, to me, seemed to be work of very great importance.[50]

Calwell went on to suggest that Dobson was linked to the Communists and to the Liberal Party, presumably on the principle that the more theories about Dobson there were, the better. In view of later events, it is not to be expected that either Calwell or the Movement should be keen to mention their co-operation, but the Parliamentary record is there. Calwell, one of the founders of the Groups,[51] had fallen out with them by 1948, but was still prepared to support their anti-Communist initiatives in 1949, the year in which the Groups caused his dumping from the Victorian state executive of the Labor Party.[52] Further documents, said to be pages from Dobson's private notebook, included such gems as "Ryan appears to get a lot of unofficial information from Security."[53] In fact the notebook was a confection by Dobson, paid for by the Communists,[54] but since some facts are now confirmed by ASIO documents, it was a confection salted with facts or near-facts known to Dobson.

Dobson had committed an extraordinary series of frauds. In 1946 he had got a trip to Europe on Royal Navy ships by posing as a war correspondent for fictitious publications. He had been jailed for fraud in Hong Kong but escaped prosecution in Manila. In Shanghai in 1948, he created a great deal of trouble with allegations of corruption against an Australian member of Parliament and an immigration official in Shanghai, and by claiming that one of the "top ten" Nazis had got into Australia as an immigrant after escaping in a U-boat to Japan. The allegations proved unfounded and Dobson eventually confessed to fabricating them in order to pressure the Australian consul to help him while he was imprisoned by the Chinese (awaiting trial for fraud, naturally). Unfortunately, one of the Dobson allegations had meanwhile turned out to be true, namely that Australia had admitted as an immigrant a Mrs Glatzel, alias "Diana Hamilton", who had broadcast on Nazi propaganda stations in Shanghai during the War (possibly as a result of threats to her husband). Since the revelation of this information would have created unfavourable publicity for the immigration program, the matter was suppressed and Dobson given a free trip home.[55] The only positive aspect from the anti-Communist point of view was that the combination of Dobson's falling on his sword and the revelation's appearing in *Tribune*, whose credibility rating was poor, caused enough doubts about the whole matter to have it forgotten among larger matters like the Coal Strike and the coming election.

Moral theology of deceitful political action

In connection with the takeovers of political bodies, there arose a subtle question of moral philosophy, disagreements over which caused much anguish in Movement and anti-Movement circles. The question is, may one vote at meetings of organisations to which one pretends to belong, but does not? James McAuley, generally supportive of the Movement, had been most worried about the question, and was assured by Santamaria that stacking of meetings with people ineligible to vote had never been a Movement tactic – or if it had once or twice happened, in Sydney, it had been put a stop to.[56] The NSW central office of the Movement did issue instructions against stacking union meetings in general; approval was occasionally given when there was considered to be a "moral certainty" that Communists would stack the meeting. The belief that stacking was widespread may be attributable to knee-jerk reactions of those defeated in union elections by Movement candidates.[57] On the other hand, students at Sydney University, where the Movement had spectacular success in 1951 and controlled all major student organisations, reported that Ryan positively encouraged Arts and Engineering students to vote at Medical students' meetings and vice versa. Father Pryke, then chaplain at Sydney University and later a critic of the Movement, recalled that "Dr Ryan had once come back from the Vatican and reported to him and some Movement people that he had consulted some top moral theologians at the Gregorian and Lateran Universities and they had advised that Catholics were morally justified in doing anything that Communists did."[58] Many Catholics were not prepared to lie on demand and left the Movement over such tactics.

Ryan's point of view should be seen in an internationalist perspective. The "top moral theologians of the Gregorian" were in a position to see the problem in terms of Hungary and Czechoslovakia (and

Italy, the subject of some very pessimistic assessments in Church circles).[59] There does seem something ridiculous in urging the future victims of Stalinism in, for example, Czechoslovakia in 1948, to watch the people planning to hang them from lampposts vote illegally at meetings, but to scrupulously avoid doing the same themselves. Ryan and his supporters, like the Communists themselves, transferred their vision of an international struggle of immense forces of good and evil to the sleepy backwater of 1950s Australia. Those who had lived all their lives in Australia found that vision out of contact with local reality. The onus of justification for dubious tactics, then, probably shifts to the question of whether the Movement really believed a takeover of Australia by Communists from within was possible. It is the moral consequences of the question that account for its ability to generate so much heat even now.[60] Another factor to take into account is that the inner Sydney branches of the ALP were not the scene of decent and civilised exchanges of views in the first place. Branch-stacking was a way of life in them long before the Communists, let alone the Movement,[61] and there would not have been much point in getting involved at all in them without being prepared to match "normal" tactic for tactic. Still, it is a high-risk strategy, to say the least. What if (as Guy Fawkes no doubt wondered) one is found out? That can be a problem even for those who do not pretend any special ethical superiority. It is far more of a problem for churchmen, whose *raison d'être* involves a bid for occupation of the high moral ground. When it was discovered that Ryan was, so to speak, subordinating morality to the struggle against the proletariat, people came to suspect that "everyone, from the Cardinal down, is guilty of conniving at arrant dishonesty."[62] Nothing came out into the full glare of publicity, but it is not difficult to understand why the Sydney bishops and the Vatican became extremely anxious to pull the plug on the Movement.

Computational casuistics is not easy.

Ryan's role in the Split

Gilroy appointed his auxiliary, Bishop Lyons, to oversee the Sydney Movement. Lyons did not get on with Ryan, nor, it appears, with many other members. In 1953 Lyons had Ryan replaced as director with a Jesuit seen to be a partisan of the Melbourne Groupers. Ryan was widely thought to have been unjustly treated and the resulting tension contributed to the parting of ways between the Sydney and Melbourne branches of the Movement that had such far-reaching consequences at the time of the Split.[63] Ryan himself resented the Melbourne takeover.[64] The tension is illustrated by an event at the 1954 conference of the Movement in Melbourne. Ryan moved that in future, not all the speeches be given by Santamaria, as happened that year, but his motion was soundly defeated.[65] Ryan was a key speaker at the meetings in 1956 at which the vast majority of New South Wales Movement men decided to accept the Sydney bishops' policy of staying with the Labor Party instead of joining their Victorian and Queensland colleagues in what later became the DLP.[66] At the meeting of seven to eight hundred Movement leaders held at St Paul's, Kensington, on 30 September 1956, which finally saw the decision to "stay in and fight" agreed to by almost all, Ryan spoke after Bishop Carroll. A participant recalled:

> The substance of Dr Ryan's address was that he would obey his Bishop even if he thought he was wrong, but on this matter he knew his Bishop was right – history proved that break-away parties never lasted – 'they were not worth two bob'.[67]

It was this meeting, as it happened, that provided the occasion for the closest the bishops came to public exposure as liars. In 1959 the *Catholic Weekly* officially denied claims in the *Sydney Morning Herald* that Catholics had been adjured to stay in the ALP "as a matter of loyalty to the Cardinal". One of the participants at the Kensington meeting offered to name the speakers and the most prominent of those present, if the claim were made again. Nothing more was heard of the matter.[68]

In a brief document of 1962, 'Why the Movement failed', Ryan argued that the original policy of purely fighting Communism was not kept to, and the Movement began to target non-Communists and thus became rightly seen by many Labor leaders as a danger to themselves. Further, in some places – though not Sydney – there was infiltration by the enemy.⁶⁹ It is not entirely clear what Ryan means by the "failure" of the Movement. If it was not intended to take control of the ALP, but only break the Communist hold on unions, then it would appear to have succeeded. If, on the other hand, its aim was to effect a spiritual transformation of Australian workers and replace monopoly capitalism with a harmonious society of medieval guilds, providing contented artisans and farmhands with the leisure to master scholastic philosophy, then doubtless it failed to do so, but the prospects of success were surely so low as to make depression at the outcome inappropriate.

Ryan was still active in 1968, complaining about the laxity of Church responses to *Humanae Vitae*; there is no possibility, he thinks, of a Catholic disagreeing in conscience with the Pope's ruling.⁷⁰ He died in 1969.⁷¹

Catholic intellectual life has become more diverse since Paddy's day. Its leaders are, in their various ways, more professional, better able to stay abreast of overseas developments. But who could get thirty thousand on the trams out to Rushcutters Bay?

---

1. C. H. Jory, *The Campion Society and Catholic Social Militancy in Australia 1929–1939* (Sydney, 1986); R. Mathews, *Of Labour and Liberty: Distributism in Victoria 1891-1966* (Clayton, Vic, 2017).

2. Jory, *Campion Society*, ch. 11; N. McDonald, *War Cameraman: The Story of Damien Parer* (Port Melbourne, 1994), ch. 4; B. F. Duncan, *From Ghetto to Crusade: A Study of the Social and Political Thought of Catholic Opinion-Makers in Sydney During the 1930s* (PhD thesis, Dept of Government, Sydney University, 1987), 221–4; see further in ch. 13 of this anthology.

3. P. Ryan, *De via morali quam ad Deum cognoscendum proposuit Eduardus le Roy*, thesis, 1932; Ryan's career at Kensington in A. Caruana, *Monastery on the Hill: A History of the Sacred Heart Monastery Kensington, 1897–1997* (Kensington, 2002), 226–31.

4. P. J. Ryan, 'The new scholasticism: its origin and history', *Catholic Press* 26/4/1934, 6, 'The fundamental tenets of scholasticism', 17/5/34, p. 12:, https://trove.nla.gov.au/newspaper/article/104375893, 'The fundamental tenets of scholasticism', 7/6/34, 6, https://trove.nla.gov.au/newspaper/article/104374216 , 'Philosophy and theology: the attitude of the moderns', 12/7/34, 10. Training of schoolgirls in apologetics at: https://trove.nla.gov.au/newspaper/article/106335061

5. O. U. Vonwiller, J. Anderson & P. J. Ryan, 'Symposium on science, philosophy and Christianity', *Science Journal* (Sydney University), Michaelmas 1936: 24–36.1

6. 'Symposium on 'The Origin of Life', *Catholic Press* 20/7/1939, 27; 'Symposium on the

'origin of life', *Catholic Freeman's Journal* 20/7/39, 30:, https://trove.nla.gov.au/newspaper/article/146377497 ; cf. 'Evolution', in Question Box, *Catholic Freeman's Journal* 18/4/40, 6–7.

[7] F. A. Mecham, 'Evolution and man', *Australasian Catholic Record* 26 (1949): 19–28, 262–8; J. Burnheim, 'Biology versus Catholic philosophy: a new approach', *Australasian Catholic Record* 27 (1950): 267–71.

[8] P. J. Ryan, 'The Existence of God: The Argument from Design', *Annals publication* no. 49 (Kensington, 1950), 22.

[9] D. Horne, *The Education of Young Donald* (2nd ed, Ringwood, Victoria, 1988) 179–80.

[10] 'Have we freewill? Lively debate at Sydney University', *Catholic Freeman's Journal*, 27/5/1939, 20: https://trove.nla.gov.au/newspaper/article/146385591 "O'Neill" is W.M. O'Neil, later Professor of Psychology, Deputy Vice-Chancellor and a dominant figure in Australian psychology.

[11] Reports on A.G. Hammer, W. H. C. Eddy and Dr Woodward, in Ryan archives, section Articles, folder Teachers' College Reports, with letter of M. D. Forrest MSC to G. R. Thomas, NSW Director of Education, 14/12/39; Dr Rumble, Question Box, 'Must teachers be agnostics', *Catholic Freeman's Journal* 19/10/39, 10; 'Is censorship immoral', 2/11/39, 6; 'Methods at Teachers' College', 16/11/39, 6; 'Man not rational!', 23/11/39, 6; 'Teachers' College dogmas', 30/11/39, 6; 'Teachers' College defended', 7/12/39, p. 6; 'Animals at Teachers' College', 14/12/39, 12; 'Action at the Teachers' College', 21/12/39, 6.

[12] P. Ryan, Question Box: 'We stand for order and sanity', *Catholic Freeman's Journal*, 3/7/41, 8:, https://trove.nla.gov.au/newspaper/article/146373777

[13] Horne, *Education of Young Donald*, 262–4.

[14] 'The cat got out', in Dr Ryan's Question Box, *Catholic Freeman's Journal* 10/7/41, 8; Horne letter in *Honi Soit* 18 (14) (27/6/41), 2.

[15] 'Enquiry not hindered: Ryan on religion and science', *Honi Soit* 15 (12) (22/4/43), 1: https://digital.library.sydney.edu.au/nodes/view/3079; '2 aspects of Ryan's 1 truth', *Honi Soit* 15 (24) (26/8/43), 1, https://digital.library.sydney.edu.au/nodes/view/3091.

[16] D. Everingham, letter, 'Dr. Ryan refuted', *Honi Soit* 15 (26) (30/9/43), 3.

[17] 'Catholic Action: Educational lectures inaugurated', *Catholic Press* 19/3/1936, 10; 'Catholic Action Association', 3/12/36.

[18] Jory, *Campion Society*, 105; Duncan, *From Ghetto to Crusade*, ch. 10; 'Rev Dr Ryan's course of public lectures', *Catholic Freeman's Journal* 13/7/39, 21; see the regular 'Secretariat of Catholic Action' page in the weekly *Catholic Freeman's Journal* during 1939 to mid-1941.

[19] P. Macphail, 'What's being done about adult education', *Catholic Weekly* 5/9/1946, 3; lecture notes of the School are in the Ryan archives.

[20] Quoted in N. Turner, *Catholics in Australia: A Social History*, (Melbourne, 1992), vol. II, 111.

[21] P. Ryan, 'Radio replies and comments', *The Southern Cross* 2/5/1941, 5; 'Rev Dr Ryan's Question Box' appeared weekly in the *Catholic Freeman's Journal* from 7/3/40 to 18/12/41; Protestant objections in 'Dr. Ryan and intolerance', *The Watchman* 2 (1) (February 1942), 8, 9, 13; 'The Loyal Orange Institution of N.S.W. replies to Dr. Ryan (R.C.)', *The Watchman* 2 (3) (Apr 1942): 10–11.

22 E. Campion, *Australian Catholics* (Ringwood, Victoria, 1987), 134–6; biography in *Who is Father Rumble?*, pamphlet (St Paul, Minnesota, n.d.), text of many questions linked at https://en.wikipedia.org/wiki/Leslie_Rumble

23 *Sydney Morning Herald*, 22/5/43, 12:, https://trove.nla.gov.au/newspaper/article/17849486

24 *Royal Commission on Espionage: Transcript of Proceedings*, vol. 3, 1329.

25 P. J. Ryan, *Dean Hewlett Johnson's Socialist Sixth: A Commentary*, (Sydney, 1943):, https://viewer.slv.vic.gov.au/?entity=IE6816222

26 Campion, *Australian Catholics*, 133.

27 L. L. Sharkey, *A Reply to Father Ryan* (1943), https://auscp.org.au//wp-content/uploads/2021/09/AReplytofatherryansharkey.pdf; also L.L. Sharkey, 'Marxism and morals: Dr. Ryan answered', *Tribune* 2/10/48, 7:, https://trove.nla.gov.au/newspaper/article/208112563

28 'Stadium's record crowd hears political debate, with big anti-Communist majority', *Sydney Morning Herald* 24/9/1948, 1, 3; 'Huge stadium crowd shows wide interest in Communism', *Tribune* 29/9/48, 8; 'Ryan versus Ross', *The Watchman* 8 (10) (November 1948): 219; full text of the speeches in 'Full report: Dr. Ryan in debate with Communist', *Catholic Weekly* 30/9/48, 1–4, 19–20: https://trove.nla.gov.au/newspaper/article/146664951 ; the Russian 'postcard divorces' were an out-of-date allegation, as other Catholic experts were well aware: F. Sheen, *Communism and the Conscience of the West* (Garden City, N.Y., 1948), ch. 7; Ryan earlier on this in 'Divorce by postcard', *Catholic Freeman's Journal* 18/12/41, 8.

29 *News Weekly* 15/9/1948, reported in ASIO file on Catholic Action, Australian Archives series A6122/30 item 1222.

30 E. Ross, *Of Storm and Struggle* (Sydney, 1982), 113; Ross's speech with photos at: https://auscp.org.au/history/communism-is-in-the-best-interests-of-the-australian-people/

31 F. Knopfelmacher, *Intellectuals and Politics* (Melbourne, 1968), 76–7

32 'Dr Ryan to lecture', *Catholic Weekly* 13/3/47, 5; 'Priest's bitter attack on communism', *Sydney Morning Herald* 9/10/1947, 4; 'Dr Ryan's attack on Communism at Religion and Life Conference', *Catholic Weekly* 16/10/47, 7, 21; 'Priest attacks Reds at Paddington', *Catholic Weekly* 6/11/47, 7; 'Public meeting', *Canberra Times* 18/2/1948; 'Civil war only aim of communists', *Argus* 2/3/1948; 'Challenge forced Ryan to retract', *Tribune* 23/6/48, 7; 'Communist debater answers "loaded" question by priest', *Tribune* 11/12/48, 8; 'The red menace in Australia', pamphlet printed by Record Printing Company, Rockhampton, 1949, with text of Ryan's address at Rockhampton of 3/5/49; 'Military conquest of Australia planned by Reds', *Sydney Morning Herald* 21/4/1950, 3; 'Communist aim – world conquest', *Honi Soit* 22 (21) (14/9/50), 2; T.P. Boland, *James Duhig* (St Lucia, 1986) 328; J.P. Maguire, *Prologue: A History of the Catholic Church as Seen From Townsville* (Toowoomba, 1990), 155

33 Dates respectively 26/5/1951; 20/8/51; 31/8/51

34 'Socialists' cure worse than disease, says priest', *Sydney Morning Herald*, 29/9/1949, 4; more fully in 'Social justice for all: Dr Ryan, MSC, expounds Christian programme', *Catholic Press*, May 1941; and P.J. Ryan, 'World Problems', Annals publication no. 14 (Kensington, 1938); C. Lewis, *People Before Profit: The Credit Union Movement in Australia* (Kent Town, S.A., 1996), 15.

35. M. Hogan, ed, *Justice Now! Social Justice Statements of the Australian Bishops, First Series, 1940-1966* (Sydney, 1990); Race Mathews, *Of Labour and Liberty: Distributism in Victoria, 1891-1966* (Notre Dame, Indiana, 2017); M. Hogan, 'Australian Catholic corporatism: proposals for industrial councils in the 1940s', *Labour History* no. 62 (May, 1992): 91-105; for a later iteration of traditional Catholic opposition to *laissez-faire* capitalism, see A. K. Dunstan, 'Guilds and other matters', *Annals Australasia* 117 (1), January-February 2006, 24-26.

36. G. Henderson, *Mr Santamaria and the Bishops* (Sydney, 1982), 71.

37. P. J. Ryan, *An Outline of Catholic Action,* Annals publication no. 5 (Kensington, 1935); summary in Duncan, *From Ghetto to Crusade,* 158-60; other Ryan pamphlets in the *Annals* series are *On creed and dogmas and all that* (no. 6, 1936); *The restoration of all things in Christ* (no. 9, 1936); *The Church and marriage* (no. 10, n.d.).

38. Jory, *Campion Society,* 119, 144 n. 6; Duncan, *From Ghetto to Crusade,* p. 232; see Ryan's Question Box, *Catholic Freeman's Journal*: 'Red attack on Catholic Action', 14/3/40, 7; 'Catholic Action versus Communism', 28/3/40, 6-7; 'Join your union', 22/5/41, 8 and 'What is Catholic Action?', 13/11/41, 9, 24.

39. P. Ormonde, *The Movement* (Melbourne, 1972), 3; G. Williams, *Cardinal Sir Norman Gilroy* (Sydney, 1971), 51; Henderson, *Mr Santamaria and the Bishops,* 26; J. T. Kane, *Exploding the Myths* (North Ryde, NSW, 1989), 23; R. Murray, *The Split* (2nd ed, 1972), 46.

40. B. A. Santamaria, *Against the Tide* (Melbourne, 1981), 85.

41. Williams, *Gilroy,* 52-3.

42. 'Liaison with Catholic Action', (27/10/53), in ASIO file on Catholic Action, Australian Archives series A6122/30 item 1222.

43. S. Arneil, *Black Jack: The Life and Times of Brigadier Sir Frederick Galleghan* (Melbourne, 1983), 131-45; A. Davies, '"Black Jack" Galleghan and the 'D.P.s': Australian immigration and a modern Major-General', *Australian War Memorial History Conference,* February 1983, 1-16.

44. M. Bialoguski, *The Petrov Story* (1955, repr. Melbourne, 1989), 36.

45. K. C. Davis (NSW State Secretary of the Movement) to author, 15/7/95.

46. 'Irregularities and improper control of sources – leakage of security information', in ASIO file on Catholic Action, as above; summary in D. McKnight, *Australia's Spies and Their Secrets* (Sydney, 1994), 202-3.

47. 'Anti-Communist union official says he was thrown off ferry', *Sydney Morning Herald* 7/8/49, 1:, https://trove.nla.gov.au/newspaper/article/28668529

48. 'Police reject story of murder attempt on ferry', *Sydney Morning Herald* 8/8/49, 1; 'Industrial group plot exposed: Australia saved from tragedy', *The Rock* 5 (33) (18/8/49): 1, 8; '"Stupid, crude": Dobson case', *Sydney Morning Herald,* 26/10/49.

49. 'Calwell linked with Dobson', *Tribune* 13/8/49, 1.

50. Commonwealth of Australia, Parliamentary Debates, House of Representatives 21 September 1949 (vol. 204, 395; further 463-6); see also 'Calwell's bid to slide out of scandal won't fool workers', *Tribune* 24/9/49: 3

51. A. Calwell, *Be Just and Fear Not* (Hawthorn, Vic, 1972), 218.

52. Ibid., 172.

53 *Tribune* 27/8/49: 3; also 7/9/49: 6; copy of latter, with denials by CIS officer, in CIS File on Dobson, Australian Archives series A432/82 item 1949/851.

54 P. Deery, 'Labor, Communism and the Cold War: the case of "Diver" Dobson', *Australian Historical Studies* 28 (1997), 66–87, summary in Brett Evans, 'The 'Ferry Plot', a secret diary and a trickster's part in a ploy for political power', *ABC Radio National*, 24/6/2020:, https://www.abc.net.au/news/2020-06-24/cold-war-william-diver-dobson-and-the-ferry-plot/12372540

55 Australian Archives series A1838/1 item 1542/36 (Dept of External Affairs, Security File on Dobson). Glatzel's activities in B. Wasserstein, *Secret War in Shanghai: Treachery, subversion and collaboration in the Second World War* (London, 2017), 145–6.

56 Santamaria, 276–7; cf. Ormonde, *The Movement*, 36–8; S. Short, *Laurie Short* (Sydney, 1992), 187.

57 K. C. Davis to author, 9/5/95 and 17/5/95.

58 Ormonde, *The Movement*, 43.

59 See, e.g., R. Hall, 'Should you ever go across the sea from Ireland …', *Eureka Street* 5 (2) (March 1995): 24–9, at 29.

60 P. Ormonde, 'A sort of healing', *Eureka Street* 4(9) (November 1994): 16, and letters of K. Davis and P. Ormonde, 5(1) (January/February 1995): 7 and 5(2) (March 1995): 8.

61 G. Richardson, *Whatever It Takes* (Sydney, 1994), 57–8; Kane, *Exploding the Myths*, 41.

62 McAuley to Santamaria, 30/8/1955, quoted in Santamaria, *Against the Tide*, 276.

63 J. Luttrell, *Norman Thomas Gilroy: An obedient life* (Strathfield, 2017), 240–4; Henderson, *Mr Santamaria and the Bishops*, 103–5; Williams, *Gilroy*, 54–5; Santamaria, *Against the Tide*, 167; Murray, *The Split*, 128–9; Ryan's complaints about Lyons in 'Memorandum to His Eminence, Norman Cardinal Gilroy, Archbishop of Sydney, October 1952, Subject: The present state of the organisation in the Archdiocese', in Ryan archives, section Articles, folder Communism.

64 K. C. Davis to author, 9/5/95.

65 G. Henderson, 'B. A. Santamaria and the cult of personality', in *50 Years of the Santamaria Movement*, ed. P. Ormonde (Sydney, 1992), 43–58, at 44.

66 Santamaria, *Against the Tide*, 204–6; Kane, *Exploding the Myths*, 127; Luttrell, *Gilroy*, 255–7; Caruana, *Monastery on the Hill*, 229.

67 M. Carroll to Santamaria, quoted in Kane, *Exploding the Myths*, 144.

68 Kane, *Exploding the Myths*, 142; Santamaria, *Against the Tide*, 206–7; cf. Kane to Gilroy, 21/12/1956: 'We are unable to reconcile your Eminence's reported intervention with the statement of your Secretary that you take no part in the affairs of political parties'.

69 P. Ryan, 'Postscript 1962: Why the Movement failed', typescript, Paddy Ryan archives, St Paul's Seminary, Kensington. I am grateful to Tony Caruana, archivist at St Paul's, for help with these archives, which have provided much of the information on Dr Ryan.

70 P. Ryan, 'Catholic conscience and "Humanae Vitae"', typescript, Ryan archives.

71 Obituary, 'Crusader for truth', *Catholic Weekly* 23/1/69, 3.

8

Convent slave laundries? Magdalen asylums in Australia*

Abstract: Magdalen asylums, set up by nuns in the nineteenth century as refuges for destitute girls and women, became transformed around 1900 into virtual prisons for girls referred by the courts and police. The institutions supported themselves with laundry work and conditions were harsh, leading to accusations of "convent slave laundries" in Protestant propaganda. Those allegations were partly true. The clash between girls brought in from mostly very disturbed backgrounds and the nuns' practices of pious regimentation led to many unhamemories by former inmates. It is also true that the nuns looked after girls for whom there were few alternatives.

A staple of extreme Protestant propaganda in the first half of the twentieth century was the accusation of "convent slave laundries". Anti-Catholic organs like *The Watchman* and *The Rock* regularly alleged extremely harsh conditions in Roman Catholic convent laundries and reported stories of abductions into them and escapes from them.[1]

In Ireland, the scandal of Magdalen laundries has been the subject of extensive official inquiries.[2] Allegations of widespread near-slave conditions and harsh punishments turned out to be substantially true.[3] The Irish state has apologised,[4] memoirs have been written, compensation paid, a movie made.[5] Something similar occurred in England.[6]

What of Australia?

The convent laundry system

Australia did have a similar system. Conditions were indeed harsh, but it remains not easy to gain a just overview of what happened. Views conflict sharply. Apparently genuine memories of very op-

---

* 'Convent slave laundries? Magdalen asylums in Australia', *Journal of the Australian Catholic Historical Society* 34 (2013), 70–90.

pressive conditions conflict with nun's recollections of their doing their best for difficult cases. This chapter aims to present both sides of the story.

Each Australian state capital had, from about the 1890s to the 1960s, a large convent which contained a commercial laundry where the work was done by mostly teenage "fallen women" who were placed in the convent, voluntarily or involuntarily, for reasons such as being destitute, uncontrollable, picked up by the police and similar.[7] Most were run by the Sisters of the Good Shepherd, an order that specialised in "wayward" girls. They included the head house at Abbotsford Convent in Melbourne (1864-1974),[8] with offshoots at Oakleigh and Albert Park,[9] the Home of the Good Shepherd, Ashfield, Sydney (1913-1969),[10] the Good Shepherd Convent, Mitchelton, Brisbane (1931-1978),[11] Mount Saint Canice, Sandy Bay, Hobart (1893-1974),[12] 'The Pines', North Plympton, Adelaide (1941-1974); the Home of the Good Shepherd, Leederville, Perth (1902-1979),[13] and St Aidan's, Bendigo.[14] Similar establishments run by other orders were those of the Good Samaritans in Sydney – Pitt Street (1857-1901), Manly (1881-1910) and St Magdalen's, Tempe (1888-1980),[15] and St Joseph's in Adelaide, run by the Sisters of St Joseph.[16] Information on most of these is available in the two professional institutional histories of the orders, Christine Kovesi's *Pitch Your Tents on Distant Shores: A History of the Sisters of the Good Shepherd in Australia, Aotearoa/New Zealand and Tahiti* and Margaret Walsh's *The Good Sams: Sisters of the Good Samaritan 1857–1969*.

They were large operations. In 1904, Abbotsford had about 366 "Magdalen penitents" (with another 154 at Albert Park), with 110 nuns (including novices) – that did not count 310 children in the "Industrial and Preservation" class and 290 in a day school for the surrounding area.[18] At its height in the years after WWII, there were 1000 women and children (that includes the orphanage and other parts as well as the refuge) plus 120 nuns and novices.[19]

Laundry work was regarded as suitable as it did not need much training and made money without great capital expense. The moral point of it was explained by the head nun of Abbotsford about 1890:

Interior of the laundry, St Magdalen's Retreat, Tempe, 1899[17]

the inmates are principally engaged in laundry work, this being, in the opinion of the sisters, the most suited to all, and calculated to occupy the mind and body, leaving little time for melancholy reflection on the past or anything except the work of reformation.[20]

Memories of harsh conditions

Memories of conditions in the convent laundries by those who were in them are overwhelmingly negative. The complaints detail a pattern of verbal abuse, shaming, lack of love and extremely hard work. Any one recollection might be put down as exaggerated, but the story is consistent.

An inmate of Abbotsford recalls:

> We girls got up early, went to mass, came back, attended the refectory where we all had breakfast (such as it was) then we went to work. I was only a kid back then and didn't know better, I just accepted their slavery as normal! … We had a huge bath and toilet area. We had a bath once a fortnight from memory and even so the water we used had been used several times before we got in Y…..UCKO! The crows, usually called auxiliaries, would drag us down there and beat the bejes-s out of us if some nun had a complaint against any of us. Never mind if it was true or not. Biff! Bash! And cop that! Until we grew older and now and then fought back.[21]

Typical are the memories of Janice Konstantinidis, an inmate of Mount Saint Canice in the 1960s:

> Other forms of punishments took were the extra cleaning of the dormitory floors. Used tealeaves were thrown over the floors, which we would then have to sweep and polish. There was a large, red cement hallway that ran through various areas of the home. Scrubbing this hallway while on my hands and knees was a job that I came to know well. It would take me over two hours, and I was expected to use a toothbrush for the grouted areas. I would be given this punishment for simply asking "why?", or for taking too long in the toilets. They did not consider the fact that I suffered from constipation and that hurrying was, therefore, impossible for me.[22]

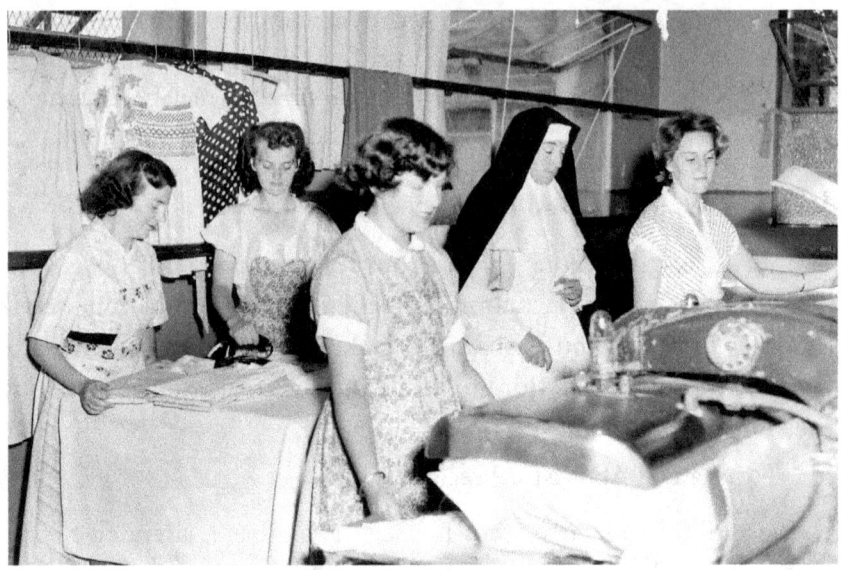

Ironing room, Mount Saint Canice Magdalen laundry, Hobart, c. 1960s
Good Shepherd Archives, Abbotsford

From 'The Pines', Plympton:

> The nuns' constant vilification branded us – as livestock are branded – by fire. We were treated as mere objects of contempt, there to earn our wretched keep in Magdalene Infernos around the world.[23]

And recalling the first day at 'The Pines':

> Mother Superior materialised. It was as though she glided into the room from out of nowhere, with her long black habit flowing all round her, she startled me. 'Your name will be Jane' she instructed. Then she opened THAT door which led to a concrete court yard. Before I could ask a single question the door was slammed and bolted behind me.[24]

From Leederville:

> It was a bugger of a life. The nuns were cruel. They belted us, hit us with bunches of keys and put us in straitjackets like Chinese dolls. I'm still deaf in one ear after a belting. I cut my plaits off so they couldn't pull me up by them. I was very miserable as a child.[25]

There are a few less negative comments. Victoria Stuart, who was in Mount Saint Canice from the ages of 15 to 18 in the early 1960s, found it an improvement after a very difficult time in a Salvation Army home, which followed a disturbed home life that included rape by a neighbour. She felt cared for by the nuns, saying "the nuns did care about what happened to us" (though she resented the long hours of work without pay). She saw the wall around the convent as "to stop blokes coming in", not to confine the girls. When she became pregnant later she returned to the nuns.[26]

A positive view of Abbotsford may be inferred on the part of former laundry inmate Mrs Cecilia Ryan, who returned to stay temporarily at Abbotsford in 1967 at the time of the execution of her son Ronald Ryan.[27] (There are also some more positive memories from those in other parts of the complex, such as the orphanage.[28])

Almost entirely absent from the recollections are stories of sexual abuse and of serious physical assaults and beatings[29] (although there are some memories of corporal punishment of the kind then common in schools, such as "They used to belt you with wet towels").[30] That agrees with the Irish experience, where there are almost no such allegations (contrary to some popular perceptions).[31] In many cases, that contrasted with the girls' lives before entry. The negative memories involve instead mental cruelty, confinement and very hard work.

Then, as in any underfunded institution, there was the food. 'Breakfast [at Abbotsford] was luke-warm porridge with a slice of STALE bread. Lunch on the other hand was soup, with the morning's left over porridge added for volume!'[32] Regular doses of Epsom salts are remembered with particular loathing.[33]

One aspect of deprivation that may not be expected by modern readers was the silence. In accordance with the traditions of the nuns, work and much of the rest of the day proceeded in silence. Some of the allowed talk was strictly supervised. A visitor to the Tempe asylum in 1890 explains one purpose: "One great element of success in the system of the refuge is the impossibility of the relation of experiences among the inmates. When at work, or at meals, or in the dormitories, silence is compulsory. Proper periods are allowed for conversation, which is carried on in, and improved by, the presence of the nuns."[34]

Another aspect of the deprivation suffered by inmates was the very poor quality of education, or for more senior girls, the total lack of it. The visitor to Tempe, while praising all other aspects of it, "regretted to notice an absence of books or means of wholesome recreation" (he is told that lack of money is the cause). One of those who made a submission to the Senate's Forgotten Australians inquiry says she worked from the ages of 8 to 12 in Mount St Canice without any schooling.[35] That was of course illegal.

Other dangers of life in the homes included diseases and industrial accidents (which were of course common in outside workplaces too). Doris Dyer lost her right arm in an accident with the mangle shortly after starting at the Leederville laundry in 1942 (she says the nuns treated her well afterwards).[36] Sister Mary of St Columba at Abbotsford badly injured her hand in the laundry machinery in 1889 and had to have it amputated; she "bore her cross with admirable fortitude, offering her sufferings for the conversion of our loved Penitents to whom she is so devoted."[37] Physical effects of the heavy work could show up later: "I worked in the laundry. I did the slave child labour for them. I worked on the presses. I'm definitely paying for it now ... physically I'm just no good. I'm 56 and I can barely get around."[38] Victoria Stuart at Mount Saint Canice believed her lungs were damaged by the high levels of bleach used on the laundry from the infectious diseases hospital.[39]

Conditions of manual work were harsh everywhere, even if pay was better. Lynette Kluck, at Leederville in the 1950s, says she found the work just as hard later in a commercial laundry.[40]

The alternative homes for girls in trouble no doubt varied but some were worse. The state-run Parramatta Girls Home, which also had a laundry, had similar harsh conditions but a worse record for assaults.[41]

Confinement and escape

A profound change in the nature of the institutions goes some way towards explaining what happened. They began as refuges but turned into prisons. In early years, there was emphasis on the freedom of inmates to leave, and the conditions from which inmates came were often not such as to invite return. The visitor to the Magdalen Asylum at Tempe in 1890 reported:

> ... the applicants shall be fallen women, and that they undertake to remain in the refuge for two years. There is nothing, however, in connection with the place, which is open on all sides, to compel them to keep this promise ... Upon my inquiring of several women, "Why do you stay here when you could earn good wages outside?" The reply was invariably "We are happy here; there is no temptation; we get plenty of everything; the sisters are good to us."[42]

The Good Shepherd order was originally founded to provide asylums to destitute women, that is, places of voluntary refuge in something the same way as modern women's refuges. They were only with some difficulty persuaded to expand their work to involuntary cases – Bishop Goold in Melbourne encountered resistance in 1864 when he asked the nuns at Abbotsford to add a Reformatory to their work, but succeeded in overcoming it.[43] The Good Samaritans faced the same problem. Their founder, Archbishop Polding, had visited an establishment in England what was "prison-like with bars and locks", and rejected that model for New South Wales.[44] The Good Samaritans continued that policy for the early decades of their Magdalen institutions. But from 1907 they became involved with the Children's Court and accepted girls who were sentenced to custody for a fixed period. Those came to dominate the intake.[45]

As the laundries came to be used as dumping grounds for girls picked up by the police, got rid of by their parents and step-parents, or sent on by jails and other institutions, they turned into penal institutions with locks, barred windows and walls. The attitudes of inmates followed suit: "I was in Abbotsford and it was little more than a prison. There was no way to walk out the door, they were all locked. I was forcibly restrained more than once trying to get away."[46] An institution where inmates are forcibly confined is very different from one full of the willing. It is necessarily full of resentment on the part of the inmates, many of whom are also the kind of people already resistant to authority and routine by the time of arrival. No-one loves their jailers. As a counterpart, such an institution encourages desperate and aggressive disciplinary strategies on the part of the (untrained) warders.

The context is that the mid-twentieth century was the high point of belief in the benefits of forcible institutionalisation – of mental patients, removed aboriginal children, child migrants and others. In the twentieth century, some 500,000 children are believed to have undergone institutional care in Australia.[47]

Inevitably, escapes and attempted escapes were frequent. Convent escape stories were sometimes reported in the newspapers: Abbotsford in 1905,[48] Abbotsford again in 1920 and 1923,[49] from Ashfield on a rope of knotted sheets in 1954.[50] Escapees caught were usually sent back.

One of the more difficult cases in Mount Saint Canice, Evelyn (in the late 1960s), recalls:

> The authorities decided the Salvation Army wouldn't be able to handle me, so I was eventually sent to Magdalene Girls Home in Sandy Bay ... After a couple of years I started to run away, I would scale the fences, undo the bars on the windows, get out through the laundry, whatever way I could, I was always taken back by the police, boy, then I would cop it. The nuns chopped off my hair with garden sheers, I would be made to scrub corridors with a toothbrush, I would be placed in a shoe cupboard for hours at a time ... Eventually I was given Largactuyl this was a drug to sedate me and to quieten me down, I was given 50mg at first, then increased it to 100mg, they would stand over me and watch me take it to make sure that I had taken it. On one of my escapades, I actually got to Burnie met this guy and I had sex with him, I don't know why, maybe I was looking for someone to love me. Well the moral of this story is I got pregnant. I was taken back to Mt, St. Canice (Magdalene Home renamed).[51]

(She was sent to the Salvation Army home and the baby forcibly adopted.)

Sometimes the authorities were over-enthusiastic about rounding up escaped girls. The Melbourne *Argus* of 1927 reported an escape that came before the courts:

ESCAPE FROM CONVENT.
Girl Swims Yarra.

Maisie King aged 17 years, recently an inmate of the Abbotsford Convent, appeared in the Fitzroy Court on Thursday on a charge of having been without sufficient lawful means of support.

Policewoman Connor said: -Defendant was placed in the Abbotsford Convent by her mother who declared that she was unable to control her. On the morning of April 11, defendant, in company with five other girls, swam the river and escaped from the convent. In company with Constable McGregor I arrested defendant at Fairfield on April 12.

King said: -My home life was unhappy, and some time ago I asked the sergeant of police at Richmond if I would be justified in leaving home. He explained that if I left home and kept myself respectably I could not be taken back against my will. I obtained a position with a drapery firm and left home. I was paid £2/10/ a week, and I rented a room at Port Melbourne for which I paid 12/6 a week. Then at the instance of my mother I was taken into a taxi-cab under the pretext of being taken to a doctor. I was driven, however, to the Abbotsford Convent, where I was taken in, contrary to my will. In order to escape from the convent I had to cross the river. I am well able to earn my living and to look after myself.

Mr W.G. Smith: Can you get any work?

King: Too right I can!

Mr. Smith: That's the spirit. It appears that the warrant was issued for the arrest of this girl as a means of getting her back to the institution from which she escaped. I cannot say that

> she is without means. On the contrary, I believe that she is a very willing worker.
>
> The case was dismissed.[52]

The more secure the security, the more dangerous escape attempts could be. Janice Konstantinidis's memoir of Mount St Canice recalls an attempt of 1964:

> A group of three girls was planning to escape one Sunday night while the rest of the girls were watching a film. I was in my dormitory helping to bathe Kerrie Anne when they attempted to escape. I had gone to the window to see if I could see them jump. They had planned to jump from the third floor bathroom window – this was one of the few windows that had no bars – to a ledge, to another ledge, and then to the roof of the first floor, which was concrete and had been added on to the home in its later years. The first girl jumped, but lost her footing when attempting to land on the ledge. She kept falling until she landed on the concrete roof. I heard her fall and saw that she lay still. The alarm was sounded by someone and the flood lights came on. An ambulance and the police were called. We soon learnt that the girl had broken her back. We never saw her again. We were told that after being discharged from the hospital, she was sent to Lachlan Park, which was a mental institution.[53]

An escape attempt from the third floor can hardly have been a surprise, since *The Rock* had complained about exactly that sixteen years earlier. *The Rock*'s editor, Wal Campbell,[54] claimed to have interviewed two 14-year-old girls who had been severely injured jumping from the third floor of Mount Saint Canice in 1948.[55] While *The Rock* is not a reliable source, the details of the interviews with the girls agree with other accounts, so it seems that in this case Campbell came across a true story. The story was also reported in the Tasmanian press.[56]

Mary Torpy, inmate of the Good Shepherd Convent in Albany W.A. in 1899, found the ultimate escape. The coroner recorded a verdict of suicide while of unsound mind, finding that she must have thrown herself into a tub of boiling water intentionally.[57]

One possibility for escapees was to seek refuge with Protestant anti-Romanists. The Rev. George Tregear, the leading Protestant critic of convents, claimed in 1918 to have sheltered eleven escapees, "seven of whom lived in his home for some years."[58] Some of them apparently became tired of life as exhibits.[59]

Confinement was not permanent (except for some intellectually disabled girls who stayed on indefinitely), but the circumstances of leaving were sometimes not helpful for girls by then used to institutionalised living. According to one of the Forgotten Australians submissions:

> These 6 girls spent 4 years or more working as UNPAID LABOURERS in the NUNS COMMERCIAL LAUNDRY [of the Good Shepherd convent, Ashfield]. When they neared their 18th birthday, they were called out of the workrooms, told to change their clothes, they were given a small suitcase which contained all their possessions, they were given £1.00 and shown the door. These girls were just dumped on the street just a few days before their 18th birthday, they were not given a chance to tell the other girls they were leaving.[60]

(That conflicts with the statement of the Mother Prioress at Ashfield in 1954, that women who left the home to take jobs outside were given new clothing and a minimum of £30.[61])

Where the girls came from

To understand experiences in the homes, it is necessary to have some idea of where the girls came from, what had happened to them and why they were confined there.

The visitor to Tempe in 1890 (when it still had more of the character of a refuge than a reformatory), reports:

> I questioned a number of inmates very closely. I found that they were not light causes that the nuns had to deal with. Many of the women had led terrible lives—they had literally been rescued from the streets. Among the elder women I found that drink had, as might be expected, been a prime factor in their misery. Several of the young girls, however, had sad histories of deliberate seduc-

tion, which led one to regret that the punishment of flogging was not applicable to this crime.⁶²

Life outside on the streets was not "taking control of one's sexuality", as contemporary feminist mythology would have it.⁶³ A "fallen woman" found in Little Bourke Street in 1895 by the Wesley Central Mission said "I will tell the Sister how dreadfully miserable I am; I hate my life; I was *once good and pure*, but look at me now ... *we have lost our name*, our honor, our character; we have lost all."⁶⁴ (Not to mention the risks of assault and venereal diseases.)

Later, however, the girls forcibly confined in the homes often (though not always) came from backgrounds disturbed in other ways, a factor that needs to be taken into account when considering how they were dealt with and how they saw life in the homes. When poverty was endemic and before the era of the Pill, there were vast numbers of unwanted children, or children wanted but with parents unable to cope. The system of orphanages was overwhelmed by the numbers. Also, the phrase "wayward and intellectually disabled" girls means what it says.⁶⁵ The numbers of the intellectually disabled were much larger than today, for reasons still not totally clear but including malnutrition, diseases like measles, industrial pollutants, assaults and physical accidents and child neglect.⁶⁶ Violence was widespread.

So the reasons for admittance to the Magdalen institutions are often a litany of extreme deprivations. Women were admitted to Abbotsford in the 1880s for, among other things, larceny", "insulting behaviour", being "out at night with boys", "neglected and associating with prostitutes", "being found in a Chinese brothel", "concealed birth and burial of her infant with the assistance of her foster parents". Rose Hubbard, a fourteen-year-old orphan in 1885 with an artificial eye, was admitted to Oakleigh after burning down a house.⁶⁷

Janice Konstantinidis, herself placed in Mount Saint Canice by a father she describes as "a sadistic alcoholic", mentions a friend who had trouble with schoolwork: "She had been placed in the home because her parents were heavy drinkers and her mother had thrown her into a fire."⁶⁸

No doubt more girls than realised at the time had been raped by their fathers. Rachael Romero from 'The Pines', who is perhaps the most bitter critic of the laundries, describes a background of physical and sexual abuse by her father.[69] Another Pines inmate had suffered rape by a neighbour.[70]

An extreme example is Camelia M'Cluskey, who killed her three children with an axe in Bendigo in 1910. Found temporarily insane by the jury at her trial, she was confined in the Abbotsford Convent (from which she escaped by forcing a lock in 1911).[71]

The Melbourne papers of 1927 reported this case:

> Winnie O'Malley, a middle-aged woman, was charged at the Fitzroy Court on Monday with having at the Fitzroy watchhouse on the night of August 6, assaulted Agnes Dobbie … Winnie O'Malley said:-I left the Abbotsford Convent on the day in question. I am willing to return for six months.[72]

Obviously, women and girls from with such disturbed histories arrived in many cases with psychological wounds that made them very hard to deal with. A Good Samaritan nun in 1947 wrote of her charges:

> It is difficult to find even one vulnerable spot through which to appeal. The majority of them come under compulsion and they have no intention of settling down and no desire to be different.[73]

Reports by outsiders

Although the convents were generally cut off from the outside world, there were visits of an official and journalistic nature which have left reports. They tend to be generally positive. The impression of the inmates from the visitor to Tempe in 1890 is:

> They work hard from daylight till dark in the various divisions of the laundry, in each of which a sister is always present with them. They receive no wages, yet they appear to be happy and contented. There can be no mistake as to the affectionate relationship between them and the sisters.[74]

Visitors to the Industrial School attached to Abbotsford and to Oakleigh in 1902 report "The children were all looking happy and contented" and 'the girls struck us as being very cheerful and happy."[75] An unannounced visit to Abbotsford by the Charities

Board of Victoria in 1923 found that in the laundry, "Except in the case of a few unfortunates of obviously low mentality, the girls looked happier than one would expect, and all were clean and tidy."[76] A visitor from the Children's Welfare Department wrote to Mother Prioress at Oakleigh after a visit there in 1934, "Yesterday I was particularly pleased with the whole content of the convent and with the healthy and contented appearance of practically all the girls I interviewed. I was also with a great deal of pleasure impressed with the love for the Sisters these girls had and their appreciation of what is being done for them."[77]

Such reports of brief visits need to be read while keeping in mind the possibility that some evidence was hidden. According to one former inmate, "When the government came out you weren't allowed to tell them anything or you'd get belted."[78] On the other hand, eyewitness reports by people whose specific job it was to inquire into conditions cannot be ignored.

Following the escape of two laundry workers aged 25 and 29 from the Good Shepherd Convent, Ashfield, in 1954 – they sustained bone fractures after dropping from knotted sheets[79] – the *Sun-Herald* sent two female reporters to the home, with the nuns' permission. They found 180 girls there, of whom 55 were there "under restraint". The 124 voluntary inmates included 24 auxiliary nuns, 65 adult women who were "subnormal" and similar, and about 30 who were originally there involuntarily but had stayed on. The reporters found that "The bright, airy dining-room has a warm, homely atmosphere," and observed tennis courts and an auditorium for picture shows. Mother Prioress regrets that all girls have to be confined at night as there is no separation between voluntary and involuntary inmates. The dormitories are described as seriously overcrowded and the reasons why all correspondence must be censored are reported without comment. After discussion with a large groups of girls without a nun present, the reporters conclude: The girls claim to be mostly happy; they expect that the nuns will find them a job when they leave (some in typing and nursing but mostly in domestic service); many are orphans and used to the comfort and security of having things done for them; they feel they don't need money.[80]

The nuns' stories

The story is incomplete without an understanding of the nuns' perspective. Writings on the topic so far have not made an effort to explain that perspective. That risks repeating the historical travesty of the Stolen Generations apology, where people who had never done anything for the worst-off in society tearfully apologised for the actions of others, such as patrol officers and missionaries, whose reasons for acting were carefully written out of the story.

Unfortunately, the nuns have not written their story themselves. Memoirs by nuns in Australia in general are very rare,[81] and those few do not deal with the Magdalen asylums. The institutional histories of the orders, while informative, do not directly address the former inmates' allegations and say whether they believe them true or false. Requests to the Sisters of Charity and to the author of their institutional history for comment on that question for this chapter did not produce responses. The present-day Good Shepherd sisters have made an official statement (2013) that they are "deeply sorry for acts of verbal or physical cruelty that occurred,"[82] but do not expand on that. So it is necessary to make some tentative inferences from a small amount of evidence.

The brief recollections by nuns that are available paint a very different picture from that of the inmates. Old Good Shepherd nuns commenting much later say: "I worked in the packing room … For me, working alongside the women and the fun we could have as we worked was a favourite memory." "It is strange to say that a favourite place was the laundry. I didn't like the work, especially the hotel guests' personal laundry – too much could go wrong … but the whole place was full of life and energy and, mostly, good will. The packing room section of the laundry where I worked was highly organised, but not stuffy. I enjoyed the sense of connection with other Sisters and with the girls and women." "At Abbotsford I worked in several sections of the laundry providing work place training for the girls and women which I enjoyed because the Sisters worked alongside them and it was a great time for building relationships and sharing their concerns and hopes for the future."[83]

Those comments are a reminder that the nuns shared, even if on a voluntary or semi-voluntary basis, some of the conditions of the inmates, such as the bad food, the hard work, the confinement and the long periods of silence. One nun recalled, "we were working at midnight and I really thought [Sr] Vincent would die. Then we would get up at five, trying to get through the mountains of work ... it was terrible." From another, "we just slaved then, and it was very, very hard work ... We would start at 7am and work after tea as well, because we had taken on these big hotels."[84] In one respect, the nuns enforced on themselves a discipline beyond that imposed on their charges – the grotesque, uncomfortable and constricting clothes.

The sisters had in general volunteered for an extremely rigid and controlled form of life – they were thus the opposite in personality to the 'uncontrollable' girls under their charge. A nun installed as Sister Assistant at Mount Saint Canice in 1962 was given a card saying, "You no longer have a will of your own because from now on the Superior's will is your will as her Assistant."[85] The attitude to obedience required of the nuns is illustrated by the address at Abbotsford in 1901 by a nun from the head house in France:

> You know what our Holy Rule says on this subject. It tells us how to act when we are reproved. We are to kneel down at once, Kiss the ground, and listen to what is said without reply or excuse. Mind, without reply or excuse, whether we are guilty or not.[86]

The women who volunteered for that kind of regime naturally regarded extreme discipline as in the best interests of their charges as well as themselves. The "uncontrollable" women from the streets were the least likely kind of people to agree.

Nor were such women likely to agree with the nun's model of success, especially in earlier years, which was that the inmates should be vividly penitent of their former sins and expire in the odour of sanctity.[87]

Mutual incomprehension and hostility was increased by the rule of the Good Shepherd order that prevented inmates from discussing their past. So the nuns had no idea of what their inmates had been through. A nun explained decades later:

We didn't know one thing about them, which didn't make us as understanding as we could have been. I remember one day, a young girl was brought in – she would have been about fourteen or fifteen – and she was put on the mangle ... Well, after a while she got tired or something, I suppose, and she went away and sat somewhere else ... She was told to go straight back to the mangle. Now that child had been brought straight from having a miscarriage, and we didn't know. I had a little girl, she was a half-American negress, and I had to teach her. I didn't know that that little soul about twelve came to us from a maternity home. Well, you know, had you known, it would have altered my approach to them altogether. You'd have been more patient and more understanding ... See, we were taught ... that we were the nuns and we weren't allowed to even touch them. That made you sort of distant.[88]

The nuns' model of what was right for both their clients and themselves was thus inherently a rigid and disciplined one that was unlikely to appeal to women brought under duress. There was no physical contact, and no emotional contact in the sense of listening to the girls' own concerns. The rules of the order enforced not only chastity but the lack of true or "particular" friendship between nuns; nuns had a communal life but nuns did not go two by two. The vow of obedience, internally and externally imposed, could warp both those who took it on and those on whom obedience was imposed by force.

It would not be surprising if some nuns' personalities became twisted, especially when added to chronic tiredness, lack of hormone replacement therapy and the like, and reacted with cruelty.

The accounts by both inmates and nuns of the unremitting hard work in the laundries are also a reminder that, like other institutions for the poor, they operated under the pressures of extreme lack of money. Like orphanages, they received almost no government funds, and the Protestant Federation applied pressure for further reductions to all such "sectarian" charities[89] – it was regarded as the thin end of the wedge for state aid to denominational schools.[90]

Although there were complaints from commercial launderers that the convents were using cheap labour to compete with union labour paid award wages, the industrial courts recognised that the convents took anyone as labour and barely paid their way.[91] (It is true though that money could be found for some elaborate chapels and, at Abbotsford, a luxurious Bishop's Parlour.[92])

Conclusions

Three points need to be made.

First, the sisters faced an immensely difficult task, and one that only they were prepared to take on. It was a task they performed without material benefit to themselves. They took in girls whom no-one else wanted and who were forcibly confined, contrary to the wishes of both the girls and the nuns. The girls came from a variety of very disturbed and deprived backgrounds and were individually hard to deal with in many cases. Dealing with them in the mass in large numbers was doubly difficult, since any significant proportion of uncontrollables in a group makes management and discipline extremely hard, as anyone who has lived in a boarding school knows. The budgets of the convents were minimal.

Second, there is an issue about the perceptions of people from backgrounds as disturbed and deprived as many of the girls in the laundries. Put simply, those who do not receive love early have difficulty perceiving positive human interactions. They understand human interactions differently – more negatively – from others. Those helping them are well aware that gratitude is not to be expected. For similar reasons, it has to be considered whether some former inmates might be blaming the convents for effects whose causes lie elsewhere and earlier. When ex-inmates found it difficult to fit into normal society and had trouble with relationships, it may be that the reasons for that lay as much in lack of parents and previous abuse as in what happened in the convents. As with the inmates of institutions generally such as orphanages, Aboriginal missions, prisons and mental asylums, it could be asked whether those arriving from disturbed backgrounds involving a gross lack of love might see things more bleakly than those more fortunate.

Third, even when all that is fully taken into account, the consistent story of former inmates includes a high level of gratuitous positive cruelty and emotional deprivation. If we just keep to the factual matters reported and leave aside matters of perception and later effects, there is both convergence of evidence from different sources and a clear picture of emotional abuse. As the Forgotten Australians Report rightly says, "The response that times were different and that standards and people's thinking and understanding of children's needs have changed, fails to explain or recognise the severity of the documented behaviours."[93] It remains unexplained why so many individual nuns should have done that and why their culture supported it.

Afterword

A number of additional summaries and analyses of oral histories of former Good Shepherd inmates, some in Magdalen laundries, are found in Suellen Murray's 2020 report, "Remembering, honouring and acknowledging former residents of Good Shepherd Homes".[94] They largely confirm the picture of the present chapter, with memories of harsh conditions and complaints about poor education mixed with some positive views and an appreciation that the earlier circumstances of the girls were often extremely deprived.

---

[1] 'Attack on convents', *Argus* 21/1/1907, http://trove.nla.gov.au/ndp/del/article/10610696; 'Abbotsford convent again: another girl abducted', *The Watchman* 22/7/1915:, http://trove.nla.gov.au/ndp/del/article/111806210; 'Protestant Federation: Why it is needed: Charge of slavery in convents', *Maitland Daily Mercury* 23/4/1921:, http://trove.nla.gov.au/ndp/del/article/123726627; 'Founder of "The Rock" at U.P.A. rally', *Northern Star* 2/4/1947: http://trove.nla.gov.au/ndp/del/article/99154812

[2] Commission to Inquire into Child Abuse (Ireland, 2009), ch. 18:, http://www.childabusecommission.ie/rpt/pdfs/CICA-VOL3-18.pdf; Report of the Inter-Departmental Committee to establish the facts of State involvement with the Magdalen Laundries (McAleese Report, 2013), http://www.justice.ie/en/JELR/Pages/MagdalenRpt2013; summary at http://www.theguardian.com/world/2013/feb/05/magdalene-laundries-ireland-state-guilt

[3] J. M. Smith, Ireland's Magdalen Laundries and the Nation's Architecture of Containment (University of Notre Dame Press, Notre Dame Ind, 2007); older history in R. L. McCarthy, *Origins of the Magdalene Laundries: An analytical history* (McFarland, Jefferson NC, 2010). (Although the best-selling memoir of alleged abuse is apparently false: H. Kelly, *Kathy's Real Story: A culture of false allegations exposed* (Prefect Press, Dunleer, 2007)).

4 Enda Kennedy's State apology to the Magdalene women, 19/2/13, transcript at: http://www.thejournal.ie/full-text-enda-kenny-magdalene-apology-801132-Feb2013/

5 The Magdalene Sisters (2002), http://en.wikipedia.org/wiki/The_Magdalene_Sisters

6 R. Kollar, Magdalenes and nuns: convent laundries in late Victorian England, *Anglican & Episcopal History* 73 (2004), 309–334.

7 A. Gill, 'Bad girls do the best sheets', *Sydney Morning Herald* 24/4/2003:, http://www.smh.com.au/articles/2003/04/23/1050777303111.html; also ABC Radio National documentary, 'Bad girls do the best sheets', 9/4/2001, http://www.abc.net.au/radionational/programs/encounter/bad-girls-do-the-best-sheets/3479892

8 C. Kovesi, *Pitch Your Tents on Distant Shores: A History of the Sisters of the Good Shepherd in Australia, Aotearoa/New Zealand and Tahiti* (Playwright Publishing, Caringbah, 2006, 2nd ed, 2010); E. Kay, 'Containment of "wayward" females: The buildings of Abbotsford Convent, Victoria', *Archaeology in Oceania* 50 (2015), 153-61; Anon, Abbotsford Centenary 1863-1963 (Collingwood, 1963), 'The Abbotsford convent and the Magdalen asylum', *Kilmore Free Press* 13/10/1881: http://trove.nla.gov.au/ndp/del/article/57701643. Photos of the present state of the building at: http://www.abbotsfordconvent.com.au/history-heritage/buildings; a 2008 video tour at: http://www.youtube.com/watch?v=jIfJI-XGISo

9 L. Schwartz, 'A local spin on the laundries of shame', *Age*, 27/4/2003: http://www.theage.com.au/articles/2003/04/26/1051316051211.html

10 Gill, 'Bad girls'; photos at http://nma.gov.au/blogs/inside/collecting/photos/good-sheperd-dormitory-bed-making/; http://nla.gov.au/nla.pic-an24493557; brief positive recollections of former workers in 'Home from home for five faithful ladies of Glenworth', *Sydney Morning Herald* 1/7/1981.

11 http://mitchymemories.blogspot.com.au/2013/03/site-78-good-shepherd-convent-home-and.html

12 http://en.wikipedia.org/wiki/Mount_Saint_Canice

13 http://www.findandconnect.gov.au/guide/wa/WE00100; http://annfreespirit.50megs.com/custom4.html

14 A recollection at: http://nma.gov.au/blogs/inside/2011/08/19/the-nuns-thought-we-were-criminals/

15 M. Walsh, *The Good Sams: Sisters of the Good Samaritan 1857-1969* (John Garratt Publishing, Mulgrave, 2001), 162-192; H. Taylor, 'The Magdalen refuge at Tempe', *Sydney Morning Herald* 20/1/1890: http://trove.nla.gov.au/ndp/del/article/28276773; 'Death of Rev. Mother Gertrude', *Freeman's Journal* 17/9/1898, http://trove.nla.gov.au/ndp/del/article/115385376; 'St Magdalene's Retreat, Tempe', *Australian Town and Country Journal* 10/6/1899: http://trove.nla.gov.au/ndp/del/article/71329414 with photos at http://trove.nla.gov.au/ndp/del/page/5321101; records available in Records of Sisters of the Good Samaritan Convent, Arncliffe, 1877-1948 [microform] (W. & F. Pascoe Pty. Ltd., Balgowlah, for the Society of Australian Genealogists, 1982).

16 'St Joseph's Refuge', *The Register* 28/5/1903, http://trove.nla.gov.au/ndp/del/article/55429124

17 *Australian Town and Country Journal*, 10/6/1899: http://trove.nla.gov.au/ndp/del/page/5321101.

18 Kovesi, *Pitch Your Tents*, 206; also 'The Abbotsford convent', *Argus* 1/2/1907, http://trove.nla.gov.au/ndp/del/article/10612917.

[19] http://www.theage.com.au/news/in-depth/on-a-mission/2006/12/17/1166 290410670.html

[20] Report of the Royal Commission on Charitable Institutions 1890–91, 1272, quoted in J. Monk, Cleansing their souls: laundries in institutions for fallen women, *Lilith* 9 (1996), 21–32

[21] http://abbotsfordblog.com/memories-on-abbotsford-convent-on-an-ebay-discussion-forum/ A book of poems based on interviews of former Abbotsford residents (in various parts of the establishment): P. Sykes, *The Abbotsford Mysteries* (Spinifex Press, North Melbourne, 2011); a fictional version based on research in K. Greenwood, *Unnatural Habits: A Phryne Fisher Mystery* (Allen & Unwin, Sydney, 2012).

[22] J. Konstantinidis, Life in "The Mag", *Journal of the Australian Catholic Historical Society* 34 (2013), 93-104. Another hostile account of Mount Saint Canice at https://www.smashwords.com/books/view/288361

[23] http://magdalenelaundrytestimony.org/#/australian-magdalene-laundries/4576 129509; further in Rachael Romero's film In the Shadow of Eden (http://www.nma.gov.au/audio/detail/rachael-romero-on-in-the-shadow-of-eden); "The Pines" compared to a prisoner of war camp in Andrew Murray's Senate speech in 2008 (http://www.forgottenaustralians.com/pdf/AUSTRALIANDEMOCRATSPEECHES.pdf).

[24] http://nma.gov.au/blogs/inside/2011/04/19/in-the-beginning/

[25] http://annfreespirit.50megs.com/custom4.html

[26] Victoria Stuart interviewed by Rob Willis in the Forgotten Australians and Former Child Migrants oral history project , 2011, http://nla.gov.au/nla.oh-vn5751943

[27] Kovesi, *Pitch Your Tents*, 297.

[28] http://nla.gov.au/nla.oh-vn5717375; http://nla.gov.au/nla.oh-vn5017833

[29] But one allegation of sexual abuse by other girls at Abbotsford at http://www.theage.com.au/victoria/former-residents-to-boycott-nuns-reunion-20130620-2olqm.html; some memories of corporal punishment at Leederville: http://annfreespirit.50megs.com/custom4.html

[30] Schwartz, 'A local spin on the laundries of shame'.

[31] McAleese report, ch. 19.

[32] http://abbotsfordblog.com/memories-on-abbotsford-convent-on-an-ebay-discussion-forum/

[33] Konstantinidis, Life in "The Mag"; http://annfreespirit.50megs.com/custom4.html

[34] Taylor, 'The Magdalen Refuge at Tempe'.

[35] Forgotten Australians, submission 182 (Report section 4.71); also in http://magdalenelaundrytestimony.org/#/australian-magdalene-laundries/4576129509

[36] http://annfreespirit.50megs.com/custom4.html

[37] Kovesi, *Pitch Your Tents*, 157.

[38] 'Former residents to boycott nuns' reunion', *Age* 21/6/2013, http://www.theage.com.au/victoria/former-residents-to-boycott-nuns-reunion-20130620-2olqm.html

[39] http://nla.gov.au/nla.oh-vn5751943

[40] http://annfreespirit.50megs.com/custom4.html

[41] B. Djuric, *Abandon All Hope: A History of Parramatta Girls Industrial School* (Chargan My Book Publisher, Perth, 2011); earlier, N. Williamson, Laundry maids or la-

dies? Life in the Industrial and Reformatory School for Girls in NSW, Part II, 1887 to 1910, *Journal of the Royal Australian Historical Society* 68 (1983), 312–24.

42   *Sydney Morning Herald*, 20/1/1890, http://trove.nla.gov.au/ndp/del/article/28276773

43   Kovesi, *Pitch Your Tents,* 71.

44   Walsh, *The Good Sams,* 169.

45   Ibid., 172–4, 182.

46   http://abbotsfordblog.com/catherine-kovesis-book-pitch-your-tents-on-distant-shores/

47   A. Chynoweth, 'Let our histories be visible', *ReCollections* 7 (1) (2012), http://recollections.nma.gov.au/issues/volume_7_number_1/commentary/let_our_histories_be_visible

48   'The Abbotsford Convent: Story of an escaped girl', *The Watchman* 24/6/1905, http://trove.nla.gov.au/ndp/del/article/111962032; A Protestant story from Sydney of 1904 in 'Escape from a Sydney convent', *The Watchman* 15/10/1904, http://trove.nla.gov.au/ndp/del/article/111922093

49   'Escaped from convent', *Sydney Morning Herald* 17/8/1920, http://trove.nla.gov.au/ndp/del/article/15902574; 'Girl escapes from convent: climbs 18ft. wall', *Riverine Herald* 7/4/1923, http://trove.nla.gov.au/ndp/del/article/115175910; 'Escaped from convent', *Argus* 13/4/1923, http://trove.nla.gov.au/ndp/del/article/1889875.

50   'Escaped from convent to get outside job', *Mail* (Adelaide) 28/8/1954, http://trove.nla.gov.au/ndp/del/article/58101331

51   http://www.adoptionoriginstas.com/stcanice.html

52   *Argus* 16/4/1927, http://trove.nla.gov.au/ndp/del/article/3849362, combined with 'Escaped from Convent', Mirror (Perth) 23/4/1927, http://trove.nla.gov.au/ndp/del/article/76401079

53   J. Konstaninidis, 'Life in "The Mag"'.

54   http://adb.anu.edu.au/biography/campbell-john-william-wallace-wal-12837

55   Plunged from Third Storey to Freedom: the stark truth of the "inside' of a Roman Catholic slave laundry as told by girls who escaped (Protestant Publications, Glebe, 1982, reprinted from *The Rock* of 1948).

56   Kovesi, *Pitch Your Tents,* 268; 'Archdeacon defends Magdalen Home', *Mercury* 1/9/1948, http://trove.nla.gov.au/ndp/del/article/27755270; 'Laundry conditions at Girls' Home', Launceston *Examiner* 4/9/1948, http://trove.nla.gov.au/ndp/del/article/52647605

57   'Suicide in a convent', *Albany Advertiser* 16/11/1899, http://trove.nla.gov.au/ndp/del/article/69895580

58   'Protestantism', *Grenville Standard* 20/7/1918, http://trove.nla.gov.au/ndp/del/article/119673099

59   Catholic story of a return from Protestant exhibiting in 'Back to the convent,' *Freeman's Journal* 26/11/1908, http://trove.nla.gov.au/ndp/del/article/111281150.

60   Australian Senate, Forgotten Australians: A report on Australians who experienced institutional or out-of-home care as children (2004), http://www.aph.gov.au/Parliamentary_Business/Committees/Senate/Community_Affairs/Completed_inquiries/2004-07/inst_care/report/index, submission 93 (Report section 4.101).

61 'They get no pay but are mostly contented', *Sun-Herald* 12/9/1954.
62 Taylor, 'The Magdalen refuge at Tempe'.
63 J. Monk, Cleansing their souls: laundries in institutions for fallen women, *Lilith* 9 (1996), 21-32.
64 R. Howe and S. Swain, *The Challenge of the City: The Centenary History of Wesley Central Mission 1883-1993* (Hyland House, South Melbourne, 1993), 47, quoted in Monk, Cleansing their souls.
65 http://mitchymemories.blogspot.com.au/2013/03/site-78-good-shepherd-convent-home-and.html
66 http://en.wikipedia.org/wiki/Flynn_effect
67 Kovesi, 179–80.
68 Konstantinidis, Life in "The Mag".
69 http://nma.gov.au/blogs/inside/2011/02/10/in-the-shadow-of-eden/
70 http://nma.gov.au/blogs/inside/2011/04/19/in-the-beginning/
71 'Dun-Street tragedy revived,' *Bendigo Advertiser* 13/6/1911, http://trove.nla.gov.au/ndp/del/article/89848791
72 'Assault in lock-up: Woman's nose broken', *Argus* 9/8/1927, http://trove.nla.gov.au/ndp/del/article/3871747
73 Sr Paula Cadusch, 1947, quoted in Walsh, *The Good Sams,* 190.
74 Taylor, 'The Magdalen Refuge at Tempe'.
75 Department for Neglected Children and Reformatory Schools, Report of the Secretary and Inspector for the year 1902. (Good Shepherd Archives, Abbotsford; thanks to Fraser Faithfull for supplying).
76 Charities Board of Victoria, file on 'Abbotsford Female Refuge', Public Record Office file UPRS 4523/P1 Unit no. 149 file no. 1446, notes by Fraser Faithfull, Good Shepherd Archives, Abbotsford.
77 JRH, Children's Welfare Department, to Mother Prioress, Oakleigh, 22/11/1934, in Good Shepherd Archives, Abbotsford (thanks to Fraser Faithfull for supplying).
78 Schwartz, 'A local spin on the laundries of shame'.
79 'Says incident at convent "a thoughtless escapade"', *Courier-Mail* 28/8/1954, http://trove.nla.gov.au/ndp/del/article/50587538'
80 'They get no pay but are mostly contented', *Sun-Herald* 12/9/1954; also Kovesi, 271.
81 J. Franklin, Memoirs by Australian priests, religious and ex-religious, *Journal of the Australian Catholic Historical Society* 33 (2012), 142-162.
82 https://www.goodshepherd.com.au/blog/good-shepherds-150-years (2013); the nuns' process to deal with the abuse claims described in Kovesi 367-72.
83 Sr Noeline White, Sr Pamela Molony and Sr Geraldine Mitchell, in Good Shepherd Action, pamphlet for Good Shepherd Festival Day, 2013 (supplied by Good Shepherd Archives).
84 Kovesi, *Pitch Your Tents,* 280.
85 Ibid., 289.
86 Ibid., 287.
87 Ibid., 162-5.

88 Sr Felicitas Hanrahan SGS, 1995 interview, in Kovesi, 281.

89 'St Augustine's Orphanage: Dr Mannix attacks the Treasurer for reducing the grant', *Geelong Advertiser* 24/9/1921, http://trove.nla.gov.au/ndp/del/article/119754241; http://trove.nla.gov.au/ndp/del/article/3744869; http://trove.nla.gov.au/ndp/del/article/3744869; 'Another glimpse of the cloven hoof', *Freeman's Journal* 1/7/1926, http://trove.nla.gov.au/ndp/del/article/116776078; 'Convents and orphanages: Protestant Federation's objections', *Chronicle* (Adelaide) 13/5/1922, http://trove.nla.gov.au/ndp/del/article/87430005.

90 'State aid barred', *The Watchman* 15/3/1923, http://trove.nla.gov.au/ndp/del/article/112235848; 'The war on the orphans', *Freeman's Journal* 15/3/1923, http://trove.nla.gov.au/ndp/del/article/116731771

91 http://trove.nla.gov.au/ndp/del/article/1442230; 'The Victorian Protestant Federation: An Attack on Convent Laundries', *Freeman's Journal* 12/9/1918, http://trove.nla.gov.au/ndp/del/article/116785928; http://trove.nla.gov.au/ndp/del/article/15852379; http://trove.nla.gov.au/ndp/del/article/116769770; http://trove.nla.gov.au/ndp/del/article/115098015; Walsh, *The Good Sams*, ch. 5.

92 http://www.abbotsfordconvent.com.au/venues-hire/venues/bishop%E2%80%99s-parlour

93 Forgotten Australians, section 5.53.

94 Suellen Murray, 'Remembering, honouring and acknowledging former residents of Good Shepherd Homes: An oral history research study', Good Shepherd Australia New Zealand, 2020, https://goodshep.org.au/wp-content/uploads/2020/12/remembering-honouring-and-acknowledging-former-residents-of-good-shepherd-homes_pdf-1-mb-2.pdf

9

Catholics versus Masons*

Abstract: The conflict between Catholics and Freemasons in Australia in the first half of the twentieth century was legendary. Catholics believed that Masons dominated many workplaces and whole white-collar professions and that they denied Catholics jobs. The European sources of the conflict between the Catholic Church and Freemasonry are described, and the results in Australia at the time of the education controversy in the 1870s. The truth of Catholic suspicions of a vast Masonic conspiracy is examined.

As is well known, one of the most significant events in Australian Catholic history was the withdrawal of state aid to Church schools in the late nineteenth century. In 1880 in New South Wales, and at similar times in other parts of Australia, the State Governments set up systems of "free, secular and compulsory" schools, and at the same time withdrew aid they had given to the Schools of the various churches. The Catholic Church maintained its system at great expense, at the same time as Catholics paid taxes for state schools. That situation lasted for ninety years, and defined the shape of Australian education thereafter. It divided Australian youth into three categories: those in private schools, usually run by a Protestant Church, those in Catholic schools, and the majority in the secular State school system. It was one of the main reasons for the distinctiveness of Australian Catholic culture.

The high point of the Catholics' struggle against the withdrawal of State aid came with Archbishop Vaughan's First Pastoral on education, attacking Henry Parkes' plan for a free and secular school system. Education without religion, Vaughan maintained, was impossible in principle. It was, he said, "a system of practical paganism, which leads to corruption of morals and loss of faith, to national effeminacy and to national dishonou'" and – in a phrase that caused

---

* *Journal of the Australian Catholic Historical Society* 20 (1999), 1–15.

particular offence – the existing state schools were "seedplots of future immorality, infidelity and lawlessness, being calculated to debase the standard of human excellence, and to corrupt the political, social and individual life of future citizens."[1] His extreme remarks caused a great deal of indignation in Protestant circles.

So much is well-known. What is not so familiar is what Vaughan thought about the enemy he was facing.

Vaughan and the Masonic Conspiracy Theory

On 9 October 1876, he gave a speech on what he believed was really behind the campaign for secular education, later printed as a pamphlet called 'Hidden Springs'. It is one of the great conspiracy theories, combined with a vision of grand conflict of philosophical systems. The three main currents of thought, he says, are Paganism, Supernaturalism and Materialism. Paganism, whose "hidden spring" is man's animal passion, as shown by the gross immoralities of the gods of Olympus, belongs to the past. The future, unfortunately, may belong to Materialism; the threat is so great that the Catholic and Protestant churches need to co-operate against it. But Vaughan does not see Materialism as just a way of thinking into which it is natural to fall when religion begins to seem less plausible. It would soon disappear, he says, if it were not being ceaselessly revivified by its own hidden spring. "The Hidden Spring of Materialism is centred in, and derives its main energy from the Sect, the Church of the Revolution, the International Secret Society, which is weaving its network around the world," that is, Freemasonry. Promoting a Voltairean gospel of "absolute toleration", its real program is deicide, and the deification of humanity. "The Sect fixes savagely on one dogma of its own, whilst gnashing its teeth at all dogmas, it is this, viz., that absolute liberty and unlimited freedom to do, say, or think anything he likes, is the natural and inalienable right of every man." It is true that ordinary Masons do not know of the plots of the inner circle, and are often men of character, even dukes, but such men are "paraded before the world, that the world may be reassured, that, a blind oath of secrecy notwithstanding, little harm could attach to a Craft, however secret, so long as Dukes and Lords, and men of large estate, and of high character were members of it. How could that Society be subversive of the throne, which is patronised by Royalty itself?" But the truth is otherwise. "The Altar, the Throne, Civil Society as at present constituted, are, under the action of its breath, to melt down into an International Communism, when the impossible equality of all men shall be achieved, when the Almighty God, and, consequently, dogma and Christian morality shall be expunged." Earlier, the Masons sneaked out of their lodges to foment the Revolutions of 1789, 1830 and 1848. But now they have a new plan. Spreading from Belgium is an "Education League", and Masons around the world are now to rally behind their campaign. "Its watchword or war-cry is 'Universal Secular, Free and Compulsory Education.'"[2]

This outburst raises a number of questions. The first one is, is it true? *Was* Freemasonry an international communist conspiracy, plotting revolutions and the downfall of the Church, and secular education in New South Wales? If not, who were the Masons, why did the Catholic Church find itself in conflict with them, and what is the relation of that conflict to job discrimination against Catholics in the 1930s?

No, it is not true. Not of Australia, at least. Freemasonry was not an atheist communist plot. An answer on behalf of the Masons was written by Wazir Beg, earlier a Muslim of Poona but at this period a Presbyterian minister in Redfern and editor of both the *Freemason* and the *Orangeman*.[3] His reply to Vaughan denies the charges of atheism, immorality and disloyalty. Masonry inculcates a "rigorous morality" – without dispensations or indulgences – and it is hardly likely that Masonry intends to subvert the State when the last King and the present heir to the throne are not merely members, but Grand Masters.[4] Beg is right: the idea of an international communist conspiracy led by royalty is ridiculous.

All the same, Vaughan was not exactly making his theory up out of thin air. Nor was he alone. To understand what was happening we need to look at the situation in Europe on a long time scale.

The Masonic conspiracy theory is part of a plot theory that had wide appeal for the European political right from the time of the French Revolution to the Second World War. The principals in the supposed world conspiracy varied: Masons, Jews, Liberals, Socialists,[5] but the linking idea was that a world conspiracy of some or all these was behind all revolutions real and potential, and all anticlericalism. The Masonic plot theory came first. It appeared in the Abbé Barruel's *Memoirs Illustrating the History of Jacobinism* of 1797, which claimed to expose the French Revolution as a Masonic conspiracy. After a long run in the nineteenth century, where it was promoted by Pius IX as an explanation for his troubles[6] (and of course that was where Vaughan got it from), it acquired an antisemitic tinge in the last two decades of the century.[7] The most famous expression of it, the *Protocols of the Elders of Zion*, written in France probably in the 1890s, was Barruel's theory over again, with the addition that the Masonic plot was actually controlled from the inside by Jews.[8] Descendants of the Protocols theory include the Nazis' Jewish conspiracy theory, the Jewish-Bolshevik plot theory that was an issue in Helen Demidenko's *The Hand That Signed the Paper*, and the Jewish-Masonic-Communist plot believed in by such people as Franco.[9]

Those full-blown conspiracy theories are all false. The *Protocols* were a forgery, there was no world Jewish plot, and there was no secret international organisation behind all revolutions.

It might seem, then, that although Vaughan was not alone, his plot theory was a pure fantasy. That is not quite true. It does not follow that there was no basis at all for the fears of the right. To understand what was really happening, it is necessary to look at what Freemasonry was, and why the Catholic Church was in conflict with it. If it was not a communist plot, what was it?

Freemasonry in Europe

It was an institutional embodiment of the Enlightenment, or at least of one version of it. The difficulty with the common view of the Enlightenment is that it portrays it as existing purely in the realm of ideas. The *philosophes* are supposed to have written learned books full of dangerous theories and radical ideas, which somehow filtered down to the bloodthirsty souls who cut off the aristocrats' heads. Apart from making the mistake of conceiving the Enlightenment as primarily atheist and an enemy of the state, when in general it was neither, this is to take far too intellectual a view of it. A church is not simply a creed and catechism, but also an institution that supplies tradition, ritual, mutual comfort and community support for right conduct and sanction for wrong, and, at least in earlier times, a social security agency. The organ through which the Enlightenment competed in these respects was Freemasonry. After developing in a still obscure fashion out of Scottish and English guilds of stonemasons around 1700, it spread quickly to the Continent and the American colonies during the eighteenth century, and included among its members such notables as Walpole, Pope, Hogarth, Franklin, Washington, Voltaire, Haydn, Mozart and Goethe.[10] It was not the intention of Freemasons to undermine the existing political or religious order. There was nevertheless an inevitable tension between Freemasonry's ideals of internal constitutional self-government and the absolutist regimes on the Continent. There was also a philosophical conflict between Freemasonry's ideals of religious toleration and the Catholic view of dogma. As a result, there was a certain amount of police action against the lodges in countries like France, and the Catholic Church condemned Freemasonry.[11] Up to the time of the French Revolution, however, the conflict was not a matter of great importance to either side. Indeed, the Church's condemnations of Freemasonry were not promulgated beyond the English Channel, and around 1800 Irish Freemasonry was full of Catholics.

The French Revolution was not a Masonic plot in any simple sense, but it is true that Masonic ideals, symbols and organisation had something to do with the origins of the Revolution.[12] Liberty, equality and fraternity were originally Masonic ideals, which one needs to read free of associations with the Terror – in the spirit of the American Revolution, not the French.[13] In the years of the Napoleonic Wars and the Restoration, the lodges did act as covers for the spread of revolutionary brotherhoods, even if Freemasonry as a whole was not revolutionary.[14] It must be emphasised that Freemasonry does not have any international central controlling body – something which the Catholic Church found hard to understand. That means, on the one hand, that an actual international Masonic plot is unlikely; on the other hand, it means that individual lodges or groups of lodges and shadowy quasi-Masonic organisations can be captured by strange ideas, and develop in their own, sometimes revolutionary, directions. For example, around 1820, there were genuine Masonic connections to the Decembrist revolutionaries in Russia, the Carbonari in Italy, and Spanish liberals resisting the Restoration.[15] Even in early New South Wales, there were fears of Masonic revolutionary activity. Governor King feared the French might sail up the Hawkesbury, unite with the Irish at Castle Hill, and leave him defended only by the mutinous rabble of the New South Wales corps. Since all three of these threats were riddled with Masons, he took seriously the possibility of their cooperation on the basis of brotherhood, and suppressed attempts to form a lodge.[16]

For the rest of the nineteenth century, Freemasonry was associated with the anticlerical "liberal" political faction in Catholic countries. Latin America was a scene of perennial conflict.[17] An article in the *Australasian Catholic Record* of 1899 on 'The just man of the nineteenth century' tells the story of the Catholic President of Ecuador, Gabriel Garcia Moreno, who dedicated Ecuador to the Sacred Heart, gave the state education system to the Catholic Church, and then was assassinated by, it was thought, Masons.[18] It was the same in Spain.[19] The unification of Italy, with the confiscation of the Papal States, was a success for Freemasonry, among other forces.[20] By and large, the Catholic right fought a losing battle. As we saw, they did not attribute that to their being out of touch with the spirit of the age, or to a lack of concern for social problems, but to a literal plot.

The control of primary education was one of the main issues in the conflict. Vaughan's story that the Education League in Belgium was a Masonic front promoting free, compulsory and secular education is entirely true.[21] In France, laws instituted by a heavily Masonic government in 1879–82 took public money from Church schools, and instituted general moral education in public schools.[22] When the Catholics added a Jewish conspiracy theory to the Masonic one, they were discredited over the Dreyfus affair, and in the early years of the twentieth century, a vigorously anticlerical and largely Masonic government took advantage of having the upper hand to expel the religious teaching orders from France and seize their property without compensation.[23] There was much interest in these events among Australian Catholics,[24] and Australia benefited by the immigration of the De La Salle Brothers, whose first Australian school, in Armidale in 1906, included brothers just expelled from France.[25] At the same time, it came to light in the "Affaire des fiches" that there really was a Masonic conspiracy: the French Masons were keeping a huge card index on public officials who went to Mass, with a view to preventing their promotions.[26] The animosity between French Freemasonry and the Catholic Church waned somewhat in the next decades, but revived when the Vichy regime published long lists of Masons and sacked them from state schools and other employment.[27] Naturally, not much has been heard of these things since 1945.

There was, however, a problem with Vaughan's theory that what was happening in Australia was the same as what was happening in France and Belgium. It is significant that all the Masonic documents Vaughan quotes as evidence are Continental, and all Beg's British. British (and hence Australian) Freemasonry was not the same as the Continental variety. It was not in conflict with the Established Church or the state – on the contrary, kings, prime ministers and Archbishops of Canterbury have been Freemasons. There is no need to plot revolution against a state one controls already or if not "controls", at least has an easy relationship with. Catholic propagandists knew their theory had a problem here, and made the most of the occasional meeting between the Prince of Wales and an Italian Mason.[28]

Freemasonry in Australia

The story of the influence of the Masons is one of the great untold narratives of Australian history. Manning Clark, for example, though seeing Australian history as an epic struggle between Christian and Enlightenment principles, hardly mentions the main Enlightenment institution, and even full-length biographies of famous Australians often fail to mention they were Masons. Freemasons were involved in most of the significant developments in Australia. Joseph Banks was a Mason, and in the early colony, so were Governor Macquarie,

Francis Greenway, and the explorers Oxley, Hume and Leichhardt.[29] (Indeed, Macquarie laid the foundation stone of the first St Mary's Church in 1821 using a ceremonial trowel decorated with Masonic symbols.[30]) More than thirty of the hundred and eleven members of the first Commonwealth Parliament were Masons, either at the time or later, "some indication", according to Masons, "that our Commonwealth was in its beginning also based on righteousness and virtuous character."[31] Almost all of the conservative Prime Ministers up to 1972 – Barton, Reid, Cook, Bruce, Page, Menzies, Fadden, McEwen, Gorton and McMahon – were Masons.[32] Many governors were Masons, often the Grand Masters of their states.[3] Masons prominent in other fields include Edward Hargraves, the discoverer of gold, Lawrence Hargrave, the pioneer of flight, and such quintessentially Australian heroes as Sir Charles Kingsford Smith, Sir Don Bradman and Sir Edward "Weary" Dunlop. The Masonic Historical Society's web site is informative.[34]

Although Governor King regarded the Freemasons as infected by republican ideas and a threat to the state, they soon became respectable. The first recognised Lodge, the Lodge of Social and Military Virtues, arrived with the regiment it was attached to in 1814,[35] and Freemasonry was associated with wealth and the party of political reform by the 1830s, in both Sydney and Hobart.[36] The lodges spread widely, especially in the 1890s and again between the Wars.[37] Specialised lodges included Lodge Cricket, of which Bradman was a member, Lodge Literature, for newspapermen,[38] and lodges for the old boys of particular schools, such as Sydney Grammar, Fort Street, Sydney High and Shore.[39] Melbourne University, Sydney University and later the University of New South Wales had lodges for academics and graduates.[40] Freemasonry was particularly strong in the Armed Forces, the police, banks, AMP, the state and commonwealth public services, and the councils of country towns.[41] Freemasonry in the army was an issue in the conscription campaigns of 1916 and 1917, since Catholics were not enthusiastic about being drafted as fodder for an officer corps dominated by Freemasonry, "the most insidious enemy of God and country … a huge tumour growing upon the life and blood of the whole of the country" (Mannix).[42] Membership increased again after the Second War, as returned servicemen used the lodges to continue the mateship of the armed forces. A high point of membership was reached in the mid-1950s, with some 330,000 members in about 2000 lodges, or one Australian man in sixteen.[43] Since there were no Catholic members and very few blue collar workers, that represents an extraordinary penetration of the target group, the "managerial classes".

This leaves the question, what did Masonic membership mean? It could, of course, mean nothing: like religious membership, it could simply be a way of getting out of the house, meeting people who might help one get a better job, or providing security for one's widow. Masonic membership seems to have meant nothing to Menzies, for example. He was a club man rather than a lodge man. But for those who took membership more seriously, as many did, more was on offer. Freemasonry is a philosophy. It is not easy to say precisely what that philosophy is, not only because part of it is kept secret, but also because putting 'doctrines' into propositional form is not the preferred method of exposition of the Masonic point of view, even to initiates. Freemasonry is officially "a system of morality veiled in allegory".[44] The allegory and symbolism, intended to assist the imagination and memory of the initiate,[45] is the main method of instruction, and the interpretation of the symbols is to some extent left to the individual. But the general outline of the system is not secret. The only Masonic "dogma", strictly speaking, is the existence of God, belief in which is a condition of entry. Belief in immortality is, however, strongly suggested.[46] Beyond that, religious matters are left to the individual's own sect; a Mason is expected to pursue his own faith, which may be of any Christian or other theistic persuasion.

The centre of Freemasonry is not doctrinal but moral. "The whole purpose of Freemasonry is to teach the Moral Law and show that man should live rightly with his fellow man under the all-seeing eye of God."[47] The normal meanings of the symbols mostly concern morality. The well-known symbols of square and compasses, for example, symbolise respectively rectitude in general and the circle separating right behaviour from wrong. Truth and honesty in dealings are crucial.[48]

Harmony has not characterised the relations of Freemasonry with the more dogmatic religions, and the reasons for conflict concern basic matters of the relation between philosophy and religion. Freemasonry insists that it is not a religion, but admits to being "religious", or having something to say in areas already occupied by religion.[49] Its tolerance of all religions can easily give rise to the impression that dogmatic differences do not matter, even though that is never asserted explicitly. Suspicion in this regard is encouraged by the phrase "the Religion in which all men agree", in the original 1723 Constitutions of Freemasonry.[50]

It is clear why Masons should have generally felt happy with a system of secular education. Vaughan's suspicion that a large-scale movement inimical to his position was under way, and that the Masons had something to do with it, was not altogether without foundation, even if there was no plot. W.C. Wentworth and John Woolley, the earlier leaders of the campaign for secular education, were Masons, while William Wilkins, the effective decision-maker on the syllabus, was a prominent Mason, who wrote in favour of the possibility of moral education free of dogma.[51] Parkes was not a Mason, but that was not much consolation for the Catholics, since his views were actually closer to those of the anticlerical European masons.[52]

The conflict between Catholics and Masons did not rest so clearly on any matters of principle. There is nothing explicitly anti-Catholic in Freemasonry (unlike the Orange lodges), and Catholic objections, other than on the secular education question, rested mostly on supposed Masonic plots in Europe and job discrimination in Australia. The main objection of principle was to Masonic oaths, committing Masons not to reveal secrets before they knew the nature of the secrets.[53] Since the 1960s, better relations have prevailed in some though not all Catholic circles,[54] mainly because Catholic theology has itself adopted a more tolerant view of other religions. The reasons for that are probably not, as some think, that the popes since then have been secret Masons.

Discrimination in Employment in Australia

This brings us to the vexed question of job discrimination. Catholics believed that up to about 1960, at least, most positions of power in organisations like the armed services, many public service departments, the private banks, and so on, were virtually barred to them by a conspiracy of Masons looking after one another.[55] It is very hard to discover any undeniable facts about it.

For one thing, it is difficult to prove that any given failure to get a job is due to underhand motives. And even if there were hard statistical evidence that there were almost no Catholics in, say, the management of the Bank of New South Wales – which there is not[56] – it is hard to demonstrate anything about the reasons for it. And even if there was discrimination against Catholics, it may have been due to Protestant sectarian feeling, or anti-Irish racism, rather than to the Masons. There seem to be no admissions by anyone of ever discriminating against a Catholic in favour of a less qualified applicant for a job, though the Masons have informally agreed that they did provide a certain amount of help to one another with jobs.[57] As one senior Mason explained it to me, Freemasonry is intended to make good men better – unlike religions that hope also to make bad men good. So being a Mason is, other things being equal, a sign of being a good man, and hence a recommendation for a job. Applicants for membership who appeared to be interested simply in improving their employment prospects were supposed to be denied membership.

There are hardly even any complaints by Catholics that they were passed over for any definite job. There is one case, though, described in some detail. It is in a life of Frank Letters, recently written by his widow. Letters was a classical scholar who applied for and failed to get university positions in the late 1930s.

> When Frank was a young graduate hoping for an academic post, there was not one practising Catholic senior staff member at Sydney University. In 1938, of the forty professors at Sydney University there was no Catholic. It was little different in the higher echelons of education departments, the police force, the

public service, banking, and in many businesses. Equally obvious, when you looked closely, was the absence of Catholics from the top legal appointments and among hospital specialists.

For a start, Catholics could not be Freemasons, and were therefore automatically excluded from the mutual help towards promotion that Freemasons gave one another. There were of course men with high ideals – and good friends of ours – who enjoyed the convivial nights out at the local masonic lodge with men friends, helping one another, perhaps even relishing a night out away from the wife. The rank-and-file Mason probably didn't realise that helping his buddy get ahead in business or career could and often did mean that a better-qualified applicant didn't stand a chance. That is not justice.[58]

It is not entirely obvious, nevertheless, that Masonic influence was responsible in this case. The Professor of Latin, Todd, was a peculiar person, who disliked Letters on personal as much as sectarian grounds. Letters eventually obtained one of the foundation lectureships at the New England University College. When the College became an autonomous University in 1954, all the pioneers were given chairs, except Letters.[59] He never did become a professor, despite his international reputation based on respectable books on Sophocles, Virgil, Thomas Mann and Huysmans, and successful essays and poetry. Academic excellence is more open for inspection than talent in, say, the public service, and it is fair to say that for Letters to fail to get a chair at a provincial university was an obvious scandal. The book presents some evidence about the role of masonic influence.

> All Armidale could see the university men's cars on Thursday nights near the Masonic Lodge on the corner of Faulkner and Barney Streets. Frank could not fail to deduce that he, a Catholic and the only one not a Lodge member, 'would never get anywhere'. The dice were loaded against his professional advancement ...
>
> Frank also recalled the invitation to a welcome for a Supreme Court judge and two barrister friends of Frank's at Tatt's Hotel. One had just won a spectacularly interesting case and offered to send some details to Frank, asking for his address. 'Send it to The Lodge'

was the answer. [The Letters family lived in a former gatekeeper's lodge at the University.] One of a nearby group, half-hearing the answer but not the question, complained, 'You university men have taken us over', assuming that Frank had meant the Masonic Lodge. This was news to Frank who had not up to that point seen the close link between Freemasonry and his colleagues.

Once, when delivering a packet of Leaving Certificate English papers to Sid Musgrove [the only other member of his department], Frank looked over the bookshelves where to his surprise he saw books to do with Freemasonry.

'Oh no! not you, Sid', he said, laughing heartily at the thought of Sid, the cynic, being caught up in a conservative secret society.

'I wouldn't get anywhere if I didn't belong', Musgrove said simply.[60]

Catholics did not take discrimination lying down. Their best chance for advancement came through the system of public service entry through competitive examination, and promotion by seniority. It is an expensive solution to job discrimination, but an effective one. The Knights of the Southern Cross, a kind of Catholic Masons, acted frequently as an employment agency as well as pressuring anti-Catholic employers.[61] In due course, there were networks of Catholics as well as networks of Masons in public service departments; if anyone had a just complaint, it was those in neither camp. The best opportunity for Catholics to use raw political power to recover territory from the Masons was in Queensland, where there were Catholic-dominated Labor governments for decades. Freemasons lost ground in the Queensland public service after 1915,[62] and in 1957 the Premier, Vince Gair, took on the University of Queensland for, among other things, an alleged bias in favour of Masons.[63] He failed.

Nationalising the banks might have helped, but Chifley and Calwell did not succeed with that particular plan. They did achieve a major change in the ethnic composition of Australia, away from the Anglo-Saxon Protestant mould that prevailed up to then, by importing 180,000 displaced Eastern Europeans, mostly Catholics.[64] It is the multiculturalism of Australia that has done as much as anything to make the old conflicts irrelevant.

Finally, a moment of speculation. Possibly the most significant effect for the Church of its long conflict with Freemasonry has been that many of the men in the highest positions in the Church have not understood the English-speaking countries. With the English kings being Grand Masters, and many American presidents being Masons and operating under a Constitution embodying Masonic ideals, how could the mind of the Roman Curia be anything but gravely suspicious of anything coming out of England or America? In particular, ideals of "freedom", conscience, toleration and constitutional government have not been well understood by the Roman mind. There has been a grave misunderstanding between the international Church and the international language, which has been a great misfortune for both.

---

[1] 'Archbishop and Bishops of N.S.W. Pastoral', *Catholic Education* Sydney, 1879, repr. in P. O'Farrell (ed.), *Documents in Australian Catholic History*, vol. 1, London, 1969, 386–99.

[2] R. B. Vaughan, *Hidden Springs, or the Perils of the Future and How to Meet Them*, Sydney, 1876; brief summary in J.N. Molony, *The Roman Mould of the Australian Catholic Church*, Melbourne, 1969, p. 150; similar later in Anon, 'Freemasonry versus Church and State', *Australasian Catholic Record* 10, 1904, 23-41; by Archbishop Kelly, in M. Clark, *Sources of Australian History*, London, 1957, 577, *Sydney Morning Herald* 15/7/1913, 8.

[3] E. C. B. MacLaurin, 'Beg, Wazir (1827–1885)', *Australian Dictionary of Biography*, vol. 3, 1969, https://adb.anu.edu.au/biography/beg-wazir-2964 .

[4] W. Beg, *Dr. Vaughan's Ignorance of Freemasonry Exposed*, Sydney, 1876, 10, 19–21, 34; other replies: D. Allen, *Reply to Dr Vaughan Upon Hidden Springs* (Sydney, 1877) (on Allen's anti-Catholic struggles, see F. Beedel, *Letters and Other Writings of the Late Pastor Daniel Allen* (Sydney, 1901), ch. 13); J. A. Downie, *Rome's Polluted Springs* (Sydney, 1877).

[5] J. Rogalla von Bieberstein, *Die These von der Vershwörung 1776-1945. Philosophen, Freimauer, Juden, Liberale und Sozialisten als Vershwörer gegen die Sozialordnung*, Berne, 1976 (see reviews in *Annales* 33, 1978, 754-6; *History of European Ideas* 4, 1983, 109–11.)

[6] R. F. Esposito, *Pio IX. La Chiesa in conflitto col mondo. La S. Sede, la massoneria e il radicalismo settario*, Rome, 1979 (see review in *Catholic Historical Review* 68, 1982, 667–8); L. Leoni, *La massoneria e le annessioni degli Stati pontificii*, Viterbo, 1892-3; summary in F.A. Ferrer Benimeli, *Masoneria español contemporanea*, Madrid, 1980, vol. 2, 36–41; Australian comment in T.A. Fitzgerald, 'The present condition of Italy', *Australasian Catholic Record* 4, 1898, 361–79, 460–74, at 467.

[7] R. F. Byrnes, *Antisemitism in Modern France* vol. 1, New Brunswick, 1950; 126–40, 187-92; R. Millman, 'Jewish anticlericalism and the rise of modern French antisemi-

tism', *History* 77, 1992, 220–36; J. Katz, *Jews and Freemasons in Europe*, trans. L. Oschry, Harvard, 1970, chs. 10–11.

[8] N. Cohn, *Warrant for Genocide*, 2nd ed, London, 1996, ch. 3.

[9] J. A. Ferrer Benimeli, *El contubernio judeo-masonico-comunista: del satanismo al escandalo de la P-2*, Madrid, 1982?; Ferrer Benimeli, *Masoneria español contemporanea*, vol. 2 ch. 5; M.R. Marrus & R.O. Paxton, *Vichy France and the Jews*, N.Y., 1981, 76, 199.

[10] European background in M.C. Jacob, *Living the Enlightenment: Freemasonry and politics in eighteenth-century Europe*, N.Y., 1991; W. R. Weisberger, *Speculative Freemasonry and the Enlightenment*, Boulder, 1993; R. van Dülmen, *The Society of the Enlightenment*, trans. A. Williams, N.Y., 1992, 52–65, 151–65; S. C. Bullock, 'Initiating the Enlightenment?: recent scholarship on European Freemasonry', *Eighteenth-Century Life* 20, 1996, 80–92; Australian knowledge of it in M. Conway, 'Freemasonry and the Age of Enlightenment', *Masonic Research in South Australia*, (South Australian Lodge of Research) 1, 1990–4, 19–21; K. Brindal, 'Brother Mozart, Freemason', *Masonic Research in South Australia* 2, 1995, 27–9; N. J. McDonald, 'Desaguliers', *New South Wales Freemason* 29, 1934, 81–2; American background in S.C. Bullock, *Revolutionary Brotherhood: Freemasonry and the transformation of the American social order, 1730-1840*, Chapel Hill, 1996.

[11] J. A. Ferrer Benimeli, *Los archivos secretos vaticanos y la masonería*, Caracas, 1976; G. Adilardi, *Un'antica condanna. le origini di un conflitto tra Chiesa Cattolica e massoneria*, Foggia, 1989; R.E. Jenkins, 'The evolution of the Church's prohibition against Catholic membership in Freemasonry', *Jurist* 56, 1997, 735–55.

[12] *Annales historiques de la revolution française*, special issue July-Sept 1969, especially D. Ligou, 'Structures et symbolisme maçonniques sous la révolution', 511–23.

[13] Jacob, *Living the Enlightenment*, p. 12; emphasised in J.E. Carnegie, *Freemasonry: its origin, history, principles and doctrines*, Melbourne, 1862, 7; also P. Carter, 'Visions of God – a Masonic perspective', *Theosophy in Australia* 58, 1, Mar 1994, 16–19.

[14] J. H. Billington, *Fire in the Minds of Men: origins of the revolutionary faith*, London, 1980, 91–9.

[15] L. G. Leighton, *The Esoteric Tradition in Russian Romantic Literature: Decembrism and Freemasonry*, University Park, PA, 1994; Billington, 141–2, 330; R. Lansdown, 'Byron and the Carbonari', *History Today* 41, May, 1991, 18–25; B.R. Hamnett, 'Liberal politics and Spanish Freemasonry, 1814–1820', *History* 69, 1984, 221–37.

[16] J. Franklin, 'Sydney 1803: When Catholics were tolerated and Freemasons banned', *Journal of the Royal Australian Historical Society* 107 (2), 2021, 135–155; A. Atkinson, *The Europeans in Australia*, Melbourne, 1997, ch. 12; King to Sullivan, 21/4/1804, *Historical Records of Australia*, series I vol v 142.

[17] C. Gazmari, *El '48' chileno: igualiterios, reformistas, radicales, masones y bomberos*, Santiago, 1992; J.A. Ferrer Benimeli, 'Bolivar y la masoneria', *Revista de Indias* 43, 1983, 631–87; J.-P. Bastian (ed.), *Protestantes, liberales y francmasones: Sociedades de ideas y modernidad en América Latina, siglo xix*, Mexico, 1990; P. Rich & G. de los Reyes, 'Freemasonry's educational role', *American Behavioral Scientist* 40, 1997, 957–67.

[18] J. Brennan, 'The just man of the nineteenth century', *ACR* 5, 1899, 162–72.

[19] M. A. Ortiz de Andres, *Masoneria y democracia en el siglo xix: el Gran Oriente Español y su proyeccion politico-social, 1888-1896*, Madrid, 1993.

[20] R. F. Esposito, *Le grande concordanze tra Chiesa et massoneria*, Firenze, 1987; L. Braschi, *La massoneria e la Chiesa cattolica: un terribile scontro, un possibile incontro*, Firenze, 1984; A. Luzio, *La massoneria e il Risorgimento italiano*, Bologna, 1966; A. Lattanzi, *Bibliografia della massoneria italiana e di Cagliostro*, Firenze, 1974.

[21] R. Desmed, 'A propos du mémoire de la Loge des Amis Philanthrops sur l'enseignement primaire obligatoire et laïque', *Revue belge de philologie et d'histoire* 53, 1975, 357–401, especially 385, 395–401.

[22] J. S. Schapiro, *Anticlericalism*, Princeton, 1967, 56, 60, 153–6; E. Acomb, *The French Laic Laws, 1879-1889*, N.Y., 1941; T. F. Power, *Jules Ferry and the Renaissance of French Imperialism*, N.Y., 1966, 16-21; J. Fulton, 'The revival of church/state hostility in France: the affair of the religious decrees, 1879–80', *Journal of Religious History* 20, 1996, 20–31; P. Nord, 'Republicanism and Utopian vision: French Freemasonry in the 1860s and 1870s', *Journal of Modern History* 63, 1991, 213–29.

[23] M. Larkin, *Church and State After the Dreyfus Affair*, London, 1974, 23–8, 91–101, 138–41; C.S. Phillips, *The Church in France, 1848-1907*, 1936, repr. N.Y., 1967, ch. 9.

[24] J. J. Norris, 'The Catholic Church and liberty', *ACR* 3, 1897, 564–72; letter of Leo XIII, *ACR* 2, 1896, 149–53; D. Lynch, 'Freemasonry in France', *ACR* 8, 1902, 529–46; P. S. Cleary, 'Freemasonry — the enemy of throne and altar', *ACR* 17, 1911, 467–510; M.Q., 'A few notes on Freemasonry', *Austral Light* 4, 1903, 672–4; 'Hiram', 'Sidelights on Freemasonry', *Austral Light* 5, 1904, 403–12, 467–73, 515–21, 609–14, 772–8.

[25] Br Aloysius, *The De La Salle Brothers in Australia, 1906-1956*, Sydney, 1956, 19-27; Fogarty, *Catholic Education in Australia*, vol 2, 274.; P.V. Dwyer, 'The Marist Brothers and their work in France', *ACR* 12, 1906, 461–9; Count de Mun, 'The religious persecution in France', *ACR* 13, 1907, 398–421, at 414–16; R.S., 'France and the Catholic schools', *Austral Light* 3, 1902, 726–9.

[26] Larkin, *Church and State after the Dreyfus Affair*, 138–41: 'Freemasonry in France', *Austral Light* 6, 1905, 164–72, 241–50.

[27] D. Rossignol, *Vichy et les francs-maçons. La liquidation des sociétés secrétes, 1940-1944*, Paris, 1981; R. O. Paxton, *Vichy France*, N.Y., 1972, 4, 102, 156, 172–3, 255.

[28] T. A. Fitzgerald, 'The Jewish Masonic combination in France', *ACR* 6, 1900, 342–88; Molony, 150; A. McLay, *James Quinn*, 2nd ed, Toowoomba, 1989, 135–9.

[29] G. H. Cumming, *The Foundations of Freemasonry in Australia*, West Pennant Hills, 1992, 1–10; 'Was Sir Joseph Banks a Mason?', *NSW Freemason* 47, 1952, 185; 'Francis Greenway', *NSW Freemason* 46, 1951, 133–6; P. Krüger, 'Ludwig Leichhardt: a German geologist of the "Vormärz" period', in H. Lamping & M. Linke (eds), *Australia: studies on the history of discovery and exploration*, Frankfurt, 1994, 127–38.

[30] Silver trowel used by Governor Macquarie, State Library of NSW, https://archival.sl.nsw.gov.au/Details/archive/110321288

[31] K. R. Cramp, 'Federation and Freemasonry', *NSW Freemason* 46, 1951, 441–6, 47, 1952, 313, 48, 1953, 5.

[32] *Freemasonry: Australia's Prime Ministers*, Masonic Historical Society of N.S.W., booklet 2, Sydney, 1994.

[33] K. Henderson, *Masonic Grand Masters of Australia*, Bayswater, 1988, *passim*.

[34] http://www.uglnsw.freemasonry.org.au/historic/historical.html [dead link: see https://www.mof.org.au/articles/famous-freemasons/43-famous-australian-freemasons.html and https://linfordresearch.info/masonic-historical-soc/]

35 Cumming, 6; K. R. Cramp & G. Mackaness, *A History of the United Grand Lodge of New South Wales*, Sydney, 1938, ch. 4.

36 A. Atkinson & M. Aveling, eds, *Australians 1838*, Sydney, 1987, 330-1, 314; Clark, *History of Australia*, vol. 2, 300-1; G.M. Dow, *Samuel Terry: the Botany Bay Rothschild*, Sydney, 1974, 215, 225-6.

37 *The Tongue of Good Report: Lodge Zion no. 218, Gunnedah 1894-1994*, Gunnedah, 1994, and similar histories of individual lodges; A. Richards, *The Centennial Story: the history of Freemasonry in Queensland*, Brisbane, 1959; D. Lauder, 'Freemasons and Freemasonry in Queensland', *J. of the Royal Historical Society of Queensland* 14, 1990, 33–40; R. W. Bell, 'Freemasonry and early Ballarat', *Ballarat Historian* 4, 2, March 1989, 17–21 & 4, 10, Mar, 1991, 6–12; W. C. Vahland, *History of Freemasonry in the Bendigo District*, Bendigo, 1904; M. Chapman, 'Jews and Freemasons in the Colony of Victoria 1840–1900', *Journal of the Australian Jewish Historical Society* 11, 3, November 1991, 415–91; R. J. Linford, 'Freemasonry in the Queanbeyan-Canberra area, 1877–1939', *Canberra Historical Journal* 36, September 1995, 18–27.

38 *Lodge Literature no. 500*, Sydney, 1938.

39 Cramp & Mackaness, 475, 587–8.

40 Ibid., 475; K. R. Cramp, *Lodge University of Sydney*, Sydney, 1945.

41 J. Maguire, *Prologue*, Toowoomba, 1990, 63; R. Haldane, *The People's Force*, 2nd ed, Melbourne, 1995, 56, 171; B. Winter, *The Intrigue Master*, Brisbane, 1995, 174; Lieut-Gen H. G. Bennett, 'Anzac Day, 1953', *NSW Freemason* 48, 1953, 133–6; R. J. W. Selleck & M. Sullivan, *Not So Eminent Victorians*, Melbourne, 1984, 127; Henderson, *Masonic Grand Masters*, 89, 91; M. Cannon, *The Long Last Summer*, Melbourne, 1985, 62; 'Clarke, W. J', *ADB*, vol. 3, 422–4; G. Davison, J.W. McCarty & A. McLeary, eds, *Australians 1888*, Sydney, 1987, 196; Bill Gammage & N. Spearritt, eds, *Australians 1938*, Sydney, 1987, 237; D. Armstrong, 'Freemasons on the march again', *Bulletin*, 3/10/78, 44-6, 51–4; M. Hogan, 'The Sydney style', *Labour History* 36, 1979, 39–46, at p. 42; P. O'Farrell, *Catholic Church and Community*, Sydney, 1985?, 380; D. Horne, *The Education of Young Donald*, rev. ed., Melbourne, 1988, 20.

42 *Age* 15/2/1916, 8 repr. in O'Farrell, *Documents in Australian Catholic History*, vol. 2 p. 265; cf. 107–9; reply in *Argus* 17/2/16, p. 9; also 10/7/16, 9; 'The coadjutor-archbishop and the freemasons', *Austral Light* 17, 1916, 185-6; some facts about Catholics in the officer corps in D. J. Blair, 'An Australian 'officer-type'? A demographic study of the composition of officers in the 1st Battalion, First AIF', *Sabretache* 39, March 1998, 21–7.

43 N.S.W. membership figures in M. H. Kellerman, *From Diamond Jubilee to Centenary: history of forty years of the United Grand Lodge of Freemasonry in New South Wales, 1948-1988*, Sydney, 1990, vol. IV, ch. 5.

44 M. H. Kellerman, 'Freemasonry', in *Australian Encyclopaedia*, 4th ed, Sydney, 1983, 241–4; C.D. Morpeth, 'A peculiar system of morality', *NSW Freemason* 30, 2, February 1935, 43-5. W.C. Bowler, 'Immortality', *NSW Freemason* 22, 1927, 169–70.

45 E. A. Hough, 'What is Freemasonry?', *NSW Freemason* 33, 1938, 561–2; F. A. Maguire (ed.), *Masonic Foundations*, Redfern, 1940.

46 W. C. Bowler, 'Immortality', *NSW Freemason* 22, 1927, 169–70.

47 'Masonry and the moral law', *NSW Freemason* 42, 1947, 185.

48 F. S. McDowell, 'Masonic philosophy', in K. R. Cramp, *From Jubilee to Diamond Jubi-*

lee: history of ten years of the United Grand Lodge of Freemasonry in New South Wales, 1938-1948, 2624; further in J. Franklin, *Corrupting the Youth: A history of philosophy in Australia*, Sydney, 2003, 253-7.

49. 'Masonry not a religion', *NSW Freemason* 28, 1933, 208, 223.

50. 'The charges of a Freemason', Anderson's *Constitutions* of 1723, repr. in M.C. Jacob, *The Radical Enlightenment: pantheists, Freemasons and republicans*, London, 1981, 280; see L. Vibert, 'Anderson's Constitutions of 1723', *NSW Freemason* 47, 1952, 397-404, 451-8, 467, especially 453.

51. 'Woolley, John', *ADB* vol. 6, 435-7; 'Wilkins, William', *ADB* vol. 6, 400-2; W. Wilkins, *National Education: an exposition of the National System of New South Wales*, Sydney, 1865, 12; elsewhere, L. Fletcher, (ed.), *Pioneers of Education in Western Australia*, Perth, 1982, 72, 159; for Queensland, T.L. Suttor, *Hierarchy and Democracy in Australia, 1788-1870*, Melbourne, 1965, 302-3.

52. H. Parkes, 'Darkness or light — which is to conquer?', *Empire* 13 October 1851, 250, partly quoted in Martin, *Henry Parkes*, 105-6; discussion in A.W. Martin, 'Henry Parkes and the political manipulation of sectarianism', *Journal of Religious History* 9, 1976, 85-92; *NSW Parliamentary Debates* 1879-80, vol. 2, 1284; discussed in P.F. Cardinal Moran, *History of the Catholic Church in Australasia*, Sydney, 1895, 875, cf 869.

53. P. J. Lynch, *Freemasonry: its incompatibility with practical Catholicism*, Sydney, 1923, 30-2; A. J. Dunn, 'Christianity and Freemasonry', *Austral Light* 8, 1907, 179-90; E. Cahill, *The Truth About Freemasonry*, Australian Catholic Truth Society pamphlet, Melbourne, 1936; L. Rumble, *Radio Replies in Defence of Religion*, Sydney, 1936, 292-9, text of pamphlet at https://www.ecatholic2000.com/cts/untitled-79.shtml

54. M. Baume, 'Masons and Catholics: a new understanding', *Bulletin* 13/1/68, 20-2; Jenkins, 'The evolution'; K. Clubb, 'Bishops' permission for Freemasonry was hiding in plain sight', Family Life International website, https://www.fli.org.au/bishops-permission-for-freemasonry-was-hiding-in-plain-sight/ accessed 19/07/2022.

55. M. Hogan, *The Sectarian Strand*, Ringwood, 1987, 197-202, 217.

56. A preliminary attempt in Anon, 'Catholics in the Australian public service', *Australian Quarterly* 32, 3 September 1960, 16-22.

57. 'The practical side of Freemasonry', *NSW Freemason* 31, 1935, 19.

58. K. Letters, *History Will Out: F. J. H. Letters at the New England University College*, Armidale, 1997, 37-8; see also E. Campion, *Australian Catholics*, 1987, 152.

59. Letters, *History Will Out*, ch. 10.

60. Ibid., 67-8.

61. C. Baxter, *Reach for the Stars 1919-2009: NSW Knights of the Southern Cross Bold Men of Faith, Hope and Charity*, Ballan, Vic, 2009; C. Kierce, 'The men in the know?', *Observer* 12/12/59, 7-9; 'The silent knights', *Nation* 13/1/60, 8-10; 'The meeting at Chapter Hall', *Nation*, 6/10/62, 5-6; see also ch 13 in this anthology.

62. R. Fitzgerald, *From 1915 to the Early 1980s: a history of Queensland*, Brisbane, 1984, 13.

63. B. Costar, 'Vincent Clair Gair', in *The Premiers of Queensland*, P. Murphy et al (eds)., 2nd ed, Brisbane, 1990, 459-74, at 467; M. I. Thomis, *A Place of Light and Learning: the University of Queensland's first seventy-five years*, Brisbane, 1985, 138; cf. P. O'Farrell, *UNSW: a portrait*, Sydney, 1999, 133.

64. See 'Calwell, Catholicism and the origins of multicultural Australia', ch. 12 in this collection.

10

Archbishop Mannix and the politics of social justice*

Abstract: Catholicism holds that objective ethical theory applies not just to personal morality but to the economic and political organisation of society. Leo XIII's 1891 encyclical, *Rerum Novarum*, laid out a vision of society as a cooperative complex of interest groups constrained by justice. Only a minority of Australian Catholics, lay or clerical, have been enthusiasts for this plan of social justice. The most prominent exceptions are Archbishop Mannix and three of his associates, Scullin, Calwell and Santamaria.

There is probably no aspect of Catholic theory as poorly understood by Protestants and other outsiders as its teaching on "social justice". Most Catholics too have either ignored it or, like Tony Abbott, dismissed talk of social justice as mostly just 'socialism masquerading as justice".[1] Yet it is one of the most significant and unique contributions of Catholicism to modern thought. Mannix showed an enthusiasm for it, an enthusiasm not always evident in his views on some other Catholic doctrines. He shared that commitment with some of his closest and most politically influential associates, Scullin, Calwell and Santamaria.

The social justice tradition is an aspect of the Catholic natural law tradition of ethics, itself poorly understood in general. On that view, ethics is not fundamentally about rules, or divine commands, or the greatest happiness of the greatest number, or habits ingrained by evolution and custom. It is about the irreducible worth of persons – the equal worth of persons – and what follows from that. Because a human being is of immense value, a human death is a tragedy. That is in contrast to the explosion of a lifeless galaxy, which is just a firework. So humans have a right to life and (to put the same thing from the point of view of others) murder is prohibited. Because humans have a particular nature, their rights and duties are of particular kinds. For

---

* *The Real Archbishop Mannix: From the Sources*, ch. 9.

example, because they are intellectual beings, knowledge is central to a full human life, which is to say they have a right to education.[2]

That objective view of ethics applies not just to personal morality, the actions of individual persons. It extends to social, economic and political systems, which are collective human creations for the purpose of serving the common human good. Humans are essentially social beings in a certain way, and it follows that certain ways of organising society are ethical and others not. So at least the most general features of economic and political organisation are conceived to be, not matters of "policy" to be decided at will by democratic political processes, but absolutely right and wrong as much as murder is wrong and charity right.

As industrialisation pushed generations of men into poorly-paid, dirty and dangerous assembly line and labouring work, conflict arose between capitalism and revolutionary socialism. Marxism advocated violent overthrow of the system, while *laissez faire* capitalism argued that any interference with economic forces would make things worse. In contrast to both sides of the conflict, Leo XIII's 1891 encyclical *Rerum Novarum* laid out a cooperative vision of society that respected the rights of workers but also the right to private property. A society should consist of many independent institutions of different sizes and purposes cooperating in the context of an acceptance of moral rules. Families, trade unions, guilds, businesses, churches, clubs, and the state should pursue their own aims, respecting each other's spheres of action and working together to build a just society.[3]

In Australia, one thesis of *Rerum Novarum* in particular struck a chord – its teaching on the right to a minimum wage, enough to support a "frugal and well-behaved wage-earner". The phrase was taken over in the 1907 Harvester judgement, which laid down a basic wage "enough to support the wage earner in reasonable and frugal comfort".[4] Debate continues on the economic effects of the basic wage, but it became an essential part of the "Australian settlement", ensuring that workers gained a share of increased productivity.[5]

The ideology of the Australian Labor Party had certain synergies with the ideas of *Rerum Novarum*. It was against revolution in the cause of socialism – drawing Lenin's ire, as he understood the competition for the workers' allegiance that would arise if workers began to achieve gains by working within the system.[6] Initially, Labor's support for nationalisation of industries posed a problem of incompatibility with the popes' defence of the right to private property.[7] That problem was solved with the party's 1921 adoption of the "Blackburn interpretation" of the socialist objective, which stated that instruments of production would not be socialised if they were used "in a socially useful manner and without exploitation". Mannix stated that the Blackburn interpretation was "exactly what the bishops in their pamphlet [*Socialisation*] have set out."[8] The way was free for Catholic men of the working class to join – sometimes dominate – the Labor Party.[9]

'Hard-headed' ideologues of both Left and Right regarded it as ludicrously naïve to address the urgent problems of capitalism, labour and depression by forming study groups to discuss a papal encyclical. Nevertheless, Catholics interested in political and economic questions who took their faith seriously maintained interest in Church social teaching.[10] A few took it very seriously indeed, and Scullin, Calwell and Santamaria, in different ways, saw their work as advancing the Catholic understanding of social justice.

Political developments in the later twentieth century, from the social engineering of Chifley's government to the Hawke Government's Accord and present-day "regulated capitalism" or "market socialism"[11] are closer to Leo XIII's vision of a cooperative society than they are to either of the extreme nineteenth-century options of revolutionary socialism and *laissez faire* capitalism.[12]

The close fellowship between the Church, as interpreted by Mannix and Catholic Labor men, and the workers' cause had important consequence for both Australian Catholicism and for politics. The situation was entirely different from countries like France, where the Church became identified with monarchism and reaction and lost the support of the working class.[13] That was not going to happen in Australia, where the Church *was* the working class, or a significant part of it. There was an element of self-interest in the Vatican's comment in 1918, that as "Monsignor Mannix, wrongly or rightly, enjoys a great influence upon the working classes," it would be imprudent to take action against him for his vigorous intervention in Irish politics.[14] There were not many Catholic archbishops in the early twentieth century who could draw tens of thousands of cheering workers.

Mannix on the Church and the workers

Mannix's 'Catholic principles' speech of November 1917 was his major extended statement on issues of theory. After dealing with strictly religious issues, he went on to address social questions. He repeated Leo XIII's ideas but went much further in advocating government intervention in the economic system, especially on behalf of the unemployed. Quoting him at some length will show the logical development of his thought and his understanding of how religion has to show itself not an opiate of the masses but their supporter in the fight for justice:

> The Church stands, first of all, for the worker's right to a living wage. (Applause.) Leo XIII seems to have opened the eyes of the world when he boldly proclaimed, not so many years ago, that the workman had a right to a living wage – a first claim on the wealth that he produced. (Applause.) And, of course, his right to a living wage gives him a right to such a share of the wealth he produces as will enable him to bring up his family in decent surroundings and in reasonable comfort. All this the Pope said, was due, not merely by reason of the wealth produced, but also by reason of what is due to man's nature. Man has a right to live upon the earth, and it is by his labour that this right is exercised. Now, though I feel that I am treading on ground which many call dangerous, I am convinced that the principle on which Pope Leo XIII relied has a wider application than it sometimes receives. It seems evident to me that, on the Pope's principles, the Government is strictly bound to see that industry is organised so that those who are willing to work will find work, or, failing to find it, will have a right to decent sustenance. (Applause.)

> To my mind, Governments are bound to provide against unemployment so far as may be, and then to provide for the unemployed. (Applause.) It is very poor consolation to tell a man that when employed he has a right to a living wage, if at the same time he is starving for want of work. (Applause.) If as Pope Leo says,

the inherent dignity of man's nature entitles him to a living wage when he is at work, the same requirement of his nature should imperatively demand for him a decent sustenance when he is willing to undertake, but, through no fault of his own, is unable to find work. (Applause.) If the right to work and the right to support during unemployment were recognised, as I think they ought to be recognised, I promise you that Governments and capitalists would try to find work for all. (Laughter and applause.) I know that people will say that I am playing fast and loose with the rights of property. Of course, I am putting upon the State, and upon society, duties which they are naturally reluctant to undertake. But the problem of unemployment has never been frankly faced, and it once and for all must be faced, and with the conviction that a man's life is more sacred than the rights of property. (Loud applause.) Of course, we shall be told – it is the old story – economic society would go to pieces. (Laughter and applause.) Yet those who stand aghast at the demands of the worker – we know it is now to our cost – those same people are able to find untold millions in order to wage war in Europe. (Applause.) Heaven and earth would have been moved and all the devices of Parliament exhausted before an hundredth part of that expenditure would have gone to improve the lot of the poor man who labours for a living. (Loud applause.) When the war is over, will the workman, who has had his eyes opened, and has seen what has happened, be satisfied with the excuse that money cannot be found – that the old system must go on?

Voices: No! (Applause.)

The Archbishop: I do not think he will. (Applause.) I believe that great changes will come as a result of the war, and as a result of the awakening that has come to a great many of us – myself amongst that number. (Applause.) It is true that the condition of the workers has been improved in some respects – old age pensions are provided and the doles are given in times of accidents and sickness. But all these benefits come from the fund – from the wealth – which the worker has himself produced. It only shows how distorted is our view of economic relations, if we claim credit for giving the worker what is really his due. (Applause.) These things are his right, and it is really no credit to the State to have provided them. (Applause.) Even now the worker is getting less than he is entitled to, and much less, probably, than he will insist on having himself before many years are over. (Loud applause.) Doubtless, even in the very best form of society, there will be inequalities, hardships, suffering. But that is no reason for leaving things as they are, for saying that the workers have no grievance; that they have nothing to complain of; that they ought to be patient; and that their religious guides should keep them quiet in this world, and offer them a great reward in the other. (Laughter and applause.)

When I read what is sometimes written by the capitalist press, and when I read between the lines, as I always try to do, I seem to discover that we have many who value religion mainly – perhaps solely – for keeping the proletariat quiet. (Applause.) That is the religion they believe in (Applause.) They believe that religion is a good thing for the poor man because it will help to keep him quiet. Even if he were quiet, we would not be absolved for giving him what is justly his due. [15]

Mannix recognised that if the existing system did not protect the workers, they would be tempted to try another.[16]

Even more dramatically, he wrote in his foreword to the first issue of a new Catholic monthly *Australia* in 1917, supporting workers' control of industry:

The War had made men and women think much and think hard: They would not cease thinking when the war was over. They would not be satisfied to be cogs in a wheel. More and more they would try to control the industries in which they were engaged. It would be hard to convince them or convince anyone that they were not entitled to industrial control as they were to political power … it was never more necessary than it was now that the public mind should be leavened by Catholic principles. [17]

During the wave of industrial unrest at the end of the War, he asked whether "any of the sneering critics would undertake to balance the family budget on the strikers' wages and at the present cost of living: Would they live in the conditions, in the holds, or in the slums, on sea or land, in which the strikers had been living?"[18]

Mannix was fully informed by Leo XIII's principles, but it was his own work to draw implications that justice for the workers implied a degree of socialism driven by government. He did not advocate the core socialist aim of nationalisation of industry, but preferred a form of workers' control supplemented by government social security.

Capitalism and the Depression

Less was heard from Mannix on the workers during the 1920s, as he spent more effort on Irish affairs. But with the onset of the Depression, the issues resurfaced. In 1931 he said:

> All over the world, people were experiencing a very anxious time: They were only now beginning to realise how wise Pope Leo XIII was when he told the world, about forty years ago, that if radical change were not made in society, much trouble, and even revolution, might have to be faced. There was more unemployment in the world than had ever existed before, and people were worse off than when slavery existed. Slave owners had to feed, clothe and look after those subject to them, but many who called themselves free men today had scarcely anybody to look after them. Until the unemployment problem was solved, the world would never be at rest. [20]

Mannix (centre, with lamp), with some workers, Broken Hill, 1922[19]

By 1933, the danger of the workers turning to a radical apparent solution, Communism, was more acute. Mannix realised more than most churchmen that a credible answer to Communism required a Catholic alternative that also critiqued capitalism. The failure of capitalism made a search for alternatives necessary:

> One could well understand how people were driven to extremes in times like the present. Millions of men and women in all lands were actually starving while the world was full of wealth.
>
> The first line of defence against Communism and Socialism was to acknowledge humbly and sorrowfully that the system under which they were living had been a complete failure ... People who were genuinely alarmed about Communism and Socialism should first put their own house in order ...
>
> Countries that prided themselves on being most progressive, such as Germany, England and the United States had been badly affected by the depression ... This was due to the capitalistic system, which concentrated the wealth in the hands of the few. His Holiness Pope Leo XIII and his successors had pointed out that concentration of wealth in the hands of the few left the multitude without the wherewithal to pay for the things that could be produced ... [21]

Speaking in Newcastle in 1938 he again condemned the failure of unrestricted capitalism, even though by this time the problem of Communism was moving to centre stage. He said

> I am old enough to remember when Pope Leo XIII was regarded by many people as a socialist or Communist of the time because he told us that human labour was not merely a commodity to be bargained for, but that human dignity had to be considered, and that a man was entitled to a living wage for himself and his family. [22]

He called for child endowment to make up for the fact that the basic wage was premised on the amount needed for a couple with just two children.

The young B. A. Santamaria, accompanying Mannix, said that the three requirements for social justice in Australia were redistribution of income, redistribution of property, and the installation of vocational groups as the controlling force in industry.

Women's role in public life

While supportive of women's "primary" duty in the home, Mannix believed it should be complemented by active roles in wider society. At the conclusion of one of a series of adult education lectures in 1917, he spoke after a lecture titled 'Woman and the state', which was presented by a woman guest lecturer. He said:

> ... women have a very great work to do, not merely in the home, but also, in the conduct of public affairs ... It is only by taking her proper place in every public movement that she can make her own home – and the homes of other women – what these homes ought to be. [23]

In his 'Catholic principles' speech, Mannix connected the Church's support for women with its protection of the weak and its opposition to divorce.[24]

The education of women was of concern, including university education:

> In respect of education, women had not been catered for in the same manner as had the men, and he thought they should be. (Applause.) The £1000 that he had received from a leading Catholic in Melbourne was given to him as a protest against the malicious and unprovoked attacks made upon him by various people in different grades of society. Thus the attacks in question had not been without some good effect. (Laughter and applause.) He proposed to hand this £1000 over to the Catholic University College committee for the benefit of Catholic women's education, to be used in the form of scholarships, or in another form the committee and himself might decide. If scholarships were decided upon, he would suggest that they should be called the 'Argus' scholarships. (Loud laughter and applause.) [25]

(Reference is to the *Argus* newspaper's long campaign against Mannix's alleged disloyalty.)

Mannix would not however count as a feminist in modern terms because of his strong opposition to contraception.[26]

Colonialism and Aborigines

In 1922, Mannix addressed colonialism and the fate of the indigenous inhabitants. As an Irish nationalist, he was more sceptical than most Australians of the civilising influences of the British Empire:

> Some nations boast of their great civilising influences in the outposts of the world. How did some of these nations acquire their colonial possessions and what use have they made of them? What has been the lot of the original inhabitants, the previous owners of these colonial possessions? In many cases these races of people were civilised out of existence. Indeed we do not have to go far from Australia for an example ... And if I may return again for a moment to Belfast ... [27]

In 1933, he joined protests against the proposed sending of an expedition to Arnhem Land in search of the "Caledon Bay blacks" who had murdered some whites. The expedition appeared to have the character of a punitive expedition to conduct reprisals, though the government denied that was the case.[28] *The West Australian* reported:

Objection to punitive force: Church and Trades Hall Opinions

The Roman Catholic Archbishop of Melbourne (Dr. Mannix) has sent the following telegram [sent on 5 September 1933] to the Prime Minister (Mr. Lyons) concerning the Caledon Bay blacks.

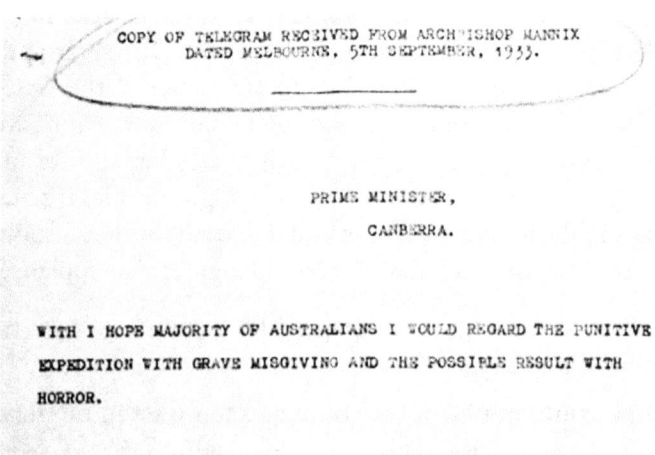

"With, as I hope, the majority of Australians, I would regard the proposed punitive expedition with grave misgiving and its possible results with horror."[29]

The protests, which came from many sources, were successful and the expedition was not sent.

In 1940, Mannix took the opportunity on Social Justice Sunday to remind Catholics that justice applied to Aboriginal Australians too:

ARCHBISHOP FEARS FOR SAFETY OF ABORIGINES

The fear that bomb experiments might harm aborigines in the Kimberley areas was expressed by Archbishop Mannix when he opened a fete at the Pallottine Missionary College, Kew, on Saturday. The aborigines were not likely to take kindly to the destruction of their old haunts, he said. The Government should be careful with the experiments, and not remove natives from their old roaming ground, where apparently they found happiness and contentment.

> I wonder if anybody else ... thought that we owed something in the matter of social justice to the Aborigines of Australia. I believe in social justice, but I believe in it all round. I do know that the Aborigines of Australia would be able to furnish a very strong indictment against the present rulers and inhabitants of Australia and those who have gone before us. I hope that if social justice ever comes, that it will reach them as it reaches the rest of us ...[30]

He supported the work of missionaries in remote indigenous communities as a work of redemption for the "original sin" of dispossession.[31]

In 1946, questions arose about atomic bomb tests in the remote outback and their effect on the inhabitants. Mannix joined expressions of concern.[32]

Jewish refugees

In March 1939, Mannix appealed on behalf of Jewish refugees fleeing Hitler's tyranny. A few thousand of them had been admitted to Australia and there was some ill-feeling about "reffos". He said:

> The unfortunate Jews were hunted post and pillar out of every country of Europe. Many of them were coming here, although some people did not seem to offer them a welcome.
>
> These people should ask themselves, what was to become of those unfortunate wanderers? It was not the Christian spirit to

have distrust and an inborn hatred of the Jews. The founder of the Christian religion Himself was a Jew, and His Mother was a Jewish maiden. People should remember these things when they were inclined to be hard upon the Jews, and when, perhaps, they were not as sympathetic with them in their sufferings as they ought to be as Christians. All of them were children of the One Eternal Father, whether they were Jews or Christians, Catholics or Protestants. There was no distinction. They should all give a helping hand to those who were afflicted and those who were heavily burdened. This was their duty as Christians.[33]

The threat of Communism

The political issue that came to define the older Mannix was anti-Communism. In the mid-century, Catholics in Australia were known for their implacable hostility to Communism. Where many on the left preferred to ignore the news from Russia of famines and show trials, and others were apathetic about such a distant country, Catholics had an international network of information about Stalinist horrors. Mannix was in the lead from an early stage, as in his 1931 address at the annual Communion breakfast of the Catholic Young Men's Society:

COMMUNISM AND SLAVERY.
EXAMPLE OF RUSSIA.
ADDRESS BY DR. MANNIX.

The Catholic Church was conservative in everything that was good, Dr Mannix said, but it is progressive and had always thrown its influence on the side of the working man. While the Church stood for the rights and progress of the workmen of Australia it was fundamentally and necessarily opposed to many of the doctrines that were being preached not so much by Australians as by aliens coming into the country. If those people should succeed it would not be good for Australia and if they were to be defeated it would be by the Catholic men. He knew that those preaching revolutionary doctrines in Australia formed a real hotbed of communism and Communistic ideas. The failures of capitalism had been great but the failures of communism would be infinitely worse. Centuries ago slavery was practically abolished but the worst slavery the world ever saw was in Russia today. A system to be successful must increase the production of the world's resources, and should distribute them to the benefit of humanity. Production of the world had increased under the capitalistic system, which, however, had failed to distribute the wealth to the benefit of humanity. There was more unemployment in the world now than had ever existed before, and people were worse off than when slavery existed. Slave-owners fed, clothed and housed their slaves and looked after them, but how many people who called themselves freemen had scarcely anybody to look after them. Until unemployment problems were solved the world would never be at rest. He did not think it would be solved along communistic or socialistic lines. The Federal and State Governments deserved credit for their efforts to steer a middle course between the different parties. He sincerely trusted that members of the society would give generous aid and intellectual support to those who were trying to do the best for Australia. They should not be led away by foolish propaganda.[34]

Mannix, as an aged prelate, was not in a position to directly translate his Catholic thought into Catholic action. But younger men inspired by him were. The story is now well-known of how these ideas prompted Mannix to support his protégé Santamaria in directing the semi-secret "Movement" to fight Communists for control of the unions, and how Mannix and Santamaria opposed both the ALP and the Vatican in the "Split" of the mid-1950s.[35]

It is less appreciated how Arthur Calwell's work in child endowment, immigration, anti-Communism and other areas was also a continuation of the work of his mentor Mannix.[36] James Scullin too had been close to Mannix over *Rerum Novarum* while warning him of the dangers of a separatist Catholic party.[37]

The 1961 Interview

Mannix reflected on his role in these events in an interview on 29 December 1961 in his study at *Raheen* by Gerald Lyons. He was then aged 97.

Mannix interviewed by Gerald Lyons at Raheen, late 1961

Gerald Lyons: When did you first become aware of the danger of Communism in Australia?

Archbishop Mannix: In the 'forties. Of course, it was public knowledge that Communism was winning all round the world, and that without firing a shot. They were piling up great armaments but they didn't have to use them. Just by infiltration and propaganda they were succeeding all round the world. They conquered a great part of Europe. They were invading Asia, Africa and, later on, even South America, and all round the world they seemed to me to be achieving all that they wanted without going to war.

GL: Did you see this onward march of Communism in the world and Communist influence in politics and trade unions in this country, in particular, as more serious than the issue of conscription and Irish independence?

AM: The most serious problem that I had to face in 100 years of my long life.

GL: There's a Catholic organization which was set up in 1941, I understand, to fight Communism in the Australian Labour Party, in the Trade Unions, which I'll call "The Movement". Now was the idea of "The Movement" originally yours?

AM: No, I don't claim that it was originally mine, but when it originated I was in favour of it because in Australia the labour unions are very important. They really control the Labour Party. They may be in opposition now but next day they may be in power. In Australia, therefore, the activities of Communism are extremely important because they were so successful in winning to their cause the labour unions, and by winning the labour unions they were on the way to winning the Australian Government some time.[38]

Archbishop Mannix was unique among Australian churchmen in a number of ways – his involvement in Irish nationalism, his defiance of Vatican directives to be less involved in politics, his populist speeches, his promotion of lay initiatives, his scathing public wit. He is no less unique in his understanding of and commitment to Catholic principles of social justice, and his direct involvement with lay people and organisations attempting to realise them through political activity.

---

[1] http://www.abc.net.au/news/2007-09-12/health-minister-tony-abbott-says-that-whenever-the/696326

[2] James Franklin, *The Worth of Persons: The foundation of ethics*, Encounter, New York, 2022.

[3] Bruce Duncan, *The Church's Social Teaching: From Rerum Novarum to 1931*, Collins Dove, North Blackburn, 1991.

[4] Kevin Blackburn, The living wage in Australia: a secularization of Catholic ethics on wages, 1891–1907, *Journal of Religious History* 20 (1996), 93-113.

[5] Paul Kelly, *The End of Certainty: Power, politics, and business in Australia*, 2nd ed, Allen & Unwin, St Leonards, 1994, introduction; Geoffrey Stokes, The 'Australian settlement' and Australian political thought, *Australian Journal of Political Science* 39 (2004), 5-22.

[6] Rick Kuhn, Lenin on the ALP: The career of 600 words, *Australian Journal of Politics & History* 35 (1989), 29-49.

[7] A. E. Cahill, Catholicism and socialism: The 1905 controversy in Australia, *Journal of Religious History* 1 (2) (1960), 88-101.

[8] Duncan, *Crusade or Conspiracy? Catholics and the Anti-Communist Struggles in Australia*, University of New South Wales Press, 2001, p. 120.

[9] Celia Hamilton, Irish-Catholics of New South Wales and the Labor Party, 1890–1910, *Historical Studies* 8 (1958), 254-67, section VI; Judith Brett, Class, religion and the foundation of the Australian party system: A revisionist interpretation, *Australian Journal of Political Science* 37 (2002), 39-56.

10. Michael Hogan, *Australian Catholics: The social justice tradition*, Collins Dove, Melbourne, 1993; Race Mathews, *Of Labour and Liberty: Distributism in Victoria, 1891-1966*, Notre Dame University Press, Notre Dame, 2017.
11. James Franklin, Regulated capitalism, market socialism, *Dissent* no. 5 (2001), 1113.
12. Recent developments in James Franklin, ed, *Life to the Full: Rights and social justice in Australia*, Connor Court, Ballan, 2007; *Solidarity: The Journal of Catholic Social Thought and Secular Ethics*.
13. J. N. Moody, The dechristianization of the French working class, *Review of Politics* 20 (1958), 46-69.
14. Cardinal Gasparri, Secretary of State, to Count de Salis, 22 Aug 1918, in *The Real Archbishop Mannix*, 121.
15. *Advocate*, 3 November 1917, 6-7; also *Tribune* 1 Nov 1917, 4, https://trove.nla.gov.au/newspaper/article/154382979 .
16. *The Advertiser* (Adelaide), 29 January 1917, 7.
17. Frank Murphy, *Daniel Mannix: Archbishop of Melbourne 1917-1963*, Polding Press, Melbourne, 1972, 63-64, quoted in Race Mathews, Socio-political aspects of the Mannix Episcopate 1913-1931 Part I, *Australasian Catholic Record*, 88 (2011), at 5-6.
18. As quoted in E. J. Brady, *Dr Mannix: Archbishop of Melbourne*, Library of National Biography, Melbourne: 1934, 129-130, quoted in Mathews, Socio-political Aspects of the Mannix Episcopate, 6.
19. Original image supplied by Michael Gilchrist.
20. As quoted in Brady, *Dr Mannix*, 244-5, quoted in Mathews, Socio-political Aspects of the Mannix Episcopate, p. 6.
21. Speech of 4 June 1933, Gilchrist, *Portrait of Archbishop Mannix*, 45.
22. *Maitland Daily Mercury*, 17 February 1938, p. 8, https://trove.nla.gov.au/newspaper/article/131273578 .
23. *Advocate*, 25 Aug 1917, 16, https://trove.nla.gov.au/newspaper/article/152185024 .
24. *Advocate*, 3 November 1917, 6.
25. *Catholic Press* (Sydney), 12 April 1917, 15, https://trove.nla.gov.au/newspaper/article/105172220 .
26. *The Real Archbishop Mannix*, 194-5.
27. *Advocate*, 6 July 1922, 15, https://trove.nla.gov.au/newspaper/article/176519829 .
28. *Sydney Morning Herald*, 6 September 1933, 13, http://trove.nla.gov.au/ndp/del/article/17004771
29. *West Australian*, 8 September 1933, 19, http://trove.nla.gov.au/ndp/del/article/33325805
30. *Advocate*, 25 April 1940, 7, https://trove.nla.gov.au/newspaper/article/172040914 .
31. *Argus*, 17 November 1941, 6, https://trove.nla.gov.au/newspaper/article/8217062
32. *Argus*, 9 December 1946, 3, http://trove.nla.gov.au/ndp/del/article/22398488
33. *Freeman's Journal*, 6 Apr 1939, p. 18, http://trove.nla.gov.au/ndp/del/article/146383596
34. *Argus*, 26 October 1931, 6, https://trove.nla.gov.au/newspaper/article/4426750, and reported in many other newspapers.
35. E.g. Duncan, *Crusade or Conspiracy?*; Franklin, Nolan and Gilchrist, *The Real Archbishop Mannix*, ch. 13; Gerard Henderson, *Santamaria: A most unusual man*, Mel-

bourne University Press, Melbourne, 2015, chs 4-10; Brenda Niall, *Mannix*, Text, Melbourne, 2017, chs 12-13.

36 *The Real Archbishop Mannix*, ch. 12.

37 *The Real Archbishop Mannix*, 166–7, 246; caricatured in Frank Hardy, *Power Without Glory: The Real Archbishop Mannix*, 264–5.

38 Frank Murphy, *Daniel Mannix: Archbishop of Melbourne 1917–1963*, Polding Press, Melbourne, 1972, 255–6; video excerpts at https://aso.gov.au/titles/tv/interview-archbishop-mannix/notes/

11

Memoirs by Australian priests, religious and ex-religious*

Abstract: Up to the mid-twentieth century, thousands of young Australian Catholics became priests, brothers and nuns. They committed themselves permanently to a hard, self-sacrificing life for the promise of spiritual goods, both for themselves and those in their charge. Some of them – most, it is true, ones who ultimately left religious life – have told their stories at length. An examination of their stories, especially their accounts of their initial commitment, gives an insight into the phenomenon of mass commitment to religious life which did so much to form the tone of Australian Catholicism.

Autobiography is history from the inside. Real history – how events appeared to those who took part in them. That is not to say that memoirs are always true, or fair, balanced and unbiased. As Clive James says, "all attempts to put oneself in a bad light are doomed to be frustrated. The ego arranges the bad light to its own satisfaction."[1] Nevertheless, what people say about themselves is at the historical front line – the primary evidence of what it was really like to be there.

The article selects some interesting parts of a few of the memoirs by Australian priests, brothers and nuns. And by ex-priests, ex-brothers and ex-nuns, who sometimes write the most dramatic stories. Perhaps ex-religious can speak more freely than those still under vows. Or maybe to write a gripping autobiography requires a strong fascination with oneself that does not fit ideally with the mental attitudes appropriate to persistence in religious life.

I have included simply what I find interesting. But I have looked especially at the accounts of first commitment to the religious life, in the hope of understanding the huge wave of vocations around the 1950s and the sudden receding of that wave. Another theme that

---

* *Journal of the Australian Catholic Historical Society* 33 (2012), 142–162. The original article included a list of memoirs which is omitted here.

emerged of its own accord is the extraordinary separation between life "inside" a religious order and what was going on in "the world".

The range of views on religious life arranges itself naturally according to how angry the writers are about their time "in religion". Let us start at the angry end of the spectrum. Readers should correct for any bias resulting from that; those with more positive stories will be heard later.

Ex and Angry

John Hanrahan, author of *From Eternity to Here: Memoirs of an Angry Priest*, plainly should never have persisted with his "vocation". That is clear from every page of his book. For example, he writes, at about the midpoint of his training, "Poverty was no problem, but the vows of chastity and especially obedience were becoming increasingly difficult, especially when I considered successive superiors devious morons."[2] Certainly, the intelligence of his superiors is called into question by their decision to allow him to proceed to ordination.

Hanrahan joined the Missionaries of the Sacred Heart Juniorate at Douglas Park in 1953, aged 13. Already he complains about the Christian Brothers who taught him in Albury: "But I think I ran away to become a priest partly to escape the sadists, who wielded their tailor-made straps with rampant piety."[3]

Out of the frying pan, into the fire. In the Juniorate and Novitiate, there were no straps, but he found more sadists:

> Apart from rules, Father Master was passionate about humiliation (ours) and loved acting-out. One day he came onto the sanctuary to perform Benediction. He approached the altar, and went into a ritual of his own. As sacristan, I knew I was approaching some scrabbled moment of destiny. Father Master raised the altar cloth and peered under it. He searched that vase of hydrangeas. He peered into them. He raised the skirts of his chasuble and probed the pockets of his religious habit. He knelt down and raised a piece of the sanctuary carpet. He turned to us with an Orson Welles' shrug.
>
> 'OK, Brother Hanrahan, I give up. Am I getting hot or cold, or are you going to let us in on the secret of where you have hidden

the monstrance so I can expose the Sacred Host and the rest of us interested can get down to worship?' In my rush from the sacristy I dropped the sacred vessel and bent a couple of the gold spikes.[4]

Another very garrulous complainer is Chris Geraghty. It takes him two volumes to cover the period to not long after ordination – the first is *Cassocks in the Wilderness,* set in St Columba's Seminary, Springwood, and the second *The Priest Factory,* about St Patrick's, Manly. The first explains what it took for the seminarians to get involved in the local community – a bushfire: at one point they were side by side with the young Communists saving the hall of the Eureka Youth League. *The Priest Factory* has ten pages of abuse of Bishop Muldoon and an account of taking the anti-Modernist oath in 1962.[5]

It is interesting to compare Geraghty with Paul Crittenden, a near-contemporary of his at Manly, later Professor of Philosophy at the University of Sydney. His memoir *Changing Orders* has thirteen pages on Muldoon's faults, but they are not as colourfully rude as Geraghty's.[6] He does say that the skills he learned in organising and money-raising as Muldoon's curate in Mosman came in useful later when he was Dean of Arts at Sydney University.

Heaven, Where the Bachelors Sit is Gerard Windsor's widely read and highly coloured story of life in the Jesuit Seminary. He makes it clear that the vow of chastity was never going to suit him. Another unhappy-Jesuit memoir is titled *Give me a Child When He Is Young.*[7]

Morris West

One last troublemaker, Morris West, was born in 1916 and joined the Christian Brothers who had taught him, at the age of 13. He writes, "On my part, the decision to join the Congregation was an act of fugue. For the Congregation it was part of a programme called 'fostering vocations', but in fact, as I see it now, a seduction of the young and immature into a choice which they were quite unready to make."[8]

... in the Congregation I had my first experience of techniques designed to wash the human brain and bend the human spirit. They were practised by my novice-master, who, though he is long dead, I still regard as an ignorant and coarse man, psychologically maimed, anti-intellectual, spiritually blind, who did grave and sometimes irreparable damage to many of the youths in his charge.

He humiliated them with gross penances: shaving their heads, sentencing them to extra field labour, making them take meal after meal on their knees. He bullied them at lecture time. He tyrannised them with spiritual fears: damnation in every sexual thought, double damnation for every impulse of pride and revolt.[9]

West proceeded as far as teaching in schools but had the good sense to leave in 1939, just before my final vows. "My departure was timed for the hour when students and masters were in chapel. The Brother Provincial gave me a cool handshake and a reminder – somehow almost comic in the circumstances – that I was still under vows until their term expired at Christmas."[10]

He joined the Army, married, wrote a novel (about life in a religious order, what else?), divorced and requested an annulment. It was refused and thus he became officially excommunicate on remarriage.

Then he created trouble. Big trouble. The best-selling novel in the United States in the year of the Vatican Council, 1963 was not Mary McCarthy's *The Group* nor J D Salinger's *Raise High the Roof Beam, Carpenters*, but Morris West's papal wish-fulfilment fantasy, *The Shoes of the Fisherman*. And that followed his huge success in 1959 with *The Devil's Advocate*.

Perhaps the work of Morris West and Graham Greene should be seen as important in preparing the public mind for "the spirit of Vatican II", at least in the English-speaking world. As is clear from the history of the Soviet Union, making the old order look ridiculous is an important prelude to changing it. (Edmund Campion recalls acquiring an addiction to Graham Greene in Manly Seminary, of all places.[11])

Of nun memoirs, the most negative is a much later one, Colette

Livermore's *Hope Endures*. She joined Mother Teresa's Missionaries of Charity in 1973 and left eleven years later, having worked with the very poor in Manila, Papua New Guinea and Calcutta. She argues that the order did not take care of the physical and mental health of its own sisters.[12]

Balanced views?

Now let us hear from two ex-religious who took a reasonably balanced view. They have criticisms of the long period they spent in religious life and are glad to have left, but they say they generally enjoyed it and that most of their fellow religious were good and dedicated people.

Paul Brock was the son of the editor of the *Newcastle Sun* and school captain of Marist Brothers, Hamilton, in 1959. Like three of his siblings and the two immediately previous captains of the school, he entered religious life, in his case joining the Marist Brothers. He writes (much later) of his sense of vocation at that time:

> The overwhelming idea that kept burning in my brain and which galvanised my decision to enter religious life was a saying that St Ignatius Loyola, the founder of the Jesuit order, used to repeat to the young Francis Xavier … The telling saying used by St Ignatius was a quotation from the Bible: 'What doth it profit a man if he gains the whole world, yet suffers the loss of his own soul?'

> Why struggle to achieve and gain things here on earth if life is really fundamentally a preparatory testing ground to see if we could avoid being condemned to a life of eternal pain and misery in Hell, and graduate to an eternal afterlife of happiness in Heaven? Why waste time pursuing the normal aspirations of things like physical possessions, marriage and ambition? Therefore it seemed to me far better to pursue a life of self-denial through the religious vows of poverty, celibacy and obedience and, as a result, have more assurance of gaining Heaven. Furthermore, I was living within an environment where I was constantly being told by priests, nuns and brothers that the finest thing that anybody could do with his or her life was to give it all up to God as a priest, nun, or brother.[13]

(Compare Edmund Campion: "What I remember [from Riverview] is the men who taught us by their lives the moral absolutism of that saying of Jesus about the world having nothing that compensates for losing one's soul.")[14]

Brock lived as a brother for fifteen years and says of his fellow brothers, "Notwithstanding the tiny minority of Brothers whose covert acts of wickedness ended up being exposed and condemned by the courts, by and large my memory of the Brothers I knew and lived with is of very fine men of integrity, generosity and whole-hearted commitment to the education of the boys and girls, young men and women they served as teachers."[15] After several years with the thankless task of teaching poetry to the ungrateful masses at St Joseph's, Hunters Hill[16] he left the Brothers in 1975, concluding, "In retrospect, I should have realised from my earliest monastic years that I was really not cut out for a life long commitment to celibacy."[17] He married twice and had three daughters, and a successful career as an academic in education and then a policy adviser in education in Canberra and Sydney. In 1997 he was diagnosed with Motor Neurone Disease. Most sufferers die within three years, but his form of the disease was much slower to progress and he continued working from a wheelchair. He is more forthcoming than many ex-religious on his subsequent faith situation. He writes:

> By the time I was diagnosed I no longer believed in a personally interventionist deity. I think it's illogical, for example, to thank God for the survival of one person in a car crash that killed all the other occupants ... But I remain a spiritual person ... I am still as much driven today by the essential truths of Christ's Sermon on the Mount as ever I was during all my years as a devout practising Catholic.[18]

Cecilia Inglis's memoir opens in 1981. She is in the office of the Mother Superior of the Mercy convent in Singleton. She is about to leave after thirty years of religious life. It takes the reader a few moments to realise that she is not in the office to say goodbye to Mother Superior. She *is* Mother Superior.

Her book *Cecilia: An Ex-Nun's Extraordinary Journey* was published by Penguin in 2003. It is well-written and she is an attractive personality: interested in lots of things and in people, able to work on self-knowledge and reinvent herself, in some ways tough but never self-satisfied.

She was born in 1935, the seventh in an Irish-Catholic working-class family in Newcastle. An elder sister became a Mercy nun and a brother became a priest.[19] At sixteen she decided to become a nun. She writes:

> There was that sense of 'calling' I had – a vocation to save the world, or at least my corner of it. There was the Jesus of the Gospels that I loved to imagine: sitting among His disciples, at weddings, tired by the well, having compassion on the hungry and tired multitude, talking about the ways His father in Heaven cared about us. I think I wanted to share this Jesus with other people who didn't know Him.
>
> There were also those feelings of peace and devotion during the family rosary, at morning Mass, and during retreats. I looked forward to living in a place where this devotion was cherished and nourished, and where people cared about each other.
>
> On the other hand, religious life was a drastic choice. It meant leaving behind family and friends, and everything familiar – even the clothes I was used to. It meant wearing all this funny black stuff, being locked away behind walls, and I couldn't even imagine what I'd be doing all day there.[20]

Her account of her eighteenth birthday (14 February 1953) explains what they did do all day:

> That day I rose at 5 a.m. when the bell clanged out…
>
> I got up, but not with the leap exhorted in the novices' guide – 'as if the bed was on fire'. I struggled out, still three-quarters asleep, and splashed my face with cold water … I got dressed as quickly as I could organise myself. Voluminous undies, a bra and singlet,

black stockings fastened to my newly acquired lace-up corset, a long black half-petticoat ... So far, as required for the sake of modesty, I had been dressing under my calico nightie ... though the screens were still closed around my cubicle ...

I only got one clean coif and veil a week. I didn't have to worry about it covering my crowning glory because my hair was cut off the previous September at my reception as a novice ...

I moved very quietly when I pulled back the screens around my bed and left the dormitory, as we were still in the Great Silence. This was a very solemn time from night prayers till the end of Mass when the whole house was in profound silence ... stories were told – perhaps apocryphal – of saintly nuns in the olden days who lay on the floor all night with broken hips rather than break the Great Silence.

Most of the nuns were already kneeling in the stalls along the sides of the chapel waiting for the prayers to begin. There were about thirty-five or forty of us ... I faced the altar, and the folded high seat of the stall stuck into my back. It was uncomfortable – probably meant to be – but not uncomfortable enough to keep me awake at this time of the morning ... Sometimes the sister behind me would give me a poke in the back when I looked in danger of rolling right out of the stall into the aisle.

I was supposed to be meditating, but I was not quite sure what that meant, so I was always glad when the 6 a.m. Angelus bell rang ... We sat on the high stall seats, faced the centre, and said the Office – Prime, Terce, Sext and None – all in Latin ... When Office finished we filed out of the chapel – still in complete silence – to the community room for the 'lecture'. This was a ten-minute or so gathering where the novice mistress could correct us for anything ... For instance, she might think we were not walking quietly enough in the Great Silence, or she might have noticed some sisters not keeping the 'custody of the eyes' (that is, eyes cast down at all times). Then she read from *The Lives of the* Saints ... I liked story time, and sat and listened with my eyes down, concentrating on my sewing ...

Mass in Latin was always the real beginning of the day, and on special feast days we had singing too ... I loved the singing. Some sisters, especially the music teachers, had exquisite voices and the harmony would swell to fill the chapel ... There was no singing on the day of my eighteenth birthday, however, as it was already Lent – the season of silence and penance preparing for Easter, when my parents would be permitted to visit me. I saw them last on Boxing Day for three hours when they came by train from Newcastle.

After Mass I went back to the dormitory to make my bed and tidy up before breakfast. [we're still not up to breakfast!] ... Breakfast was cereal with milk, which often tasted slightly off because the day's milk had been mixed with the day's before ... cold toast and a little butter ... we ate in silence ... After breakfast we did my charge (chores ...) ... By nine o'clock we were ready for the proceedings of the novitiate to begin. There were talks by the novice mistress on religious life, study of the rule of our Order, meditation, and learning the customs to be observed.

We broke for 'lunch' ... No biscuits today, and Lenten silence was everywhere until recreation time at 4.30 p.m. ...

On this day I walked close behind Sister Julie and whispered, 'Today's my birthday!' as we went up the steps to the novitiate. She half-turned to me and whispered, 'Happy birthday!' and we both had a quiet grin – until we ran slap-bang into the novice mistress. She said nothing but froze us with a look ...

Before the 1 p.m. dinner there were more prayers ... It was my turn to read in the refectory – a real ordeal ... At a sign from Reverend Mother – a tinkle on her small bell – I began to read from the assigned book. Today it was on the life of Saint Thérèse ...

Then it was back to the novitiate for the afternoon of study, music practice and private spiritual reading ... At 4 p.m. I went to have a cup of tea again. Today there was fresh bread and jam – a real treat for hungry young people. By 4.20 I was back in the chapel for Vespers before recreation, when Mother suggested a walk around the farm, and we were free to walk and talk as much as we liked. We sauntered along in threes – 'No twos, please!' – and at last I could legally tell people it was my birthday. We laughed and joked as we walked, and in spite of the stresses of silence and regimentation, life was good among my friends. Our friendships were meant to be general, however, not exclusive, so there were no 'best friends'.

Recreation was short but we always packed a lot into it, and let off steam. We went to Office again at 5.05 … After Office we had a lecture again – another story from The Lives of the Saints. Some of the stories were a bit weird … At study between six and seven o'clock we had set topics and time flew till the bell rang for supper … I was hoping it wasn't just beetroot as it sometimes was, but was relieved to see bowls of salad with cold meat on the table … I joined [the nuns in the chapel] to struggle with evening meditation till night recreation began at eight o'clock. This hour was my favourite time of the day. I'd talk and laugh with the others as we sat and did our sewing or some other craft … Promptly at nine o'clock the night prayer bell rang out and we all went into immediate and deep silence. We'd go back to the chapel for some more Office (called Compline) and a litany of the saints … By nine-thirty I was changing my shoes for slippers … I fell into bed as fast as I could because I was always tired, and knew 5 a.m. would come all too quickly.

At 10 p.m. the lights went out.[21]

Inglis – or Sister Mary Scholastica, as she then was – with minimal teacher training, was given a mixed kindergarten-first class of 75 at Tighes Hill.[22] She learned to cope with and like teaching and became a high school geography teacher. She graduated from Newcastle University with study on top of a full teaching load. But eventually, following her mother's death, she became severely depressed. She was admitted to St John of God Hospital Burwood and had sixteen treatments of ECT. Someone new took over the treatment and after stopping the ECT, asked if she thought she should leave religious life. She says "The idea of leaving had never occurred to me."[23] She recovered and went back to the convent. By then the major changes in religious life resulting from Vatican II were well under way. She was all for them, and took to counselling work and generally interacting with the wider community. At one point she is looking after a friend's small boys while the friend is away. The boys barge into the bathroom and see her topless. One of them says "My mummy's are only little ones. You've got big fat nippies." She shoos them out, falls about laughing, and comments that she didn't know whether she had big ones or not as she'd never seen other women's breasts.[24]

She became Mother Superior at Singleton but had had enough after a while, among other reasons, because of conflict with more conservative nuns. She left and obtained dispensation from her vows.

She had a hard time at first, with glandular fever, living alone, a long struggle to find a job, and a conviction for shoplifting. She got a teaching job and gradually sorted it out. She found a good husband through an ad in the paper, after some gruesome experiences on the singles scene ("a lot more toads out there wanting to be kissed than handsome princes"[25]). Some psychotherapy was helpful. She concluded from it that her father was more important to her than she had realised, and she hints that a wish to please him was significant in her decision to enter the convent. Here she explains to the therapist something about how different things were in the convent:

> I told him how the superior opened our letters, and had the right to read or even withhold them from us, both the letters which arrived for us and the letters we wrote. How we had to ask permission to write a letter. Permission might be refused, and if it was permitted, you were given just one sheet of paper. You then put your unsealed envelope and letter on the superior's desk for posting. This was a humiliating way for grown professional women to live, but again *it was just the way it was.*[26]

(It should be appreciated that "the way it was" was due not just to immemorial custom and the decisions of superiors but to the provisions of the 1917 Code of Canon Law, which decreed the censorship of letters, travelling in twos, eating separately from "seculars" and not attending the funerals of family members. Archbishop Kelly in Sydney insisted that nuns should not visit their dying parents.[27])

A rather similar story is by Eileen Jones. She was born in 1927 and grew up poor and poorly educated in Coogee. After some jobs and a near-engagement to a non-Catholic man who refused to marry in a Catholic Church, she joined an order of nuns (which she does not name but is the Brigidines). She was then just over 30 so needed a dispensation. Two features in common with Inglis's story are the role of choral music as an attraction of the religious life; and the problems of harsh decisions by superiors when she needed something, especially, in her case, treatment for serious medical conditions. She obtained a PhD in psychophysiology and left the order aged almost 70.[28]

Happy Souls

What is needed for a fair view of religious life is stories from, for example, ordinary parish priests who had their ups and downs but mostly just got on with their work and were overall happy with their lives. There are some such memoirs, but they are hard to find – they are published by small presses and not found in most libraries. Maybe they are not especially well written. Maybe the reading public wants something more salacious.

One example: Kevin Condon was born in Ireland in 1932 and grew up on a poor farm. He gained a scholarship to high school, which he says came with a tacit expectation of joining the Dominicans,[29] an expectation which was reinforced by a talk from his uncle, a Dominican prior. Although he is clear that that was unreasonable pressure, he says he has no regrets. He was sent off to Australia, which he was happy enough with though he would have preferred Nigeria. He was generally happy with everything he was ordered to do later, such as being parish priest of Wahroonga. His superiors seem to have been generally cooperative with him too. He is obviously blessed with a positive personality and a knack of getting on with people; though he does see himself as lacking in self-confidence, and soon after arriving in Australia he took a written course in "positive thinking" advertised in a newspaper (without telling his superiors).[30] As to celibacy, he mentions some challenges but keeps to it and thinks it worked well for him, though he is against it being compulsory.

Another priest happy enough with his lot is Noel McMaster. From suburban Melbourne, he joined the Redemptorist Juniorate in Galong in 1954. He describes a style of training somewhat similar to Morris West's but less severe. While agreeing it was narrow, he is less concerned by it. He describes himself at that time as "phlegmatic, callow, casual", personality traits no doubt useful in the context.[31] After some years teaching at the seminary and as an army chaplain – activities he sees as worthwhile but not entirely suiting him – he found more fulfillment in the Kimberley as parish priest of Kununurra and later Halls Creek. He came to see the typical church style of operation as somewhat out of tune with aboriginal culture and spirituality. That and his liking for the liberation theology of Juan Luis Segundo were factors in certain tensions between him and successive Bishops of Broome, but there was no serious falling out and he completed his mission successfully.

A different kind of story is the very detailed account of study in Rome in the Sixties by Peter Brock, younger brother of Paul Brock. It includes this story about canon law and the separation of clergy from laity. The very pious Italian spiritual director at Propaganda College explained to the students how pastorally broad-minded he was: once when cycling through the countryside he was approached by a young woman who asked him to hear her confession. Canon law of course did not permit a priest to be alone with a woman – confession could only be heard with the two separated by a wire grill. So, he upended the bicycle and heard confession through the back wheel.[32] (Peter Brock later apologised for an inappropriate relationship with boys and was charged but not convicted of sexual abuse.[33])

Much more on Rome from an Australian perspective can be read in two of the volumes of autobiography by the Jesuit theologian Gerald O'Collins, *A Midlife Journey* and *On the Left Bank of the Tiber*.[34]

A positive nun memoir, very focused on the inner life, is Mary Lalor's *The Inner Road*. In 1928 when she was six, her mother died, soon after giving birth to the last of ten children. Her father remarried and had six more children and she helped care for them. At the age of sixteen she discovered a vocation to the contemplative life.[35] Her father refused to allow that but did permit her to join the Sisters of Charity, which her elder sister, aunt and great-aunt had already joined. She completed the novitiate and taught primary school for some years, but retained her feeling that she was called to a contemplative order. She was allowed to join the Carmelite Monastery at Parkes in 1955. Although happy there, she felt in 1973 an "inner instruction" to live a Carmelite-like life outside the monastic setting. She left and founded a community in a shared house in inner-city Melbourne to pursue "Carmelite contemplative life in an open setting".[36] That proved to be the foundation of a small order. Throughout, most of the text is not about these facts of what she did, but expressions of her love for God and especially of her devotion to Mary, such as:

> Beloved Lord, Father All-Holy, Jesus Lord, Holy Spirit, I desire to do as You have said: Rest in our oneness, so that I may become more completely love, more completely light, for Your Glory and the good of my brothers and sisters.
>
> Mary, you tell me also: Rest in our oneness. O thank you![37]

It is obviously such thoughts that fill her mind most of the time.

Finally, my two favourites.

The first is *Banished Camelots: Recollections of a Catholic Childhood: A Celebration and a Requiem*, by John Redrup. Its account of boyhood between the wars combines a fine recall of detail with a sense of the child's point of view without too much adult reinterpretation. It includes a very positive, even starry-eyed, view of his years in the Marist Brothers' Juniorate in Mittagong, 1932–37. He recalls his reaction to the recruiting talk at his school by the head of the Juniorate. He is aged 11:

> As Brother Hubert told the story, his Juniorate seemed to me to combine the best features of all the English Boarding Schools I'd been reading about for years past in *Magnet, Gem, Champion, Nelson Lee, Boys' Own*, and *Chums*. There were playing-fields for every conceivable sport, a dam for swimming in and illimitable surrounding bushland in which to adventure. To be sure, Brother Hubert made no mention of Billy Bunter-style dormitory feasts … but my imagination amply corrected that oversight.
>
> I'm sure that the gentle Brother must have spoken of the more serious and spiritual aspects of training for a Marist Brother's life and of the subsequent vows of Poverty, Chastity and Obedience that would serve to separate new disciples utterly from 'the

world' that I'd hardly begun to be aware of; but I suspect that I absorbed little of this side of his message. What I did carry away ... was the notion that God determined whether a boy should become a Marist Brother by granting him the privilege of a 'vocation' ... In that class-room, on that day, I decided that I loved the Marist Brotherhood and that God wanted *me* to become a Marist Brother.[38]

He is too young at that time to join, but after a while the Brothers visit his parents, then hard-hit by the Depression. His father is not keen but agrees, saying to him, "The Brothers have explained to us that if we allow you to follow your wish and go to their Juniorate at Mittagong, you'll be assured of a finer education than perhaps we could otherwise afford to give you."[39]

He did enjoy the Juniorate, even if conditions were not quite as he had originally imagined them. His account of the daily regime resembles that of Cecilia's in the convent, except that it starts at 5.30, there is a lot more farm work, and there is a usual school day – the boys all study for the Intermediate and Leaving Certificates and high academic standards are expected. He writes "I developed a deep affection for the prayerful round of life that the Brothers maintained at their Juniorate. Until the storm-clouds of adolescence began to gather, I could still picture no better life for myself than to join their calm Order and doubts about my vocation never entered my head ... a large part of our vocation, I feel sure, stemmed from frank hero-worship."[40]

Of course, with teenaged boys, you still needed discipline. It worked like this. A series of coloured Monthly Behaviour Cards were given out, and too many pink or red ones meant days taken off the annual 10-day holiday at home. Points were lost for faults on the following scale:

Special Friendships	20	Unkindness	10
Breaking Silence	10	Irreverence	10
Disobedience	10	Unpunctuality	5
Inadequate effort	5	Bad language	5
Lack of frankness	5	Poor Demeanour	5
Un-sportsmanship	5	Untidiness	5

Does all this seem to suggest that the average Junior felt oppressed? Certainly not I … I regarded our playing-field as reassuringly level, the boundaries clearly marked, and the goalpost luminously clear and firmly-set.[41]

But he does criticise one aspect: the prohibition of special friendships, which he believed badly affected his ability to make lasting friendships in later life.[42]

He completed the Leaving Certificate in the Juniorate, but was told that he was too young to join the Novitiate and would have to repeat the year. The disappointment added to a summer holiday with girls around, and he found his vocation had disappeared. He became a radical university student, a senior journalist on *The Age*, and a consultant to UN development agencies.

My last example is François Xavier Gsell's *The Bishop with 150 Wives*. His story is told in an earlier chapter in this collection.

Final remarks

The selection of memoirs that has been published has some biases. As mentioned, there are more by ex-religious than religious, especially in easily available books, which gives a certain negativity of tone to the selection. There is a general shortage of nuns' stories.

There are none by an abuser of children (although there is a partly autobiographical book by an alleged abuser.)[43] A later article in this anthology describes Gerald Ridsdale's evidence to the Royal Commission on his life of offending.

Also lacking is anything much from the more distant past, before the 1930s. Apart from Gsell, the only one I have seen that goes back to "Around the Boree Log" days is Archbishop Duhig's string of anecdotes (starting on page 1 with the housekeeper at his first presbytery who "cooked fish better than anybody I have since known", and continuing with the importance of a good horse in a priest's life and his successes in buying real estate, and an interview with "the then-famous duce").[44]

One of the most dramatic effects of Vatican II was the collapse of vocations. That has often been taken by conservatives as a sign of the evil effects of the Council. In the light of the stories above, it may well be asked, was the decline of vocations a good thing or a bad thing? It is true that very many people benefited from the ministries – sacramental, educational, nursing – of the vocations of earlier times, so there is much to regret in the decline. But it is clear from the stories that before 1965, many people joined religious life who should not have done so. That should be taken into account when discussing the high level of vocations at that time.

---

[1] C James, *Unreliable Memoirs* (1980), 20.

[2] John Hanrahan, *From Eternity to Here: Memoirs of an Angry Priest* (Bystander Press, Northcote, Vic, 2002), 71.

[3] Hanrahan, *From Eternity to Here*, 16.

[4] Ibid., 59.

[5] Chris Geraghty, *The Priest Factory: A Manly Vision of Triumph, 1958-1972 and Beyond* (Spectrum Publications, Melbourne, 003), 141–151, 324–6.

[6] Paul Crittenden, *Changing Orders: Scenes of Clerical and Academic Life* (Brandl and Schlesinger, Blackheath, 2008), 138–41, 182–92.

[7] Ian Guthridge, *Give Me a Child When He Is Young* (Medici Publications, Port Melbourne, 1987).

[8] Morris West, *A View From the Ridge: The Testimony of a Pilgrim* (HarperCollins, Sydney, 1996), 6.

[9] Ibid., 6–7

[10] Ibid., 32.

[11] Edmund Campion, *Rockchoppers: Growing Up Catholic in Australia* (Penguin, Ringwood, Vic, 1982), 15–16.

[12] Colette Livermore, *Hope Endures: An Australian Sister's story of leaving Mother Teresa, losing faith, and her on-going search for meaning* (Heinemann, 2008); synopsis at http://www.colettelivermore.com.au/book.htm

13 Paul Brock, *A Passion for Life* (ABC Books, Sydney, 2004), 96–7.
14 Campion, *Rockchoppers*, 4.
15 Brock, *Passion for Life*, 106.
16 A brief recollection, possibly exaggerated, of Brock's teaching in *Oxford Book of Australian Schooldays*, ed. B. Niall, I. Britain and P. Williams (Oxford University Press, 1997), 265.
17 Brock, *Passion for Life*, 106.
18 Ibid., 107–111.
19 Without intending anything negative by the comparison, the phenomenon of multiple vocations in families could be compared to copycat suicides, in the sense that early teenagers can make dramatic decisions about their lives and do so in imitation of others. A study of vocations in families is Beverley Zimmerman, 'She came from a fine Catholic family': religious sisterhoods of the Maitland diocese, 1867–1901, *Australian Historical Studies* 31 (115) (2000), 251–272.
20 Cecilia Inglis, *Cecilia: An Ex-Nun's Extraordinary Journey* (Penguin, Camberwell Vic, 2003), 49.
21 Inglis, *Cecilia*, 71–84.
22 Ibid., 100.
23 Ibid., 175.
24 Ibid., 208–9.
25 Ibid., 325.
26 Ibid., 294.
27 Anne O'Brien, *God's Willing Workers: Women and Religion and Australia* (UNSW Press, Sydney 2005), 190.
28 Eileen Jones, *The Accidental Poet* (Ginninderra Press, Canberra, 2007).
29 Kevin Condon, *Here I Am Lord: Memories and Musings of a Wandering Dominican*, 8.
30 Ibid., 27.
31 Noel McMaster, *From Coburg to the Kimberley* (David Lovell Publishing, Kew East, 2010), 16.
32 Peter Brock, *Home Rome Home* (Spectrum, Melbourne, 2001), 62.
33 http://www.brokenrites.org.au/drupal/node/120
34 Gerald O'Collins, *A Midlife Journey* (Connor Court, Ballan, 2012); *On the Left Bank of the Tiber* (Connor Court, Ballarat, 2013).
35 Mary Lalor, *The Inner Road (A Legacy of Love): Autobiography of Sister Mary Lalor, Foundress of the Little Sisters of Our Lady of Mount Carmel* (Little Sisters of Our Lady of Mount Carmel, Hawker SA, 1984), 1–16.
36 Ibid., 56.
37 Lalor, *The Inner Road*, 141.
38 John Redrup, *Banished Camelots* (Bookpress, Sydney, 1997), 228.
39 Ibid., 245.
40 Ibid., 266, 271.
41 Ibid., 279.

42 Ibid., 280.

43 John I. Fleming, *Convinced by the Truth: Embracing the Fullness of Catholic Faith* (Connor Court, Ballan Vic, 2010)

44 James Duhig, *Crowded Years* (Angus and Robertson, Sydney, 1947); it can be compared with his biography: T.P. Boland, *James Duhig* (University of Queensland Press, St Lucia, 1986).

12

Calwell, Catholicism and the origins of multicultural Australia*

Abstract: Arthur Calwell's postwar immigration program transformed Australia from an Anglo-Celtic monoculture to a multicultural nation. It is argued that he intended that result, and that his and his government's motivations included not only a perceived need for more population and for more workers for nation-building, but a Catholic belief in the rights of refugees to a share of rich lands and a desire to assist the anti-Communist, largely Catholic, refugees from the Red Army.

In the middle of 1947, Australia was an Anglophone country with very few immigrants from anywhere except Britain and Ireland. On a wave of "populate or perish" sentiment driven by the Japanese near-invasion five years earlier, it had its first Minister for Immigration, Arthur Calwell. But despite his energy and ability, few immigrants had arrived, mainly due to shipping problems, and it was unclear where large numbers could come from or how they could get here. He had also promised the Australian people ten British migrants for every non-British one.

At the same time, there were a million "Displaced Persons" (DPs) in camps in Western Europe. They were Eastern European anti-Communist refugees who had fled the Red Army and then had avoided being sent back East by the victorious Western allies. They had been surviving in basic camps as an unsolved minor problem of the early Cold War. 60% of them were Catholics (Ukrainians, Lithuanians and Poles, typically).[1]

By early 1950, the camps were empty and some had been burned down. In contrast to the usual persistent failure of the international community to solve refugee problems, almost all the DPs had been resettled. 180,000 of them were "New Australians", as Calwell cun-

---

* *Proceedings of the 2009 Australian Catholic Historical Society 2009 Conference*, 42–54.

ningly called them. They constituted some 2% of the Australian population.[2] Australia had started on the road to multiculturalism and it never looked back.

So what happened? How did the Australian people, without being asked, suddenly find themselves taking in nearly two hundred thousand refugees from countries they had barely heard of and from which there had been virtually no migrants before?

Let us step back and look at the background in three parts: what was happening in Europe where the DPs came from, then the situation in Australia, then the Catholic aspects.

Europe after devastation

In the summer of 1945, central Europe was a very disturbed place, and it looked like staying that way. In hindsight, we know that the Iron Curtain locked into place approximately along the line of the disposition of forces on the day of Hitler's death, and that Europe to the West of that line quite quickly recovered to a long period of peace, prosperity and democracy. That seemed an unlikely outcome in mid-1945. The thirty years of continuous disasters since 1914 had culminated in the discovery of the Holocaust. There was a power vacuum in central Europe with the collapse of the Nazi regime. Power lay with the Red Army in the East and the Anglo-American army in the West, neither of which was equipped to run civil governments. The Anglo-American army planned to go home as soon as possible. The British, in any case, had run out of money and their new Labour government was full of pro-Soviet sentiment. The Communist parties in the West were very strong and working on seizing power, probably with the aid of the Red Army, which had done the main job of defeating Hitler and was aggrieved that the Anglo-American army had somehow got as far east as Berlin and Vienna. Germany was in the grip of famine and its industry and infrastructure were bombed flat. Stalinist regimes were consolidating in Eastern Europe.

There were millions of people in the wrong place, the main groups being forced labourers in German industry and those who had fled West in front of the Red Army's advance. There was a distinct mass of

Jewish refugees, mostly keen to live anywhere except Europe. In 1945 and the few years following, nearly all the *Volksdeutsche*, the ethnic Germans who had lived in Eastern Europe for centuries, fled or were expelled west; at around 12 million people, it was (and still is) arguably the largest mass movement in history.

In the next two years, 1946 and 1947, the dust cleared and the worst fears for Western Europe were not realised. However, there was not much improvement and things still hung in the balance. It remained very unclear how to find a functioning government in Germany and Italy. Where were there experienced leaders who were neither Communist nor tainted with fascism? The American, British and French zones of Germany were put together as a new "West Germany" despite intense Russian opposition. In Italy, it looked close to certain that the Communist Party would win the election due in 1948 – and at the same time that an isolationist Republican would win the US Presidential election due for the same year, leaving Western Europe with hardly any military or economic protection against Soviet ambitions. Economic revival was proving very slow, both in Europe and in Britain, where bread rationing was introduced, a measure that had never been needed in the War. On top of that, the winter of 1946–7 was horrendous.

So government leaders had a lot on their minds. One problem that nearly slipped off the radar was the remaining mass of refugees in camps in Germany, Austria and Italy. Most of the millions of people displaced by the war were sent home very quickly, sometimes willingly and sometimes not. But with the development of the Cold War, the Western allies quickly lost their appetite for forcibly repatriating anti-Communists refugees to be shot. A million Eastern European refugees thus stayed in camps as an unsolved problem. Jewish refugees were not going to be resettled in Europe either, and advocates for them in the United States agitated to have a homeland found for them. Among many smaller-scale refugee problems, the Polish Second Army Corps of over 100,000 men remained in Italy, armed and keen to invade Poland.[3]

In those dark times, it would have been easy to give in to pessimism and repeat the mistakes of the period after the Armistice of

1918. The world could have plunged into another round of the shabby compromises and lost opportunities of the decades between the Wars. Instead there emerged a number of remarkably intelligent and energetic men who collaborated to solve all the main problems and create the peaceful and prosperous democratic West that we live in today. Their leader was Harry Truman, who had become President when Roosevelt died and lacked relevant experience, but quickly worked out which way was up in dealing with Stalin; he was assisted by two very competent Secretaries of State, George C. Marshall and Dean Acheson. He managed to survive isolationist trends to just win the election of 1948, pour money into war-ravaged Western Europe through the Marshall Plan, and contain Communism in Greece, Korea and elsewhere. In Britain, the Prime Minister, Clement Attlee, and his Foreign Secretary, Ernest Bevin, also ran an anti-Communist line and preserved a British army on the Rhine. In Western Europe, leaders were found among Catholics with solid anti-Fascist credentials: Konrad Adenauer in Germany, Alcide de Gasperi in Italy (who had survived the War in the Vatican Library), and Robert Schuman in France. They had the support of the equally able man in the Vatican who ran its foreign policy, Under-Secretary of State Mgr Giovanni Battista Montini, later Pope Paul VI. By 1950, under their stable leadership and with the help of the Marshall Plan, Western Europe had not only shown astonishing economic recovery but was embarked on an ambitious plan that would have looked ludicrous ten or even five years earlier: political unity. The European Coal and Steel Community was formed, the forerunner of the European Community.

In Australia

Australia had some leaders of the same calibre, men equally determined to make a new, peaceful and just world out of the wreckage of the past, with a realistic understanding of Cold War problems and a grasp of the need for international cooperation. Like the Western European leaders, they were Catholic: Prime Minister Ben Chifley and his Minister for Immigration and for Information, Arthur Calwell. Australia was of course far from the Cold War and not capable of playing any major part in it. But it did have one relevant resource:

space. Space was useful in two ways in the Cold War: to test atomic bombs in, and to send unwanted people to.

Let us go back to survey the Australian scene, especially with regard to immigration. Australia between the Wars was well out of the mainstream of history, and glad of it. In the Depression of the 1930s, Australia had a low birthrate but was not keen to supplement the population with immigration, because of the fear of foreigners taking Australians' jobs. There had been a great deal of fuss just before the War about a mere 7000 Jewish "reffos".

The Labor Party in particular supported immigration restriction, with a certain amount of simple racism being supplemented by fears of cheap foreign labour. An incident from the federal election campaign of 1928 is a vivid illustration of the attitudes of those times. The Labor candidate for the seat of Macquarie in central New South Wales had fought a clean campaign in 1925, only to see it buried by conservative scares about Labor links with Communists. In 1928 he fought back with a campaign against the "invasion of 30,000 aliens" sponsored by the Bruce Government. A stream of "Jugo-Slovakians" and "Czecho Slavs", "scabs of the worst kind", were being brought in to displace Australian workers. A fight between Dagoes and Australians in Melbourne was a "forerunner of what was likely to happen in the future unless the stream of these most undesirable immigrants was stemmed"; "Australia was supposed to be a white man's country, but Mr Bruce and his Government were fast making it a hybrid." There were "hundreds of Italians, Jugo-Slavians and Czecho-Slovakians" working on the Melbourne waterfront, while Australians were left to walk the streets and their wives and children starved.[4] The campaign was successful, and that is how Ben Chifley first gained a seat in Parliament.

Australia's complacency was rudely shattered by the fall of Singapore and the bombing of Darwin, and at the end of the War there was a consensus expressed in the phrase "Populate or perish": that Australia would have to find white immigrants to strengthen itself against the Asian hordes to the north. As one aspect of vast plans for postwar reconstruction that came to include such high-profile projects as the Snowy Mountains Scheme and the first Holden car (and less happily bank nationalisation), immigration plans on a large scale were announced. Arthur Calwell was appointed Australia's first Minister for Immigration and vigorously set about finding immigrants. It proved not so easy. While initially there were many Britons keen to come, it was impossible to find shipping. A good proportion of Britain's merchant navy was at the bottom of the Atlantic where U-boats had put it, while the rest and new ships built were desperately needed to revive Britain's shattered export industries. What passenger ships were available for migration were not likely to be spared for the long voyage to Australia. Calwell tried many ideas, including a plan for 50,000 child migrants and another to hire an aircraft carrier, but by well into 1947, very little had been achieved. The difficulties of having non-British immigrants were underscored when a single ship, the *Misr*, arrived in Melbourne in April 1947 after a chaotic voyage from Haifa and Mombasa, leading to a media storm about the filthy conditions on board with overtones relating to the somewhat suntanned complexions of the refugees.[5] If there was to be any more than a trickle of immigrants, someone was going to have to think of something.

Meanwhile back in the camps of Europe, the Displaced Persons' natural belief that they had fallen down a memory hole proved not to be true. Despite the large number of more major problems occupying the minds of Western leaders, the DP problem received recurrent attention. The Vatican, especially, kept informed about the camps and repeatedly reminded Western governments of the problem. When Justin Simonds, Coadjutor Archbishop of Melbourne, visited Europe on behalf of the Australian bishops in 1946, Montini provided him with a car to tour the camps and see for himself. The Catholic Church also a number of times put forward its teaching that rich countries with space had an ethical obligation to take in refugees, and indeed that they had no moral right to refuse to take reasonable numbers. For example Pius XII wrote to the American Catholic bishops in 1948:

> You know indeed how preoccupied we have been and with what anxiety we have followed those who have been forced by revolu-

tions in their own countries, or by unemployment or hunger to leave their homes and live in foreign lands.

The natural law itself, no less than devotion to humanity, urges that ways of migration be opened to these people. For the Creator of the universe made all good things primarily for the good of all. Since land everywhere offers the possibility of supporting a large number of people, the sovereignty of the State, although it must be respected, cannot be exaggerated to the point that access to this land is, for inadequate or unjustified reasons, denied to needy or decent people from other nations, provided of course, that the public wealth, considered very carefully, does not forbid this. [6]

At some point around the beginning of 1947, the Truman and Attlee administrations reached a number of hard decisions about the Cold War. They included a decision to build a British atomic bomb, which the British economy could ill afford, and to finally name a date for Indian independence. Included was a decision to clean up the Displaced Persons problem once and for all. For the Jewish refugees, the British would give up their opposition to a Jewish state in Palestine and the Jews would go there. The rest, the East Europeans, would be parcelled out to countries around the world, as far as they could be leaned on to take them. Britain itself took a large number, including most of the Polish ex-servicemen. Truman was keen for the United States to do its share, but it was initially impossible because of quotas previously imposed by Congress and it was not until 1948 that a new act made it possible for large numbers to go there.[7] Canada and some South American countries proved reasonably hospitable, helped by their traditions of European immigration. But the British remembered another country, distant certainly and unused to European immigrants, but with plenty of space, prosperity and with a long record as a place to dump people.

Viscount Addison, Secretary of State for Dominion Affairs, wrote to the Australian High Commissioner urging that Australia sign up to the International Refugee Organisation, the new body tasked with resettling the DPs. Signing carried the implication of taking some of the DPs:

SECRET
DOMINIONS OFFICE
DOWNING STREET
S.W.1
14th March, 1947
Dear Mr. Beasley,

We are naturally hesitant to appear to be urging the Commonwealth Government to accept additional obligations in the matter of provision for displaced persons, having regard to the extensive plans that they are making for the reception of various classes of immigrants, which, as you know, we very much appreciate, and we fully realise the difficulty which they may feel in accepting any further burdens.

In view, however, of the important considerations in the international sphere referred to in the enclosed memorandum, I should be grateful if you would bring the matter to the notice of your Government in the hope that they will give the fullest consideration to the possibility of signing and accepting the Constitution of the Organisation, which would be a most valuable and appropriate contribution to the re-establishment of political and social security, not only in Europe, but throughout the world.

Acceptance does not, of course, involve any commitment on the part of accepting countries to receive immigrants which they do not wish to take.

Sincerely yours,

(sgd.) ADDISON [8]

The request was taken seriously but nothing happened about signing. In May Addison wrote again, not quite so politely:

If it [the IRO constitution] cannot be brought into force within next two or three weeks, it looks as though the whole scheme for an International solution of refugee problem on which we have been working so hard for past eighteen months, might have to be abandoned with most disastrous consequences, not only from social and economical, but even from the political point of view. Indeed, if no solution of refugee problem is found, these unhappy people will constitute a disturbing element which may well prejudice and delay economic, social and political recovery of Europe and constitute a further element of potential friction in a situation which is already quite dangerous enough.⁹

Australia signed as requested within a fortnight. Calwell visited Europe and on 21 July 1947, signed an agreement with the IRO to take 12,000 Displaced Persons, soon increased to 20,000. With an amazing feat of organisation, the system was put in place and one ship full of refugees, the *General Heintzelman*, arrived in Fremantle on 28 November.¹⁰

That left a number of problems. How were the people to be selected? Where was the shipping to come from? What was to be done with the refugees when they arrived? And last and most awkwardly, how were the Australian people to be persuaded that they would love to take them?

The shipping problem was solved by the Truman administration, which provided half a dozen converted army transports. The reception problem was solved by housing them in converted army camps in Australia and bonding them to work for two years as directed by the government, which made for a convincing case that they were of benefit for national development (and possibly also ensured they didn't create anti-Labor feeling in marginal electorates before the election of 1949). Calwell believed that the hardest problem lay in keeping public opinion onside. He threw everything into it. Only an old Labor man of the strictest orthodoxy such as himself could have kept the unions on side, always suspicious as they were of immigrant workers – only the Communists objected, with *Tribune* spouting Moscow's line about "Calwell's Balt concentration camp guards".¹¹ The RSL was persuaded not to worry about which side the refugees had been on during the War.¹² The media bought a series of feel-good stories about the benefits of "New Australians" for the Snowy Mountains Scheme. The *Sydney Morning Herald*'s 'Young migrants from Baltic countries revel in Australian outdoors ... first camp wedding ... all fine swimmers'¹³ was exceeded by the *Catholic Weekly*'s editorial on the "amazing similarity" between the Balts and the Irish (referring not so much to racial characteristics as to their flight to the ends of the earth from the heel of a foreign oppressor).¹⁴ And a great deal of effort was put into carefully selecting the first shiploads of immigrants for their media appeal. The 844 passengers on the *General Heintzelman* had, by deliberate choice, a very strong bias towards young, blonde, blue-eyed Baltic people (hence mostly Protestant). There were no Jews.[15] Calwell later wrote in his autobiography:

> After deliberating the issue we decided to select a 'choice sample' of displaced persons as migrants. We would bring one shipload with nobody under fifteen and nobody over thirty-five, all of whom had to be single. ... Many were red-headed and blue-eyed. There was also a number of natural platinum blondes of both sexes. The men were handsome and the women beautiful. It was not hard to sell immigration to the Australian people once the press published photographs of that group.[16]

When they arrived, Calwell rushed to the dockside to be photographed with them, which made them look even better. They danced

Arthur Calwell with the Latvian Kalnins family
(50,000th New Australian), 1949[18]

fetchingly in national costume for the movie cameras and expressed in excellent though accented English their gratitude for being allowed in such a wonderful country as Australia. Once that was over, the selection criteria were quickly extended without fanfare to include Ukrainians, old people, almost anyone without TB.

Then, just as the program was getting into its stride in 1948, it nearly fell apart. Stalin decided to push the envelope in Europe. He blockaded West Berlin, which was completely surrounded by the Russian-occupied zone of Germany. Because of the extra tension, the Americans secretly ordered that the troop carriers they had loaned should not go into the southern hemisphere in case they were needed to evacuate Europe.[17]

The crisis blew over when the Americans supplied Berlin by a massive airlift, but in the meantime Calwell had taken a bold step. To affirm Australia's place as a major player in the Displaced Persons emigration, he took the figure of 20,000 that Australia had agreed to take, and added a zero.[19] With increasing speed, almost all the refugees were selected by the different countries and sent out to their new homes. Australia took more than any country except the United States and more per head of its own population than any country except Israel. Australia's 180,000 or so were distributed approximately as follows:[20]

Poles	60,300	90% Catholic
Yugoslavs	23,300	64% Catholic
Ukrainians	19,600	57% Catholic
Latvians	19,600	12% Catholic
Hungarians	13,300	74% Catholic
Lithuanians	10,100	74% Catholic
Czechoslovakians	9,900	80% Catholic
Estonians	6,000	2% Catholic
Russians	4,900	15% Catholic
Romanians	2,200	42% Catholic
Others	12,900	
Total	182,200	

Calwell's intentions

What remains not entirely clear is the extent to which Calwell intended to have the effect that his actions actually did have, of creating a multicultural, less than true British, Australia. For obvious reasons, he would not have revealed any such intentions to the public, if he did have them. There is some evidence, nevertheless.

It is inherently unlikely that Calwell should have been enthusiastic about his promise of 10 Britons for every non-Briton, given for example his arrest during the First World War as a suspected Irish agitator. He had written confidentially to Chifley in 1944 of his "determination to develop a heterogeneous society: a society where Irishness and Roman Catholicism would be as acceptable as Englishness and Protestantism; where an Italian background would be as acceptable as a Greek, a Dutch or any other".[21] Calwell later acknowledged Chifley's support, saying "Had we had an anti-immigration man as prime minister, or a lukewarm one, we would still be a dull inbred country of predominantly British stock." [22] (This was in a comment to the *Auckland Star* newspaper; the New Zealanders could reasonably have taken offence at that as their country took only 5000 DPs.)

Calwell once replied "Yes" to the question, "Do you think that the Australian way of life will suffer any change as a result of the great migration movement?",[23] and his secretary gave the same answer to the question whether Calwell had intended to change the orientation in Australian society away from a narrowly British mould.[24]

Some direct evidence of Calwell's thinking comes from correspondence between him and Montini in 1949, after the displaced persons immigration scheme was well under way. Montini's letter concludes:

> His Holiness prays that Your Excellency's activity in the field of immigration may continue to open up new avenues of life for the many thousands of people whose future at the moment seems bereft of hope, and, as a token of his paternal benevolence, He imparts to you His Apostolic Blessing.[25]

It would be possible to regard this as no more than a piece of polite Italianate officialese. On the face of it, the language is far from effusive. That is not how Calwell read it. He wrote requesting a cleaner copy, and distributed copies of it to those in the Catholic Church who had most enthusiastically worked to promote immigration: Mannix, Duhig and others. His covering letter says that the Pope's words apply to "everyone who like yourself has given such willing and helpful co-operation in the implementation of the plans which have excited the interest and won the commendation of the Supreme Pontiff". He replied to Montini:

> I was deeply touched by the expression of the Supreme Pontiff's paternal regard when he bestowed His Apostolic Blessing on me and on the work in which I am engaged as Minister of State in the Commonwealth of Australia. It is most gratifying to know that the work of arranging for the settlement of an ever increasing number in Australia of Displaced Persons from European countries meets with such august approval and evokes such touching commendation ... I ask you to accept the assurance that no letter which I have written in the six years in which I have been privileged to hold Ministerial office in this country has given me greater pleasure than this acknowledgement of the Holy Father's appreciation of my humble efforts in the cause of distressed humanity.[26]

Calwell's reaction – or overreaction – to the Pope's commendation is more significant than Montini's letter itself. The most difficult thing to know about is Calwell's private motivation, so the superlatives in which he expresses his pleasure at the Pope's message are of great interest.

Epilogue #1

In 1964, a brown paper parcel arrived at Calwell's office. It proved to contain a document from Rome in Latin. When translated, it revealed that Calwell was now Knight Commander of the Order of St Gregory the Great with the Grand Silver Star. Though it has no detailed citation, he later heard it was awarded in honour of his general devotion to the Church, the possibility (by then remote) of becoming Prime Minister, and his work on post-war immigration. It was well deserved.[27]

Epilogue #2

In the late 1970s, the Vietnamese government proved itself a typical Stalinist regime. By 1979 50,000 people a month were fleeing in boats and the countries of south-east Asia were starting to tow them back out to sea. The Catholic bishops and B. A. Santamaria, among others, urged Australia to take some. The U.S. State Department organised a solution to the problem, involving bribing the Vietnamese to stop sending them and distributing the refugees to countries willing to take them.[28] Australia signed up for a few thousand, though there was little support in opinion polls. They eventually took a number hard to determine but possibly about 150,000. Sydney became an Asian city.

---

[1] M. Wyman, *Europe's Displaced Persons*, 1945–1951 (Ithaca, 1998).

[2] A. Markus, 'Labour and immigration 1946–9: the displaced persons prram', *Labour History* 47 (1984), 73–90.

[3] W. Anders, *An Army in Exile* (London, 1949).

[4] D. Day, *Chifley* (Sydney, 2001), 230–2

[5] 'The first wave: beyond a White Australia', *Sydney Morning Herald* multimedia feature, 2007: https://web.archive.org/web/20070901181905/http://www.smh.com.au/multimedia/misr/main.html

[6] Pius XII to Cardinal McNicholas, 24/12/48, in *Acta Apostolicae Sedis* 41, 69-70, quoted in 'Exsul familia', *Constitutio apostolica de spirituali emigrantium cura* (30 Sept 1952), in *Acta Apostolicae Sedis* 44 (1952), 649–704, at 675–87; trans. in *The Church's Magna Charta for Migrants*, ed. G. Tessarolo (Staten Island, NY, 1962), 23–100, at p. 51.

[7] H. Genizi, America's Fair Share: The Admission and Resettlement of Displaced Persons, 1945–1952 (Detroit, 1993).

[8] Australian Archives, series A698014 item S250104, last (i.e. chronologically first) document.

[9] In Beasley to Chifley, 1/5/47, repr. in W. J. Hudson & W. Way, eds, *Documents on Australian Foreign Policy 1937–49*, vol. XII (Canberra, 1995), 484.

[10] 'The General Heintzelman and the Kanimbla', in J. Jued, *The Australian People: An encyclopedia of the nation, its people* (2nd ed, Cambridge, 2001), 74–5.

[11] 'Imported Nazi bullies are ready to run Australian Belsen for Calwell', Tribune 3/8/49, 3; 'Calwell brings in stormtroopers', 29/1/49, 7.

[12] Refugees for Australia: R.S.L. attacks proposal', Age 24/7/47, 3; 'Calwell gives defence of migrants' plan', Sydney Morning Herald 26/7/47, 4; A.A. Calwell, 'Populate or perish: Japan can rise again', *Reveille* 21 (5) (Jan, 1948), 6–7.

[13] *SMH* 17/12/47, 2, further in J. Persian, *Beautiful Balts: From displaced persons to New Australians* (NewSouth, Sydney, 2017).

[14] 'Editorial: For some New Australians', *Catholic Weekly* 18/12/47, 4, https://trove.nla.gov.au/newspaper/article/146605881: cf. 'Cardinal urges migration', *SMH* 2/10/47, 3.

[15] S. D. Rutland, *Edge of the Diaspora: Two Centuries of Jewish Settlement in Australia* (Sydney, 1997), 238–40; S.D. Rutland, 'Subtle exclusions: Postwar Jewish emigration to Australia and the impact of the IRO scheme', *Journal of Holocaust Education* 10 (2001), 50–66.

[16] A. A. Calwell, *Be Just and Fear Not* (Melbourne, 1972), 103.

[17] 'Shipping for displaced persons: agenda for meeting of Commonwealth Immigration Advisory Council', in AA A6980/4 item S250105.

[18] (National Archives of Australia, image no. 8318052, in the public domain at: http://commons.wikimedia.org/wiki/File:KalninsFamily%26Calwell1949.jpg)

[19] Chifley to Truman, 2/7/48, and Truman to Chifley, 19/7/48, and Calwell's public statement, 8/7/48, AA A6980/4 item S250105; Foreign Relations of the United States 1948 vol VI, 3; '200,000 Balts if ships given', *Argus* 9/7/48, https://trove.nla.gov.au/newspaper/article/22678526

[20] Figures for total arrivals from Table 48 of M. Proudfoot, *European Refugees, 1939–52* (London, 1957); figures for religion from E. F. Kunz, *Displaced Persons: Calwell's New Australians* (Sydney, 1988), table 4.2, 'Religion of displaced persons in Australia in conjunction with nationality', taken from Zubrzycki's 10% survey.

[21] Quoted in J. Zubrzycki, *Arthur Calwell and the Origin of Post-War Immigration* (Canberra, 1995), 4–5.

[22] Calwell in *Auckland Star* 26/1/65, quoted in Kiernan, *Calwell: A political and persona biography* (West Melbourne, 1978), 119.

[23] *Australasian Post* 17/11/49, quoted in Kiernan, Calwell, 118

[24] Recorded interview with Joan O'Donnell, 15/5/75, quoted in Kiernan, 118.

[25] Montini to Calwell, 4/4/49, in Calwell papers, National Library of Australia, Box 62.

[26] Calwell to Montini, 30/6/49.

[27] Calwell, *Be Just and Fear Not*, 159–61.

[28] G. Loescher & J. A. Scanlan, *Calculated Kindness: Refugees and America's Half-Open Door, 1945 to the Present* (New York, 1986), ch. 7; B. Wain, *The Refused: The Agony of the Indochinese Refugees* (New York, 1981), ch. 11; N. Viviani, *The Long Journey: Vietnamese Migration and Settlement in Australia* (Melbourne, 1984), ch. 5.

13

Catholic Action, Sydney style: lay organisations from friendly societies to the Vice Squad[*]

Abstract: Sydney Catholics in the mid-twentieth century were organised into a large number of active and effective associations, from parish sodalities and professional guilds up to the Cahill government. Parish-based and larger organisations supplied a body of people accustomed to uniformity of beliefs and to coordinated action in support of those beliefs, easily mobilised against Communism and in favour of Catholic moral and political positions. Pragmatic, informed by implicit moral views rather than explicit theory, and clerically controlled, Catholic Action in Sydney proved more able than its Melbourne counterpart in controlling the levers of political power. The heavily Catholic Cahill government and its police force, spearheaded by the Vice Squad, built on this organisational infrastructure to implement in law and policing a conservative moral agenda, including a vigorous pursuit of homosexuals and the music conductor and sexual experimenter Sir Eugene Goossens.

The mid-twentieth century was the high point of lay Catholic societies in Australia. The best known are those associated with B. A. Santamaria and based in Melbourne, the Campion Society and the anti-Communist "Movement" with its various offshoots such as the National Catholic Rural Movement. The wide array of mass lay organisations in New South Wales are much less known, but in their time they had a huge membership and influence.

It is often said that Catholic Action in Sydney lacked the vigour of the Melbourne organisations, and that "Catholic Action in Sydney remained diffuse and uncoordinated"[1] and stunted by its strict clerical control. That judgement may be strictly true, but behind the

---

[*] *Journal of the Royal Australian Historical Society* 108 (2) (2022), 172-201, slightly edited. I am grateful to John Luttrell, David Hilliard and Edmund Campion for helpful comments.

scenes a remarkably effective collection of interconnected organisations was coming into existence. When the Victorian Movement's independence as a vast organisation out of external control led to disaster in the Labor Split of 1955, the close clerical connections of Sydney Catholic Action meant it survived, as did its ally, the Catholic-dominated state government of J.J. Cahill (premier 1952-59). As David Hilliard puts it,

> Sydney Catholicism had its own distinctive style: pragmatic, unintellectual, ultramontane in piety, closely linked to the Labor Party, which had ruled in New South Wales since 1941. The Catholic community, with its own system of primary and secondary schools, was reinforced by scores of pious societies, social and sporting clubs, and guilds for Catholics in particular professions and occupations. During the 1950s Sydney's Catholic subculture expanded rather than dwindled and new societies were formed ...[2]

Michael Hogan writes similarly,

> It is the reinforcing coincidence of political styles which has led both Church and party leaders to be pragmatic, bureaucratic and moderate. This can be contrasted with the situation in Victoria where completely different styles in the Church and in the party have reinforced both in a confrontational, radical (left and right), separatist mould of symbolic politics.[3]

The Sydney style was less confrontational and ideological than Melbourne's, more pragmatic (but not aimless or lacking in coherent goals) and reliant on quiet backroom negotiations. Not coincidentally, it was more successful in achieving its aims.

PART I: Organised Catholic laity in Sydney, 1900–1960

Benefit societies and sodalities

In common with the Church in many European and colonial countries,[4] the Australian Catholic Church in the late nineteenth century and early twentieth century saw an extraordinary flourishing of lay societies designed to create a complete Catholic culture covering all aspects of life.

Those associations built on an older tradition. In 1845 Archbishop Polding founded the Australasian (later Australian) Holy Catholic (AHC) Guild. It operated mainly as a friendly society, that is, in return for regular contributions from working men it provided sick pay, medical and pharmaceutical benefits and funeral benefits. It competed with the Victorian-based Hibernian Australasian Catholic Benefit Society, which Polding considered too Irish.[5] In the decades before state social security, such "friendly societies" played a crucial role in enabling working people to survive health disasters. The societies, including non-Catholic ones such as the Oddfellows, also had a spiritual and social aspect.[6] The reach and importance of the many branches of those societies can be seen in the long account of the annual communion breakfast of the Australian Holy Catholic Guild in Boorowa in 1907, which had 49 members and a credit of £772. (It was attended by representatives of the opposition, the Oddfellows.)[7] Friendly societies survived into the later twentieth century, but became less relevant with better state social security and private health insurance.

From the late nineteenth century there was a strong tradition of parish-based sodalities such as the Holy Name Society, Children of Mary for purely spiritual purposes,[8] the St Vincent de Paul Society for charitable work,[9] and the Catholic Youth Organisation (CYO) for a combination of spiritual and social purposes.[10] Every age group above the age of reason was catered for, with older infants enrolled in the Holy Angels Sodality.[11] Even small and remote parishes usually had a range of active sodalities. In its centenary year, 1952, the parish of Mudgee had an AHC Guild, St Vincent de Paul Society, Children of Mary, a school Parents and Friends Association, Holy Name Society, Sacred Heart Sodality, Catholic Women's Club, Legion of Mary, Sewing Guild, Altar Society, the People's Eucharistic League and the CYO.[12] All from a Catholic population of around 1500.[13]

The Catholic organised laity were on show in their thousands at the International Eucharistic Congress in Sydney in 1928.[14] In 1934, a series of impressive photos were taken by the celebrated press photographers Sam and Ted Hood at the annual Corpus Christi procession at St Patrick's College Manly:

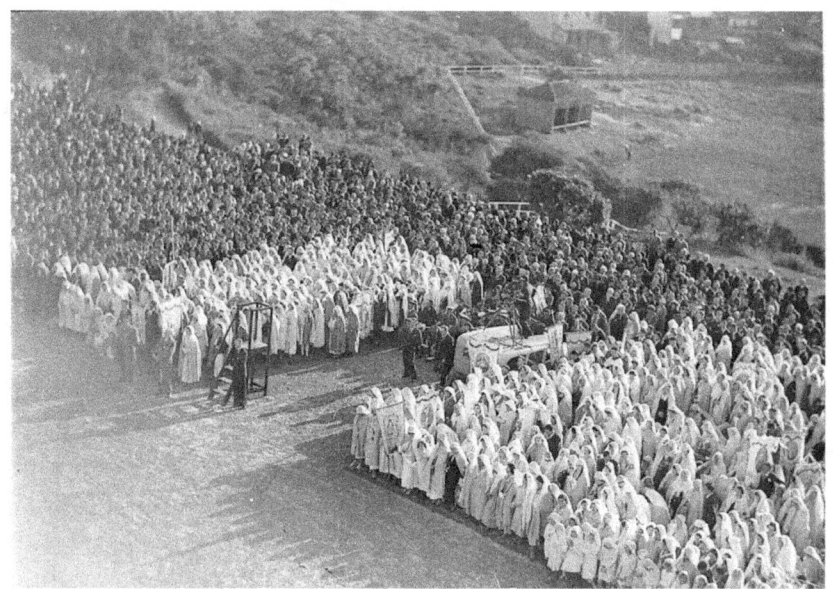

Corpus Christi Procession, St Patrick's College Manly, 3 June 1934
Photographer Ted Hood. State Library of New South Wales: https://collection.sl.nsw.gov.au/record/94R7mO01

Members of Holy Angels Sodality, Corpus Christi, St Patrick's College, 7 June 1934
Photographer Ted Hood. State Library of New South Wales, https://collection.sl.nsw.gov.au/record/npA2Gol1

Some organisations were for more than purely spiritual and charitable purposes. A major attempt at a Catholic political party around 1920, the Catholic Federation, was unsuccessful.[15] Action moved behind the scenes. The Knights of the Southern Cross – by the 1930s "by far the most powerful and cohesive lay organisation in New South Wales", according to Patrick O'Farrell[16] – was formed largely to combat employment discrimination against Catholics. As a Catholic counterpart and rival to the Freemasons, it put pressure on anti-Catholic employers as well as acting as an employment agency for young Catholic men in need of a job.[17] Large Catholic Clubs in the city and suburbs had little spiritual activity and resembled typical sporting, social and gambling clubs such as Leagues Clubs, but had the effect of segregating Catholics from mainstream society.[18] Dr P. J. Ryan MSC – a philosophy lecturer who was to become the intellectual leader of Catholic Action in Sydney as well as a prominent anti-Communist speaker and organiser[19] – criticised the laity as the "church dormant" and organised some to teach Catholic children in state schools from 1932.[20] Also established with the aim of evangelisation was the Catholic Evidence Guild, brought from London by Frank Sheed in 1925 to train speakers in debating opponents in the Domain.[21] A Catholic Debating Society trained members in spoken argument.[22]

Women's groups included the Catholic Women's Social Guild and the Catholic Women's Association[23]; an umbrella Legion of Catholic Women was formed in 1941.[24] The more independent women's movement, The Grail, evoked less clerical enthusiasm and in the 1950s found itself in a chilly relationship with Cardinal Gilroy.[25]

Between the wars and especially in the 1930s, a huge range of specialist lay groups were founded, mainly on clerical initiative, wherever a critical mass of Catholics with some special interest could be found. Catholic Boy Scouts Movement, affiliated with but separate from the Boy Scouts, ensured that Catholic youth were not influenced by what some considered "Masons in shorts" with their semi-Pantheist ideology.[26] 500 marched in 1941.[27]

Catholic boy scouts, Corpus Christi, St Patrick's College Manly, 7 June 1934
Photographer Ted Hood, State Library of New South Wales:
https://collection.sl.nsw.gov.au/record/nM7BVKKY

A Catholic Bushwalking Club was formed in 1943 (and still exists).[28] Central coordination of these groups increased with the appointment of Fr A. R. E. Thomas (later Bishop of Bathurst) as Director of Catholic Action in 1940.[29] It was his role to rule on such contentious questions as whether the Bushwalking Club could conduct mixed camping trips. (The answer was no; and furthermore that was not to be written in the constitution or rules.[30])

These Sydney groups did not see the split, visible in Melbourne and Adelaide, between sodalities devoted to personal spirituality and groups of intellectuals discussing *Rerum Novarum*, Chesterton and Belloc[31] (except for a very small Sydney Campion Society). Sydney did not produce a theoretical organ like the Melbourne *Catholic Worker* (instead producing the clerically-oriented *Australasian Catholic Record*). The practical Sydney style was more devoted to rolling the Masons and stacking Labor and union branches.

That raises the complex question of the extent to which the New South Wales ALP was itself a Catholic-dominated organisation. It cannot be said that the party was "taken over" by a Catholic bloc, in the sense that Santamaria aimed to take over the federal ALP in the early 1950s in order to implement his vision of Catholic social policy.[32] That is clear from the failure of NSW Labor governments to deliver state aid for church schools. However, in the relevant period about half of NSW Labor parliamentarians were Catholic,[33] and at the local level the large overlap between Catholic and ALP networks is undeniable. Cahill's biographer writes:

> In those days [the 1920s] Marrickville was very Irish-Catholic and very Labor, some said it was an Irish-Catholic-Labor ghetto of which St Brigid's was the epicentre. The 9 o'clock Mass every Sunday was the politicians' Mass. Afterwards, local members and hopefuls and union bosses would gather near the steps to be seen and to trade gossip and caucus and maybe assassinate a few reputations.
>
> It is relevant for me to recall here the story told of a little old lady who, arriving late for a Marrickville Labor branch meeting, genuflected as she entered the hall, causing the meeting to erupt into a gale of laughter. "They're all the same faces," the poor flustered woman protested. And it was true. Most of the people attending branch meetings could be seen also at St Brigid's on Sundays, often taking up the plate or with the Holy Name sodality. Joe Cahill was always among them.[34]

It is those long and close connections in personnel that make the history of Catholic organisation relevant to explaining government policy in the 1950s. The parish-based nature of the anti-Communist Movement[35] is just one instance of how pre-existing Catholic organisational structures could be used for new purposes.

Professional and workers guilds 1930s–50s: blue-and white-collar

This article will concentrate especially on the industry-specific guilds formed from the mid-1930s to encourage Catholics in particular industries to form a community, for their spiritual benefit and as a help in evangelising their workplaces. In most industries, there was no definite Catholic perspective on the work being done, but in a few important cases, there was. The non-controversial cases will be surveyed first. Most of the information that survives comes from reports of the main spiritual activity of each guild, its annual communion breakfast. Members would attend mass and receive holy communion together and afterwards gather for a meal and an address by a bishop or other church dignitary. A common theme was the need to act ethically in professional life. The speeches are not always platitudinous and can sometimes reveal the hopes of the hierarchy for Catholic Action.

Some successful guilds were for blue-collar workers. 300 railway and tramway employees attended a communion breakfast in 1937 to found a Transport Guild.[36] In 1938 700 members attended and a principal activity was the awarding of bursaries for members' children to complete school. At the annual breakfast of 1947, at the height of industrial unrest, Cardinal Gilroy attacked communism and urged fighting it.[37] A record number of 420 attended the sixteenth annual breakfast in 1952, where Gilroy said "Individually each one should take a pride in his work. Whether you drive a pen or an engine, whether you build a carriage or clean it, do every phase of your work to the best of your ability."[38] There were branches in Goulburn[39] and Newcastle.[40] The taxi drivers' Guild of St Christopher and St Anthony devised a taxi-blessing ceremony "similar to that enacted when fishing fleets put to sea."[41]

Guilds were formed in many white-collar industries. The Postmaster-General's Mission Guild attracted 500 to its Communion Breakfast of 1939.[42] A Stamp Duties Guild is mentioned in 1940.[43] The Catholic Insurance Guild of St Anthony held a ball in 1954 attended by 400.[44] The Catholic Bankers Guild of St Matthew was formed in 1946;[45] H.C. Coombs spoke to 430 at its 1950 gathering.[46] Cardinal Gilroy addressed 450 members at the 1951 breakfast, reminding them that "attachment to money … never brings real happiness," but agreeing that "Banks today are far removed from the money-changer or money-lender mentioned in Scripture."[47] 600 attended mass in 1954.[48]

Other white-collar guilds were the Qualified Accountants and Secretaries' Catholic Guild of St. Vincent de Paul,[49] the Journalists' Guild of St Francis de Sales, the Catholic Radio Guild of St John

Chrysostom,[50] and the Assisian Guild of Catholic Teachers (that is, teachers in state schools), which numbered 125 in 1940.[51] At its breakfast in 1946, members were urged to confront Communist control of the Teachers Federation.[52]

(Where possible the founders of the guilds tried to name them after an appropriate saint: thus the Postal Guild of St Gabriel because the Angel Gabriel was a messenger and the Dentists Guild of St Apollonia, called after an early Alexandrian martyr whose tortures included having her teeth pulled out.[53])

One of the longest-lived and most successful professional guilds was the St Thomas More Society for lawyers. It was founded in 1945 "to spread the knowledge of the principles of Christian ethics and morality in relation to the profession of the law."[54] 110 attended its Red Mass in 1954.[55] The Society published a journal up to 1988 and remained active for decades, including in Thomas More scholarship.[56] It still exists and holds an annual Red Mass.[57] Catholic-inspired natural law principles of legal philosophy had an impact in changing the law, notably in the Mabo case.[58]

There was no need for a guild of academics, as the number of Catholics employed by universities was negligible. However there was a Newman Society (of students) at Sydney University[59] and a University Catholic Federation of Australia in which Rosemary Goldie was prominent,[60] and a Newman Graduate Association active from 1944.[61] Its journal *Manna*, edited mostly by Patrick O'Farrell, sustained a high intellectual level around the early 1960s.[62]

A Catholic Soldiers' Guild achieved official recognition by the Minister for the Army in 1940.[63]

The Australian Catholic Historical Society, founded in 1940,[64] remains among the most active of the mid-century Catholic organisations.

Professional guilds at the moral cutting edge: Medicine and pharmacy

Catholic ethical views on "life" issues like eugenics, contraception, abortion and euthanasia differed from the mainstream, then as now. Catholic members of the medical and pharmaceutical professions therefore saw a need to gather together to support one another and to put their point of view both within and beyond their professions.

The Medical Guild of St Luke was formed 1934, "aimed at the efficient organisation of the Catholic medical profession; to strengthen their faith; to educate in medical matters involving the Church's teaching: to encourage, help and advise senior students; to co-operate for common spiritual and material good for the welfare of the nation and the glory of the Church."[65] It emphasised the need for doctors to follow moral law especially when the general opinion of the medical profession might be against it.[66] It published a journal for many years, up to about 1970.[67] A Junior Guild of St Luke was formed to support medical students.[68]

St Anne's Catholic Nurses Guild was formed in 1939 by the Women's Group of Catholic Action,[69] and later extended to Canberra and Broken Hill.[70]

Pharmacy was very much at the cutting edge, since Catholic opposition to contraception was opposed to normal practice in the profession.[71] Catholic pro-natalism also opposed the body of opinion represented by the Family Planning Association of Australia (still called, up to 1960, the Racial Hygiene Association).[72] The Catholic Pharmacists Guild of St Francis Xavier was founded in 1935 "to purge the chemists' business of all unclean dealings and of all practices contrary to the laws of Catholic morality"[73] It soon produced a guidebook on 'Moral problems of Catholic chemists'.[74]

In a speech at the Communion breakfast of 1953, Gilroy told them "Your guild asks more of its members than any other," referring to the loss of business sustained by pharmacists refusing to stock contraceptives. In reply, pharmacist Nelson Johns said that Catholic pharmacists, in opposing birth control, were engaged in a battle against "a greater evil than Communism – an evil which cheats God of His greatest power, the power of creating souls."[75] The next year, Bishop Lyons said "anyone who deliberately and directly prevents or destroys life is guilty of a grave sin."[76] It is stretching Catholic orthodoxy to equate preventing life with taking it, but these remarks show the depth of opposition to contraception in the lead-up to *Humanae Vitae*.

In the health professions, Catholics remained in a minority and there was no question of their views on morality becoming legislated (unlike in Ireland, where the sale of contraceptives was illegal). But in one other profession, Catholics did capture governmental policy.

The Police Guild of St Christopher

The Catholic police founded their Guild of St Christopher in 1934, with 120 present.[77] At the 1939 breakfast, the philosopher Dr Ryan said "As Catholics, they realised the divine origin of all law and that its continuity came from Catholicism … By what law could they better be guided in doing their duty than that of God. Who was the source of all authority?" A friendly message was received from the Police Commissioner, Bill McKay, a Freemason, and he was praised for his creating a Christian force.[78] 200 members of the Guild escorted Archbishop Kelly's funeral in 1940.[79]

Gilroy's speech at the 1940 breakfast declared them "perhaps the most physically perfect body of men in the whole city", the sight of which would give a salutary lesson to "those larrikins who hang round street corners and who declare that religion is all right for women and old folk." Like the Communists, Catholic men should seek to "indoctrinate others in the principles of their faith." The men of the Guild will not imitate those of a certain association in the Force "that is formed simply to push forward members, independent of their worthiness for that office."[80] His audience knew he meant the Freemasons. (The Colonial Police Act 1850 had required police to swear not to belong to "any secret society whatsoever unless to the Society of Freemasons"[81] and Masonic domination of the force from the Commissioner down was well-known.)

At the 1944 breakfast Gilroy attacked Communism and the press duped by them.[82] At the 1948 breakfast, attended by 500 including three policewomen, he urged them to "respect the human dignity of the wrong-doer": "no matter what may be the crime of which a person seemed to be guilty, there should be respect for human personality." The police must respect the law themselves.[83]

The 1952 breakfast, again attended by 500, had something to

celebrate. The Freemasons were outfoxed and a foundation member of the Guild, Colin Delaney, was congratulated on becoming the first Catholic Commissioner of Police.[84] One of the famous Sydney rumours is that there was an arrangement that Masonic and Catholic Police Commissioners alternated. An approximate alternation is observable, but the existence of an "arrangement" is unclear. The affiliations of Commissioners are listed in Table 1:

William McKay	1935–48	Mason
Fred Scott	1948–52	Mason
Colin Delaney	1952–62	Catholic
Norman Allan	1962–72	Mason
Fred Hanson	1972–76	Catholic
Merv Wood	1977–79	Mason
Jim Lees	1979–81	Mason
Cec Abbott	1981–84	Catholic

Table 1. NSW Police Commissioners[85]

Police Commissioner Colin Delaney with Albert Namatjira, c. 1952
NLA obj-146941269

PART II: The Cahill Government's moral agenda

The police service was far from the only branch of government under Catholic control or at least strong influence. For some years from 1952, the Police Commissioner, Attorney-General, Premier and Lord Mayor of Sydney were Catholic. Michael Hogan notes that in 1954 the Departments of Public Works, Attorney-General, Justice, Police and the Housing Commission had Catholics both as their respective responsible Ministers and Permanent Heads.[86] Equally important was the consummate skill behind the scenes of Bishop, later Archbishop, James Carroll, who handled negotiations with politicians for the Cardinal.[87] Some vertical integration of legislative and police policy became possible, based on shared assumptions.

One thing Labor did when it gained control of both houses of parliament was to abolish the death penalty. Whereas Victoria conducted executions up to 1967, there were none in New South Wales after 1939 and in 1955 the death penalty was abolished except for very rare crimes like treason, with Attorney-General Bill Sheahan arguing that the risk of hanging an innocent was unacceptable.[88]

Background: Catholic theory and practice on the confessional state and morals legislation

Before addressing the legislative policy on morals of the Cahill government and its implementation by the Vice Squad, it is useful to survey briefly some background issues of Catholic theory and its relation to the social mores of the 1950s.

First, the decade was, as everyone agrees, morally conservative, worried about moral decay, and in favour of state interventions. It was the decade of the Call to Australia by leading citizens hoping for a "restoring of the moral order",[89] Fr Peyton's Family Rosary Crusade[90] and the Billy Graham Crusade, White Australia and government assistance for the integration of "New Australians", fears of Communism and juvenile delinquency, the widespread institutionalisation and forced adoption of children. The heightened expectations of paternalist state action were also seen in positive policies like baby health centres, child endowment, mass polio vaccination, free and compulsory school milk and slum clearance. From later ideological perspectives, the combination of conservative values and large-scale government planning informed by what was taken to be science may look incongruous, but it was characteristic of the 1950s in many Western countries.

Second, Catholic doctrine up to the 1965 Vatican II declaration on religious freedom, *Dignitatis humanae,* favoured a close connection between Church and state, ideally a confessional state which granted special privileges and support to the Catholic Church. That doctrine was naturally soft-pedalled in Anglophone countries with a tradition of liberal democratic polities involving separation of Church and state;[91] indeed, it was Anglophone writers who were largely responsible for the change of doctrine towards freedom of conscience, such as the American John Courtney Murray and the Australian Eric D'Arcy.[92] Nevertheless in principle Catholic leaders in Australia remained supportive of government action in the interests of what they took to be the common good, such as increasing the birth rate and "morals" legislation.[93]

Third, Catholic doctrines on sexual morality were especially severe. Many ex-Catholic schoolchildren have complained in their memoirs of Catholic "sexual repression", but we can go to the source by looking at the Australian Catholic Truth Society pamphlet 'Can I keep pure?' by the Irish Jesuit Fr Robert Nash. An ACTS pamphlet was both officially approved and intended for wide distribution among the laity.[94] He emphasises the seriousness of sins concerning sex: they are all mortal sins: "Deliberately to seek the pleasure accompanying that power outside of marriage, even in the smallest degree, whether when alone or with others, is a mortal sin against God's law. And, even in marriage, it is a mortal sin to seek the pleasure in a manner devised to frustrate God's design in instituting marriage." A sin's being mortal means it is serious enough to merit eternal hellfire, if it is indulged in with full knowledge and consent. He explains why even the smallest degree of sexual sin should be mortal: "But why do we say that the smallest degree of such deliberate seeking is a mortal sin? The question seems to answer itself. Let a man give way in this matter, even the smallest degree, and very soon he will find to his bitter sorrow that he has let loose a wild beast in his heart. That beast becomes more and more insatiable. Let small gratifications be lawful, and very soon, men and women are swept into a very inferno of vice and passion." Then he discusses some of the results of sexual sins in this life, such as imbecile children of parents with sexually transmitted diseases.

It is commonly said that Irish Catholicism was of a specially "Jansenist" or puritanical variety. It is also true however that at the time of Fr Nash's writing, thousands of unwanted children of casual sexual liaisons formed a major problem, many of them looked after in Catholic orphanages without government subsidy, and that syphilis and other STDs were widespread and largely incurable.

Despite the gravity of sexual sins, the Catholic Church was not in favour of criminalising all of them, in the manner of early Puritan Massachusetts. Nor did Catholic writing single out particular sexual sins such as homosexuality for special attention.[95] When in the 1970s decriminalisation of homosexuality became a political issue, Catholic church leaders did not comment. The Church did however approve of legislative action to preserve public morals, for example by censorship. The general theory of state intervention in morals is explained by Dr Ryan in connection with the banning of James Joyce's *Ulysses* in 1941:

> Public authority has the right and the duty to secure the well-being of its citizens, to promote the good of the community as a whole, to preserve the moral standards without which civilisation would lapse into savagery and anarchy, and to foster religion which is the necessary basis of morals. It has, therefore, both the right and the duty to ban and proscribe everything which is subversive of right order and good morals. This right has its origin in the very nature of civil society, the Author of which is God. And this right and duty must be exercised in accordance with the law of God.[96]

Ulysses, he says, "is a grossly obscene and blasphemous work; the product of a diseased and perverted mind; breathing the atmosphere of the sewer and the brothel and of perversions which cannot be named." His attitudes were widely shared in Catholic and other circles. The Cahill government was to strengthen the Obscene and Indecent Publications Act.[97]

Fourth, a crucial political fact of the 1950s was that the close Catholic Church-Labor nexus held in New South Wales through the Split, when it fell apart in Victoria and Queensland. When the crisis of the Split broke and threatened to consign Labor to the political wilderness, "loyalty to the Cardinal" was called in to keep good Sydney Labor Catholic men in the Party.[98] In addition, Joe Cahill's Catholicism meant there could be no suspicion of Communist sympathies, as there was with Evatt.[99] The Cahill government owed the Cardinal one. The Church did not however gain its main political objective, substantial state aid for Church schools. As a policy for the 1956 State election, Catholic schools were allowed to purchase books and equipment from the government stores at the lowest price – a decision reached with a very smooth and fast operation between church and politicians[100] – but that was the limit of aid allowed by the Labor Federal Executive. State aid remained off the agenda until the early 1960s when Menzies made political capital by initiating it.

Background: Police culture

It was not new for the police and especially the Vice Squad to be vigorously policing the morals of the community in respect of obscene publications, prostitution, abortion, homosexuality, gaming and SP bookmaking. Those activities had not been of much concern to the law or police in the mid-nineteenth century, but in the hundred years from 1850 there was increasing community concern, tightening of laws and police crackdowns.[101] Nor were Masonic police any less vigorous than Catholic ones in pursuing those vices – Freemasonry is a deeply conservative ideology, though less theoretical than Catholicism.[102] The nature of these "vices", most of them not criminal since about 1980 and not obviously seriously wrong to everyone even in earlier times, meant that enforcement did not always meet with willing cooperation in the community, and thus that opportunities for corruption were rife.

The Vice Squad – well before any special prominence of Catholics in the force – had in particular a history of keen pursuit of homosexuals, patrolling gay beats and conducting theatrical raids on venues like "Black Ada's", a "dancing academy" in Wentworth Avenue run by a large African-American which was a cover for a gay nightclub.[103] In 1937 the Commissioner for Motor Transport was found naked in the bush with a police decoy and jailed.[104] In 1943, the editor of the *Daily Telegraph* was arrested in a Lang Park urinal and Sir Frank Packer had to intervene.[105]

Another relevant matter was that police were not well educated – no university graduates joined the police – putting them at a disadvantage in dealing with such matters as allegedly obscene literary and artistic works and in understanding the sort of people who produced them. Bill Dovey KC (Gough Whitlam's father-in-law), cross-examined Det Sgt Munro of the Vice Squad in 1946 on *We Were the Rats*, a literary work which represented the gallant heroes of Tobruk as sometimes using rude words and viewing pornographic pictures. He said:

> Have you ever heard of Chaucer? — No.
>
> You never met him while in the Vice Squad? — No.
>
> Have you ever heard of Byron? — No.
>
> He was a lord. — Yes, I've heard of him.
>
> Do you know if he was on Lord Louis Mountbatten's staff? — I don't know.
>
> Do you know if he was a writer? — I don't know.[106]

In dealing with vice, as in some other matters, the police conceived themselves as having a pastoral role as well as one of simply apprehending criminals. The name "Guild of St Christopher" alludes to the saint's role in helping people. Addressing the Newcastle branch of the Guild in 1952, Bishop Gleeson of Maitland said:

> Think of the power given you to prevent sin. There is scarcely a commandment whose observance you have not a part in securing. You have a share in preventing blasphemy, improper language, abuse of the Lord's Day, quarrelling, revenge, intemperance, immorality, dishonesty, and so forth. How many young girls do you not save from the hands of the wicked?[107]

The Vice Squad in Sydney conducted "dawn patrols" to warn and sometimes rescue women in near-prostitution situations.[108] In 1947 they took two women from a café on Pitt St at 8am, questioned them beside a police car and demanded to look in their purses. It transpired that they were GPO telephonists who had just come from early mass on Ascension Thursday and did not appreciate being treated in public as prostitutes. *The Catholic Weekly* made a scene.[109]

Not everyone enjoyed the well-meant attentions of the police. A first-year pharmacy student ventured into the Royal George pub, frequented by the Sydney Push, in 1962:

> I spoke to no-one all evening and no-one spoke to me until just before closing time when I went outside ... and two policemen seized me. I was flung into the back of a Black Maria and driven to the back of Darling Harbour. I expected that something dreadful would happen. But the police had identified me correctly as a decent young man from the Western Suburbs. They tipped me out into the cold night air and gave me a lecture: "Look, son, don't you go near that pub again – it's full of loose women, social diseases and drugs." I thought "Terrific!" and was back there next night.[110]

That aspect of police work was associated especially with the legendary Vice Squad man, Frank "Bumper" Farrell. Farrell grew up in Catholic Marrickville between the Wars, in the same community as Joe Cahill. A story from his childhood indicates the style of direct action that characterised his later working life:

> Bumper and I and some other kids were playing cricket in the street. We saw some well-dressed men and women open the gate, march up the path, climb the steps and knock on Bumper's door. They were carrying a gramophone, one of those you crank up with a lever and the music comes out of a horn, and a stand. Meg Farrell [Bumper's mother] answered their knock, her face thunderous. The kids crowded closer, sensing that something exciting was about to happen. One suited man told Mrs Farrell that surely this was her lucky day because he intended to play her a record. Bumper's mother's eyes narrowed further, but she motioned for him to proceed. He ceremoniously placed the

gramophone on the stand and turned the handle, which caused a voice to blare out of the gramophone declaring that Seventh Day Adventism was the one true religion and Catholicism was a disgrace borne of Satan that was leading the world to ruin. The speaker didn't get to finish his spiel. Meg picked up the gramophone and pitched it as hard and as high as she could over the picket fence and out onto the road, where it smashed into pieces. The stand followed the gramophone. She then chased the Seventh Day Adventists, cursing at the top of her voice and throwing haymakers, off her property.[111]

He had a very successful career in Rugby League but missed selection for the Kangaroos tour of 1948, allegedly due to Masonic selectors.[112] His police career was largely as sergeant in the Vice Squad at Darlinghurst station (that is, in charge of Kings Cross). He did things his way.

His Catholicism was very public:

Bumper continued to pray morning and night, and went to confession once a week, stopping in at whichever Catholic church was handy. He once impressed his family when they attended a service for the Little Sisters of the Poor at St Mary's Cathedral and he parked in a car space reserved for the Archbishop of Sydney, Cardinal Sir Norman Gilroy. "She'll be right," he assured them, and it was. The cardinal and Bumper went way back.[113]

That influenced his views on who was deserving of help and who wasn't. "The plight of the poor and put-upon of his police beat weighed heavily on Bumper. 'The people the old man helped … prostitutes, the homeless, the nuns and nurses at St Vincent's and St Margaret's, people from all walks of life.'"[114] People of a Bohemian nature were less favoured, such as the performers at the drag venue Les Girls.[115]

Farrell's biographer explains the police sense of a twilight zone between the legal and the illegal where a degree of toleration applied:

They believed that prostitution, gambling and having an alcoholic drink after 6 p.m., even though against the law, were minor crimes, part of the Australian way of life, and that those providing and enjoying these activities should be left alone so long as other more serious crimes, such as murder, grievous bodily harm and extortion, were not committed in their execution. 'There was no trouble in the brothels and SP shops and gambling clubs because the proprietors feared Bumper and adhered to the standards he insisted on.'[116]

With those understandings of background matters in hand, we can examine what the Cahill government and its new Commissioner of Police planned to do about vice.

The Vice Squad and imposition of moral order on gays and others

Colin Delaney had a firm view on what the greatest menace facing Australia was. It was homosexuality.[117] In a speech to the Vice Squad in 1952, he said that homosexuality was "damaging to the moral welfare of the community and must be checked at all costs."[118] In 1953 he ordered an "intensive drive to stamp out growing homosexuality in Sydney," with all 84 members of the Sydney vice squad "switched to almost full-time duty locating the haunts of homosexuals."[119] He appointed a new and energetic team to the Vice Squad headed by Ron Walden,[120] former assistant treasurer of the Guild of St Christopher.[121] Like Bumper Farrell, Walden was a noted footballer, but in Rugby Union, which Bumper thought "a poofter's game."[122]

Sunday Telegraph, 6 December, 1953

The government backed him up, although the politicians do not give the impression of being as viscerally angry with homosexuals as Delaney. The Crimes Act had already been amended in 1951 to ensure that a defence of consent was impossible for an attempt to commit "the abominable crime of buggery,"[123] and when the Supreme Court inconveniently held that "soliciting" meant only soliciting female prostitutes, work was undertaken to fix the problem.[124] In 1954 Cahill and the Cabinet agreed to Delaney's request for harsher penalties,[125] and in 1955 Attorney-General Bill Sheahan told Parliament "the Police Commissioner holds the view that remedial legislation is an urgent necessity to combat the evil."[126] "The Government has acted," he said, "because it considers that the homosexual wave that unfortunately has struck this country – though not to the extent of continental countries – must be eradicated,"[127] especially to protect the young. The effect of the campaign is visible in court records, with convictions for homosexuality in the lower (magistrates) courts rising from about one hundred in 1946 to over five hundred in 1958.[128]

Everyone in authority took it for granted that homosexuality was a perversion needing at least some degree of prohibition. There was no discussion of possible decriminalisation (until the publication in

Sydney Morning Herald Archive, Wednesday, June 11, 1958

HOMOSEXUAL MENACE IN AUSTRALIA

Homosexuality was Australia's greatest menace, the Commissioner of Police, Mr C. J. Delaney, said yesterday.

Mr Delaney was discussing "crime detection

"We hope soon to have a communication system which

Sydney Morning Herald, 11 June, 1958

1957 of the UK Wolfenden Report). But when the need for harsh measures was argued for, there was one theme that recurred: pedophilia. It was not that homosexuality and pedophilia were simply equated or conflated, but they were thought of as continuous, as if it was obvious that homosexuality had a strong tendency to lead to pedophilia. The 1951 article that originally used the phrase "greatest social menace" (not then attributed to Delaney) reported on two men convicted of assaulting children.[129] An unnamed psychiatrist commenting on Delaney's policies does distinguish between the secretive type, "to be pitied, poor devil" and the "defiler of children" who "deserves no mercy".[130] Delaney in 1951, then still CIB Chief, said that the "Tragic feature of the perversion is the number of young boys involved."[131] In a 1953 speech, he said that the main problems faced by the police were the growing road toll and "growing cancer" of perversion, which he described as meaning offences against boys.[132] A 1953 *Daily Telegraph* article picturing Delaney and headlined 'Vice Squad ordered to rid Sydney of male perverts' says that "many complaints are from managers of theatres where perverts prey on young boys." However the same article reveals also a quite different cause of concern, the inducement of youths to join a homosexual subculture. Unsuspecting young men are said to be invited to "join in discussions on matters ranging from art and ballet to philosophy and literature" and to then find it hard to break away when the "real reason" for sociability is revealed. The Vice Squad will set traps for them.[133]

To understand what needs explaining, the situation in Sydney needs to be compared with policy on homosexuals elsewhere. It was broadly comparable to other places in the Western world, but had some special features. All Western countries saw rising concern about homosexuality and other forms of "vice" in the 1950s, and Australia did not share the widespread fear in the US that homosexuals would be blackmailed by Communists.[134] Broadly similar policies of police persecution of homosexuals were in operation in Melbourne, Brisbane and Adelaide,[135] not all of which experienced Catholic dominance of political life or of policing. So the overall shape of policy on that and other forms of "vice" is to be explained by wider currents, which remain controversial as they involve large multinational shifts in culture. However developments in New South Wales did have some unique features. They included Colin Delaney's personal crusade against homosexuals, with his ability to direct Vice Squad resources and to gain political support through his close relationship with ministers, and, as described below, a homosexuals-only jail. Those are both unique to Sydney. Whatever broader factors were in play, decision-making in Sydney was in the hands of a particular small group of people with a shared organisation and shared theory.

The Vice Squad's biggest scalp: the Goossens case

The Vice Squad's highest-profile scalp came in 1956, when they picked up Sir Eugene Goossens at Mascot airport with a briefcase full of pornography, ruining his hitherto stellar musical career. That is not a story about homosexuality, but the Squad was disappointed that they were unable to jail Goossens for buggery despite having the evidence.

Goossens, an English conductor and composer of international stature, in 1947 took up the positions of Director of the Conservatorium of Music and first permanent conductor of the Sydney Symphony Orchestra. With great energy he raised standards in both and dominated classical music in Sydney. He gave Joan Sutherland her stage debut in his opera *Judith*. He convinced Cahill that Sydney needed an opera house sited on Bennelong Point and Cahill drove the project through against widespread opposition in his own party.[136] Goossens had also become involved with Rosaleen Norton, the "Witch of Kings Cross" and recorded in letters and photographs his affair with her and her lover, Gavin Greenlees.[137] Norton did not follow his instructions to destroy them but stuffed them behind a sofa, from where they were stolen by petty criminals who offered them to the *Sun*.[138] On developing the photographs the *Sun* declined to print them but passed them to the Vice Squad.

The inside story of what happened next is told in a long interview many years later with Bert Trevenar, the Vice Squad man in charge of the case. Goossens visited Buckingham Palace to receive a knighthood and the Soho area to buy pornographic material. Although the

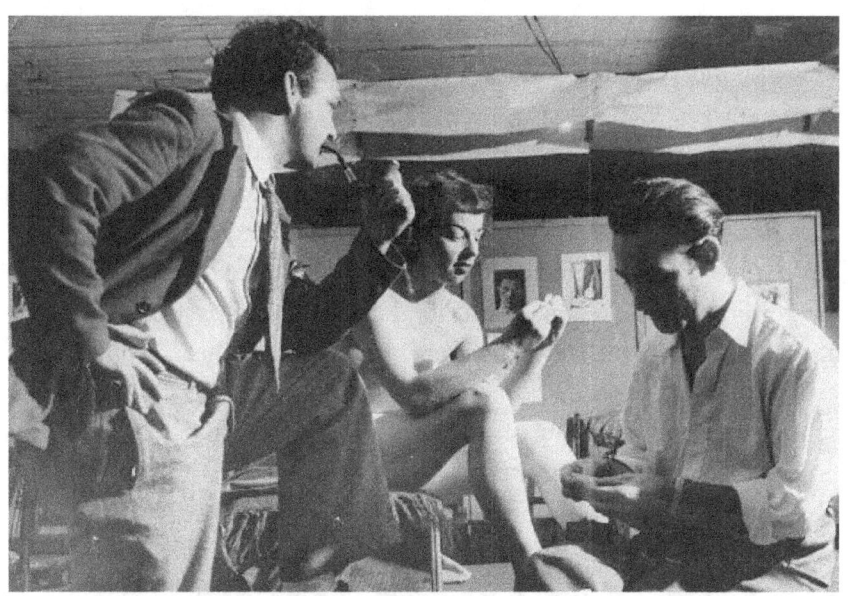

Rosaleen Norton modelling at Studio for Realist Art, Sydney, 1948
Photograph by Ted Hood; Wikimedia Commons

Rosaleen Norton and Gavin Greenlees, Darlinghurst Rd, 1950
Sydney Morning Herald

police did not have the resources to observe him, the *Sun*'s journalistic acquaintances in London did. Trevenar and his superior Walden (a Mason and Catholic respectively, but Trevenar says there was no animosity) were ready to meet Goossens as he stepped off the plane at Mascot. Some thousand pornographic photos and other items were found in his briefcase with the Brahms and Beethoven. They have since been destroyed in accordance with the provisions of the Customs Act but Trevenar described a few, taking particular offence at one showing a policewoman getting on a bike where "you can see everything." There was no suggestion of child pornography. Goossens admitted everything and later pleaded guilty to the customs offence of importing prohibited goods. He was fined £100, resigned his positions in a blaze of publicity and returned to England.

Sir Eugene Goossens facing charges, 3 March 1956
Alamy

However, the Vice Squad had bigger fish to fry than a mere customs offence with a fine. They had solid evidence of Goossens' sexual acts with Norton and Greenlees that would have justified a substantial jail term. They applied for a warrant to the Attorney-General, Reg Downing (who had just succeeded his cousin Sheahan in the office). Trevenar describes what happened:

> So anyway I was summoned with Ron Waldren [sic] to the Attorney General's office. We were waiting in the anteroom, waiting about an hour and Ron Waldren was spitting chips. And he's saying, not sotto voco [sic], but very loud about being kept there. And after a while Delaney storms along the corridor and I thought 'ello, 'ello, 'ello.
>
> Interviewer: As Cops do.
>
> As Cops do. Any road he was in there about quarter an hour and he came out with a look of thunder on his face. He walked past the anteroom, stopped, came back, looked in and beckoned me. So I followed him out to the footpath and he says "Sergeant, you've been dudded. You've done a fantastic job and I want to congratulate you on a job well done, but you're not getting a warrant. So you can just get back to your station."[139]

Detective and Mrs Trevenar, 1968[141]
State Library of New South Wales

Trevenar attributed the result to papal knights looking after one another. Delaney complained to the press that Downing had instructed him to drop charges; Downing replied that he would never direct the police but had given legal advice that the evidence did not disclose any crime committed by Goossens.[140]

Lady Goossens, tracked down by the *Sun* at a convent in France where she was on retreat, said she would stay with her husband. That did not happen as he brought from Australia the 26-year-old SSO pianist with whom he was having an affair.[142]

The two lowlifes who had robbed Norton's flat were put away for offering an obscene publication for sale; Norton and Greenlees were eventually acquitted.[143] Goossens died in 1962 and was buried with Catholic rites. Norton died in the Sacred Heart Hospice, Darlinghurst in 1979, tended by nuns.

Both of them had been taken on a difficult journey by their libidos. Father Nash would have said, I told you so.

Sydney's reputation in the international music world was confirmed the next year when Claudio Arrau, one of the century's leading pianists and father of two, was fined £5 for winking suggestively at a policeman in a Lang Park toilet (dismissed on appeal).[144]

The Cahill government regarded itself as modern and enlightened. As Cahill had said in arguing for the Opera House, "This State cannot go on without proper facilities for the expression of talent and the staging of the highest forms of artistic entertainment which add grace and charm to living and which help to develop and mould a better, more enlightened community."[145] An enlightened approach to homosexuality, as understood in the 1950s, implied a move away from purely moral and policing actions to a more "scientific" approach. That involved two innovations: segregation of homosexuals in jail, eventually in their own jail, and consultation with the profession newly establishing itself as the scientific experts on all matters to do with deviance, the psychiatrists.

Downing, then Justice Minister, announced the segregation of homosexual prisoners in existing prisons in 1953.[146] The old jail at Cooma was reopened in 1957 and designated for homosexuals only.

It contained single-celled accommodation for 128. It is believed to have been the only jail in the world exclusively for homosexuals.[147] Downing defended segregation – for low-risk prisoners at Cooma and for the "intractable" in a special section of Maitland jail – on the grounds that "otherwise there is always a danger to other prisoners."[148] Some homosexual prisoners who had experienced severe assaults in non-segregated prisons regarded segregation as an improvement,[149] while Robert Adamson, later a noted poet, recalled pretending to be a homosexual to avoid bashings in Maitland jail.[150]

Psychiatry, a profession rapidly establishing itself in the mid-twentieth century as a properly scientific field, mostly agreed with traditional views that there was something seriously wrong with homosexuality. It was classified as a disorder in the standard Diagnostic and Statistical Manual of Mental Disorders up to 1973. The profession put forward a range of allegedly scientific theories of its causes, and offered or imposed treatments such as aversion therapy.[151]

The state government set up an expert committee in 1958 to investigate the "causes and treatment" of homosexuality. In accordance with contemporary views on an enlightened approach, it was headed by William Trethowan, the Professor of Psychiatry at Sydney University, who had been active in reforming the primitive conditions in the state's mental hospitals. The inmates of Cooma were to be among the subjects studied.[152]

Five years later, after extensive delays, the *Sydney Morning Herald* reported on the imminent release of the Committee's interim report. The newspaper's apparently well-informed discussion of the report's contents hinted that it would recommend decriminalisation of homosexual acts between consenting adults, but said that Police Commissioner Norman Allan was strongly against legalising this "abominable crime".[153] Nothing further was heard. The Trethowan Report never appeared and no copies of it have been found despite extensive searching. Homosexual acts were not decriminalised in New South Wales until 1984.

The Cahill government's desire to be enlightened and scientific coincided with the Wild West period of psychiatry, when rash pioneers experimented with ill-tested experimental drugs and psychosurgery. If Cahill's best big spend was on the Opera House, his worst was on the Cerebral Surgery and Research Unit, established at Callan Park under the directorship of Dr Harry Bailey. Bailey was to become notorious later for the many deaths resulting from his "deep sleep" insulin therapy at Chelmsford Hospital, but at this earlier period his main interest was in brain operations like lobotomies to "cure" a range of psychiatric conditions. There were plans to send Cooma inmates to be treated by Trethowan and Bailey at the CSRU, but it is not known if that happened.[154] Someone rang Bailey in 1973 and asked about his brain operations; he said his team had performed 150 cingulo-tractotomy operations, 15% of which were on homosexuals.[155] However, Bailey was a notoriously unreliable informant.

Conclusion

The memories of everyone old enough to remember are correct: the 1950s were a deeply conservative era in the Western world, especially in comparison with the late 1960s and later. Indeed, they were in most ways a time of increasing rather than relaxing conservatism. Many benefited, especially the baby-boomers brought up in stable family environments. But some paid a heavy price for not fitting the mould laid down by society's dominant values, notably illegitimate and institutionalised children, unmarried pregnant women and homosexuals.

The causes of that conservative dominance are varied and in the main common to all Western countries. Anglophone countries without any special Catholic influence, such as the UK, US and New Zealand, and other Australian states such as South Australia, saw broadly similar attitudes and legislation, so it cannot be argued that if there had been no Catholic government in New South Wales, there would have been significantly more liberal legislation. Nevertheless, the cases of de Valera's Ireland, Salazar's Portugal, Franco's Spain, de Gaulle's France and Christian Democrat Western Europe show that political dominance by conservative Catholic leaders was one way of ensuring social conservatism by government decree.

One element in the political success of those policies, in New

South Wales as overseas, was Catholic moral theory and its reach into practice through the Catholic tradition of powerful mass organisations. Though a less extreme case than Ireland and Portugal, New South Wales in the 1950s saw a Catholic influence in politics which provided exceptional opportunities for Catholic moral theory to be implemented in government policy. The results were benign in areas like infant health and the abolition of capital punishment, but disastrous in the campaign against homosexuals.

---

[1] John Luttrell, *Norman Thomas Gilroy: An Obedient Life* (St Pauls, Strathfield, 2017), 81.

[2] David Hilliard, 'God in the suburbs: The religious culture of Australian cities in the 1950s,' *Australian Historical Studies*, 24 (1991), 399–419.

[3] Michael Hogan, 'The Sydney style: New South Wales Labor and the Catholic Church', *Labour History* 36 (1979), 39–46, at 42.

[4] 'Western European background in Hugh Macleod, Building the "Catholic ghetto": Catholic organisations' 1870-1914, in W.J. Sheils and Diana Wood, eds, *Studies in Church History*, Vol. 23: Voluntary Religion (1986), 411–44.

[5] 'Overview of benefit societies and sodalities in Newcastle area in Beverly Ruth Zimmerman, The Making of a Diocese and the Moulding of Its People: The Maitland Diocese During the Episcopacy of James Murray, 1866-1909', PhD thesis, University of New England, 1998, ch 8 https://rune.une.edu.au/web/bitstream/1959.11/10818/2/open/SOURCE11.pdf

[6] James Franklin, *Corrupting the Youth: A History of Philosophy in Australia* (Macleay Press, Sydney, 2003), 257-8.

[7] https://trove.nla.gov.au/newspaper/article/114460907; AHC and Catholic Club debate "Is capitalism a failure?" 1940, https://trove.nla.gov.au/newspaper/article/146102911

[8] Edmund Campion, *Australian Catholics* (Penguin, Ringwood, 1987), 115-6, 120.

[9] Campion, Australian Catholics, pp 116-8; Stephen Utick, Captain Charles, Engineer of Charity: The remarkable life of Charles Gordon O'Neill (Allen & Unwin, Crows Nest, 2008).

[10] K. Coen, Monsignor John Leonard and the Catholic Youth Organisation (Strathfield, 2000).

[11] https://trove.nla.gov.au/newspaper/article/146389173

[12] A. W. Maher, 'Mudgee Catholic Centenary: A short history of the parish of Mudgee over the past century and a guide to St Mary's, Mudgee', (*Mudgee Guardian*, Mudgee, 1952), 62-8, https://nla.gov.au/nla.obj-2203193212; an account of a similar range in Richmond, Victoria, in *Richmond Catholic Parish History* (Richmond Parish, Richmond, 2020), 55–60., https://www.ignatius.org.au/about/community/publications/category/3-richmond?download=14:richmond-catholic-parish-history,

[13] 'Population of Mudgee Municipality, 1950-4370; 1951-4460', *New South Wales Statistical Register, 1950-1951, Part VII. Population and Vital Statistics*, S. R. Carvers, Govern-

ment Statistician, Published by Authority of The Government of New South Wales, A.H. Pettifer, Government Printer, Sydney', pp 616: https://www.ausstats.abs.gov.au/ausstats/free.nsf/0/DAB4F568806C6494CA2579E2001837D8/$File/33111_1950_51.pdf) and estimating 30% Catholic. (The surrounding shire had a similar population but rural dwellers would have found it hard to get to town to participate in meetings.)

[14] The story of the Twenty-Ninth International Eucharistic Congress, Sydney, Australia, 5-9 September 1928: a Pictorial Record and a Review of the Congress, Sydney, 1928, compiled by P. C. Cregan, L. Rumble and J. Meany (Green Press, Sydney, 1928); summaries in Samantha Frappell, 'International Eucharistic Congress 1928', Dictionary of Sydney, 2012: https://dictionaryofsydney.org/entry/international_eucharistic_congress_1928 and Campion, Australian Catholics, 93-96.

[15] Jeff Kildea, Tearing the Fabric: Sectarianism in Australia, 1910 to 1925 (Citadel Books, Sydney, 2002); Jeff Kildea, Troubled Times: A history of the Catholic Federation of New South Wales, 1910 to 1924, PhD thesis, University of New South Wales, 2002: http://hdl.handle.net/1959.4/65387

[16] Patrick O'Farrell, *The Catholic Church and Community: An Australian History* (UNSW Press, Sydney, 1985), 380.

[17] Campion, Australian Catholics, 118-20; Cliff Baxter, Reach for the Stars: 1919-2009, NSW Knights of the Southern Cross: Bold men of faith, hope and charity (Connor Court, Ballan, 2009); Luttrell, Gilroy, 162-4.

[18] *Freeman's Journal*, 2/5/1914, https://trove.nla.gov.au/newspaper/article/111291022; *Catholic Press*, 21/6/1934, https://trove.nla.gov.au/newspaper/article/104375336; Mike Davis, *Dooley's Lidcombe Catholic Club: Our History*, Dooley's Lidcombe Catholic Club, Lidcombe, 2012; Mike Davis, *Liverpool Catholic Club*, (Liverpool Catholic Club Pty Ltd, Prestons, 2014.

[19] James Franklin, 'Catholic thought and Catholic Action: Dr Paddy Ryan MSC and the Red Peril', *Journal of the Australian Catholic Historical Society* 17 (1996), 44-55 and in this collection.

[20] https://trove.nla.gov.au/newspaper/article/104497504

[21] https://trove.nla.gov.au/newspaper/article/114744280: 1935 report on Catholic Speakers Guild, https://trove.nla.gov.au/newspaper/article/104506902

[22] https://trove.nla.gov.au/newspaper/article/146506986

[23] https://trove.nla.gov.au/newspaper/article/108163902: Catherine O'Carrigan, Barlow, Mary Kate (1865-1934), *Australian Dictionary of Biography*, vol. 7: https://adb.anu.edu.au/biography/barlow-mary-kate-5134

[24] Luttrell, *Gilroy*, pp 156-8.

[25] Luttrell, *Gilroy*, 154-5; Campion, *Australian Catholics*, 113—5; Alison Healey, 'The Grail-75 years in Australia: An international women's movement and the Australian Church', *Journal of the Australian Catholic Historical Society* 31/32 (2010-11), 27-38.

[26] Franklin, *Corrupting the Youth*, 253-6; https://trove.nla.gov.au/newspaper/article/116779946

[27] https://trove.nla.gov.au/newspaper/article/17741493

[28] Peter Blayney, 'A history of the Catholic Bushwalking Club', *Journal of the Australian Catholic Historical Society* 31/32 (2010/11), 39-52.

[29] Luttrell, *Gilroy*, 85; https://trove.nla.gov.au/newspaper/article/146098840

30 Blayney, 'A history of the Catholic Bushwalking Club', 47.
31 Described in Melbourne in Race Mathews, Of Labour and Liberty: Distributism in Victoria 1891–1966 (Monash University Publishing, Clayton, 2017), chs 7–8 and Colin Jory, The Campion Society and Catholic Social Militancy in Australia 1929–1939 (Harpham, Sydney, 1986); in Adelaide in Katharine Massam, Sacred Threads: Catholic Spirituality in Australia 1922–1962 (UNSW Press, Sydney, 1996), 237–9.
32 Santamaria to Mannix, 11 December 1952, in *B.A. Santamaria: Your Most Obedient Servant*, ed. Patrick Morgan (Miegunyah Press, Melbourne, 2007), 73–79, at 75.
33 Hogan, 'The Sydney style', 40.
34 Peter Golding, 'They called him Old Smoothie: John Joseph Cahill', *Journal of the Australian Catholic Historical Society* 31/2 (2010/11), 75–82; origins of the Catholic–Labor alignment in Celia Hamilton, 'Irish-Catholics of New South Wales and the Labor Party, 1890–1910', *Historical Studies, Australia and New Zealand* 8 (31) (1958), 254–67.
35 B. A. Santamaria, 'Report on anti–Communist campaign, 1944', in *B. A. Santamaria: Running the Show*, ed. Patrick Morgan (Miegunyah Press, Melbourne, 2008), 115–129, discussion at 113.
36 https://trove.nla.gov.au/newspaper/article/146399809 (protest) https://trove.nla.gov.au/newspaper/article/133554423
37 https://trove.nla.gov.au/newspaper/article/146599595
38 https://trove.nla.gov.au/newspaper/article/147087743
39 https://trove.nla.gov.au/newspaper/article/147087395; https://trove.nla.gov.au/newspaper/article/146379252
40 https://trove.nla.gov.au/newspaper/article/160489170
41 https://trove.nla.gov.au/newspaper/article/91238089
42 https://trove.nla.gov.au/newspaper/article/106364147
43 https://trove.nla.gov.au/newspaper/article/106422274
44 https://trove.nla.gov.au/newspaper/article/147159205
45 https://trove.nla.gov.au/newspaper/article/146618189
46 https://trove.nla.gov.au/newspaper/article/146738278
47 https://trove.nla.gov.au/newspaper/article/146750091
48 https://trove.nla.gov.au/newspaper/article/147160713
49 https://trove.nla.gov.au/newspaper/article/147158423; https://trove.nla.gov.au/newspaper/article/147159207
50 https://trove.nla.gov.au/newspaper/article/146734587
51 https://trove.nla.gov.au/newspaper/article/146098656
52 https://trove.nla.gov.au/newspaper/article/146617423
53 https://trove.nla.gov.au/newspaper/article/106409267 https://trove.nla.gov.au/newspaper/article/147087158
54 https://trove.nla.gov.au/newspaper/article/146484639 https://trove.nla.gov.au/newspaper/article/146483270: 'US background in St Thomas More Institute for Legal Research, The Guild of Catholic Lawyers of New York – A history of twenty–seven years', *Catholic Lawyer* 1 (2) (1955), 101–12.

55 https://trove.nla.gov.au/newspaper/article/147156123
56 J. A. McCarthy, introduction, in John McCarthy and Anthony Reynolds, eds, Thomas More: The Saint and the Society: addresses and articles on St Thomas More further published to commemorate the Golden Jubilee of the foundation of the St Thomas More Society on 14th August 1945 (St Thomas More Society, Sydney, 1995), 1-14.
57 https://stms.org.au/about-us-frequently-asked-questions/
58 Franklin, *Corrupting the Youth*, 388-98.
59 Desmond Ryan, ;The Sydney University Newman Society: the early years;, *Journal of the Australian Catholic Historical Society* 6 (2) (1979), 63-78.
60 https://www.auscatholicstudents.com/our-mission-identity
61 Anthony Young, 'The Sydney Newman Graduate Association, 1944-1979: an introductory history', *Journal of the Australian Catholic Historical Society* 6 (2) (1979), 43-62.
62 Patrick O'Farrell, 'That which was lost: *Manna* 1957-1968', *Australasian Catholic Record* 79 (2002), 155-163.
63 https://trove.nla.gov.au/newspaper/article/167763816
64 A. E. Cahill, 'The Australian Catholic Historical Society: the first fifty years', *Journal of the Australian Catholic Historical Society,* 12 (1990), 31-38.
65 https://trove.nla.gov.au/newspaper/article/261633613; overseas background in Jessica Martucci, Religion, medicine, and politics: Catholic physicians' guilds in America, 1909-32, *Bulletin of the History of Medicine* 92 (2018), 287-316, Carla Zawisch, The guilds of Catholic doctors in Europe, *Linacre Quarterly* 12 (3) (1944), 57-61.
66 E.g.: https://trove.nla.gov.au/newspaper/article/146800091
67 *Transactions of the Catholic Medical Guild of St. Luke,* 1937-55; *Transactions of the Medical Guild of St. Luke,* 1956-69; example articles at https://trove.nla.gov.au/newspaper/article/172210310; https://trove.nla.gov.au/newspaper/article/147162836
68 https://trove.nla.gov.au/newspaper/article/10439462
69 https://trove.nla.gov.au/newspaper/article/146376931; https://trove.nla.gov.au/newspaper/article/146377247
70 https://trove.nla.gov.au/newspaper/article/146482397
71 Official policy and natural law reasoning laid out in Dr Rumble's 1934 Australian Catholic Truth Society pamphlet, 'The Truth About Birth Control', http://pamphlets.org.au/docs/cts/australia/acts0662a/
72 Sylvia Bannah, Birds, bees and birth control: a history of Family Planning in Queensland 1971-2001, PhD thesis, University of Queensland, 2010, 10.
73 https://trove.nla.gov.au/newspaper/article/104496772
74 https://trove.nla.gov.au/newspaper/article/146422648 ; self-employed pharmacies argued to be in accord with Catholic social theory in https://trove.nla.gov.au/newspaper/article/146481042
75 https://trove.nla.gov.au/newspaper/article/147083756
76 https://trove.nla.gov.au/newspaper/article/147160884
77 https://trove.nla.gov.au/newspaper/article/106422274
78 https://trove.nla.gov.au/newspaper/article/146380931

[79] https://trove.nla.gov.au/newspaper/article/247486965
[80] https://trove.nla.gov.au/newspaper/article/146100925
[81] *Colonial Police Act 1850*: http://classic.austlii.edu.au/au/legis/nsw/num_act/cpa1850n38175/
[82] https://trove.nla.gov.au/newspaper/article/17932164
[83] https://trove.nla.gov.au/newspaper/article/146661066
[84] https://trove.nla.gov.au/newspaper/article/147085237
[85] *SMH* 17 May 1983; P. Molloy, 'Portrait of a police chief', *SMH* 6 June 1979, 7.
[86] Michael Hogan, 'The Sydney style: New South Wales Labor and the Catholic Church', *Labour History* 36 (1979), 39–46, at 42.
[87] Brian Croke, 'Prelates and politics: the Carroll style', *Journal of the Australian Catholic Historical Society* 22 (2001), 31–45; Brian Croke, Carroll, James Patrick (1908–1995), *Australian Dictionary of Biography* vol. 19 (2021): https://adb.anu.edu.au/biography/carroll-james-patrick-28122
[88] https://trove.nla.gov.au/newspaper/article/91195413; Jo Lennan and George Williams, 'The death penalty in Australian law', *Sydney Law Review* 34 (2012), 659–694, at 680.
[89] David Hilliard, 'Church, family and sexuality in Australia in the 1950s', *Australian Historical Studies* 27 (109) (1997), 133–136.
[90] Katharine Massam, (1991) 'The Blue Army and the Cold War: Anti-communist devotion to the Blessed Virgin Mary in Australia', *Australian Historical Studies*, 24 (97), 420–428.
[91] Except by Mannix: James Franklin, Gerald O. Nolan and Michael Gilchrist, *The Real Archbishop Mannix: From the Sources* (Connor Court, Ballarat, 2015), 142.
[92] Joseph A. Komonchak, 'The American contribution to "Dignitatis Humanae": The role of John Courtney Murray, S.J.', *U.S. Catholic Historian* 24 (1) (2006), 1–21; Eric D'Arcy, *Conscience and its Right to Freedom* (Sheed and Ward, London and New York, 1961); local debate in Henry Mayer, ed, *Catholics and the Free Society: An Australian symposium* (Cheshire, Melbourne, 1961) with comment in Austin Gough, 'Catholics and the free society', *Australian Historical Studies* 10 (39) (1962), 370–8.
[93] E.g. Franklin, Nolan and Gilchrist, *The Real Archbishop Mannix*, 193–7.
[94] Robert Nash SJ, *Can I keep pure?* (7th ed, Dublin 1939; Melbourne ACTS 1944; quoted from the 1953 reprint: http://pamphlets.org.au/docs/cts/australia/acts0947/
[95] A rare Catholic homosexual community in the Order of St Gerard Majella, an order of teaching brothers founded in Western Sydney in 1960: https://www.childabuseroyalcommission.gov.au/sites/default/files/CTJH.280.01003.0001_R.pdf
[96] https://trove.nla.gov.au/newspaper/article/146370240
[97] David Clune, *The Labor Government in New South Wales 1941 to 1965: A study in longevity in government*, PhD thesis, Sydney University, 1990, https://ses.library.usyd.edu.au/bitstream/handle/2123/2229/The%20Labour%20Government%20in%20NSW%201941-1965.pdf, 89; https://trove.nla.gov.au/newspaper/article/107517633
[98] Luttrell, Gilroy, 247–55; Franklin, Catholic thought and Catholic Action.
[99] Clune, The Labor Government in New South Wales, 119.
[100] Hogan, 'Sydney style', 44.
[101] Barbara Sullivan, *The Politics of Sex: Prostitution and pornography in Australia since 1945* (Cambridge University Press, Port Melbourne, 1997), ch. 1.

102 Franklin, *Corrupting the Youth*, 253-6.
103 Garry Wotherspoon, *Gay Sydney: A History* (NewSouth Publishing, Sydney, 2016), 45-6.
104 Michael Flynn, Maddocks, Sydney Aubrey (1881-1963), *Australian Dictionary of Biography* vol. 15 (2000): https://adb.anu.edu.au/biography/maddocks-sydney-aubrey-11031
105 Frank Cain, MacKay, William John (1885-1948), *Australian Dictionary of Biography* vol 10 (1986), https://adb.anu.edu.au/biography/mackay-william-john-7381
106 https://trove.nla.gov.au/newspaper/article/248489192
107 https://trove.nla.gov.au/newspaper/article/147084927
108 Steve Meacham, Pioneer policewoman whose virtue was vice, *SMH* 12 May 2012, https://www.smh.com.au/national/nsw/pioneer-policewoman-whose-virtue-was-vice-20120511-1yi2u.html; https://trove.nla.gov.au/newspaper/article/231551494
109 https://trove.nla.gov.au/newspaper/article/146618704; https://trove.nla.gov.au/newspaper/article/146604359
110 Sally McInerney, 'The Push revisited', *SMH* 22 Oct 1983, 33-4; Franklin, *Corrupting the Youth*, 165.
111 Larry Writer, Bumper: The Life and Times of Frank 'Bumper' Farrell (Hachette, Sydney, 2011), 14.
112 Ibid., 204.
113 Ibid., 340.
114 Ibid., 299.
115 Ibid., 281 and 286.
116 Ibid., 240-1.
117 'Homosexual menace in Australia,' *SMH* 11 June 1958, 5; the phrase used without attribution in *Sun*, 1 August 1951: https://trove.nla.gov.au/newspaper/article/230228883; G. Wotherspoon, 'The greatest menace facing Australia: homosexuality and the state in NSW during the Cold War', *Labour History* 56 (1989), 15-28.
118 https://trove.nla.gov.au/newspaper/article/18291286
119 'Vice squad ordered to rid Sydney of male perverts,' *Sunday Telegraph* 6 December 1953, 5: https://trove.nla.gov.au/newspaper/article/248833557
120 https://trove.nla.gov.au/newspaper/article/96526972: https://trove.nla.gov.au/newspaper/article/230726247
121 https://trove.nla.gov.au/newspaper/article/146380931
122 Writer, *Bumper*, 106.
123 Wotherspoon, *Gay Sydney*, 109; a 1950 acquittal after arrest by a "tall, good looking Vice Squad man" at https://trove.nla.gov.au/newspaper/article/167908817
124 Ex parte LANGLEY; Re HUMPHRIS (1953) 53 SR (NSW) 324: https://nswlr.com.au/preview/53-SR-NSW-324: https://trove.nla.gov.au/newspaper/article/18423338; Sullivan, *The Politics of Sex*, 53-4; an acquittal: https://trove.nla.gov.au/newspaper/article/183990281955
125 https://trove.nla.gov.au/newspaper/article/172054585

126 NSW Parliamentary Debates, Legislative Assembly, 23 Mar 1955, pp 3223; Wotherspoon, *Gay Sydney*, 112.
127 NSW Legislative Assembly Hansard, 23 March 1955, 3230 and 1973
128 Graham Willett, 'The darkest decade: Homophobia in 1950s Australia', *Australian Historical Studies*, 27 (1997), 120-32.
129 https://trove.nla.gov.au/newspaper/article/230228883
130 https://trove.nla.gov.au/newspaper/article/161506615
131 https://trove.nla.gov.au/newspaper/article/161381635
132 https://trove.nla.gov.au/newspaper/article/18399024
133 https://trove.nla.gov.au/newspaper/article/248833557 Brisbane parallel at: https://trove.nla.gov.au/newspaper/article/217743819
134 David K. Johnson, *The Lavender Scare* (University of Chicago Press, Chicago, 2004).
135 Graham Willett, 'From vice to homosexuality: policing perversion in the 1950s', in Shirleene Robinson, ed, *Homophobia: An Australian History* (Federation Press, Annandale, 2008), pp 113-127: https://www.google.com.au/books/edition/Homophobia/lWHOI2s9JqQC?hl=en&gbpv=1&pg=113 .
136 David Salter, Goossens, Sir Eugene Aynsley (1893-1962), *Australian Dictionary of Biography*, vol 14 (1996), https://adb.anu.edu.au/biography/goossens-sir-eugene-aynsley-10329
137 Details and documents in Neville Stuart Drury, *Rosaleen Norton's contribution to the Western esoteric tradition*, PhD, Newcastle University, 2008, https://nova.newcastle.edu.au/vital/access/manager/Repository/uon:2752 ch. 8.
138 David Salter, 'The conservatorium director and the witch', *SMH Good Weekend*, 2 July 2015: https://www.smh.com.au/lifestyle/the-conservatorium-director-and-the-witch-20150702-gi3h8y.html ; Harold Tucker, 'The sad tale of Sir Eugene Goossens', *Classical Music Guide Forums*, 2007: https://classicalmusicguide.com/viewtopic.php?t=16828
139 David Salter, 'The strange case of Sir Eugene and the witch', *Good Weekend/Sydney Morning Herald*, 3 July 1999, 16, full interview at: https://nedmccann.blogspot.com/search?updated-max=2009-04-16T20:35:00-07:00
140 https://trove.nla.gov.au/newspaper/article/138121433
141 Also pictured at https://www.gettyimages.dk/detail/news-photo/former-vice-squad-detective-albert-trevenar-75-old-stamping-news-photo/1079480380
142 Salter, 'The strange case'; Tucker, 'The sad tale.'
143 Drury, 268.
144 *SMH* 29 August 1957, 9; Wotherspoon, *Gay History*, 121-2.
145 'A competition to design a National Opera House for Sydney', *Sydney Opera House: The Competition*: https://www.sydneyoperahouse.com/our-story/sydney-opera-house-history/the-competition.html
146 https://trove.nla.gov.au/newspaper/article/194090147; implementation in Maitland jail in 1954 https://trove.nla.gov.au/newspaper/article/163294697
147 Patrick Abboud and Simon Cunich, 'The Greatest Menace: Inside the Gay Prison Experiment', *Audible Audiobook*, 2022: https://www.audible.com.au/pd/The-Greatest-Menace-Audiobook/B09S169W9J, summary at: https://www.abc.net.au/

news/2022-02-15/podcast-the-greatest-menace-reveals-cooma-jail-as-gay-prison/100830608; briefly mentioned in *Canberra Times*, 1 July 1958: https://trove.nla.gov.au/newspaper/article/136301603

[148] State govt grant for study of homosexuality, *SMH*, 24 January 1958, 4; discussion in Abboud and Cunich, ch. 2.

[149] Marcus Finnane, 'Camp prisoners: a personal experience', *Camp Ink* 3 (4) (Feb 1973), 5: https://nla.gov.au/nla.obj-788130631/view?sectionId=nla.obj-828540848&partId=nla.obj-788139731

[150] Abboud and Cunich, ch. 6

[151] Survey in Jack Drescher, 'Out of DSM: Depathologizing homosexuality', *Behavioral Sciences* 5 (2015), 565–75.

[152] *SMH* 27 February 1958, 3, *Canberra Times*, 1 July 1958, 10: https://trove.nla.gov.au/newspaper/article/136301603

[153] Controversial report on homosexuality in N.S.W., *SMH*, 1 March 1963, 2; further discussion in Abboud and Cunich, ch. 8.

[154] Abboud and Cunich, ch. 5.

[155] John Ware, Psychosurgery in Australia, *Camp Ink* 3(4) February 1973: https://nla.gov.au/nla.obj-828541003; *Gay Liberation demonstration against Bailey in Sue Wills, The Politics of Sexual Liberation*, PhD thesis, Sydney University, 1981, 182–3.

14

Gerald Ridsdale, pedophile priest, in his own words*

Abstract: Gerald Ridsdale was not only Australia's most notorious pedophile priest but the only one to give his own account of offending. His evidence to the Royal Commission into Institutional Responses to Child Sexual Abuse, apparently given honestly, is therefore a unique opportunity for insight into the causes of the abuse crisis. His story is one of out of control sexuality, inability to relate to adults, and gross failures by the many who knew of his crimes to do anything about them.

One major difficulty in understanding the clerical abuse scandal in the Catholic Church has been that the abusers themselves have not told their story. There has been virtually no account of their crimes by themselves, no apologies, no repentance.

That changed with the appearance of Gerald Ridsdale before the Royal Commission into Institutional Responses to Child Sexual Abuse on 27–28 May 2015. Ridsdale is believed to be Australia's worst priest sexual abuser of children. He was convicted of offences against 53 children, including many rapes, but that is thought to be a small proportion of his victims.

Sitting in Ballarat, the Commission heard two days of testimony from Ridsdale. He appeared by video-link from prison, where he has been since 1994. He gave the impression of being an honest and cooperative witness, though notably affectless. At age 81, his memory was very patchy, but the Commission was able to supplement it with some earlier material, especially a 1994 account he gave of his actions.[1] His oral evidence and the earlier document provide a unique opportunity to see into the mind of a pedophile priest.

Since the Commission's brief was to investigate the responses of institutions rather than the abuse itself, questioning by Gail Furness

---

* *Journal of the Australian Catholic Historical Society* 36 (2015), 219–230.

SC focused on who knew about his offending and what they did or did not do about it. In this article however we select that part of the evidence where Ridsdale talks about himself.

The testimony was streamed live. Graham Richardson wrote after watching his evidence, "I want there to be a hell and I want Gerald Ridsdale and his ilk and all those who covered up for them to burn in that dreadful place for all eternity."[2] Moral evaluation of that kind is certainly appropriate, but this article confines itself to the facts as they appear from his testimony and related documents.

Ridsdale's account of his abusing

Gerald Ridsdale was born in 1934, the eldest of eight children, and studied at St Patrick's College, Ballarat. He experienced some relatively mild sexual abuse from an uncle and from a Christian Brother (according to his 1994 statement). He left school at 14 and worked in an accountant's office but about three years later was inspired by a priest friend to consider becoming a priest. The little he recalls about it is significant:

Gerald Ridsdale appearing before the Royal Commission, May 2015

> Q. You say you talked to your priest friend, Dan Boylen, about becoming a priest?
>
> A. Yes.
>
> Q. Do you remember now anything he told you about the life of a priest?
>
> A. No. The only thing I can remember about any conversation with Dan Boylen with regard to the priesthood was, he was talking about spiritual books that I was reading, and I remember him saying, "Always remember, when you're reading books like that, that that's not necessarily how people like that lived, but that's how they would like to have lived", and I

don't know why that stuck in my mind, but that's something that I've always remembered.[3]

That was an unfortunate thing to take notice of, given that Ridsdale would go on to represent the extreme in the disjunction between priestly appearance and reality.

He is asked if he committed abuse while studying at Werribee Seminary:

> A. Not in Werribee, I can't remember anything. My biggest problem there was masturbation, and I remember going to my confessor and confessing it, and he said something like 'You will have to stop that or otherwise you have got to leave the seminary'. That was the kind of attitude there towards masturbation, et cetera.

His offences began very soon thereafter. After some study in Genoa and Ireland he was ordained in 1961 and served as assistant priest in parishes of the Ballarat Diocese. In the mid-1960s, he served in Mildura under the supervision of Monsignor John Day, another of Australia's worst pedophile priests, but there seems to be no evidence that they knew of each other's crimes. From 1974 he was parish priest in various locations.[4] Very little evidence comes to light of his priestly life apart from his offending. At one point he is asked about the only notable item on his CV other than parish work (and certain appointments made later to get him out of the way), his role as secretary of the Salary Review Board. He downplays the importance of the role:

> Q. And, to be appointed as a secretary of that committee showed, did it, that you were held in esteem by those who appointed you?
>
> A. Well, yes; I don't know how I was appointed or how I got onto the committee, but very often becoming secretary is a matter of, no one else is willing to do it.

He is asked if he agrees with a psychiatrist's description of his *modus operandi* in abusing:

> Q. Professor Ball says, and I quote: It is very clear that his subsequent career in parish work indicated that in each of the parishes to which he was appointed there was a group of five or

more children with whom he had close and ongoing relationship, plus a number of other casual contacts. His usual pattern was to become involved in one or two families, often with an absent father, develop close relationships with the children, which then merged into the sexual in the context of a variety of opportunities within the presbytery, on various outings and camps, et cetera. The targets were predominantly prepubertal or early prepubertal boys. Do you accept that is an accurate description of your pattern?[5]

A. Yes, I think so.

In his own description, he admits his manipulative behaviour. He is asked to read from the transcript of his earlier interview, concerning his offending at Inglewood in 1975:

A. Yes, I was out of control, really out of control in those years.

Q. These other ones, would they be from the school or altar boys or what?

A. Well, I had a pool table and it was just known that anyone who wanted to come was welcome to come and play pool. There is no sense in pretending, I suppose, because if there was any kind of good motive about it being a drop-in centre but it was the trap.

Q. You can see that now?

A. Yes, I can see that now.

(Presumably in the interests of retaining his cooperation as a witness, the questioning does not go into some of the more grotesque aspects of his actions that had come out in earlier court cases, such as telling a nine-year-old boy that the abuse was "the Lord's work"; describing a four-year-old girl he was abusing as "God's little angel", and giving another victim a piece of communion bread as a reward for being abused.[6])

Ridsdale is hato admit that his actions were all wrong and criminal (at the same time, without appearing notably remorseful or overcome with any sort of emotion):

Q. Now, you knew what you were doing were committing crimes against children, didn't you?

A. Yes, I did.

Q. You'd known from the very beginning in 1961 when Bishop O'Collins spoke to you that what you were doing was committing criminal acts?

A. Yes.

Q. Did you see them, in addition to criminal acts, as moral failures on your part?

A. Yes, they were serious sins.

Q. You thought they were serious sins because of the teaching you had received in the seminary and beyond about what a sin was?

A. Yes. ...

Q. You would have known it was a crime; is that what you said?

A. Yes.

Q. Thank you.

A. Well, should have anyway.

Q. Well, you did know it was a crime, because otherwise you wouldn't have been concerned about the police, would you, Mr Ridsdale?

A. Exactly that, yes, exactly. I would have known it was a crime.

As to the effects of his offending on his victims, Ridsdale answers:

Q: Did you know, Mr Ridsdale, that the effect you had on children you offended against was that they wouldn't let anyone touch them and they wouldn't let their fathers touch them. Did you know that?

A. No, I didn't know then. I didn't know that then. I do now.

Q. You didn't think about the effects on the children, did you?

A. No, I didn't.

Q. You were only concerned about your own gratification?

A. That's right.

It is arguable that there is some contradiction between his claiming not to knowing the effects of abuse and claiming to have been abused himself. However, the abuse he suffered appears to have been much less severe than that he inflicted.

The offending continued and Ridsdale was moved from place to place, including to New South Wales. In the late 1970s, he was able to take children to White Cliffs, the remote opal mining town in western New South Wales, where he had an underground house. From this period there is a near-contemporary description of the abuse as seen from both sides, thanks to correspondence received by the Bishop of Ballarat and made available to the Royal Commission. The solicitor for victim "BAF" writes:

> BAF alleges that at the age of 16 at Whitecliffs he was under the care of Father Ridsdale and because of an accommodation shortage, he was forced to sleep with Father Ridsdale in the same double bed. We quote his instructions: "That night he began touching me firstly on the arms and legs and then my genitals. I asked him to stop but he would not. He made me masturbate him and forced me to give him oral sex. I was crying and emotionally upset and wanted him to stop. He apologised and he said he would not do it again. The following night, similar events occurred."[7]

The solicitors were able to quote from letters and a card which Ridsdale sent to BAF soon after. It is the most astonishing evidence in the whole case, revealing an extraordinary level of self-deception on Ridsdale's part:

> We quote from a letter from Father Ridsdale dated May 2nd, 1979 addressed to BAF:

> "I depend on you more than anything or any-one else for support – that weekly phone call and a card in the mail gives me the energy to keep going 'straight'. I hope I don't lean too heavily on you – sing out if I do. I don't know how much you know about me or how much you've guessed, but you're the first person I've ever wanted to open up to (although I seem to do it in a roundabout way – You're the first kid I have been honest with and warned off (a bit late unfortunately, but I suppose all experiences bring some good out in us)."

In a card sent, the following statement by Father Ridsdale appears:

> "I am far from strong and hope you're strong enough – I don't want to run any risk of losing you as a friend."

In a letter posted 3rd May, 1979 from Edenhope Father Ridsdale stated:

> "The words on the front seemed to say a fair bit about Sunday night. Thanks. Even though it was December 1978 at W-Cliffs, I still sometimes wish! No harm in hoping. Good to have a weak mate, isn't it? Not much help! and, when I come to think of it, I'm pretty weak with you. I think your mum hasn't much trust in me. I suppose I really don't want to be a priest with you – a friend, or what? When I pray for you, God comes first – when I'm with you, you are first."

Who knew of Ridsdale's offending?

The evidence before the Royal Commission on knowledge of the fact and extent of Ridsdale's offending was complex. Certainly the successive bishops of Ballarat, James O'Collins and Ronald Mulkearns, received plenty of information about it. Various people in parishes came to learn about it, but it did not exactly become common knowledge and it was possible for other priests to remain unaware of it. Here we consider what Ridsdale himself says. He certainly feared exposure and made efforts to conceal his crimes, including from his confessors.

> Q. When you left the seminary, did you continue to go to confession?
>
> A. I did for a while, but not regularly.
>
> Q. When you say "for a while", for how long did you continue to go to confession?
>
> A. Maybe three, four, five years. But I can't really remember, but that's just the impression that I sort of have now.
>
> Q. And were you honest in what you confessed to your confessor?
>
> A. No.
>
> Q. What did you not confess to your confessor which you should have?
>
> A. I didn't confess the sexual offending against children.
>
> ...
>
> Q. What did you do, as an assistant priest and as a parish priest when you are offending, to keep it a secret?
>
> A. Well, I would have made sure that I was in a situation where

there was no one else around, and I would have told the children to keep quiet about it.

Q. Did you threaten the children as to what might happen if they didn't keep quiet?

A. I don't know whether I did or not; I may have.

Q. You hurt those children, didn't you, Mr Ridsdale?

A. Yes, I did. I know that.

What he feared from exposure was the loss of priesthood:

A. It's the sort of thing I wouldn't tell anyone.

Q. Why is that?

A. Looking back on it, I think that the overriding fear would have been losing priesthood.

Q. And you thought that, if you told anyone, you'd lose the priesthood?

A. Yes.

Q. Because what you were doing was a crime, wasn't it?

A. That's right.

He was caught, and caught again, but did not lose the priesthood until the time of his court cases in the 1990s. His 1994 document says, speaking of 1963:

> While I was there [Ballarat East] I remember going into his room and fondling him while he was showing me something in the cupboard, toys or whatever, and putting my hand down his trousers and touching his penis. It would have been a fairly brief kind of thing. Then later the Bishop called me in, Bishop O'Collins, and said there had been a complaint and he said, 'If this thing happens again, then you are off to the missions' and he sent me to Mildura.

In Ballarat East Ridsdale lived in the same presbytery as Fr George Pell. Ridsdale says he does not remember that. He says there were no general rumours about his offending at that time. This has been the subject of intense interest because in a much-reproduced video, Pell is seen accompanying Ridsdale to his first court appearance in 1993. Pell has expressed regret for doing so. There has been controversy as to whether Pell knew earlier of Ridsdale's offending. Ridsdale's own evidence gives no reason to think so.

But at Inglewood in 1975 things became more difficult:

> What happened there was a lady came to me one morning after a morning mass and she said that 'there is talk around the town that you've been interfering with the boys', and she said 'the police have been around making enquiries'. So I panicked, packed up a few things and then probably about midnight I called in to stay with a priest friend at Maryborough and slept the rest of the night there and went straight down to the Bishop.

Police involvement seems to have been off the agenda. The bishop and his advisers seem not to have considered reporting the matter to the police. Even the police did not report it to the police:

> Q. ... Bishop Mulkearns is recorded as saying that the first complaint he ever had was when you were at Inglewood in 1975, and he describes the complaint as being that a policeman came to see him to say that he was worried about an incident with his son, that is, the policeman's son, and that in addition you came to see Bishop Mulkearns too, and that Bishop Mulkearns said to the policeman that he would "pull you straight out of the parish and have him seek counselling" ...
>
> Q. But that police officer from Bendigo was a police officer who happened to be a father of a boy that you had offended against?
>
> A. I didn't know that, or I don't remember that now.
>
> Q. You see a bit further down on that page, it was put to you that, knowing the size of Inglewood, that the interviewer thought it would be imprudent to molest the policeman's son, and you then say: [in 1994] ...
>
> A. Well, one of them was with the policeman's son, and when you say imprudent, it's like taking an alcoholic and saying, 'Call into that hotel and get a bottle of lemonade', there's no logic to it.

(In fact the police produced a report and notified Bishop Mulkearns of Ridsdale's offending. A police investigation of 1995 into whether Mulkearns had concealed a felony found that he may have known only of lower-scale offences.[8])

Psychological treatment

During the long course of his offending, Fr Ridsdale had considerable interaction with psychologists and psychiatrists. What he tells the Commission casts light on the role of those professions in the sexual abuse crisis. He had some awareness of needing professional help. He says (in the 1994 document) of his time in Warrnambool in 1970–2:

> Well sometimes it would go on for a while, maybe with one lad over a period of some months just on and off and then you had a time when I was free of the problem. Warrnambool was probably the first place that I tried to get some help or realise that I needed help and I was out at the mental institution near Brierley and part of my job was to go out to Brierley and take communion out and probably had mass out there and I remember one day there was a psychiatrist or psychologist that I had met a couple of times, and I remember saying to him once 'Could I ask you a question, I want to talk about a problem?' and I said something to the effect that 'I think I might be homosexual' and I can clearly remember his question, 'Do you dream about having sex with men?' and I said 'No' and he said 'Well you have got no problems, you are okay' and rather than follow it up then with, 'Well, what about kids?', I just let it go. But the first time I can remember having the guts to say anything.

When his offending became known to the Church authorities, a series of therapies were tried:

> Q. You describe that, and I quote: [1994 document] One of his strongest things [his, being Father (Augustine) Watson] was to stay close to the Lord and respect your priesthood and more spiritual kind of stuff. Do you see that?
>
> A. Yes, I can see that now, yes.
>
> Q. Can you recall now what benefit you received from the therapy with Father Watson?
>
> A. No, I can't, but I did follow up that logotherapy with Viktor Frankl, and I studied that, and I think the basic reasoning behind that was, in whatever difficult circumstances a person is in, if

they have some reason for living, a good reason for living and going on with life, then that was helpful.

The 1994 document, speaking of 1980, contains some self-diagnosis:

> I took a year off and one of the reasons I took a year off was I knew my life was all screwed up and I appreciated or I thought that I had worked out for myself that part of my problem was that I couldn't mix comfortably and relate comfortably with adults. So I thought if I could go to some kind of a program or course and spend a year, a live-in year with adults, I might be able to sort of help myself that way, but it was only partially successful.
>
> I know, looking back from where I am now, that there was probably a lot of fear in mixing with adults because of the secret that I held, the secret of offending, and perhaps frightened of being questioned by them or – I don't know really, and it was also concerned with control I think, control and power, and I was a control freak and I couldn't control adults.
>
> Well, I think the whole purpose of the year was to just try to turn my life around, away from offending with children, to becoming more comfortable with adults and, if I could do that, then I thought it might eliminate the offending. But I had no idea then, as I do now, that logic and threats, they're no help to a paedophile. The only way out of it is proper treatment.

Ridsdale was eventually sent to the centre for "hard-core" problem priests run by the Congregation of the Servants of the Paraclete at Jemez Springs, New Mexico. The facility was closed down in the 1990s because of its failures in treating abusive priests, but Ridsdale takes a more positive view:

> Q. It's plain that, although you went through this treatment, it didn't work, isn't it?
>
> A. In New Mexico?
>
> Q. Yes.
>
> A. I didn't offend at all after I came back from America.
>
> Q. You didn't?
>
> A. No.

Q. So you say the treatment worked?

A. Yes, I think it did.

A final exchange between the Royal Commissioner and Ridsdale is hard to disagree with:

THE CHAIR (Peter McClellan QC):

Q. Mr Ridsdale, do you accept that someone with your issues should never have been a priest?

A. Yes, I accept that now. I'm sorry that there was nothing –

Q. What should have been in place with the church to stop you becoming a priest?

A. There should have been a better screening process that was much more thorough, a psychological process that was much more thorough than anything that was conducted then.

Q. If, when you first discussed your offending behaviour with the Bishop, he'd gone to the police, that would have brought it to an end, wouldn't it, as far as your role in the church was concerned?

A. It would have, and I am now sorry that it didn't; that it didn't happen.

Q. You might be sorry, but the offending –

A. It would have saved so many others.

---

[1] Part of the 1994 document is in the Commission's exhibits at http://www.childabuseroyalcommission.gov.au/exhibits/860eabc6-e0fc-453a-b9d4-51a89852fede/case-study-28,-february-2016,-melbourne under the heading 'Extracts of transcript of interview between Catholic Church Insurance Limited and Gerald Ridsdale'.

[2] G. Richardson, 'If there is a hell, let abusers burn for all eternity', *The Australian* 29/5/2015.

[3] This and later quotes from Royal Commission on Institutional Responses to Child Sexual Abuse, Case Study 28, Transcript of Days C083 and C084 (27 and 28 May 2015), at http://www.childabuseroyalcommission.gov.au/case-study/860eabc6-e0fc-453a-b9d4-51a89852fede/case-study-28,-may-and-november-2015

[4] Personnel documents for Fr Gerald Ridsdale, exhibits in hearing day C077 of the Royal Commission, http://www.childabuseroyalcommission.gov.au/exhibits/860eabc6-e0fc-453a-b9d4-51a89852fede/case-study-28,-may-2015,-ballarat; Broken Rites summary at http://brokenrites.org.au/drupal/node/55 (which includes some victims' stories).

5   Professor Ball's 1993 report is included in the exhibits under the heading 'Psychological reports prepared by Professor Ball'.
6   M. Russell, 'Notorious pedophile priest jailed for eight years', *The Age*, 8/4/2014.
7   Paul Cronin, solicitor for BAF of Shepparton, to Bishop Ronald Mulkearns, 19/2/1988, http://www.childabuseroyalcommission.gov.au/downloadfile.ashx?guid=edf85c42-6f3a-4351-8715-7c5d8ddea608&type=exhibit&filename=CCI.0001.00632.0179_R&fileextension=pdf, downloaded 30/5/2015; the severe effects on the victim are detailed in a letter from the victim's mother to Fr Brian Lucas of 24/10/1989 http://www.childabuseroyalcommission.gov.au/downloadfile.ashx?guid=6ba5db98-1aad-4ee4-9a68-594d1e66f0a8&type=exhibit&filename=VPOL.0014.001.0088_E_R&fileextension=pdf
8   Broken Rites site, http://brokenrites.org.au/drupal/node/55

15

Natural law ethics and the Mabo decision*

Abstract: The objectivist natural law theory of ethics at the core of Catholic scholastic philosophy implies a philosophy of law. It claims that there exist abstract principles of justice, to which actually existing law ought to conform but may not. If legal precedents fail to conform to justice, it may be necessary to overturn them in the interests of deeper principles. That philosophy of law was held by the judges in Mabo who overturned the precedent of *terra nullius* in favour of the principle of equality of persons before the law.

The earlier chapter on 'Catholic scholastic philosophy in Australia' left that tradition in an apparently decrepit state. After the Second Vatican Council, an elaborate philosophy descended from the middle ages came to be thought a hopelessly antiquated embarrassment. But in the legal world the middle ages are only yesterday. There, the scholastic method of arguing for and against propositions with lengthy citation of learned authorities is fully preserved.[1] So are practices like wearing robes and hiring champions to fight one's case. Scholastic natural law philosophy of ethics, stressing objective principles of justice, has also survived and flourished in the nourishing habitat of the Australian courts.

Consequently, the most dramatic outcome of Catholic philosophy in recent times has been the High Court's 1992 Mabo judgment on Aboriginal land rights. The fundamental issue in the case was the conflict between the existing law based on the principle of *terra nullius*, and what the judges took to be objective principles of justice. If there are principles of justice external to the law, the possible deviation of actually existing law from them raises a fundamental issue of philosophy of law. The Mabo judges believed that such a clash had arisen and that a major change in the law was necessitated.

---

* *Corrupting the Youth: A History of Philosophy in Australia*, 388–98.

The relation between law and morality is a question on which Catholic philosophy is dramatically opposed to traditional legal theories. On one older view of the relation between the two, "the King can do no wrong" by definition: the law simply is whatever is laid down by properly constituted authority. A less extreme position holds that there may be moral constraints on law, as on any other human activity, but that law is still not especially connected with morality. Instead it is a set of customs that have arisen to allow society to become organised. They could have been different, but once they arise they are fixed so that everyone can get on with life, knowing what is expected of themselves and others.[2] It is hard to see what other view is possible for those who lack the scholastic view that morality is somehow founded on the objective facts of human nature. At the opposite extreme, the scholastics hold that law and morality are so closely related as to be almost the same thing. The whole point of law, they say, is to implement the demands of justice, whose standards are external and objective. Or rather, one should not think of the standards of justice as external to law, since the aim of law is exactly to realise and internalise the principles of justice: "the precepts of law are designed to be the precepts of justice."[3] Father Farrell, a Dominican philosopher who denounced university philosophy in 1961, was one of the most active in promoting this view, and many other Australian Catholics have defended it.[4]

The two views come into conflict over the issue of whether a precedent should be followed, even when it is unjust. Generations of lawyers absorbed the fundamental doctrine of precedent: a precedent cannot be overthrown in favour of some abstract conception of "justice"; there is to be no private revelation of justice, since that would make the law unstable, as each new judge imposed his own opinions or the changeable opinions of society. Sir Owen Dixon, often regarded as Australia's most eminent Chief Justice of the High Court, expressed the old consensus in 1956:

> But in our Australian High Court we have had as yet no deliberate innovators bent on express change of acknowledged doctrine. It is one thing for a court to seek to extend the application of accepted principles to new cases, or to reason from the more

fundamental of settled legal principles to new conclusions, or to decide that a category is not closed against unforeseen instances which in reason might be subsumed thereunder. It is an entirely different thing for a judge, who is discontented with a result held to flow from long accepted legal principles, deliberately to abandon the principle in the name of justice or of social necessity or of social convenience … The latter means an abrupt and almost arbitrary change. The objection is not that it violates Aristotle's precept 'that the effort to be wiser than the laws is what is prohibited by the codes that are extolled.' The objection is that in truth the judge wrests the law to his authority. No doubt he supposes that it is to do a great right. And he may not acknowledge that for the purpose he must do more than a little wrong … It is for this reason that it has been said that the conscious judicial innovator is bound under the doctrine of precedents by no authority except the error he committed yesterday.[5]

This means, in plain terms, that if the legal system as a whole falls into a mistake, it can never dig itself out.

Dixon's works do not include a discussion of such matters as whether there is or could be any such thing as an abstract standard of justice. His view on such large philosophical issues is clear, though, from his remark, "An enquiry into the source whence the law derives its authority in a community, if prosecuted too far, becomes merely metaphysical."[6] His assumption that legal readers will not query "merely" before "metaphysical" is a sign of the anti-philosophical stance of the legal mainstream.

Such enquiries were pursued nonetheless, by those less shy of metaphysics. Besides the work of Catholics, the massive volumes and long years of teaching of Julius Stone, Professor of Jurisprudence at Sydney University, served to bring questions about the source of legal authority to the fore. Although he did not precisely agree with the view that there are moral principles that the law must implement, that view was one he took seriously and expounded sympathetically. His students, who included three of the Mabo judges, were introduced to a range of opinions and a habit of looking for the principles that informed the law.[7]

Dixon's view was upheld by his immediate successors as Chief Justice, Barwick and Gibbs.[8] Barwick did indeed allow that there is a community sense of justice and fairness that may occasionally be "pandered to" when interpreting ambiguous laws, but went on to say, "it is not for the individual judge or judges to express his or their own views as to the law, views perhaps tinged by a philosophy of one kind or another. Such a course would, it seems to me, be a complete deviation from the judicial tradition of the common law. It would lead to a rule by men rather than a rule by law."[9] But by the 1980s, doubts had set in at the highest level. Sir Anthony Mason, Chief Justice at the time of the Mabo decision, wrote of Dixon's passage, "Yet in some respects his Honour's outline resembles an elegantly constructed mansion in which some of the windows have been deliberately left open."[10] He means that Dixon has neglected the possibility of inconsistency among precedents, or between precedents and principles. "If applied too rigidly, the doctrine of precedent produces both injustice and lack of rationality – the very flaws whose purpose it is to expel. Thus adherence to a past decision which reflects either a principle undermined by subsequent legal development or the values of a bygone era, will produce an unjust result, judged by the standards of today."[11] Mason thus emphasised the conflict an outdated precedent may have with "community values" rather than with an abstract standard of justice, but the recognition that a precedent may conflict with something more basic and of legal relevance was a major step away from Dixon's reasoning.

The most detailed and explicit answer to Dixon, in terms of the conflict between precedent and absolute standards of justice, came from Sir Gerard Brennan, the writer of the first Mabo judgment and Mason's successor as Chief Justice. His theory of the relation of morality and law is that of the Catholic natural law school. In earlier works he had praised such Catholic legal heroes as Thomas More, well known for his stand on the conflict of law and morality, and the colonial Irish lawyers Therry and Plunkett, whose "impartial enforcement of the law" secured the convictions of the perpetrators of the Myall Creek massacre. He also commented favourably on Justice Higgins's adoption in the Harvester judgment of the phrase "reasonable and frugal comfort", as the standard which a basic wage ought to support, from an outside moral source, an encyclical of Pope Leo XIII.[12] Lawyers, he also said, have moral duties beyond simply applying the law they find in place. "If the law itself is an obstacle to justice, the duty of a Christian lawyer extends to seeking its reform."[13] Most remarkably, in a speech on 'Commercial law and morality', he said:

> Moral values can and manifestly do inform the law … The stimulus which moral values provide in the development of legal principle is hard to overstate, though the importance of the moral matrix to the development of judge-made law is seldom acknowledged. Sometimes the impact of the moral matrix is obvious, as when notions of unconscionability determine a case. More often the influence of common moral values goes unremarked. But whence does the law derive its concepts of reasonable care, of a duty to speak, of the scope of constructive trusts — to name but a few examples — save from moral values translated into legal precepts?[14]

The complex maze of rules that makes up commercial law may seem an inhospitable domain for moral imperatives, but the opposite is true, according to Brennan. It is for the commercial lawyer to discern the moral purpose behind each abstruse rule, and advise his client's conscience of what is just in the circumstances, not merely what he can legally get away with.

So when he comes to the specific matter raised by Dixon, whether a precedent can be overturned for conflicting with justice, it is no surprise to find him agreeing that it can: "The existing body of law may yield no relevant legal rule, or, in rare cases, may yield a legal rule which is offensive to basic contemporary conceptions of justice." In overturning it, however, the judge does not simply impose his private morality, as Dixon had claimed. "The reasons for judgment in the higher appellate courts increasingly look behind the legal rule to discover the informing legal principle and behind the informing principle to discover the basic value."[15] The answer of the innovators to Dixon's charge that judges who upset a precedent are imposing their idiosyncratic notions of morality is thus a cunning one. Overturning an unjust precedent need not be a matter of judges implementing their personal morality, but instead (in Dixon's own words) "to reason from the more fundamental of settled legal principles to new conclusions." It is simply that the judges now perceive that the offending precedent conflicts with more fundamental legal principles or values. Brennan's successor as Chief Justice, Murray Gleeson, asserts that all judges must be for Dixon's "strict and complete legalism"; what this means, however, is not an adherence to the letter of the law but that judges are appointed to "interpret and apply the values inherent in the law."[16]

In the Mabo case, such a conflict was found between the existing law, which justified the dispossession of the Aborigines by the doctrine of *terra nullius*, and principles of justice which, the judges held, conflicted with that precedent. *Terra nullius* is not a phrase of English law, but its substance is contained in a judgment of the Privy Council in 1889, according to which New South Wales in 1788 was "a colony which consisted of a tract of territory practically unoccupied, without settled inhabitants or settled law, at the time when it was peacefully annexed to the British dominion."[17] Aborigines, in other words, have no more rights to the land they walk over than tourists. To explain what is wrong with this, the Court needed first to adopt a theory of native title. Obviously, this cannot be part of the existing (British) law, and must be found in more general principles of justice. An explanation close to that adopted by the Court is found in a 1988 article by Frank Brennan, Jesuit, barrister, son of Sir Gerard and adviser to the Catholic bishops on Aboriginal affairs:

> Where a traditional tribal community has continued to reside on its traditional land, discharging its spiritual obligations with regard to that land, and that land has never been occupied by any other persons, that community is entitled to a legal title to that land in *legal recognition* of the fact that they have always lived on that land, land to which no other persons have any moral claim. To deny legal title to that land would be to complete the act of dispossession commenced 200 years ago, or else it would be to deny the rule of law operation with respect to these citizens and their most precious possession.[18]

Aficionados of scholastic philosophy will notice that the judges' theory of native title is even closer to one of the scholastic classics, and a founding work of modern international law, Francisco de Vitoria's *De Indis*. It was written in 1539 in response to the original question of this kind, the rights of the American Indians to their land.[19]

Having established that native title exists, the question of its conflict with precedent arises. Both of the two main Mabo judgments, the first written by Gerard Brennan and the second by Justices Deane and Gaudron, admit that to achieve justice in the case, the existing law will have to be overturned. Brennan writes, "According to the cases, the common law itself took from indigenous inhabitants any right to occupy their traditional land, exposed them to the deprivation of the religious, cultural and economic sustenance which the land provides, vested the land effectively in the control of the Imperial authorities without any right to compensation and made the indigenous inhabitants intruders in their own homes and mendicants for a place to live. Judged by any civilised standard, such a law is unjust and its claim to be part of the common law to be applied in contemporary Australia must be questioned."[20] Both judgments treat the overturning of precedent that this circumstance renders necessary as a serious matter, needing careful justification. Not any unjust law whatever can be overturned, they hold. "In discharging its duty to declare the common law of Australia, this court is not free to adopt rules that accord with contemporary notions of justice and human rights if their adoption would fracture the skeleton of principle which gives the body of our law its shape and internal consistency."

To overturn a law like that of *terra nullius*, it must be found inconsistent with one of the basic underlying principles of the law. That principle is a simple one: equality before the law. "No case can command unquestioning adherence if the rule it expresses seriously offends the values of justice and human rights (especially equality before the law)."[21] Even if there is such an inconsistency, one must weigh whether the disturbance to the settled rule of law would be "disproportionate to the benefit flowing from the overturning." (Even this last point, which appears at first sight to be a modern and sophisticated concession to the Dixonian view, can be found in Aquinas.[22]) One must also consider international law. While the English legal system is not strictly bound by outside decisions, an influence from them is legitimate, "especially when international law declares the existence of universal human rights."[23]

The same views are crucial to the other Mabo judgment, that of Deane and Gaudron. In writing of the natural law basis of international law, as founded by Aquinas and Vitoria, Deane had earlier said that "This basis gave international law a rich philosophical foundation which was a source of unlimited development. In it there is a reservoir of rules for all situations and cases. A law based on natural law can never grow out of touch with the current needs of nations."[24] The legal principle drawn out of the reservoir for Mabo is again that of equality before the law, on which he had written more explicitly in an earlier case:

> For one thing, there is the conceptual basis of the Constitution. As the preamble and s. 3 of the *Commonwealth of Australia Constitution Act* 1900 (Imp.) (63) make plain, that conceptual basis was the free agreement of 'the people' — all the people — of the federating peoples ... At the heart of that obligation [to act judicially] is the duty of a court to extend to the parties before it equal justice, that is to say, to treat them fairly and impartially as equals before the law and to refrain from discrimination on irrelevant or irrational grounds.[25]

The intrinsic equality of all people, he said, "might sound a bit wet, but it is just basic to the whole of my thinking."[26] Deane acknowledges the role of Catholic natural law philosophy in his Mabo judgment. "The basis of natural law", he says, "is the belief that some things are innately right and some innately wrong, flowing from the nature of things, including our nature as human beings. That approach provides a philosophical basis for seeing such things as human rights as going deeper than any particular act of Parliament or what have you. That is not exclusively Catholic. It runs through Christian belief."[27]

Similarly, Mary Gaudron writes that "equality" means more than a purely formal requirement that there be no irrelevant discriminations among litigants. The High Court, she says, has been embedding in constitutional interpretation a theory of equality "not dissimilar to that propounded by Aristotle." This theory, as she explains it, involves an active taking into account of relevant differences, so that true equality between persons is preserved; it implies, for example, the provision of legal aid and interpreter services in court to prevent discrimination by default.[28]

The inevitable outcome of this philosophical orientation was the rejection of the law's unjust past, in the passage of great moral force that became the most quoted part of the Mabo judgment:

> If this were any ordinary case, the court would not be justified in reopening the validity of fundamental propositions which have been endorsed by long-established authority ... Far from being ordinary, however, the circumstances of the present case make it unique. As has been seen, the two propositions in question [that Australia was *terra nullius*, and that full ownership vested in the Crown] provided the legal basis for the dispossession of the Aboriginal peoples of most of their traditional lands. The acts and events by which that dispossession in legal theory was carried into practical effect constitute the darkest aspect of the history of this nation. The nation as a whole must remain diminished unless and until there is an acknowledgement of, and retreat from, those past injustices. In these circumstances, the court is under a clear duty to re-examine the two propositions. For the reasons which we have explained, that re-examination compels their rejection.[29]

For giving effect to philosophical principles, the law is supreme.

Naturally, there were complaints from those who abhorred such judicial "activism". The complaints entirely ignored the careful arguments of the Mabo judges concerning the basic principles of the law. Instead they returned to Owen Dixon's jibes about the personal standards of judges. The "activists" were said to replace "strict rules with flexible standards based on their own notions of reasonableness, fairness and efficiency."[30] In assuming there were no objective standards and moving discussion instead to the sociological entity "their own standards", the conservative commentators were making the same move as postmodernists in replacing objective standards of truth with relations of power and rhetoric. Why should we accept our laws as they stand? For no other reason than this, that they are ours.

---

[1] J. Franklin, *The Science of Conjecture: Evidence and Probability before Pascal* (Baltimore, 2001), 17, 345.

[2] M. Krygier, 'Law as tradition', *Law and Philosophy* 5 (1986), 237-62; M. Krygier, 'Julius Stone: Leeways of choice, legal tradition and the declaratory theory of law', *UNSW Law Journal* 9 (1986), 26-38; summary in article 'Common law/custom' in *Routledge Encyclopedia of Philosophy*; an ethical defence in T. Campbell, *The Legal Theory of Ethical Positivism* (Aldershot, 1996); T. Campbell & J. Goldsworthy, eds. *Judicial Power, Democracy and Legal Positivism* (Aldershot, 2000); a more nuanced view in M. Krygier, 'Ethical positivism and the liberalism of fear', in Campbell & Goldsworthy, *Judicial Power*, 59-87; further in J. Finnis, 'The truth in legal positivism', in *The Autonomy of Law*, ed. R. P. George (Oxford, 1996), 195-214; defence of similar view by former logic lecturer and Chief Justice of the High Court, Sir John Latham, in *Latham papers, National Library of Australia*, series 12; J. G. Latham, 'Law and the community', *Australian Law Journal 9 Supplement* (1935), 2-8.

[3] F. G. Brennan & T. R. Hartigan, *An Outline of the Powers and Duties of Justices of the Peace in Queensland* (Brisbane, 1967), 200; discussion of such views G. Sawer, 'The administration of morals', in *Legal Change: Essays in Honour of Julius Stone*, ed. A.R. Blackshield (Sydney, 1983), 88-99; the topic avoided in *Bulletin of the Australian Society of Legal Philosophy* special issue on justice and legal reasoning (1981); other views of the question in M.J. Detmold, *The Unity of Law and Morality* (London, 1984); E. Kamenka & A.E.-S. Tay, eds, *Justice* (London, 1979); P. Cane, *Responsibility in Law and Morality* (Oxford, 2002).

[4] P. M. Farrell, *Sources of St. Thomas' Concept of Natural Law* (pamphlet, Melbourne, 1957), reprinted from *The Thomist* 20 (1957), 237-94; P. M. Farrell, 'The theological context of law', *Australasian Catholic Record* 32 (1955), 319-25; P.M. Farrell, 'The location of law in the moral system of Aquinas', *Australian Studies in Legal Philosophy*, ed. I. Tammelo et al. (Berlin, 1963), 165-94; earlier, J. G. Murtagh, *Australia: The Catholic Chapter* (New York, 1946), 252-3; M. V. McInerney, 'Natural law', *Twentieth Century* 1 (4) (June 1947), 58-68; D. P. O'Connell, 'The natural law revival', *Twentieth Century* 7 (4) (Winter 1953), 35-44; Anon, 'The natural law and Catholic social principles', *Social Survey* 3 (7) (July 1954), 13-17; later in 'The natural law as a basis of social justice', *Australian Catholic Bishops' Social Justice Statement*, 1959, in *Justice Now!*, ed. M. Hogan (Sydney, 1990), 206-12; R.D. Lumb, 'The scholastic doctrine of natural law', *Melbourne University Law Review* 2 (1959/60): 205-21; R. D. Lumb, 'Natural law — an unchanging standard?', *Catholic Lawyer* 6 (1960), 224-33; B. Miller, 'Being and the natural law', *Australian Studies*, ed. Tammelo, 219-35; F. A. Mecham, 'Philosophy and law', *Australasian Catholic Record* 46 (1969), 137-46; and *Australian Society for Legal Philosophy, Preliminary Working Papers*, 1972; D. W. Skubik, 'The minimum content of natural law', *Bulletin of the Australian Society of Legal Philosophy* 12 (1988), 101-46; J. Finnis, *Natural Law and Natural Rights* (Oxford, 1980); on which V. Kerruish, 'Philosophical retreat: A criticism of John Finnis's theory of natural law',

University of Western Australia Law Review 15 (1983), 224–44; J. Finnis, 'Natural law and legal reasoning', *Cleveland State Law Review* 38 (1990), 1–13; an unsympathetic view in M. Davies, *Asking the Law Question* (North Ryde, 1994), 59–74; Andersonian objections in W.L. Morison, 'Anderson and legal theory', *Sydney Law Review* 8 (1977), 294–304, at 302–3; see also on earlier history, G. P. Shi'Divine and natural law in Greece', in *For Service to Classical Studies*, ed. M. Kelly (Melbourne, 1966), 149–52; D. Grace, 'Natural law in Hooker's Of the Laws of Ecclesiastical Polity', *Journal of Religious History* 21 (1997), 10–22; L. Chipman, 'Grotius and the derivation of natural law', *Bull. ASLP* no. 26 (1993), 66–78; H. Ramsay, 'William Blackstone's natural law', *Bull. ASLP* 20 (1995), 58–70; T. J. F. Riha, 'Natural law and the ethical content of economics', *Australian Journal of Legal Philosophy* 22 (1997), 15–50.

[5] O. Dixon, 'Concerning judicial method', reprinted in *Jesting Pilate and Other Papers and Addresses* (Melbourne, 1965), 152–65, at 158–9; P. Ayres, Owen Dixon (Melbourne, 2003), 251–4; some doubts as to whether Dixon's practice accorded with his pronouncement in K. Mason, *Continuity and Change* (Leichhardt, 1990), 38–9.

[6] O. Dixon, 'The Statute of Westminster 1931', *Australian Law Journal* 10 (Supplement) (1936): 96–112, at 96.

[7] J. Stone, *Human Law and Human Justice* (London, 1965), 249–52; J. Stone, *Precedent and Law* (Sydney, 1985), 238–9; see L. Star, *Julius Stone: An Intellectual Life* (Sydney, 1992), 176–9.

[8] G. Barwick, *A Radical Tory* (Sydney, 1995), 224, 274–5; H. Gibbs, 'Law and government', *Quadrant* 34 (10) (October 1990), 25–9, at 28.

[9] G. Barwick, 'Judiciary law: Some observations thereon', *Current Legal Problems* 33 (1980), 239–53, at 243–4; G. Barwick, 'Courts, lawyers and the attainment of justice', *Tasmanian University Law Review* 1 (1958), 1–19, at 3–7; criticism in M. Atkinson, 'Trigwell in the High Court', *Sydney Law Review* 9 (1982), 541–67.

[10] A. Mason, 'Future directions in Australian law', *Monash University Law Review* 13 (1987), 149–63, at 155, 159.

[11] A. Mason, 'The use and abuse of precedent', *Australian Bar Review* 4 (1988), 93–111, at 94; also A. Mason, 'Courts and community values', *Eureka Street* 6 (9) (Nov 1996), 32–4; Lionel Murphy's view in G. Sturgess & P. Chubb, *Judging the World* (Sydney, 1988), 362; cf. 346, 351.

[12] G. Brennan, 'The peace of Sir Thomas More', *Queensland Lawyer* 8 (1985), 51–66; G. Brennan, 'The Irish and law in Australia', in *Ireland and Irish Australia*, ed. O. MacDonagh & W. F. Mandle (London, 1986), 18–32; Higgins and Leo XIII from J. Rickard, *H. B. Higgins: The Rebel as Judge* (Sydney, 1984), 173–4; on which see also J. Dynon, 'The social doctrine of Leo XIII and Australia', *Twentieth Century* 6 (1) (Spring 1951), 12–21; full details in K. Blackburn, 'The living wage in Australia: A secularization of Catholic ethics on wages, 1891–1907', *Journal of Religious History* 20 (1996), 93–113.

[13] G. Brennan, 'The Christian lawyer', *Australian Law Journal* 66 (1992), 259–61; cf. G. Brennan, 'Pillars of professional practice: Function and standards', *Australian Law Journal* 61 (1987), 112–8.

[14] G. Brennan, 'Commercial law and morality', *Melbourne University Law Review* 17 (1989), 100–6, at 101; see also G. Brennan, 'The purpose and scope of judicial review', *Australian Bar Review* 2 (1986), 93–113, at 104–5; P. Finn, 'Commerce, the common law and morality', *Melbourne University Law Review* 17 (1989), 87–99.

[15] G. Brennan, 'A critique of criticism', *Monash University Law Review* 19 (1993), 213-6.

[16] M. Gleeson, *The Rule of Law and the Constitution* (Sydney, 2000), 134; cf. 98; similar in M. H. McHugh, 'The judicial method', *Australian Law Journal* 73 (1999), 37-51, esp. 46; some backsliding from Dixon himself in *Jesting Pilate*, 165.

[17] *Cooper v. Stuart* (1889) *14 AC* at p. 291, per *Finding Common Ground*, ed F. Brennan et al. (2nd ed, Melbourne, 1986), 13; other philosophical perspectives in D. Ivison, P. Patton & W. Sanders, eds, *Political Theory and the Rights of Indigenous Peoples* (Melbourne, 2000); G. Lloyd, 'No one's land: Australia and the philosophical imagination', *Hypatia* 15 (2) (Spring 2000), 26-39 .

[18] F. Brennan, 'The absurdity and injustice of terra nullius', *Ormond Papers* 5 (1988), 51-5, at 54; see also F. Brennan, 'Aboriginal aspirations to land', in *Finding Common Ground*, 11-49; Frank Brennan's comments on the thesis of this article in 'Honesty and the issues', *Sydney Papers* 16 (1) (2004), 122-37.

[19] Original in F. de Vitoria, *Political Writings* ed. A. Pagden & J. Lawrance (New York, 1991), 231-92, especially 239-40 and 264-5; see J. O'Rorke, 'Francis de Vitoria', *Australasian Catholic Record* 17 (1940), 308-20; Stone, *Human Law and Human Justice*, 62; mentioned in H. Wootten, 'Mabo and the lawyers', *Australian Journal of Anthropology* 6 (1/2) (1995), 116-133, at 123 and in J. Thompson, 'The loss of Aboriginal sovereignty', *Res Publica* 2 (2) (1993), 1-8; similar in F. Brennan, *Land Rights: The Religious Factor* (Adelaide, 1993), 5; J. Malbon, 'Natural and positive law influences on the law affecting Australia's indigenous people', *Australian Journal of Legal History* 3 (1997), 1-39; G. Marks, 'Law, theology and justice in the Spanish colonies', *Australian Journal of Legal History* 4 (1998), 163-73; a slightly different discussion also from scholastic principles in E. Azzopardi, *Human Rights and Peoples* (Drummoyne, 1988), 131-2, 159-64.

[20] G. Brennan in *The Mabo Decision with Commentary by Richard H. Bartlett* (Sydney, 1993), 18.

[21] *The Mabo Decision*, 19.

[22] Thomas Aquinas, *Summa Theologiae* I-II q. 97 art. 2.

[23] *The Mabo Decision*, p. 29.

[24] W. P. Deane, 'Crisis in the law of nations', *Social Survey* 6 (1957), 8-15, at p. 12; also briefly in W. Deane, review of Oppenheim & Lauterpacht, *International Law*, *Sydney Law Review* 2 (1957), 382-4; W. Deane, 'Vatican diplomacy', *Twentieth Century* 15 (1960-1), 347-52; cf. W. P. Deane, 'An older Republic', *Hermes* 1950, 5-10.

[25] J. Deane in *Leeth v. The Commonwealth*, *Commonwealth Law Reports* 174 (1991-2), 486-7; cf. *CLR 168* (1980), 522; I am grateful to George Winterton for calling these passages to my attention.

[26] T. Stephens, *Sir William Deane: The Things That Matter* (Sydney, 2002), 94.

[27] W. Deane to author, 14/5/1996; Stephens, *Sir William Deane*, 100.

[28] M. Gaudron, 'Equality before the law with particular reference to Aborigines', *Judicial Review* 1 (1992-4), 81-9; implications in Dietrich v. The Queen, *Commonwealth Law Reports* 177 (1992), 292; similar in Gleeson, *The Rule of Law and the Constitution*, 61-3; opposite view in Barwick, *A Radical Tory*, 274; bibliography of philosophy of law and equality in A. E.-S. Tay, *Human Rights for Australia* (Canberra, 1986), 173-5; also H. J. McCloskey, 'A right to equality?', *Canadian Journal of Philosophy* 6

(1976), 625–42; K. Dunn, '"Yakking giants": Equality discourse in the High Court', *Melbourne University Law Review* 24 (2000), 427–61.

[29] Deane and Gaudron, in *The Mabo Decision*, 82; reflections in R. Gaita, *A Common Humanity* (Melbourne, 1999), 73–86.

[30] J. Gava, 'The rise of the hero judge', *UNSW Law Journal* 24 (2001), 747–59; D. Heydon, 'Judicial activism and the death of the rule of law', *Quadrant* 41 (1) (Jan–Feb, 2003), 9–22.

16

Random thoughts

On the energy of the pioneers

The impression left by Edmund Campion's *Australian Catholics* is of a Catholic culture of immense size. "The apron bar had sold 250 aprons by early afternoon," said the report of the 1967 Moonee Ponds parish fête; how many times does that item have to be multiplied to give an idea of the size of the Catholic enterprise? The impression is often of huge energy, too, especially in the early years. Like the universe, Australian Church history seems to have been a slow working out of massive clashes of elemental forces in its early minutes.

The famous conflict between Mary MacKillop and the Bishop of Adelaide, which resulted in her (temporary) excommunication, was only one of such clashes of titans. Vows of poverty and celibacy left these religious pioneers with a large surplus of energy to expend. Joined to a vow of obedience, and confined, such energy could produce a St Thérèse of Lisieux; the Australian Church represents the opposite extreme, where there was a continent to expand in. In fact, Australia did not even get a random sample of those who took vows as priests and nuns. Our presbyteries and convents were largely built by Irish who had not only taken vows, but also volunteered to go to the other end of the world for life.[1]

On Catholic Anzacs

Faith operated under different conditions in the War overseas. First, death on the battlefield was an ever-present threat. Priests could offer general absolution and Communion before a battle, an exception to the usual rules. Corporal Wilfred Gallwey wrote in 1917, "Every man gets communion and then he is fit to die. Many a time after Mass I have gone to Confession and received Communion immediately afterwards. Every chance I get I go and am always prepared for death. If I ever get killed you may be certain that I will be sure of everlasting happiness in the next world."

Secondly, denominations mixed in a way that was rare at home, and padres of both sides often impressed all kinds of soldiers. One Roman Catholic padre was "universally voted as 'one of the best'" because he "risks his life to give absolution to men out in No Man's Land, and that sort of thing," praise recorded in the diary of an ardent Protestant. Father Michael Bergin, an Irish Jesuit missionary in Syria who was deported by the Turkish authorities, was perhaps the only member of the AIF never to have set foot in Australia. He attached himself to the Australians in Egypt, serving at Gallipoli, before being killed in action at Passchendaele in 1917. Bergin was described by his senior Catholic chaplain as "tall, spare, gaunt; he looked the typical Jesuit of anti-Catholic literature … I have never known anyone to inspire such respect and admiration from such diverse characters: good men and bad, broad-minded and those devoid of that reputation.'"[2]

On interwar sectarian polemics

Sectarian tension in Sydney reached a height in 1922 with the *Ne Temere* debate, which was resolved, in a sense, intellectually. The papal decree *Ne Temere* had declared invalid marriages of Catholics performed by non-Catholic ministers, appearing to threaten a large number of New South Wales children with bastardy. After a campaign by the Protestant Federation, a bill to criminalise the propagation of the papal decree was passed in the Legislative Assembly and came within one vote of passing the Legislative Council. A compromise formula was agreed that let both sides off the hook, while its exact propositional meaning was hard to interpret.

While sectarian tension was never as high again in Sydney, it eased only gradually, especially in areas such as employment discrimination. Between the wars some of Sydney's radio stations were set up by religious entities, in part to pursue polemics: 2SM by the Catholics, 2CH by the Council of Churches, 2GB by the Theosophists. On Sunday nights the spokesmen could be heard going at it hammer and tongs: on 2CH, Archdeacon Hammond, Principal of Moore College and Grand Master of the Loyal Orange Lodge; on 2SM Dr Leslie Rumble, Catholic convert from Anglicanism. Rumble's books of *Radio Replies* were hugely successful in America and said to have sold seven million copies. "Using plain language and short sentences, and avoiding rhetoric, he spoke ninety words to the minute in a voice like worn sandpaper, giving an effect of common sense and rationality." Polemic for a popular audience it may have been, but the standard of argument was high. Higher, certainly, than in contemporary left-right debates.[3]

On WWII Italian internees

When war was declared with Italy in June 1940, the Italian population in Australia was about 26,000, making it the largest ethnic group other than the British, Irish and Australian Aborigines. Although there was no near prospect of invasion of Australia by Italy or any of its allies, the existence of an identifiable minority including many recently arrived from an enemy territory and including a few with admitted fascist sympathies posed a genuine security problem. A total of 4,721 Italians were interned, a figure much in excess of the number of real security threats but not one indicative of out of control paranoia ... Not only were Italian nationals in Australia widely used without supervision in rural industries – while Australia was still at war with Italy – but 12,000 extra Italian prisoners of war were imported for the purpose, mainly from India ... the perception that the Italians had been harmless and no "trouble" had important consequences for the postwar immigration program, as did the experiences of Arthur Calwell and the Catholic Church in helping them. In the years 1947–50, Calwell transformed Australia by importing and quickly settling about 180,000 "New Australians" ... Opinion was finely balanced, and anything less than a benign experience with the Italians during the War could have put paid to the prospects of the displaced persons in the late 1940s and the Italian and Greek mass immigration that followed in the 1950s. Multicultural Australia owes a great debt to those, on both the Italian and Australian sides, who negotiated the minefields of wartime xenophobia with restraint.[4]

On B.A. Santamaria

No other country's Catholicism produced a figure like B.A. Santamaria. And if he had been destined to exist somewhere, Australia should have been the least likely place for him to fall to earth. The sceptical, secular or Protestant, isolated Anglophone society of mid-twentieth-century Australia was stony ground for an ideologue with a European sensibility and a vast plan to reorder society according to a rational and divine order ...[5]

Santamaria was on the right side of the main international political issue of his time, the threat of Communism. He devoted his immense intellectual and organisational skills to combatting it, in an atmosphere where many were either stupidly blind to the threat or criminally covering it up. If he had lived in Czechoslovakia or Vietnam – or if he had died in 1950 – his alarmist views would have been vindicated in full and his actions proven to be justified. The question is whether the rising prosperity and political stability of 1950s Australia rendered his apocalyptic vision out of date and his infiltration of the Labor Party morally improper. It is easy to see why Stalin with an H-bomb and Evatt's office with communist moles were still cause for worry. It is equally easy to see the point of view of traditional anti-communist Labor men like Calwell who thought no good could come of single-issue conspiratorial tactics.[6]

By the late 1960s, when the leftward tide of opinion was running at its strongest, there was only one accessible media outlet where a coherently argued response could be found. It was Santamaria's weekly TV slot, *Point of View*. Many a student radical surreptitiously tuned in to it, and more than a few came to wonder if all the good arguments were on one side.[7]

On Mannix and Vatican II

The complementary nature of the Brenda Niall's *Mannix* and Franklin, Nolan and Gilchrist's *The Real Archbishop Mannix* is exhibited in their treatments of Mannix's siding with John XXIII's reform agenda, at the very end of Mannix's life. *The Real Archbishop Mannix* prints extracts from Mannix's response to the original highly conservative agenda documents for the upcoming Vatican Council. The response – probably drafted by Eric D'Arcy but approved by Mannix – is very critical of legalism and triumphalism and in favour of freedom of conscience and lay initiative. Niall tells the personal side of the story, recording Mannix agonising to Santamaria over whether he should have been more like John XXIII. "I think the whole of my policy has been mistaken, of standing up to unpopularity; this Pope shows that if you are ready to embrace the whole world you can have a much greater influence." (Characteristically, Santamaria, who was to come close to leaving the Church over the post-Vatican II changes, snaps "I thought it was a completely wrong analysis.") Too late. The avuncular Mannix, the earthy peasant Mannix, the cuddly Mannix – it was not to be.[8]

On Catholic schooldays

The real Jesuits are there [in *The Oxford Book of Australian Schooldays*], of course. The Jesuit memories of Robert Hughes and John Funder are among the best pieces. But perhaps the only regrettable omission also lies in the area of Catholic education. Jennifer Dabbs' *Beyond Redemption* is a lightly fictionalised recollection of the author's education at Star of the Sea College, Gardenvale, and is a classic account of the Catholic childhood of legend. It is at first glance unbalanced by its portrayal of a classmate of the narrator who is quite impossibly sassy, intelligent, tall and pushy. At least, that is how it looks until one learns that Dabbs was a school friend of Germaine Greer. Germaine's own opinions are included in the *Oxford Book*. Like Dabbs', they are by and large positive in their view of the school and the nuns. Carmen Callil's account of the same school at almost the same time is much bleaker. The three together make Star of the Sea in the fifties one of Australian childhood's sacred sites.[9]

As Wanda Skowronska remembers – with a vivid recall whose accuracy I as a contemporary can vouch for – a Catholic education created a total world of devotion which permeated all of life. "Culture" does not express the depth of penetration aimed at. The point of the "sensurround" of nuns, angelus, incense, hymns, sodalities, feast days, novenas, saints, first communions and confessions and the catechism was to create souls completely oriented to God and his commands. If some students let it wash over them or reacted against it, with many, like Wanda, the lesson took and flourished. Her memoir is a perfect insight into the Australian Catholic past, as seen from the inside.

The second part of her story concerns the disappearance of that world, an event which occurred quite suddenly around 1969. The rebellious spirit of the times (as embodied, according to the nuns, in the Johnny O'Keefe Show) combined with the currents of change from the Second Vatican Council and the impact of *Humanae Vitae* to pull the rug from under the old order. As a child of refugees from Communist Eastern Europe, Wanda had a particular horror of socialist challenges to authority. Why would anyone throw over the splendid Catholic vision of the eternal for a mess of Communist-inspired agitprop and a few sub-pop hymns?[10]

On ignorance of the religious aspects of Australian history

Roy Williams's book, *In God They Trust?*, describes how Australian prime ministers have, without exception, understood the significance of religion. Nearly all were Christians (of a tolerant and not very sectarian variety), while even the non-religious ones, such as Gough Whitlam and Julia Gillard, had a good understanding of religion in their upbringing and an attitude similar to Clement Attlee's "Believe in the ethics of Christianity. Can't believe the mumbo jumbo." Prime ministers are just an example. Until only yesterday, most people had a general idea of what religion was about and how religious people saw it bearing on ethics and public policy.

Now they don't. A secular mindset has grown up that instantiates not just hostility to religion but an unteachable incomprehension of it ... historians should be giving a comprehensive view of the thought-worlds of the past, but aren't. Although there is some excellent work on the religious history of Australia, such as Patrick O'Farrell's books on Catholics, Stuart Piggin and Robert Linder's recent *The Fountain* of *Public Prosperity: Evangelical Christians in Australian History*, and Wayne Hudson's *Australian Religious Thought*, the topic has remained a sectional interest. The mainstream of Australian historiography (except for Manning Clark and Geoffrey Blainey) has been and remains a religion-free zone. It is dominated by a narrative according to which Australians since the noble founding convicts have been inspired by ideas such as imperialism, socialism, mateship, racism, nationalism, environmentalism, "social justice", and money, but not religion.[11]

On the lack of explanation of the sexual abuse scandal

One absence in Cardinal Pell's book, *Test Everything*, is any mention of the sexual abuse scandal. That may disappoint those who have heard little else about the Catholic Church in recent times. It is a pity, since a proper account of the crisis from the official spokespersons of the church is still awaited. There have been apologies and plans put in place to prevent any recurrence, which are of course the first steps needed, but there has not exactly been an official account reflecting on how it happened and what to make of it.

A retired auxiliary bishop of the Sydney Archdiocese, Geoffrey Robinson, published in 2007 a book, *Confronting Power and Sex in the Catholic Church*, arguing that the institutional church had gone very wrong on those two matters. The Australian Catholic Bishops Conference expressed their disagreement with some of the more theological aspects of his views, but have not exactly put forward an alternative analysis.

What does the official church think was the cause of perhaps one in twenty priests and brothers in the 1960s and 1970s committing abuse? Was there something in seminary training and the circumstances in which priests lived that left them somehow vulnerable to the temptation to abuse? What was the thinking behind the policy of dealing with the cases internally to "avoid scandal"? Was there some point to the policy in the historical circumstances? Does the policy call in question the Catholic Church's claimed divine guidance, or at least the wisdom of taking all Vatican pronouncements with total seriousness? Those are questions to which there could be different answers. A serious official historical and theological investigation would give both Catholics and others an insight into an issue that will be with us for some time.[12]

On Cardinal Pell's wrongful conviction

[Published on the announcement of Pell's conviction for child abuse in February 2019. The text is left unchanged.]

Australian Catholics have been appalled over the last three decades at the revelations of abuse by some priests and religious and the cover-ups by many church leaders. So they have been grateful for the efforts of those bishops who first took action to sack perpetrators and put in place safeguarding mechanisms. Two bishops stood out, George Pell and Philip Wilson. Both initiated vigorous action when they took charge of dioceses, despite obstruction from the Vatican. Pell startled the Royal Commission into child abuse by telling them that it was hard to get action from Pope John Paul II because he thought the abuse scandal was a Communist plot.

It was therefore surprising to Catholics when Wilson and Pell were the very bishops convicted by the Australian justice system. Wilson's conviction on charges of concealing a complaint of child abuse was overturned on appeal. Pell's conviction for sexual penetration of a child is currently subject to appeal …

All Australians should consider the strength of the evidence against Pell for themselves. It is possible to do that because the evidence is essentially available and there is so little of it … One of the two alleged victims died of an overdose after saying no-one had abused him. The surviving alleged victim claims Pell assaulted him in circumstances which the defence believed they had proved could not have happened. The layout of the cathedral and sacristy made the crime close to impossible. The elaborate vestments Pell was wearing at the time made it more so. There is no corroborating evidence … The problem is simply a mismatch between the jury's verdict and the objective relation between the evidence and the conclusion. The evidence is inadequate to support the verdict.[13]

On hope for the future

Jude Dougherty recalls an earlier thinker who lamented that the gods have departed from the earth, faith and temperance have been abandoned, oaths are no longer reliable, and if the only remaining divinity, Hope, were to depart, civilisation would collapse. "The parallels to our present are obvious," Dougherty comments. The thinker he refers to is Theognis of Megara in the sixth century BC. That is a long time ago. If virtue and piety were declining catastrophically as much in Theognis's day as in ours, it follows (from the mathematical theory of functions) that they must have recovered substantially somewhere in between. If that was possible once, it is possible again.

Hope is not lost, because the resources of civilisation are still available. Each new generation faces its own choice of what among the smorgasbord of traditions to accept and what to abandon. The Internet, for all its tendencies to vacuity and pointlessness, does make available and easily accessible a range of intellectual resources unimaginable in the past. Young brains are not as damaged by malnutrition, blows to the head, measles and arsenic in the wallpaper as they were in earlier generations. A proportion of young intellects will grasp the truth.[14]

---

[1] 'Australian Catholics', review of E. Campion, *Australian Catholics, Quadrant* 32 (1/2) (Jan/Feb, 1988), 114–6.

[2] Review of D. Reynaud, Anzac Spirituality, *Journal of the Australian Catholic Historical Society* 39 (2018), 210–12.

[3] The Sydney intellectual/religious scene, 1916–2016, *St Mark's Review* no. 242 (Dec 2017), 20–55.

[4] Preface to A. Cappello, ed, *Enemy Aliens* (Melbourne, 2005), iii–vi.

[5] Review of Santamaria: The Politics of Fear ed. P. Ormonde, *Journal of the Australian Catholic Historical Society* 22 (2001), 82–3.

[6] Review of G. Henderson, 'Santamaria: A Most Unusual Man', *Journal of the Australian Catholic Historical Society* 37 (2) (2016), 243–5

[7] Review of *Santamaria: The Politics of Fear* ed. P. Ormonde, *Journal of the Australian Catholic Historical Society* 22 (2001), 82–3.

[8] Review of B. Niall, *Mannix, Journal of the Australian Catholic Historical Society* 36 (2015), 295–7.

9. Earls cool, review of *The Oxford Book of Australian Schooldays*, *Quadrant* 42 (10) (Oct 1998): 85–6.
10. Preface to Wanda Skowronska, *Angels, Incense and Revolution: Catholic Schooldays of the 1960s* (Connor Court, 2019), xi–xii
11. 'Incomprehension of religion in Australian society', in Bryan Turner and Damien Freeman, eds, *Faith's Place: Democracy in a religious world* (2020), 177–185.
12. Cardinal directions, review of George Pell, *Test Everything*, *Quadrant* 54 (7-8) (July/Aug 2010), 38–40.
13. The cloud of doubt over Pell's conviction, *Quadrant Online* 28 Feb 2019, https://quadrant.org.au/opinion/qed/2019/02/the-cloud-of-doubt-over-pells-conviction/
14. Hope is not lost, review of Jude Dougherty, *Interpretations*, *Annals Australasia* (Jan/Feb 2019), 41–2.

Index

Abbotsford Convent 129-46
Abbott, Tony 171
Aboriginal issues, see missions, Mabo judgment
Anzacs, 285-6
apologetics 82-3, 92, 111
Aquinas Academy 89-91
ASIO 116-7

Bailey, Dr Harry 250
Bathurst Island mission 27-9, 32, 36, 46-55
Beagle Bay mission 25, 29, 32, 36
Beg, Wazir 155
Bligh, Governor William 11
Boorowa 64-65, 69
Brennan, Fr Frank 277
Brennan, Gerard 275-9
Brock, Paul 192-3
Brock, Fr Peter 200

Cahill, J. J. 223, 228, 237, 244, 248-50
Calwell, Arthur 118, 183, 207-21, 287-8
Campion, Fr Edmund 191, 193
Campion Society 88, 105, 222, 227
Carroll, Archbishop James 122, 234
Castle Hill Rebellion 1, 10-11
casuistry 95-7, 120-1
Catechism 84-5
Catholic Action 115-6, 183, 222-8
Charlesworth, Max 93

Chifley, J. B. 75-6, 96, 210, 218
Chisholm, Caroline 64
Communists 32-3, 51-3, 61, 110-122, 182-5, 209, 233, 243, 288, 290, 292
Condon, Fr Kevin 199
contraception 96, 123, 231-2

Deane, William 279
Delaney, Colin 233, 241-4, 247-8
Dixon, Fr James 1-11
Dixon, Owen 273-7
Dobson, W. T. "Diver" 118-20
Downing, Reg 247-9
Duhig, Archbishop James 204, 219

Farrell, Frank "Bumper" 239-41
Farrell, Fr P. M. 91-3, 273
Filipino missionaries 25, 32, 47
Fisher, Archbishop Anthony 87, 97
Fitzpatrick, Catherine, Columbus and Ambrose 21-3
Freemasons 12, 154-70, 226, 233, 237, 246
future prospects 293

Garden Point mission 27, 29, 52-3
Gaudron, Mary 279-80
Geraghty, Chris 190
Gilroy, Cardinal Norman 116, 120, 226, 229-31, 237, 240
Goossens, Eugene 244-8
Greer, Germaine 85, 289

Gsell, Bishop F.X. 27, 29, 32, 35-7, 46-55
guilds, professional 228-33

Hanrahan, John 189-90
Hartigan, Fr Patrick, "John O'Brien" 56-7, 68, 70-1
Hayes, Michael 13, 22
Hobart, Lord 1, 4, 7
homosexuals 238, 241-4, 248-50
Horne, Donald 109-10

immigration, postwar 207-19, 287
Inglis, Cecilia 193-8
Irish influence 1-4, 9, 18, 20, 32, 56-7, 64-66, 74, 228

"John O'Brien", see Hartigan

Kelly, Ellen and Ned 73-5
Keneally, Thomas 83
King, Governor Philip Gidley 1-10, 158
Konstantinidis, Janice 131, 138, 140

Lalor, Mary 200-01
leprosariums 28
Letters, Prof Frank 163-5
Liddy, Marjorie 40

Mabo judgment 277-80
MacKillop, Mary x, 25, 69, 285
Macquarie, Governor Lachlan 12-13, 21-2, 159
Magdalen laundries 128-52

Mannix, Archbishop Daniel 4, 62, 160, 171-87, 219, 288-9
Marsden, Rev Samuel 2, 5-6, 12
Martina, Bathurst islander 47-50
McAuley, James 94-5, 120
McGarry, Francis 34-5
McMaster, Fr Noel 199-200
Meehan, James 13, 64
"Men of '98" 13, 20
missions to aboriginals, 24-55, 181, 200
Murray, Les 57

natural law ethics viii, 86, 272-3, 279; see also social justice theory
New Norcia 25, 29, 32
Norton, Rosaleen 244-48
nuns 28-32, 39, 46, 50, 69, 75, 85, 114, 128-52, 193-8, 200-1, 240, 248, 285-90

O'Connor, Eileen 70
O'Farrell, Patrick 91, 230, 290
O'Reilly, Bernard 71-2

Paul VI, Pope 210, 212, 218-19
Pell, Cardinal George 266-7, 291-2
philosophy, Catholic scholastic 82-109, 272-3, 278
Polding, Archbishop J. B. 25, 86, 135
Police Guild of St Christopher 232-3, 241
problem of evil 91-3
Protestant attitudes to Catholics 2, 5-6, 21, 65-6, 75, 128, 286-7

Redrup, John 201-3
Rerum Novarum viii, 171-2, 183, 227, 276
Ridsdale, Gerald 259-71
Royal Commission into Institutional Responses to Child Sexual Abuse x, 259-71
Rumble, Dr L. 109, 111, 287
rural virtue 56-72
Ryan, Dr P. J. 86, 105-127, 226

Salazar, Antonio 59-61, 250
Santamaria, B. A. 57-9, 62-3, 82-3, 122, 178, 183, 228, 288-9
Scullin, James 171, 183
sexual abuse scandal x, 259-71, 291-2
sexual ethics 235-7; see also contraception
Sheahan, Bill 234, 242, 247
Sheehan, Archbishop M. 83, 87, 92

Skowronska, Wanda 289-90
social justice theory viii, 115, 171-82, 212-3
sodalities 224
Split, Labor 121-2, 183, 223, 237
state aid for church schools 153, 237
Stolen Generations 36-8, 50-1, 143

Therry, Fr John Joseph 20-2
toleration of Catholicism 2-10

Vaughan, Archbishop R. B. 86, 153-5, 162
Vice Squad, NSW 237-48

West, Morris 190-1
Windsor, Gerard 87, 190
women's role 179; see also nuns
Woodbury, Dr Austin 89-91

www.ingramcontent.com/pod-product-compliance
Lightning Source LLC
Chambersburg PA
CBHW061946300426
44117CB00025B/2170